GREEK SANCTUARIES AND TEMPLE ARCHITECTURE

Also available from Bloomsbury

AN INTRODUCTION TO GREEK ART
Second Edition, by Susan Woodford

GREEK ARCHITECTURE
by R. A. Tomlinson

Supplementary resources for *Greek Sanctuaries and Temple Architecture* can be found at www.bloomsbury.com/Emerson-Greek-Sanctuaries-2E

Please type the URL into your web browser and follow the instructions to access the Companion Website.

If you experience any problems, please contact Bloomsbury at contact@bloomsbury.com

GREEK SANCTUARIES AND TEMPLE ARCHITECTURE

AN INTRODUCTION

Second Edition

Mary Emerson

BLOOMSBURY ACADEMIC
LONDON • NEW YORK • OXFORD • NEW DELHI • SYDNEY

BLOOMSBURY ACADEMIC
Bloomsbury Publishing Plc
50 Bedford Square, London, WC1B 3DP, UK
1385 Broadway, New York, NY 10018, USA

BLOOMSBURY, BLOOMSBURY ACADEMIC and the Diana logo are trademarks of Bloomsbury Publishing Plc

First edition published by Gerald Duckworth & Co in 1997
This second edition published in 2018
Reprinted 2018

A catalogue record for this book is available from the British Library.

Library of Congress Cataloging-in-Publication Data
Names: Emerson, Mary, author.
Title: Greek sanctuaries and temple architecture : an introduction / Mary Emerson.
Description: Second edition. | London ; New York : Bloomsbury Academic, an imprint of Bloomsbury Publishing Plc, 2017. | Includes bibliographical references and index. | First published as 'Greek Sanctuaries: an introduction' in 2007.
Identifiers: LCCN 2017024385| ISBN 9781472575289 (pbk.) |ISBN 9781472575296 (epub) | ISBN 9781472575302 (ePDF)
Subjects: LCSH: Temples--Greece. | Architecture, Ancient--Greece. | Architecture, Greek. | Decoration and ornament, Architectural--Greece. | Sculpture, Greek. | Sculpture, Ancient--Greece. | Greece--Religious life and customs.
Classification: LCC NA275 .E45 2017 | DDC 722/.8--dc23 LC record available at https://lccn.loc.gov/2017024385

ISBN: PB: 978-1-4725-7528-9
ePDF: 978-1-4725-7530-2
ePub: 978-1-4725-7529-6

Typeset by Deanta Global Publishing Services, Chennai, India
Printed and bound in Great Britain

To find out more about our authors and books visit www.bloomsbury.com and sign up for our newsletters.

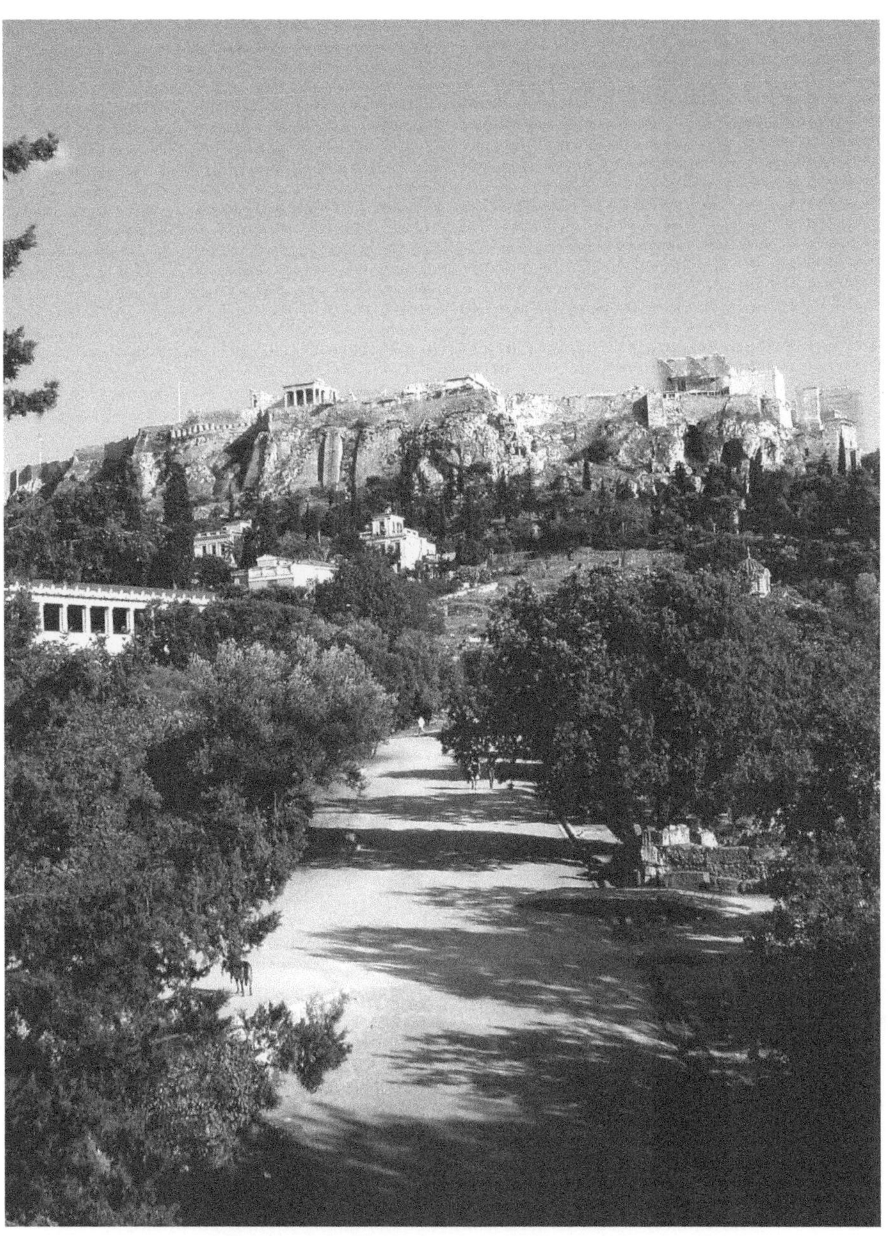

The Panathenaic Way crossing the Agora, Athens. The north face of the Acropolis is in the background.

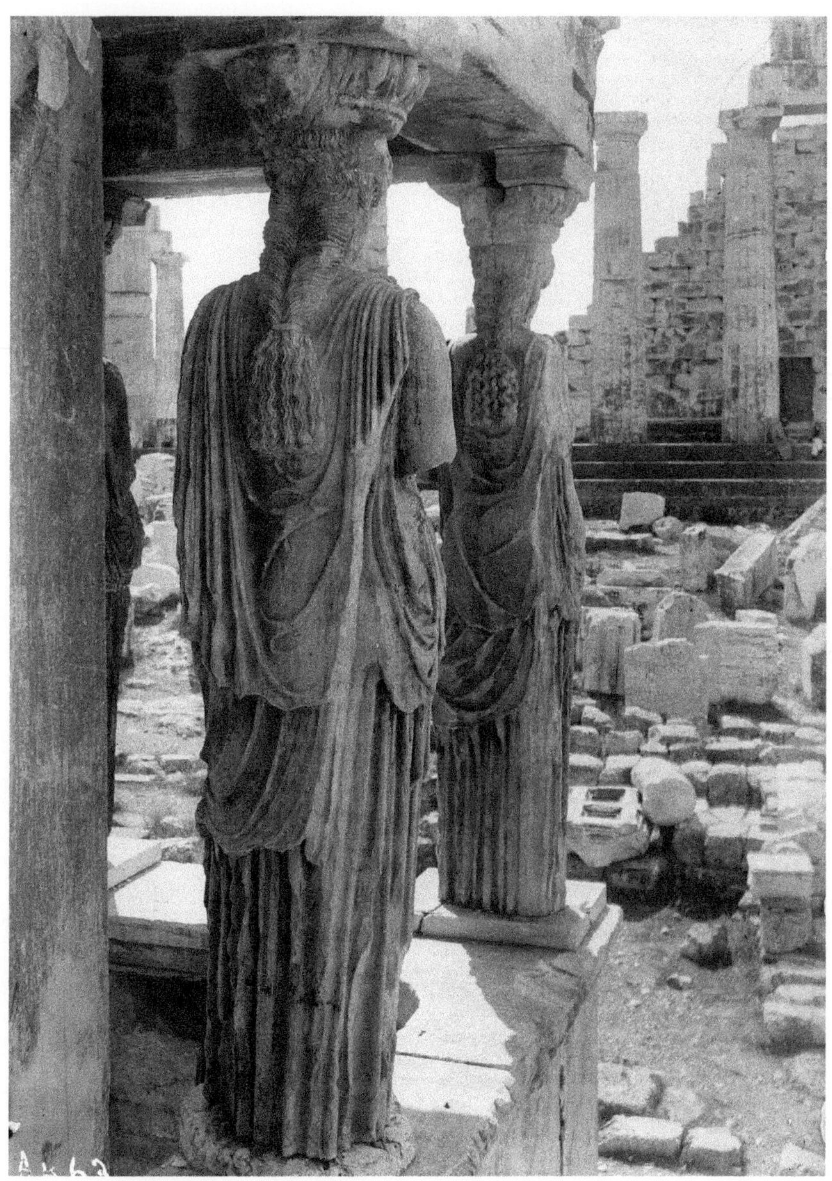

Erechtheion Caryatids seen from behind, looking towards Parthenon.

CONTENTS

PREFACE TO THE SECOND EDITION

This book is primarily about buildings – the temple buildings, treasuries and other structures to be found in ancient Greek sanctuaries. It aims to describe those buildings in a clear and detailed way, and to enable the reader to gain a good general understanding of their design and construction. It also aims to put the buildings into context, in several ways. First is the landscape context and then the surrounding built environment (usually but not always an elaborate sanctuary). Second, the social, historical and political context is touched upon. Third, the religious purpose and uses of sanctuaries are discussed. Finally, the meaning of the buildings for the original viewers is explored, in terms of the aesthetic appearance of both the overall architecture and the architectural sculpture. This last aspect is of great interest but of course is necessarily speculative.

It must be emphasised that this book is very much 'an Introduction'. It is aimed at the reader who knows little or nothing about the topic, but who would like to gain reasonably in-depth knowledge quickly. For this purpose, there is a glossary of terms used. Technical terms have been used throughout so the reader can build up a useful working vocabulary as these terms will be found everywhere in the scholarly literature, often without explanation. No previous knowledge of the subject matter is assumed here, and hopefully the presentation of material will be clear and self-explanatory.

The book is arranged by topic. The opening sections give a brief account of the history and theory of Greek architecture. Then, each site or building is dealt with separately in a self-contained chapter. The treatments may be found to vary slightly, in accordance with the nature of the site and the evidence available. Although there is some cross-referencing, each case study should stand alone as a presentation of that topic. It is hoped that this method will be useful and practical. It certainly means that sections can be skipped or that the reader need not read the material in a linear fashion.

Two new sections have been added to this edition, covering the site of Poseidonia (Paestum) in Magna Graecia (Southern Italy) and the unusual temple of Zeus at Akragas (Agrigento) in Sicily.

Commentary on architectural sculpture has been added in this new edition. This has been done mainly to expand upon how the sculpture relates to its building, rather than as an autonomous artefact.

This new edition also has a greatly expanded bibliography. For the reader who wishes to go on to tackle the large body of scholarship, it should be easy to enter the field by making a start on the books and articles listed. Reference to particular discussions has been made in the text, but the reader will soon find their own way according to their particular interests.

I cannot overstate how heavily this book depends on the scholarship of others. As an introduction to the field, it is necessarily somewhat cursory in discussion, and many sacrifices had to be made about the selection of sites. In order to cover the most notable examples, only buildings from the sixth and fifth centuries BC are dealt with. The aim of the book is not to be exhaustive, but to equip readers new to the field with a working knowledge for further reading, or for site visits.

A few difficulties always occur with writing about the classical world. A big problem is the spelling of classical names, especially difficult when transliterating Greek. There is not much attempt here to follow a consistent method. Recognisable names are spelt in their most recognisable form: e.g. Athens, Bassae, Heracles. Other spellings attempt to be more accurate transliterations: for example, Akragas, Iktinos, Kallikrates.

All dates are BC unless marked AD. Mostly BC has been inserted, but not every single time.

All translations from Greek tragedies are by the author. Line references are to the original Greek texts. The passages will be found in published translations close to the original line numbers.

ACKNOWLEDGEMENTS

Finally, I owe hearty thanks to my dear friend Frances Van Keuren who, as well as being a constant source of encouragement, has offered very valuable criticism of the new chapters in this edition. I would like to thank Bloomsbury academic department who thought an enlarged edition was worthwhile, and thanks to the two anonymous readers who made many helpful suggestions. I am very grateful to the director and staff at the Parco Archeologico at Paestum for their kindness and help, both at the site and afterwards. Looking back into the distant past, I would like to thank Joyce Reynolds and Professor Pat Easterling for setting my feet on the path of Classical study at Newnham College, and for remaining interested, kindly, scholarly inspirations through all the years since. I would like to thank Dr Richard Cocke and the late Professor Andrew Martindale of the University of East Anglia for an eye-opening education in looking at art and architecture. I thank my family for their interest in the project, and especially Zak Emerson for his great help with pictures, and my husband Peter Emerson for his constant encouragement and support and particularly for his enthusiastic company on our western trips to Paestum and Sicily. Thanks also to Natalia Vogeikoff of the American School at Athens, Katharina Brandt at the Deutsches Archäologisches Institut, Athens, and to Calliopi Christophi at the Ecole Française à Athènes, who all generously provided pictures.

ACKNOWLEDGEMENTS TO THE FIRST EDITION

I would like to offer my grateful thanks to the many people who have helped me along the way towards producing this book, but especially to Frances Van Keuren of the University of Georgia, for her encouragement, criticism and inspiration at an early stage of writing, to Jennifer O'Hagan and Charles Relle, fellow Classicists, for their meticulous and critical reading of the text, to Jan Jordan and Natalia Vogeikoff-Brogan at the American School of Classical Studies in Athens, and to Oliver Pilz of the Deutsches Archäologisches Institut and to Kalliopi Christophi of the Ecole Française à Athènes for their kind and cheerful help with locating pictures, to Zak Emerson for much artistic and technical help with the figures, to Deborah Blake of Duckworth for her support and enthusiasm as well as ironing out of errors, and to Peter Emerson for generous and time-consuming help of all sorts.

LIST OF ILLUSTRATIONS

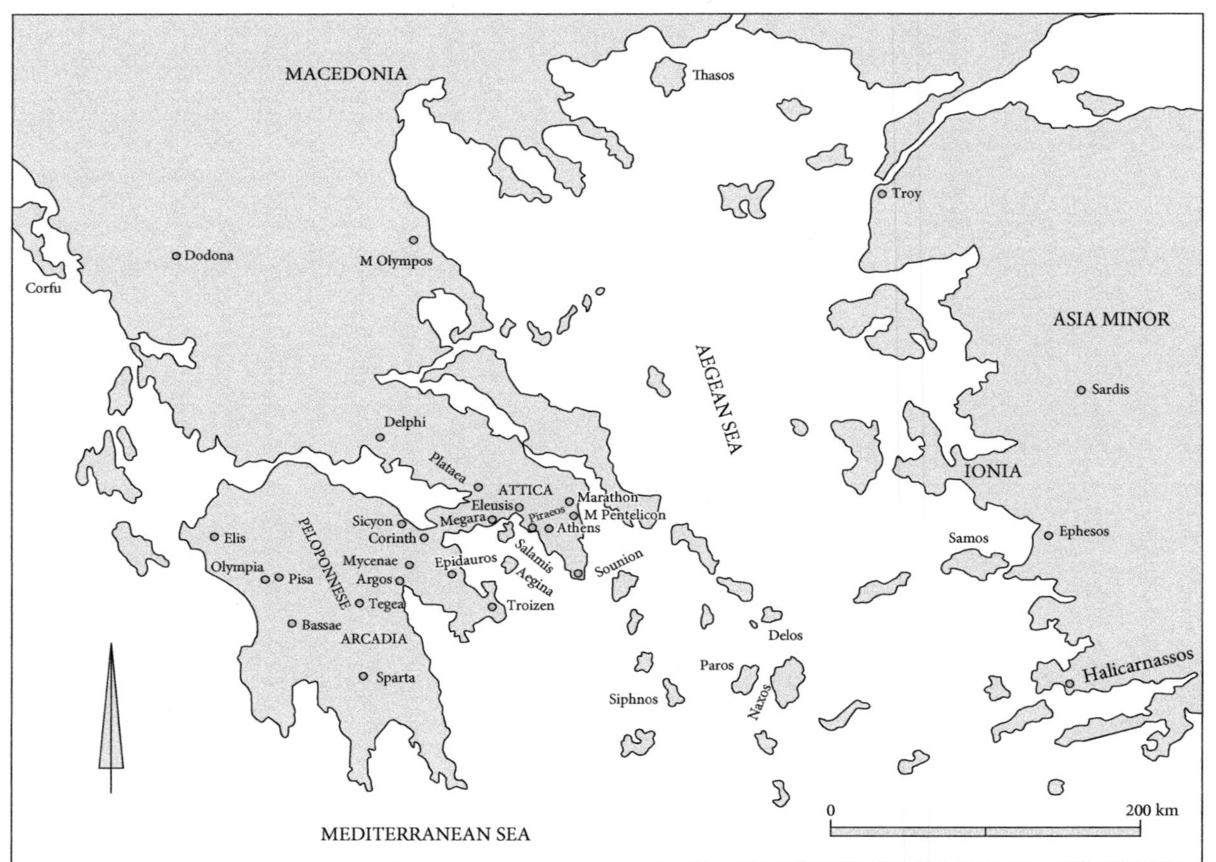

Map 1 Central and East Greece.

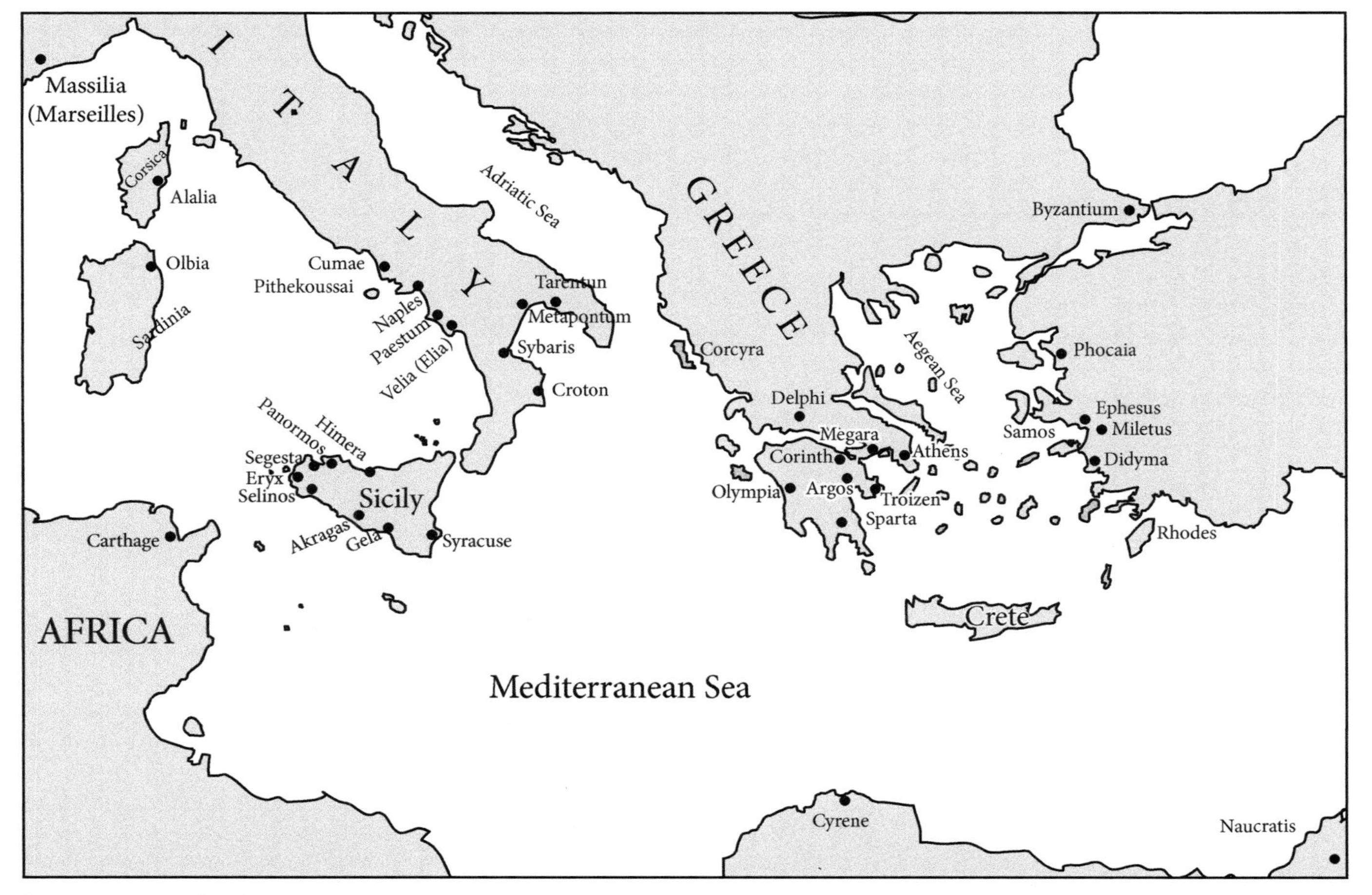

Map 2 Western, Central and East Greece.

CHAPTER 1
INTRODUCTION

'Temples of the mind'

The mainland buildings of Delphi, Olympia and the Athenian Acropolis, chosen for study in this book, are 'classics' of Greek architecture: they date from the sixth and fifth centuries BC (the archaic and classical periods). A study of Greek architecture could scarcely bypass them, as they are so central to the Greek experience. The well-preserved temples of Paestum in Magna Graecia (Southern Italy), and the unusual Olympieion of Akragas, Sicily, provide interesting parallels with the temples of mainland Greece. Dating from the same centuries, they have developed within the same general tradition, yet have their own local architectural character, possibly with some aspects dictated by alternative rituals and patterns of worship. By the end of the fifth century, designers of temples began to use the design vocabulary in yet more creative ways, even, in a sense, playful ways: examples of this would be the temples at Bassae and Tegea in Arcadia, mainland Greece. Yet, even at the beginning of the sixth century, experimentation was taking place, as monumental carved stone architecture first began taking over from its more perishable predecessors: examples would be the early octostyle temple of Artemis on Corfu (Corcyra) or the later-sixth-century 'mixed' temple of Athene at Assos, neither of which are mainland buildings. In the ancient world, temples were ubiquitous. A choice has had to be made from a very wide range of possible examples.

It is hoped that a close look at these few select examples will provide a useful introduction to the design vocabulary of Greek architecture. Technical terms for the architectural features are used throughout. Since many of these may be unfamiliar, a Glossary is provided: terms explained in the Glossary appear in bold type the first time they are mentioned in the text. The book aims to equip the reader to use these technical terms with confidence, and to confront any Greek temple with understanding and pleasure.

There is a great deal of accident in what remains to us of ancient Greek architecture. Most buildings that remain are incomplete and sculptures are fragmentary. Very often, buildings and their sculptures are separated. Some important temples have left only the scantiest traces or have disappeared completely; the unique architectural aspects of those temples may have vanished, or be traceable only by experts. To appreciate the real character of Greek temples takes some reconstruction work and some imagination. We shall be, as it were, building 'temples of the mind'.

Sources

In this book, some use has been made of ancient travel authors, so they should be introduced here. Although Greek architects quite often wrote books about their work, tantalisingly, no examples have survived. The work of the Roman architect Vitruvius (first century BC) may preserve material from those books. What does survive is later travel-writing, above all, the work of Pausanias (*c.* 110–180 AD) who wrote *Guide Book to Greece.* He offers a very detailed coverage of mainland sites, giving invaluable information which would be lost to us otherwise. To quote two obvious examples, without Pausanias we would not know the subjects of the pedimental sculpture of the Parthenon or the temple of Zeus at Olympia, even though this sculpture survives. At the same time, he does not always tell us what we would like to know. His own interest is very much directed towards myth, ritual, genealogies and ancient lore. He is much less concerned with the visual aspect of buildings. His work is therefore a well-stocked treasure-house to be explored gratefully for what it offers: he is quoted quite frequently in this book.

Another author from the ancient world with a strong interest in Greek and Roman past is Plutarch (46–120 AD). He too has much to offer, and was in fact a priest at Delphi in its last phase, who was intimately involved in the day-to-day workings of the Delphic shrine.

Both these writers had a nostalgic fascination with Greece, and a desire to immortalise its history, though both were living under Roman rule, and in almost the last flowering of the Classical pagan culture. Both were Greeks who wrote in Greek, and both were educated men of private means. Plutarch was a native of Chaeronea, a few miles from Delphi, and purchased his Roman citizenship. Pausanias came from the Mediterranean coast of Asia Minor, but travelled within mainland Greece for his researches. It is sometimes evident in his writing that he is recording his actual experience of a site, as he traces a recognisable itinerary, and this adds vividness to his account. In his extensive work, mistakes can occasionally be detected. Even this gives the reader a vivid sense of the traveller himself, in his attempts to transmit a full understanding of sites whose first flowering usually pre-dated his own time by 500 years and more. Pausanias clearly gathered information from locals, 'sacred guides' and other personnel on the spot, and the reader may well sympathise with these efforts. Though ancient, he is a source that needs weighing, like any other.

Strabo the geographer, another Greek writer of uncertain date, but living during and after the reign of Augustus, and Diodorus Siculus (first century BC), a Sicilian historian, whose extensive works survive in part, both have useful information on western sites.

The author of the present book followed the example of Pausanias by visiting all sites discussed. The fundamental references for the buildings described are Dinsmoor (1975) and Lawrence (1996) and the reader is directed to those monumental works for further information. The Bibliography will be found a useful start for further targeted study and detailed discussion.

Some use has been made also of literature contemporary with the buildings themselves, with the aim of bringing to light the kinds of issues that may have been important to the users of the sanctuaries. Tragedy and other works have been quoted, not for the stories, but for sidelights which are hopefully illuminating. (All quotes from tragedies have been re-translated by the author. Line numbers given are those from the original Greek texts.)

The sameness of Greek temples

A complaint can be made that all Greek temples are the same. Certainly, they are all composed of similar elements: steps, platforms, columns, architraves and friezes, pitched roofs and pediments. However, to the interested eye, each temple is unique. Even Doric temples, though said to conform to strict rules, all differ. As in any field of interest, what seems uniform to outsiders is – on inspection – full of nuance, innovation and individuality. The temples mentioned above will illustrate this.

The apparent sameness of Greek temples did not result from lack of imagination; the ancient Greeks are not known for a lack of creativity, so positive causes for sameness should be sought. A building usually declares its purpose by corresponding to a type; a response is aroused in the viewer as a result. A Gothic cathedral for example will be clearly recognisable as such, whatever personal responses a particular viewer brings to it. Another building may 'borrow' a response from the known type: for example, the Houses of Parliament, which were designed with Gothic features in order to 'borrow' the venerability associated with a medieval cathedral.

It is quite normal for building design to contain not only innovation, but also deliberate conformity to a type, sufficient to arouse certain emotional and practical responses from the viewer. There were additional reasons why this conformity should be true of Greek temples. Greeks, while intensely proud of their Greekness, had no political or even geographical unity. What bound them together was cultural: their language, religion, literature, ideas. They were insistent on their 'difference' and their superiority as a group: all others were 'barbarians' – non-Greek-speakers. Greeks lived on the mainland area now called Greece, but also all around the Mediterranean coasts, from Turkey to Sicily, Italy and even France, and on islands. Every city – or **polis** – was self-governing and formed an independent mini-state with the territory around it. The Greek people were not isolated from each other by these great distances but in fact did a lot of travelling, mainly by sea. Trade encouraged constant communication, and so did cultural events such as the four-yearly festivals in the great religious sanctuaries: the Olympic games, the Pythian games with the oracle at Delphi, and the lesser games of Nemea and Isthmia.

When worshippers came, for example, from Sicily to Olympia, they would feel quite at home, because the great temple of Zeus would be a supreme example of the kind of temple they expected to see. And the visitor to Sicily would be delighted by the similar temples found there and would also feel perfectly at home. There would be stimulating differences – but no doubt about the shared Greekness.

Landscape

One element, closely bound up with the character of each temple, is less likely to have suffered destruction – its setting. Even the Acropolis in the heart of modern Athens retains much of its natural surroundings, above all, the astonishing rock on which it sits. Delphi, a sanctuary whose site was chosen entirely for the impact of the place itself, retains virtually all its effect for the visitor. Much understanding can be gained from books and photos: yet the physical experience of the place, scents of trodden herbs, sunshine and keen mountain air are unforgettable to the lucky visitor, and are an important dimension of what the designers intended in the first place. In studying Greek temples from a book, this essential element is necessarily missing: the landscape.

The Greeks of our period did not go in for architectural landscaping, that is, they did not alter the landscape setting around their buildings much, as far as we can tell, apart from some planting schemes. They did not carve its contours (as the Romans did) into conformity with their building plans, levelling hills, bridging gullies and creating straight lines from one area to another. Instead, they were sensitive to what was there already, and placed their buildings to maximum effect, so that nature and art would work together as a satisfying whole. Whether the sanctuary was in remote countryside or busy city centre, buildings were planned to accord with the existing contours and character of the site.

Each sanctuary is very different and often expresses something of the nature of the god worshipped there: the site fits the deity.

Ancient and modern

Buildings were sited carefully, not only with reference to the view and to near and distant natural elements, but also in relation to other buildings or areas of significance close by. It will make sense to pay attention to these relationships. Most major sanctuaries were built over centuries, so the kind of planning which went into them was gradual and may even appear haphazard. Yet the antiquity of buildings sometimes gave them significance beyond mere appearance. The reverence due to an ancient monument, as with us today, could be played off against the smartness of a new building with interesting effect.

Ancient as the ancient Greeks seem to us, they did not seem so to themselves: they looked back from, say, the fifth century BC to more ancient times with nostalgia and pride in their past, just as we do, and liked to see it embodied and preserved in ancient monuments. They also liked to add something of their own, in the spirit of their age. Monumental buildings represented cutting-edge art and technology, implied political and military power, and were used to transmit messages about cultural identity. Designers of temples aimed for a physical perfection of beauty, which would speak of divinity and inspire the soul. Patrons wanted to impress visitors with the wealth and sophistication of the city, and to delight the citizens who owned and used the sanctuaries.

CHAPTER 2
WHAT WAS A SANCTUARY?

This book is about the architecture of the Greek sanctuary, which mainly – though not entirely – means the architecture of Greek temples. We shall be looking in some detail at temple buildings, but also at the layout and function of Greek sanctuaries.

An ancient Greek sanctuary was a marked-out sacred precinct (**temenos**), in which primarily an altar, but also temples – and a range of other specialised structures – might be found. For ancient Greek religion to function, sacred spaces were necessary where people could gather and rituals be celebrated. Rituals varied more than we would expect, including not only religious ceremonies with processions and choric performances, but also cultural activities such as sport, music events and drama festivals.

Who used sanctuaries?

Those who used the sanctuaries would not have made a particular choice to be religious. A city shrine belonged to the citizen body as a whole; a national shrine existed for all Greeks. Civic religious festivals would be part of a citizen's day-to-day life; participating in them would belong to his identity as a citizen of that city, it would not necessarily be a spiritual choice. Similarly, those who travelled to a more distant sanctuary like Olympia or Delphi were expressing their Greekness and claiming an experience which was theirs by right. There were many facets to the experience, some 'religious', others 'athletic' or 'cultural', some unique to that shrine, others common to all. The sanctuaries we shall be looking at offered ample recreation, a chance for Greeks of widely scattered city-states to mingle and (of special interest for this book) to experience the finest art and architecture available. For a more specifically religious experience, concerning issues of life, death and afterlife, the interested Greek would turn to a mystery religion such as the Eleusinian mysteries, which made special promises and special demands, and for which initiation had to be sought. Such mystery religions were not at all in conflict with civic religion but were additional to it.

What was in a sanctuary?

The most basic elements of a sanctuary were an altar and a boundary (**peribolos**). The altar was essential for the primary act of worship – the animal sacrifice. The boundary separated the sacred area off for its special purpose: dedication to a particular god or gods. Many other ingredients could be in a sanctuary, but these two were absolute requirements.

There might be a visible boundary such as a wall, or a series of boundary stones, or just a local understanding of where the boundary was. In a sanctuary of some importance, a monumental gateway (**propylon**) marking the entrance point, the transition from secular to sacred, could heighten the sense of significance. In order for processions of worshippers to reach the altar, a Sacred Way might be planned, or might develop informally over time. The altar would routinely be open-air and situated where there was plenty of room for crowds to gather; altars came in many shapes and sizes. We shall meet a few of these in the case studies, ranging from the time-honoured ash altar of Zeus at Olympia to the beautifully stylish altar of the Chians at Delphi.

To increase the visible importance of the altar and to house the **cult statue**, a temple could be added. But the temple was not a necessity as it probably had no particular function in open-air ceremonies. Even a large one was far too small to accommodate the kind of numbers that would attend a public sacrifice: it was not intended to house crowds, and was probably more the preserve of the temple staff. The extent of public access to the interior of temples varied quite considerably from example to example, and is a question that needs more research. A fine building as backdrop would add dignity to a ceremony, and it would normally contain the cult image of the patron god. A temple could also embody visual messages and so add to the meaning of the sanctuary. It could do this by means of the architecture itself, and also by the sculpted decoration which was part of the design. The building was also intended to delight the viewer by its aesthetic qualities. By its beauty, a carved temple also justified the enormous trouble and expense of its making.

One of the Greek words for 'statue' is agalma, whose literal meaning is 'pleasure' or 'delight'. It was expected that a carved statue would give delight – maybe to the god to whom it was offered, but certainly to its human viewers. The statue would represent the god of its temple, and be seen through the open doors as though the god were 'at home' – and the god could also see out through the open door. The appearance of the statue would obviously be very important, but it would not always be expensive or impressive. Yet it could indeed be phenomenally impressive: we will meet a wide range of statues in sanctuaries, in and outside of temples. At one end of the scale, a piece of driftwood of curious suggestive shape, the sort that gets people guessing at resemblances, could become a 'statue'. At the other end of the scale were the colossal **chryselephantine** works of Pheidias, artworks which represented the utmost that man could produce in terms of artistry, craftsmanship, ingenuity, impressiveness and expense. In between were shapeless **diapeta** ('fallen from the sky'), probably stone meteorites; **xoana**, early archaic wooden 'plank-shaped' sculptures that could be dressed up in clothes and jewellery to give them a more dignified appearance; like the ancient olive-wood Athene Polias, they could be taken down to the sea to be washed (and give their worshippers more opportunity for intimate service of the god); life-size archaic **kouroi** and **korai** who stood about in sanctuaries, and first seemed to replicate the human worshipper in art; major classical marble works which illustrated the perfection and beauty of the gods; small votive terracotta copies of cult statues which gave the ordinary person a chance to make their gift to a god; bronze figures mainly reserved for outdoor use, such as the colossal Athene Promachos with her glittering spear, which stood on the Athenian Acropolis, or the many life-size bronze heroes who stood in awesome gatherings in Delphi or Olympia.

A temple (normally locked) could serve as a treasury or bank for precious offerings made to the god. This could be a very important function in a rich sanctuary such as the Athenian Acropolis. In a large or complex Panhellenic sanctuary, there would also be individual treasuries: very small – but also architecturally eye-catching – temple-like buildings donated by other cities in which to keep their valuable offerings safe.

Any sanctuary would have gradually acquired a large number of smaller offerings. While buildings would mainly be offered by cities, individuals could make smaller offerings ranging from statues or gold or silver artefacts down to the humblest terracotta figurines or even baby-garments. Facilities such as theatres, club-houses, gymnasia and racing tracks were all an integral part of sanctuaries, and the events which they hosted were a part of the religious ritual.

Local or Panhellenic

Sanctuaries were either local or Panhellenic. Local sanctuaries were maintained by a polis mainly for the use of its own citizens; Panhellenic sanctuaries were intended for the use of all Greeks who wished to come, and they functioned as meeting places for the Greek community as a whole.

Of the sanctuaries we shall be looking at, two were Panhellenic, open to all Greeks. Both were famous for their four-yearly sports events: Olympia held the most important games of all, while Delphi was also famous for its oracle. The Athenian Acropolis, though clearly a showpiece, was a local sanctuary, primarily intended for the benefit of the people of Athens and its territory, Attica. Of the other sanctuaries, some were remote, like Bassae, others served their cities more centrally like the temples of Paestum, or the temple of Zeus in Akragas.

Sacred places

Here are two quite well-known passages from Greek drama which describe a 'sacred place'. In the first, Antigone and her old blind father Oedipus have wandered to the outskirts of Athens and stumbled on a shrine. In this case, there was no boundary marked out and Antigone recognises it as a shrine only by its untouched natural beauty.

> This place is holy, as I guess; it bursts
> with laurel, olive, vine; and fluttering
> around are many sweet-voiced nightingales.
>
> (Sophocles, *Oedipus at Colonus* 16–18)

Although Antigone recognises the spot as sacred, she does not know to whom it is dedicated. A local person explains:

> All this place is holy ground; awesome
> Poseidon dwells here; and the divine fire-bringer
> Titan Prometheus; the spot you stand on
> is called the Brazen Threshold of this land,
> Bulwark of Athens; and the neighbouring fields
> claim for themselves this horseman as their leader,
> his name to be their own – Colonus …
> (Sophocles, *Oedipus at Colonus* 54–9)

A sanctuary can be dedicated to multiple deities and heroes, some of major importance such as Poseidon, and some never heard of outside their own village, like Colonus.

In the next example, Socrates has taken an unaccustomed (for him) walk outside the city. He recognises a particular place as special by the same kind of natural features as Antigone noticed, this time including water. For him, what clinches it as sacred is the man-made evidence he sees – the statues and other votive offerings, proof of worship.

> By Hera, what a lovely place to stop! This plane tree so spreading and high, and the lovely shadiness of the willow … in full bloom, it makes the place so fragrant. And besides, the spring is really charming, the way it flows from under the plane tree – very cold water judging by my foot! The place seems to be sacred to the Nymphs and to Achelous because of all the statues of girls and the other votive offerings. And … how pleasant and sweet the fresh air … Clear and summery, it is humming with the chorus of cicadas. But the nicest thing of all is the grass, the way it grows on a gentle slope, thick enough to be just right when you lay your head on it. (Plato, *Phaedrus* B-C)

The sacred place seems to be what we would call a beauty spot. The natural elements come together in a way that particularly impresses the viewer. In both of these examples the response of the visitor is actually to sit and enjoy the place.

Mountains, caves, groves, springs: these were the kind of natural features which attracted worship. There was a sense of the **numinous** – that is, a feeling that the place was somehow haunted by an unseen unexplained spirit. In the shrines we shall look at, built up and sophisticated as they were, it is often still possible to sense the special natural character that had first attracted attention.

Sacred events

Socrates tells us something else about ancient Greek worship: it was interesting and fun – it was a bit of a show. At the opening of Plato's *Republic*, Socrates has gone down to the Piraeus to see the procession for a new goddess – Bendis – a sort of Thracian Artemis. He says his motive in going was:

> 'to offer prayers to the goddess; and also because I wanted to see how they would celebrate the festival, as this was the first time they were doing it. I was delighted with the procession of the locals; but that of the Thracians was equally beautiful'.

More is to come. A young man asks,

> '"Has no one told you of the torch-race on horseback in honour of the goddess which will take place in the evening?" "On horseback!" I replied: "That's a new idea. Will horsemen carry torches and pass them one to another as they race?" "Yes", said Polemarchus, "and there will be an all-night festival, which will be worth seeing"' (Plato *Republic* A. 327).

There is an element of showmanship, of spontaneity and excitement, as well as of piety and respect to the gods.

Another example which demonstrates the range of spectacle and showmanship is found in Plutarch's *Life of Nikias*. Although written 500 years after the event, it seems to highlight several authentic aspects of the sacred festivals. Nikias was a very rich and generous man, of genuine piety, who took a leading role in Athenian affairs after the death of Pericles. Rich citizens were expected to finance various public works, such as theatre performances or warships, but Nikias's generosity on this occasion obviously was especially memorable:

> When cities would send choruses (to the sacred island of Delos) to sing for Apollo, they would just arrive, and as soon as the crowd of islanders came down to the ship, they would bid them to start singing, haphazardly, disembarking in a rush, at the same time as getting their garlands on and changing into their costumes. But when Nikias led a **theoria** (417 BC), he disembarked at Rhenaia (an island next to Delos), with the chorus and the animals for sacrifice and the rest of the equipment, and he had with him a bridge of boats already prepared at Athens, made to measure and decorated splendidly with gilding, with paintwork, with garlands, with hangings. By night, he set it in place to bridge the narrow channel between Rhenaia and Delos, and at daybreak, leading the procession and the chorus, gorgeously dressed and singing as they went, he crossed by the bridge. After the ceremonial sacrifices, and the competition, and the feastings, he dedicated and erected a bronze palm tree for Apollo. (Plutarch: *Life of Nikias*, 3)

This bronze palm tree, commemorating the birth of Apollo and Artemis on Delos, became celebrated, and its granite base, with Nikias's dedication inscription, can still be seen today.

The anecdote gives a clue as to expectations of a festival: the sacred song and dance, special costumes, sacrifices, competitions and feastings. Spectacle, panache, choreography, colour, music – all these and much more are the human element, the sound effects, the personalities and the massed movement which was part of sanctuaries, and should not be forgotten as we look painstakingly at the temples and other buildings, trying to piece them together into something of their former appearance.

The meaning of public worship

Worship is something that went on in the sanctuaries we shall be looking at. The above-quoted passages suggest that worship was not generally seen as a chore, but in fact was a delightful element of people's lives. It included specialised activities such as athletic competition, theatre performances, feasting (at public sacrifices) and musical performances. A great animal sacrifice was in effect a public barbecue. The gods received their portions while the worshippers feasted on the grilled meat. The general citizen was involved, as spectator and partaker. Children and young people would be trained to take part in the choruses and the dances. Adults would serve in various ways, ranging from joining processions to doing a stint at priesthood. Joining in would be an expected part of being a citizen, not a choice to be especially religious.

The singing and ritual would form a continuum with the architecture and sculpture. The songs would tell the stories of the gods, some of the rituals would re-enact them and the same stories were sculpted on the buildings. Every element reinforced the whole. All this created a loose 'cosmic' structure in which the individual could expect to live safely. The prayers, songs and sacrifices requested protection from the gods, and some would be aimed at fertility and prosperity of the city. Individuals could make their own sacrifices, offerings and specific requests for their personal benefit. Additionally, the festivals could be seen to form a continuum with the way things should be done in society. In *Oedipus the King*, Sophocles has his chorus cry out at a moment of high tension and despair:

> CHORUS: If such [evil] doings are held in honour,
> why should I join the sacred dance (*choreuein*)?
> I will go no more in worship to the sacred shrine of earth [i.e. the **omphalos** at Delphi]…
> … or to Olympia.
> Godly things are on the wane. (Sophocles *Oedipus the King*, 895–910)

The Chorus of old men links the good ordering of society, the trustworthiness of the gods' utterances, and the willingness to worship and the honouring of sacred things. For them, it is a single chain that must not be broken. Of course, this is poetry, but it offers a sense of what worship might ideally mean at one level, to the person in the street.

Priests

Another aspect of sanctuary life is of course the need for priests. Their role was to get the sacrifices done properly, sacrifice being the core activity of a sanctuary. They would be appointed to a particular priesthood, usually attached to one temple. If taking a long-term post, they would be responsible for the good running of their precinct and their temple, and even be expected to do repairs and improvements out of their own pocket. At the other end of the scale, Pausanias mentions priests at Olympia who were only appointed for one month (Pausanias 5.15.10). Whatever needed to be known for the practical task would have been very important, as the welfare of the city depended on successfully performed public sacrifices. The task was functional, not moral or didactic. There was no body of doctrine for priests to learn, or impart. Even so, some priests may have become outstanding. Only one example can be quoted however, and that is the highly regarded priestess of Athene Polias, Lysimache, who served for 64 years, at the end of the fifth into the fourth century, recorded by an inscription on her statue base (Pliny *Nat. Hist.* 34.19.143). She is thought to have been the model for Aristophanes's strong-minded heroine, Lysistrata, in the play of that name.

Priests were men or women, usually in accordance with the gender of the god they served. At home, the father of a family would act in a priestly way, making small offerings at family altars and shrines. The mother also might tend a household altar, giving flowers or cakes. In tragedy, we often see women making offerings, for example, Clytemnestra at the start of *Agamemnon* visits all the altars around the palace, and Queen Jocasta in *Oedipus the King* (OT 911-913) takes garlands and incense to the shrines of the gods in fear for her husband.

Thus, there is not so much distinction as we might expect between priests and laypersons. The community would in general be behind them, and was very contributory to sacred events. The effort was for the sake of all and of each.

Access to temples

Linked with the thought of the 'priest-in-charge' is the practical question of who had access to temples. It seems that there could be as many answers to this as there were temples. Priestesses were depicted in art holding a large key, and this indicates that priests and priestesses controlled their buildings. However, each temple would have had a laid-down directive, linked with its situation and ritual function. Some would have been open every day, some as little as once a year. They may well have had specific ritual uses, however there would not have been room to accommodate the general public attending a sacrifice. Later writers such as Pausanias or Diodorus imply that they had access to certain temples, for example Pausanias describing the statue of Zeus at Olympia, and viewing it from the upstairs gallery. A great temple like Olympia would have had plenty of personnel to monitor the flow of visitors, and besides that, crowds were controlled by a substantial barrier surrounding the famous cult statue. Other temples had these barriers, but not all did (Mylonopoulos 2011). There was also a halfway situation where the visitor could look through grilles fixed between porch columns and get some kind of impression of what lay within. Seeing the statue was probably a significant experience in itself.

CHAPTER 3
FROM MUD HUT TO MARBLE TEMPLE: DORIC AND IONIC ORDERS

Predecessors

The origins of Greek architectural style are much studied yet remain obscure. What seems clear is that monumental buildings entirely of carved stone in recognisable architectural style began to be built around the beginning of the sixth century BC. As we shall see, there were basically two styles: **Doric**, a plain and sturdy style developed first; **Ionic**, more graceful and decorative, soon followed.

At that time, Greeks would have had some notion of monumental stone buildings in Greece from the still visible remains of masonry dating from the Bronze Age, or, as they would have called it, the Age of Heroes. Impressive architectural ruins were to be seen at Mycenae, with its monumental Lion Gate, and elsewhere, some of which are still visible today (Fig. 1). The walls of these ruins are composed of enormous boulders, roughly shaped and fitted together, held in place by gravity, small pieces of rock stuffed into any gaps. **Cyclopean** fortification walls of this date were still in use in the early fifth century on the Acropolis of Athens.

However, with the collapse of Mycenaean civilisation (*c.* 1200–1100 BC), knowledge of how to make buildings of massive stone seems to have been lost for several centuries. During this period walls were made of mud brick or wattle and daub, and roofs of thatch, with wood as a framework. Unbaked mud reinforced with straw and hair can be shaped in moulds into large rectangular blocks that fit together neatly. When kept fairly dry, but not too dry, mud is a strong and durable material; however, it dissolves in water. This factor would dictate such safety measures as overhanging roofs, protective surfaces and stone rubble foundations. For extra strength and protection from damp, stone blocks could be used in lower courses of walls, and little cylinders of stone might be used as **bases** for wooden columns. Such building methods are obvious ways of using readily available materials; they were used by the Greeks for buildings of every size, during the period between the Mycenaean era and the early sixth century BC. Even after the introduction of stone and marble for temples, perishable materials continued to be used for private houses and humbler public buildings. Such buildings disappear leaving little apparent trace, yet archaeologists can detect, and, to some extent, reconstruct them.

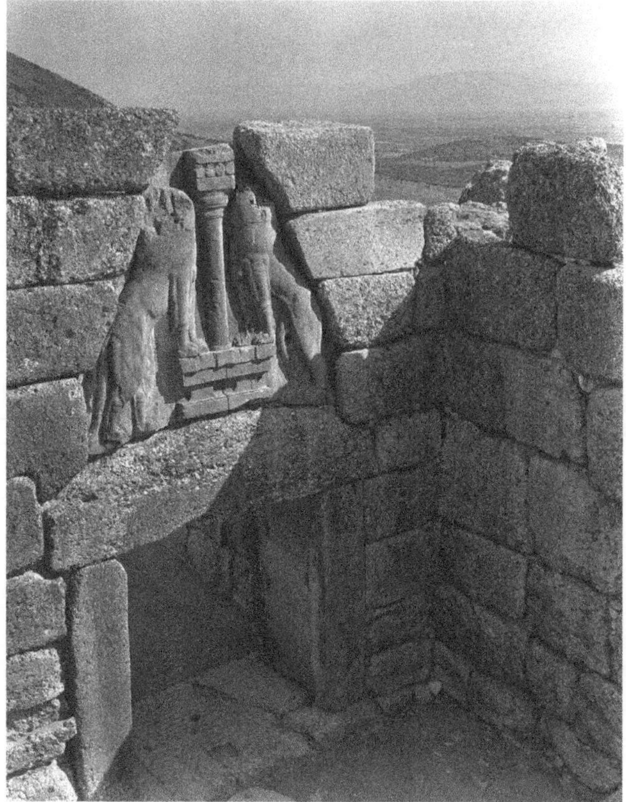

Fig. 1 The Lion Gate at Mycenae, *c.* 1250 BC.

'Dark Age' temple building

It is thought that Mycenaeans did not build temples, but worshipped in open-air sacred areas around an altar, or else incorporated shrines into the palace-buildings that characterised their civilisation. Homer, composing *c.* 750 BC, mentions a temple on the Trojan citadel containing a seated statue of a goddess (*Iliad* 6.300). Though the poet may have pictured his Trojan temple among palaces 'of polished stone', real temples throughout the so-called Dark Ages (*c.* 1100–800 BC) were probably made of wood, thatch and mud with some use of stone for foundations.

The ground plans of such wood-framed buildings have been traced. The construction method and materials limit the width (because wooden beams were needed to span the roof, whether flat or pitched) but do not limit the length; it would be easy to add extra rooms or sections by elongation. On a large-scale building, the pitched roof would need a central internal row of columns as support, probably reaching up to the ridge beam. The thatch would lend itself well to a rounded **apse**-end at the rear. However, at the front, the face of the pitched roof would be a flat triangular gable end, perhaps left open for a smoke-outlet. Additionally, a porch could be added to protect the entrance, and an all-round colonnade could support the overhanging roof at the sides. The overhang, having begun as a protective measure for mud walls, would then become a useful shaded space for social activity. The wooden props to support the overhang would not need to be very strong or very close together.

Evidence for buildings of this sort is also found in the form of eighth-century painted terracotta models (two are displayed in the National Archaeological Museum, Athens) which feature the steep apse-ended roof, apparently thatched, the open triangular gable front, and the porch with slim, apparently wooden columns.

Changes came with the invention of terracotta roof tiles to replace thatch. The enormous weight of a tiled roof made more demands on the substructure, so the wooden elements would need to become more massive. In addition, tiles – which are held on a roof largely by gravity – need to lie at a shallower angle than thatch – which requires a steep pitch for run-off of water. Tiles also fit more easily into a rectangular arrangement, so the apse-end would become outdated.

Some elaborate temples were built using terracotta to protect, and then to decorate, the exterior wooden parts of the structure. Terracotta could easily be painted and moulded. An example of this was the wooden temple of Apollo at Thermon dated to the late seventh century, which had impressive roof ornaments in painted baked clay and a set of painted clay panels as well (also in the National Archaeological Museum, Athens). A conjectural reconstruction of this building suggests a fairly finished Doric form, realised in wood and terracotta.

Stone-working

An essential factor in the move towards stone building was the discovery of stone-working skills. Monumental sculpture began to appear in the mid-seventh century. Masonry and sculptural skills overlap and both were necessary if stone architecture was to be developed. All elements of a stone building, whether decorative or 'plain', had to be hand-carved. It cannot be emphasised enough that the high-precision carving of a Greek temple is a large part of its aesthetic effect. The joints, if visible, are planned, not randomly placed. On the whole, they are so precise that they can hardly be seen. (A method called **anathyrosis** was used to help achieve this efficiently: the margins of the blocks fitted precisely, while the hidden inner face was less finely fitted (see Fig. 75).) Every block fitted a particular position on the temple; they were not interchangeable. This fine fit was to a large extent what kept the building together, since no mortar was used. For this reason, a collapsed temple can be successfully re-erected.

The development of stone sculpture might in itself have influenced temple design. A large-size carved cult statue would lose some of its visual impact when placed to the side of a central row of columns; a central position between two framing rows of columns would provide a more dramatic focus. The double row of columns would then suggest or require a more complicated roof structure, involving horizontal cross-beams (Fig. 30). These beams would increase the stability of the whole structure, and the idea of a horizontal ceiling could then naturally develop, filling in between the beams, closing off and hiding the roof-space. The ceiling could then eventually become a decorative feature in itself.

'Petrification' of wooden forms

It is broadly agreed that the forms of the wood, mud and tile temples were converted into carved stone. The details of this process are far from clear.

As we saw earlier, it was desirable for temples to be easily recognised as such. Since they had no function other than to house a statue and to indicate the 'presence' of a god, their appearance and the impression they created were the most important thing about them.

Stone was a far more impressive and durable material than mud and wood or even than painted moulded terracotta. The idea of carved stone buildings must have been derived from the disciplined architecture of Egypt (where Greeks were first allowed to settle in the mid-seventh century) as well as from Asia Minor, with perhaps some inspiration from the rugged stonework of the Greek heroic age (Mycenae, etc.). Stone buildings making use of columns, decorative carving and impressive statues were to be seen widely in Egypt. Luckily for the Greeks, their local **limestone** and subsequently marble lent themselves to fine and fluid carving very readily, unlike the hard granite of Egypt.

The move to stone necessitated much more serious foundations to bear the great weight. A wood and mud building might make use of stone rubble for foundations under the weight-bearing sections, and make do with beaten earth for the floor. But the solid platforms on which stone temples are raised have the double benefit of displaying the temple and of providing a firm basis of finely fitting squared blocks which hold together well in an earthquake. Under the more weight-bearing sections, that is, the walls and the colonnades, the stone foundations go deeper (see Fig. 30).

In the pre-stone temples, colonnades were made of wood. Wooden columns could be thin props or whole tree trunks, shaped with an axe. It is speculated that either the natural tree-shape or the downward strokes of the axe on a rounded trunk could have given rise to the downward grooves on Greek stone columns, termed **fluting**. To support the enormous weight of a stone and tile roof structure, columns had to be both sturdy and carefully spaced. Engineering calculations would be made as to size and closeness of supports for the weight-bearing stone beams that lay across them; an appearance of combined strength and ease was desirable. Such calculations led eventually to the complex and subtle system of proportions which characterises Greek architecture, and which goes way beyond practical necessity.

While a wooden structure would hold together by means of joinery, a stone structure relied a great deal on gravity. The structural method of a Greek temple is known as post and **lintel**, meaning that horizontal members rest upon vertical props. The simplest example of this method is Stonehenge, where it is easy to see the principle at work. The weight, if fully supported, actually holds the structure together. This method of building continued unchanged for centuries among the Greeks, just being refined in certain details.

It was the Romans who took classical architecture finally in new directions with their exploitation of the arch, **pier**, and vault, the decorative column and the use of concrete.

Use of materials

Stone columns were at first **monolithic**, that is, made from a single block. Later it was found more practical to fit together several **drums**, giving the effect of a single block; together they made up the shaft. At the top of the shaft was the **capital**, a crowning element, which was broader and spread the weight of the superstructure more widely. This extra section became decorative and gave character to the building. Upon it rested the heavy horizontal beam (**architrave**), with another beam above (fronted by the decorative **frieze**); they supported the roof structure. The roof was pitched, that is, it consisted of two slopes resting against each other at the high **ridge,** leaving at each end a triangular space which was filled in with an upright wall (**tympanum**), or gable end. This triangle is the pediment, which, together with the colonnade, is a 'trademark' element of classical architecture (Fig. 2).

Even in a stone temple, the hidden parts of the roof were usually constructed of wood. This would lighten the heavy load a bit. Roof tiles would be terracotta or marble. Everything else would be of stone except the interior ceiling and the doors. The ceiling

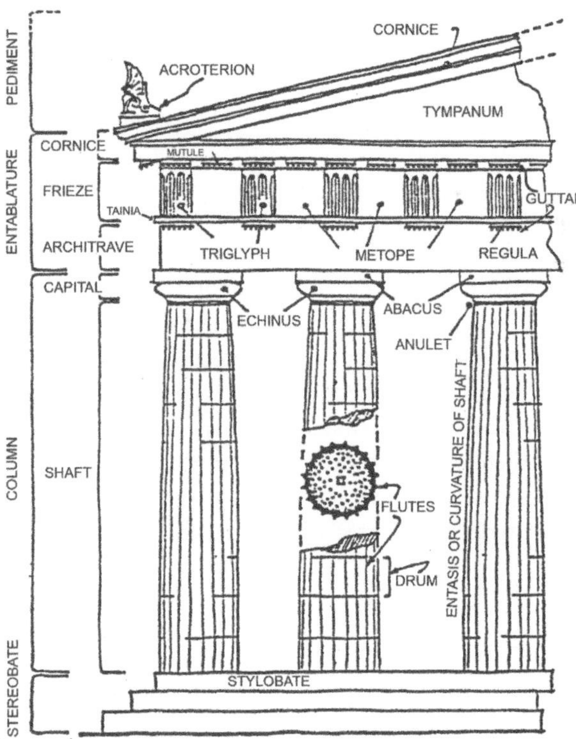

Fig. 2 Drawing of a generic Doric elevation.

would be made in a complicated 'box' construction called **coffering** which would be realised in wood indoors (Fig. 76), and in stone in the covered colonnade area. The doors would be made of imported wood: ebony, cypress or cedar of Lebanon, with inlay of ivory, metal or other precious material. Wood was not necessarily a cheap alternative for the Greeks, since suitable timber was not plentiful. Pine might be imported from Macedonia or the Black Sea for general carpentry, and the exotic showy woods from the Eastern Mediterranean.

The stone for a temple was usually local for the sake of cheapness. But very often the sculptured parts would be of marble imported from the Cycladic islands, probably Naxos or Paros. **Parian** marble was the favourite because of its pure white brilliance, while **Naxian** was greyer. In Athens, after about the first quarter of the fifth century, the local **Pentelic** marble was used. Having this readily available fine material, Athens had a natural advantage.

Marble takes a very fine finish. Where the stone was not marble – and this was mostly the case – a smooth surface could be obtained by coating columns with marble-dust **stucco**. This was done with great finesse, preserving sharpness of the flutes. It was so strong that even today it can be seen intact where unweathered (see Fig. 117).

The provision of stone, whether imported or local, was a complicated process. It had to be ordered well beforehand in specific sizes to be quarried by skilled workers, then roughly shaped at the quarry to reduce the bulk for transport (Fig. 119). Labour and transport were vital elements of cost in the planning of a temple. Marble was often used for sculpture on a building, and sometimes for other parts, even when the main part of the building was **poros** or limestone. It was worth the trouble of bringing marble over from an island, because of the fine effects that could be obtained.

The Greek architectural orders

There are two main styles in ancient Greek architecture: they are known as the Doric and Ionic orders. Doric is associated with the Greek mainland while Ionic originates from Ionia, Greek city states of the islands, and eastern coast of the Aegean. Doric is considered to be sturdy, 'masculine', rule-based, uniform. Ionic is considered to be elegant, 'feminine', decorative, inventive. These are of course stereotypes. The two styles have plenty in common. Eventually there will be a third style – **Corinthian**. This style took its name from the elaborate foliate capital, which could be viewed from all round. Apart from the capital, it resembled the Ionic style. We shall see the first example of this in Chapter 14, at Bassae.

Doric ground plan

Study of a ground plan of a Doric temple will show that the peripheral part of the roofed area is open-air (Fig. 3). The relatively small indoor part, enclosed by walls, is the **cella** or **naos**. It was lockable and contained the statue, and perhaps precious offerings too. Access

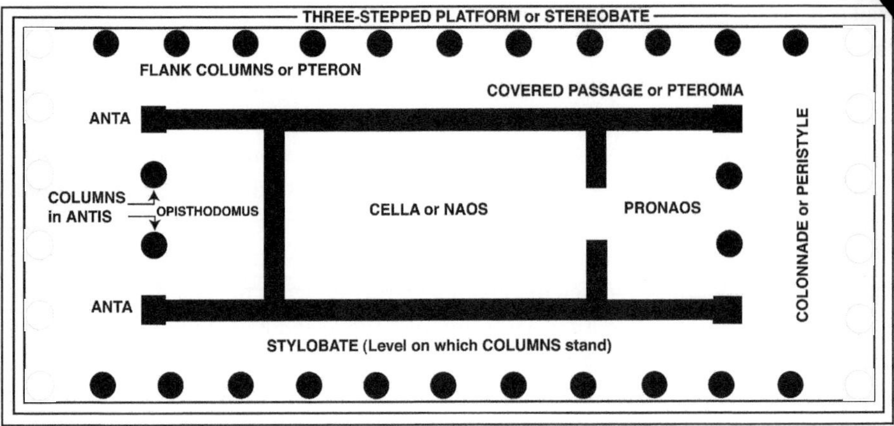

Fig. 3 Ground plan of a generic Doric temple.

was controlled, and the small size of the cella or naos did not matter since worship took place outside, and was focused on processions and sacrifices.

The ground plan of a temple or treasury is simple, not so different from the Dark Age hall, except that measurement and proportion become ever more calculated and sophisticated. The cella is an enclosed, rectangular, roofed chamber, usually single, sometimes double. It may be surrounded by a colonnade or **peristyle** on a raised platform, reached by steps. There will probably be a porch at the entrance (**pronaos**) and perhaps a matching porch at the other end (**opisthodomos**). Porches are defined by the protruding ends of the cella walls and these protruding sections are called **antae**. Porch columns may be arranged between the antae: **in antis**. Or they may be more numerous and spread right across the façade: **prostyle**.

Doric style

Doric is characterised by its columns and its frieze (Fig. 2). The pediment is common to both orders, Doric and Ionic. Doric columns are tapered and **fluted**; that is, the shaft is wider at the bottom than at the top, and is carved with shallow concave grooves running downwards which meet at sharp vertical ridges called **arrises**. The columns sit firmly on the **stylobate** or top step of the platform (**stereobate**), with no separate base or other element. The joint with the platform is elegant and economical (Fig. 75). The capitals consist of two sections, a cushion-like circular lower section (**echinus**) which supports a square flattish element above (**abacus**). On this sit the architrave and frieze, two horizontal beams which, together with the decorative projecting **cornice** above, make up the **entablature**. Below the echinus are some unobtrusive rings around the thinnest part of the column: these are necking rings or **anulets**. The square abacus juts slightly beyond the architrave which rests on it. Since the column foot aligns with the edge of the platform, it is easy to see that the abacus is slightly more spreading than the column

…est part. The column, as well as tapering overall from bottom to top, usually …lled **entasis:** this is a slight swelling towards the middle of the shaft, more … the sixth-century archaic period, and more subtle in the fifth-century …assical period.

Above the plain architrave is the **Doric frieze**, a horizontal band of decoration divided into alternate sections – **metopes** and **triglyphs**, both roughly square or oblong. Triglyphs are divided vertically into three strips divided by two carved grooves (and normally two half-grooves on the edges), hence the name. Metopes are slightly recessed flat plaques which can be painted or carved with mythological figures. Below the frieze runs a thin projection called a **tainia** or 'ribbon'. Above and below the frieze are some strange features with the appearance of blocks with pegs sticking out of them. They are arranged at regular intervals: under each triglyph, a thin **regula** with peg-like **guttae** adheres to the tainia; and above every metope and triglyph, a **mutule** adheres to the bottom surface of the cornice (**soffit**); it looks like a larger block, from which two or three rows of little 'pegs' can be seen hanging down. These features have such a utilitarian appearance that the conviction arises that they are functional wooden structures copied in stone. They have no function in the stone system of the Doric order, yet are an invariable part of the Doric frieze.

The metopes and triglyphs arouse similar discussion. Vitruvius, the first-century AD Roman architectural writer, derived the triglyph form from the wooden roof beam-ends resting on the architrave (Vitruvius: 4.2.1–3). The triglyph grooves would be a reminder of the rough natural texture of the cut wood; the metopes would be plain or decorative slabs masking the spaces between. While this explanation holds quite well for the frieze running along the bottom of the sloping roof, it makes no sense on the façade under the pediment, where no beams would end. But these functional-looking forms probably became conventionalised, retaining only a distant relationship to any real structural parts.

Another reminiscence of wooden forms is the thickened anta. The antae are the extensions of the cella walls, which form the porch area. When the walls were made of mud brick, these sections were vulnerable to damage and so were cased in wooden planking. This thicker casing is copied in stone.

The cella walls also reflect the old mud-brick construction. Mud brick could rest on a lower course of worked stone which lifted it away from the harmful damp of the ground. The lowest few feet of an **ashlar** wall are often differentiated with a taller course of blocks called **orthostates**. These preserve tradition, and also the base of the wall is emphasised and appears sturdy.

Another mud-brick feature was the gradual tapering of the wall towards the top: this is sometimes imitated in stone.

Ionic style

The Ionic order is also distinguished by its columns and its frieze (Fig. 62). The columns are typically tall and slender. They may taper only slightly and will probably not have the faint curve (entasis) of Doric. They stand upon fairly elaborate **bases**. In the old wood and mud construction, stone bases had served the practical purpose of protecting wooden columns from rotting at the bottom, especially when standing on an earth floor. While Doric abandoned this feature, Ionic developed it. Varied 'rings' of convex and concave sections were piled into an interesting shape (Fig. 72). On a grand temple, such as that of Artemis at Ephesus, the column shaft just above the base might even be sculpted with narrative.

The Ionic capital is the most eye-catching feature of the order (Fig. 4). Like the Doric capital, it has an abacus and an echinus. But the abacus is so small it is hardly noticed – while the echinus is prolonged into two delightful scrolls (**volutes**) curling down; a decorative band fills the space between.

The flutes of the Ionic column are also more elaborate than the Doric and there are more of them on a slimmer shaft. The ends of the vertical grooves are rounded, top and bottom; between the grooves are flat sections called **fillets**. As the shaft meets its base, it is likely to flare out slightly, unlike the Doric, which maintains its steady simple line. The Ionic column is elegant but definitely 'busier' than the Doric.

Fig. 4 A marble Ionic capital; Delphi.

The entablature resting on the columns will be divided as before into architrave and frieze with cornice above. The architrave will probably be divided into three plain steps, imitating overlapping wooden boarding. The frieze will be continuous and may be topped with a carved **dentil** design of alternating tooth-like blocks and spaces (Fig. 67). These perhaps represent the small roof rafters, just as the triglyphs represent the heavier beam-ends. In Ionia, the frieze itself will be left plain; on the Greek mainland, a sculptured narrative often replaced the dentils. Similarly, the Ionic pediment was usually left empty in Ionia, but often sculpted in mainland Greece.

The examples of Ionic style examined in this book will all be mainland ones, and display a certain Doric influence. Ionic temples in their homeland of Ionia are often very vast, so much so that they may even be unroofed in the central area. While the elements used are like Doric, the overall effect must have been very different indeed.

Major Ionic temples in East Greece

The important Temple of Hera on Samos (38 × 85 metres), built in the last quarter of the sixth century, illustrates Ionic layout (Fig. 5). Its restored ground plan shows that it was **dipteral** on the flanks, that is, the colonnades are two deep. On the short ends, it was **tripteral**, that is, there was a third row of columns. At the back end, these rows were of nine columns each, uniformly spaced. On the entrance front, the rows were of eight columns each, and the spacing varied, being wider at the centre; this was achieved by removing a notional central column and then readjusting the spacing of the central four. This more open front arrangement threw a strong emphasis onto the entrance.

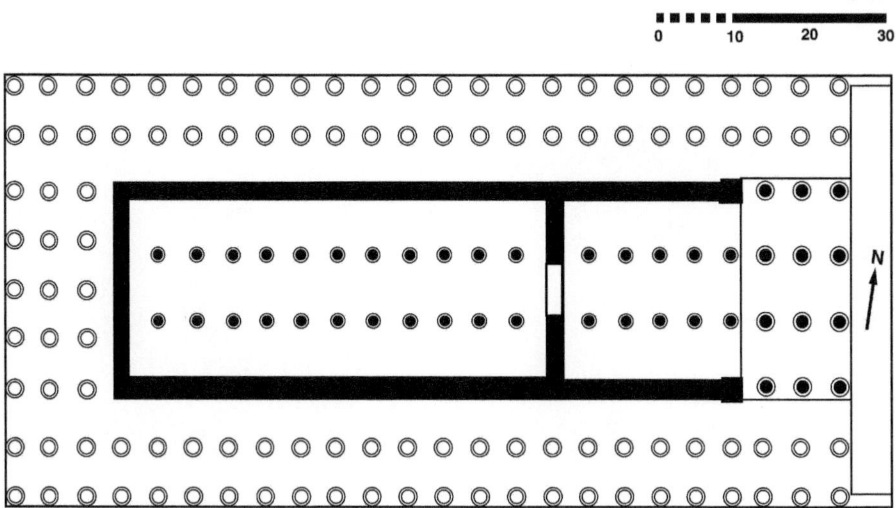

Fig. 5 Restored ground plan of the later archaic temple of Hera of Samos.

Through the three rows of porch columns could be seen inner depths – the extended antae enclosed two smaller-scaled colonnades of five each side, leading to the door itself. Overall, the effect would have been of a 'forest of columns' – it is speculated that a temple like this was even intended to recall a sacred grove. Furthermore, the emphasis was on the front and the entrance, whereas a Doric temple did not draw special attention to its entrance.

The varied spacing of Ionic façade columns just described was easily achieved because of the flexibility of the continuous frieze above. The disciplined arrangement of the Doric triglyph frieze encouraged much greater regularity in spacing. Nevertheless, it will be seen that the great Ionic temples of the east had a certain influence on mainland Doric, mostly at Athens, and also in the west, Sicily and Southern Italy.

CHAPTER 4
ARCHITECTURAL SCULPTURE

Architectural sculpture is often studied out of context. This approach is prompted and reinforced by the fact that very little architectural sculpture remains in situ. The typical location for admiring such works is in a gallery or museum where they appear as relief or free-standing sculptures in their own right, studied for their place in the evolution of sculptural style as a whole. Here, we shall consider architectural sculpture only in its intended role as part of a building.

Architectural sculpture in its original context can be viewed formally as a way for the designer to highlight particular parts of a building; or it can be seen iconographically as a vehicle for specific messages, interpreting or reinforcing the meaning of a building. In both aspects, it should be seen as an integral part of the architecture. Equally, we can reverse the idea: since every inch of a Greek temple or treasury was skilfully carved and shaped with sculpting techniques to fit a unique slot in the whole, we could view the entire building as a complex piece of sculpture, combining both abstract and organic forms.

Sculptured components of a temple

The buildings we will be considering are for the most part temples and treasuries (which have the form of miniature temples). The buildings vary but, as we have seen already, are made up of similar components: a stepped platform, columns supporting an architrave topped by a frieze, a cornice and a pediment. Originally the three corners of the pediment were finished with roof sculptures (**acroteria**): these tend to be forgotten as there are none left in situ to remind us of their position; and there was further decoration along the roof edge on the flanks (Figs. 2, 11 and 40).

The areas on the building where we can expect to see major sculpture are the triangular pediments, the rectangular metopes (if the frieze is Doric) or the long ribbon of the continuous **Ionic frieze.** Each building differs in the amount of sculpture it carries and on which of the likely areas of the building it is found; this is a design point to which the ancient viewer would have been immediately sensitive.

The Greeks were very conscious of structures and the structural components of a complex whole. Temples come in all sizes, yet the elements and their proportions are constant. Sculptures on a temple always emphasise the component parts.

Doric decoration

In a Doric temple, the pediment is likely to be the major focus. Second to that, the viewer will check the metopes. If the pediment is empty, more emphasis will fall on the metopes, or vice versa. The viewer might also check the inner porches for a second sculptural sequence, especially if the outer metopes were blank (Figs. 28 and 29).

The platform and columns of a Doric temple remained undecorated. Since columns were fluted, this was considered decoration enough: no one would want to interfere with the pure vertical sweep of the column with its subtle curve from pavement to entablature. However, the Doric capitals and anulets, though plainly carved, were marked out with paint.

Above the capitals comes the architrave, topped by the frieze. The Doric frieze is divided into triglyphs and metopes. The metopes, whether sculpted or not, would have been picked out with paint. The horizontal of the frieze is therefore always emphasised by these decorative segments, which partly interrupt the horizontal with groups of mini-verticals (the triglyphs), echoing the fluted columns.

At each narrow end of the building rises the triangular pediment. In a Doric temple of any importance, this will probably carry sculpture. In any case, there is a nice geometric contrast of the elongated flattened triangle with the rectangular building it crowns. As mentioned above, the pediment will usually be punctuated by acroteria on the central peak and at each corner. These will obviously vary in size in accordance with the building's size and may therefore be enormous or quite small. Acroteria are often in the form of winged or windswept figures because they are viewed against the sky; or for the same reason they may be elaborate floral motifs with a pierced design through which light shows.

Meanwhile the side view of the building was routinely enriched with a decorative **sima** or gutter, lion-head waterspouts or rows of decorative **antefixes** edging each line of tiles where they end above the architrave. These will be marble if the tiles are marble or sometimes terracotta if the tiles are terracotta.

The typical three-quarter view of a temple will include all this decoration, both front and side. This may well be why Doric temples are often placed obliquely to their approach path – for example, the initial view of the Parthenon – instead of head-on as we might expect (Fig. 40).

Ionic decoration

The Ionic order (Fig. 61), while similarly furnished with columns and pediments, differs in emphasis. In Ionia, the Ionic pediment was normally left empty, though the borders were probably decorated. The frieze might be topped with dentils but will probably not be carved. However, in mainland Greece, Ionic pediments and friezes are very likely to be carved, through the influence of Doric style. The capitals are of course very decorative and varied with their volutes and other ornaments. The slender shafts are fluted more elaborately and have bases with more or less elaborate **mouldings**. Steps will be undercut. There will be more mouldings, and border patterns may be richly carved where Doric would make do with paint. Overall, the effect is lighter and the decorative carving is spread more evenly over the whole, while Doric concentrates attention around the entablature.

The Ionic order retains the key elements of column and pediment, but is allowed to aim at more dazzling effects. Thus, the sequence of elements is less inevitable than the Doric. There may be more surprise, more variation or more profusion: as we have seen, the great Ionic temples of Ionia could duplicate colonnades till the eye must have been confused and amazed. Ionic style could also vary its spacings and play with the ideas of interior and exterior. Interiors were sometimes unroofed; a grove might be growing there with perhaps another smaller temple inside the grove. Therefore, the viewer of an Ionic temple might have approached with a more open mind where the viewer of Doric might be surer of his expectations. However, some temple-designers of Doric have played upon this expectation to surprise the viewer. We shall be seeing some examples of this, especially in West Greece.

Colour

The use of colour is easily forgotten when imagining the original effect of Greek art and architecture. There is plenty of evidence that it was there, but attempts to reproduce it look crude. Red and blue were the major colours, with black, white, yellow and some green. Gold leaf was used, too. Sculpture, including of course the figures in friezes, metopes and pediments, would have had realistic facial details added in paint (Fig. 6), and could be enhanced with gilded bronze accessories; coloured robes or painted borders emphasised the forms of drapery. On a building, it seems likely that red or blue backgrounds marked out the main architectural formatting: for example, the tympanum of a pediment, the long friezes, the thin horizontal tainia and so on, while triglyphs and metopes would have alternated red and blue. Uncarved Doric architraves and cornices would have carried painted patterned borders, similar to those on drapery. Ceiling coffers of marble or wood were also painted and gilded. All these details would have helped the eye both to assimilate the geometric forms of a building and to identify the sculptural narratives, since the figures would have stood out clearly against the solid-colour background. The colour might also have relieved the glare of the sun on marble buildings of freshly cut whiteness.

Both orders were decorated with colour in this way. It can be seen from the above that, though Doric is considered to be the 'plain' order of Greek architecture, it would actually have been rich and lively with plenty of interest for the eye. The overall effect was sturdiness and strength below, with strong colour effects above, while Ionic was jewel-like and decorative throughout.

Fig. 6 Archaic sphinx head with preserved painted facial detail, *c.* 530–520 BC, Acropolis Museum, Athens.

An early archaic Doric pediment: The temple of Artemis at Corcyra

Coming to specific examples of architectural sculpture, we find that the first known stone-carved temple in Greece not only carries its full complement of Doric detail with guttae, **mutules**, etc.., but also has a pediment fully sculpted in limestone. This is the **octostyle** temple of Artemis at Corcyra (Corfu) dated *c.* 580 BC (Fig. 7).

This early archaic pediment is sometimes treated dismissively as 'primitive', yet it already displays some of the ongoing characteristics of pedimental design. The most obvious is symmetry, together with conformity of the design to the triangular field. The symmetry is not precise but is dominant: the most prominent section is the central winged Gorgon who faces frontally but races towards the viewer's right; the largest area is taken up by the mirror image pair of flanking leopards. There are also two smaller narrative scenes placed, one at each corner, where the pediment narrows. Interest carries right to the extremities and all the figures are adjusted to the available space, though not uniform in scale.

Limestone is more difficult to carve successfully than marble because the texture is rougher. The sculptors of this piece have achieved a surprising degree of fine detail, for example Medusa's ringlets (Fig. 8). They also used undercutting, that is, a little stone is cut from underneath and behind the figures, creating very strong shadows. This makes the figures seem separate from the background with a life of their own. Medusa herself is in an archaic kneeling-running position, and her head overlaps the confining decorative

Fig. 7 Reconstruction drawing of the 'Gorgon pediment', temple of Artemis, Corfu, *c.* 580 BC.

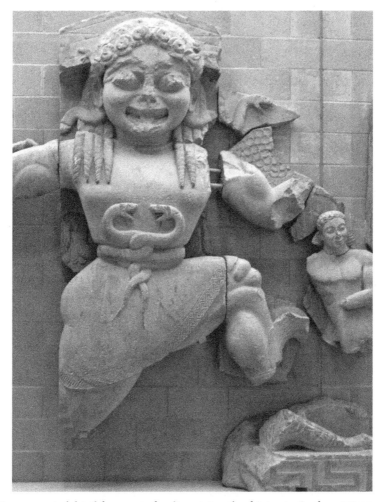

Fig. 8 Gorgon, central detail from cast of pediment, temple of Artemis, Corfu, *c.* 580 BC.

border at the apex so that she can be understood to be bursting dynamically out of the pediment towards the viewer. The spots on the leopards are lightly outlined, so we can deduce once-brightly coloured spots on them and bright colour on the Gorgon too, especially her hideous lolling tongue. In the right-hand corner, Zeus battles Giants and

Titans in his early struggle for supreme power. He is small but deeply carved; parts of him are almost completely free-standing from the background.

The whole scene, despite the inconsistency of scale, can easily be read as a thematic illustration of divine power at work, offering both protection and a warning. The powerful Medusa is alive and well, sheltering her two children, Chrysaor and Pegasus. This adds a political dimension since Corinth, (the mainland city which planted the colony at Corcyra), often used the winged horse Pegasus as an emblem.

So, in this earliest example of a pedimental sculpture, we already find:

- An intriguing tension between the confining geometric format and the exuberant liveliness of the figures. Although these figures are in the stiff early archaic style, the sculptor has made a real effort to suggest that they are capable of independent life away from their limestone background. Pure geometry confines organic figures that are constantly on the verge of escape.
- Decorative forms which would certainly have shown up clearly and effectively from a distance and were designed to do so.
- Concern for balance and symmetry, combined with dramatic narrative.
- Recognisable themes which have both 'theological' and political reference.

All these design principles will be carried forward throughout the development of architectural sculpture.

CHAPTER 5
DELPHI

Delphi was a Panhellenic sanctuary, and home to a major oracle. It was also the venue for the second most important of the quadrennial 'crown games' – the four very prestigious Panhellenic sports events where the prizes given were simple garlands of leaves. Today, as a fairly complete and significant site in a spectacular mountain setting, it is well worth study and well worth visiting. In ancient times, it was likely that most Greeks who had the funds and ability to make a visit would have done so, either for the games or for the oracle. We can still attempt to recover something of what such a visit would have meant to the ancient worshipper/visitor.

The sanctuary site included a main temple, furnished with an oracular cell, which must always have been at the heart of the shrine. There was a variety of architecture and architectural sculpture, a wide range of buildings, including many treasuries, two of which we will examine. Hundreds of precious offerings were added over the years, including monumental columns, large statues, and the like and eventually purpose-built sports facilities – a theatre, a stadium and in a separate location, a hippodrome. There was another smaller sanctuary, Athene Pronaia, and a sacred washing place, the Castalian Spring.

The oracle was held in the highest respect, and was consulted by clients from every level of society. Over the years, it became increasingly important for projected overseas colonies to have the approval of Apollo, and this too added to the importance and prestige of Delphi.

Apollo was the god of Delphi and lord of the oracle. By killing the resident dragon, Pytho, he had won for himself the title 'Pythian', which also was given to the prophetess and the quadrennial festivals.

The site seems to have been continuously active from about the tenth century BC, the oracle by the eighth century, but the Pythian games only from about the early sixth century. They were not as old as those of Olympia and came second in importance. However, Delphi will be dealt with first, because of the age and influence of its main temple and some of its other buildings.

The landscape

Many sanctuaries are remarkable for their natural setting, but Delphi must be the most dramatic of all (Fig. 9). Placed high on a steep mountainside where the terrain has to be steeply terraced for building, the site is difficult to reach. However, it also has amazing

Fig. 9 Delphi: the theatre, temple and panoramic view from the site.

advantages. The air is keen and bracing. The view is stunning and far-reaching. Just to be at Delphi feels like a spiritual experience, where the mind grows sharper, the outlook clearer.

Views are varied and varying: to the south a vast and open panorama of usually blue mountains and sun-filled green valley far below. To the north – and very close – the sheer rock face of the Phaidriades ('Shining ones'), and the twin peaks of Mount Parnassus. These cliffs and crags are dark and ominous, not quite as shining as their name suggests, and they loom upwards, pathless, inaccessible.

These two aspects reflect the many-sided Apollo. He is the sun-god and patron of music, harmony, rationality, and a friend of the Muses. But as the archer-god, he is sudden death, as well as healing. He is the darkness as well as the clarity of prophecy. We shall visit two of his sanctuaries; both are in harsh mountain settings.

Today the visitor arrives at Delphi by a mountainous but modern road and walks comfortably from the car park to the shrine. In ancient times, she or he could have arrived by sea, landing at the nearby coast, or have travelled overland nearly 200 kilometres by the ancient road from Athens. Pausanias, a Greek speaker and indefatigable traveller who lived in the Roman era in the second century AD, wrote a guidebook to Greece which is invaluable for understanding the Greek sites. He tells us, with a display of feeling unusual for him: '… the high-road … to Delphi gets more precipitous and becomes difficult even for an active man' (Pausanias 10.5.3). Despite the difficulty of the journey, Delphi was at least as attractive to visitors then as now. It held great significance throughout the Greek world and even beyond.

The main 'selling point' of the Delphic shrine was its oracle, the foremost oracle of the Greek world. In the temple sat the prophetess, the Pythia, who became ecstatic and prophesied as the mouthpiece of Apollo; priests then interpreted her messages. According to ancient accounts, she descended into an oracular chamber, sat on a tripod, perhaps chewed laurel leaves or just waited for the god to come to her, maybe in the form of an 'exhalation'. For years, this process was recorded with scepticism. Recently, however, French geologists together with American scholars have identified small fissures in the ground as a possible source of 'oracular' fumes, a mind-bending mixture of natural gases, and these fissures were located precisely under the temple and the prophetic seat. Since antiquity, geological shifts in the rocks have closed off the source of inspiration. The discovery, if correct, explains the location of the shrine.

It will be seen from the plan (Fig. 10) that the sanctuary area was extremely crowded. The various features had to be carefully fitted into a limited space, and this was done over a long period of time. Buildings accumulated, were destroyed and replaced in a kind of organic process. What is not apparent from the plan, and is hard to convey in a photograph, is the steep ascent. The Sacred Way makes two hairpin bends, and the first two legs of the path are sharply ascending. As the closed-in view is crowded with monuments and treasuries, it is clear that visitors are constantly confronted with something new and unexpected. At certain points, they will be able to pause and appreciate a broad view of the mountain surroundings. But to take in the entirety of the site at once is impossible and so it appears much larger than it really is.

A distant view of the shrine suggests a few tiny buildings, huddled on a series of terraces in a cup of the mountain. However, when the visitor stands on the Sacred Way, surrounded by elaborate buildings and monuments, the skill of the planners is revealed. A 'sacred landscape' has been created on a human scale within the vast inhospitality of the mountain. This 'landscape' held potency throughout the Greek world for a thousand years.

In the prologue of Aeschylus's play, *Eumenides*, the Pythia stands outside the temple entrance praying; in her prayer, she makes reference to what she sees. Any previous visitor to Delphi – and there would have been many in the audience – would immediately recognise the famous view from the terraces. This is interesting, as it suggests an appreciation of landscape not found in any surviving visual art and alerts

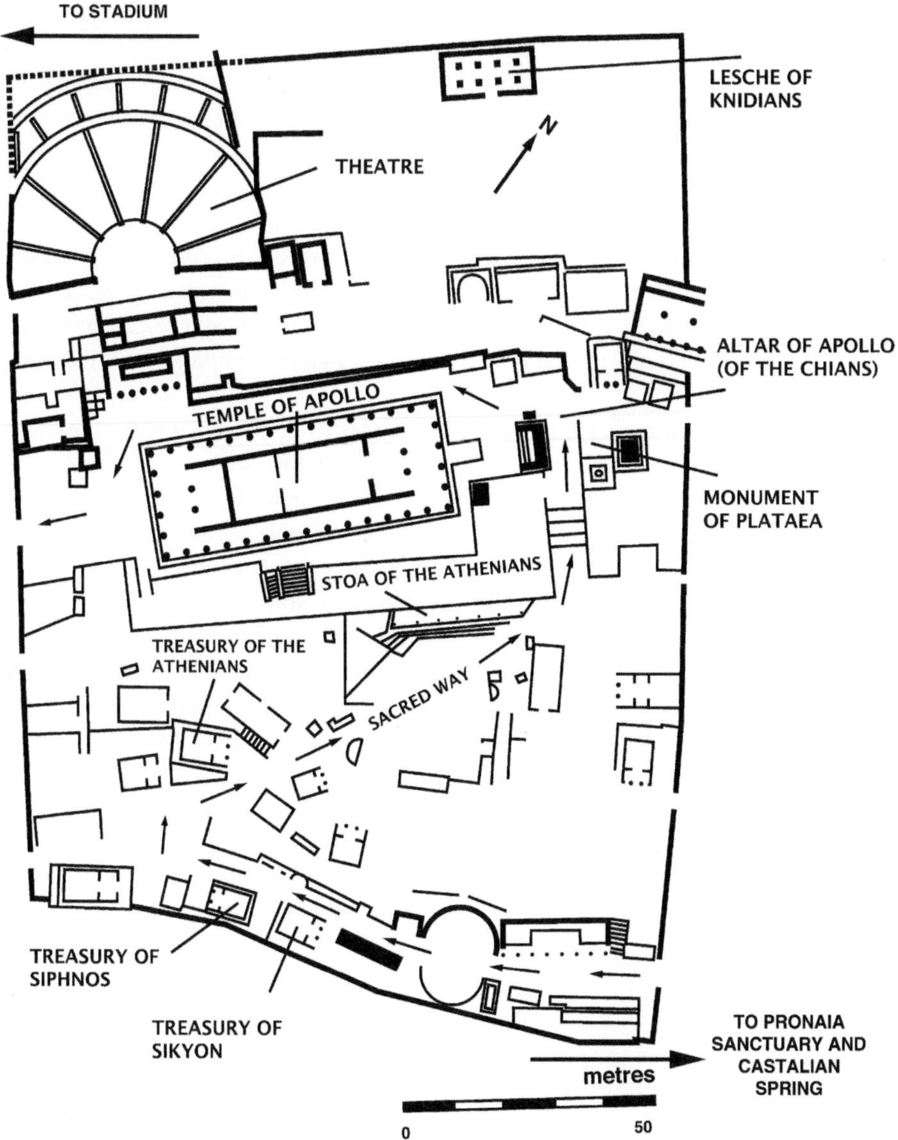

Fig. 10 Site plan, Delphi.

us that an ancient Greek would have been fully aware of the Delphic panorama. The priestess weaves into her speech mythical references to Apollo and his first coming to Delphi. She pictures him, sailing from Delos, his island birthplace, to the headlands of Attica, continuing in triumphal procession along the very same road that an Athenian visitor would have taken to Delphi and which is clearly visible from the temple platform (Fig. 9). The Pythia's speech also reminds the audience of the late archaic pediment sculpture in front of which the drama places her, for the entrance façade did indeed feature the arrival of Apollo by chariot, surrounded by a divine assembly (Fig. 20). So, by means of sculpture and myth, the temple itself is seen as an interpreter of the place, its surroundings and the experience of arriving there.

The Castalian Spring

The sacred Castalian Spring on the main road was a stopping-off point for worshippers, just before they reached the main sanctuary. The location of the spring is a wooded dell bounded by cliffs, which narrows at the back to a mysterious cleft in the mountainside, possibly once the lair of Pytho. This spot is numinous, permanently twilit, because of the trees and the cliffs, a suitable spot for an encounter with the god. The sense of awe and mystery is reinforced by real danger, as rocks can fall without warning from the cliffs.

The ritual importance of the spring is shown by two separate arrangements for approaching the spring water. The more extensive one is Roman, demonstrating the continued popularity of the shrine in the period of Roman rule (*c.* second century BC onwards). The simpler archaic one (which would have been used in classical times) is right on the edge of the modern road. Water is channelled down from the wooded bank into a semi-subterranean masonry tank reached by stone steps. The ancient worshipper descended into the tank to reach the water, which is pure and chilly, fresh from the mountain. Here he or she was supposed to wash hands and hair in imitation of the god Apollo before entering the main sanctuary. The Pythia herself would bathe here, before beginning her duties in the temple.

The Sacred Way

The modern visitor now enters the main sanctuary through the remains of the Roman Agora, just outside the original starting point of the visit. There is no monumental entrance or propylon to be seen, just an opening in the peribolos wall; but the Sacred Way is clearly defined as it rises steeply between walls and terracing on each side. The path will take the visitor through the whole site in three zigzags or 'legs'.

Clustered around the entrance there were in classical times several major groups of life-size sculptures, arranged on raised stone platforms like little theatre stages. They were mainly victory monuments for wars between Greek city states, but included the Marathon monument dedicated by Athens (after 490 BC), which featured more than a dozen impressive life-size bronze figures by Pheidias and others: Athene, Apollo, the general Miltiades, Erechtheus, Cecrops – to name a few. They included the 10 Eponymous heroes, so seem to be connected with the organisation of the 10 tribes and the set-up of the democracy. (The particular 10 heroes, incidentally, were chosen by the Delphic oracle.) This display commemorated Marathon and was paid for, as Pausanias tells us, with 'the tithes of Marathon' (Paus 10.10.1). One huge group commemorated Tegea's victory over Sparta, and another Sparta's victory over Athens. The semicircular plinths which embrace both sides of the path were the Argive offering. These were dedicated in two phases: first, the Seven against Thebes, and, later, kings of Argos. This area was a good chance for cities to score off each other in recording their successive victories. An unusual offering was the bronze Bull of Corfu, in thanks for an amazingly good catch of tunny fish. Pausanias's list of statues here is almost endless. After statue groups, a little higher up on the left, the visitor reaches treasuries.

The treasuries

Delphi was very rich in treasuries – tiny ornate buildings, like mini-temples. They had a twofold purpose. They were in themselves offerings to the god of the sanctuary and they contained offerings. They were also showcases for the far-flung cities which offered them: they formed a permanent presence for that city in the international centre and meeting place which a Panhellenic sanctuary was, and stood in permanent competition with the treasuries of other cities. These were all good reasons for a city to lavish the best it could of money, materials and craftsmanship on its treasury.

There were also the precious or dedicated contents. Sometimes offerings were of no monetary worth, such as a used helmet which a successful general might dedicate. An inscription recording his victory would give it value, and make it interesting to the visitor. Other offerings would be precious and desirable. The fact of dedication to the god would give homogeneity to the motley contents of a treasury. Very often, a treasury was left open at the front so it could be appreciated at all times. Grilles of wood or metal would give security to the display. Plutarch (*Pythian Responses* 12) has his characters peering into the Corinthian treasury, at a highly elaborate golden palm tree with frogs at its base, now 'the only remnant of the offerings'. The treasury is clearly locked, but open to view. The characters surprise themselves by the amount of time that passes while they do this detailed sightseeing.

At Delphi, there were 30 or more treasuries whose foundations can still be seen; but many are unidentifiable. The donors were cities, some from the Greek mainland, but many being colonies from the wider Greek world. We shall look at two outstanding examples with substantial architectural remains; one of them has been reconstructed using much of the original material – the Athenian treasury. The other – the Siphnian – is demolished nearly down to its foundations, but the very exquisite carved decoration is well preserved in the site Museum.

The Siphnian Treasury

The Siphnian Treasury (Fig. 11), an extremely sophisticated building in Ionic style, stood on the edge of the terracing to the left, on the first leg of the Sacred Way as the visitor faces uphill; it was raised on a high base of local limestone to bring its entrance up to the level of the path. Above the base, it was impressively all marble, the first mainland

Fig. 11 Reconstruction drawing of the Siphnian treasury, Delphi, *c.* 525 BC.

building to be so. We know from Herodotus (*Histories* 3.57) that the islanders of Siphnos built it with a tithe of their profits from gold and silver mines at their time of greatest prosperity, and it was probably complete by 525 BC. Though, like all treasuries, it was small, it is easy to see how luxurious it was and how totally it would put its neighbours in the shade. (Its fine fragments, now dismantled, are on show in the Delphi Museum.)

The building was designed, small though it is, to give delight to the viewer on all sides. Visitors would see the east side of the treasury (the back) as they approached, with sculpted pediment and frieze; they would then walk alongside the north frieze, which would not be too high up to admire in some detail. As visitors reached the west front of the building – which was spectacular – they could turn aside into a little paved forecourt, and there enjoy the famous view as well as a display of architectural wonders: a super-elaborate façade with colourful maiden columns (**Caryatids**), a crowded little pediment and general air of sophisticated elegance.

Architectural detail

In plan, the treasury is a small temple-like rectangle with a single space inside, fronted by a **distyle in antis** porch. The two columns, however, are caryatids or statues of maidens (korai), standing on rectangular plinths and supporting the entablature and pediment on ir cylindrical hats (poloi) and tiny capitals. These delightful korai were once brightly decorated with paint, gilding and even little coloured glass gems, and actual jewellery. Piercings for their earrings can be seen in their ears. They stand in an upright columnar posture, pulling at their elaborate **chitons** (Ionic dresses) with one hand to reveal their figures – the fashionable pose for archaic girls. Even their **polos** hats and the capitals are carved with little scenes.

The Siphnian Treasury is enriched with unique narrative carving and with elaborate mouldings (Fig. 12), which articulate and emphasise every element of the architecture:

- The base of the exterior marble wall, just where it sits upon its limestone podium, has a colossal **bead-and-reel** moulding.
- The narrative frieze runs almost at the top of the exterior walls. Above is a small bead-and-reel under a larger 'tongue' or leaf border.
- The overhang (soffit) of the roof is carved underneath with a bead-and-reel and a large **lotus-and-palmette** border (**anthemion**). Richness of decoration could hardly go further than this: the crispness of the carving alleviates the rich and heavy mix.
- The lateral sima (gutter) was a double anthemion with lions' heads.
- The acroteria were probably sphinxes on the corners with central Nikai (victory figures).
- The door frame is wide and surrounded by extremely rich decoration; it acts as a dramatic frame for the kore-columns. Its uprights carry an anthemion with a small bead-and-reel; the lintel has a plain moulding with a band of spaced **rosettes** above; the lintel is supported at each corner by an inverted volute or scroll decoration.

The marble for the building was from Siphnos itself, the decorative borders are of Naxian and the sculpture is of Parian, the finest of island marbles. Although Parian marble itself

Fig. 12 Drawing of mouldings from the Siphnian treasury. *From top*: egg-and-dart, bead-and-reel, lotus-and-palmette (anthemion).

was a luxury material, the transport of this heavy mass – undamaged – to the mountain site was the main expense. Island sculptors probably accompanied it to execute the work with the required skill and understanding of the marble. This material was known to enable a finer finish than local limestone, so it was often used for sculpture: but the planners set a new benchmark for mainland opulence by using marble also for the whole building. Furthermore, they provided a full set of sculpture incorporating a continuous narrative frieze on all four sides, two tiny carved pediments and kore-columns, all bound together decoratively by the exquisite carved mouldings.

Pediments

Both pediments contained sculpture but only the scene from the east (the back) is preserved (Fig. 13). This pediment faced the ascending visitor and showed the rather odd but popular scene of Heracles attempting to steal the Delphic tripod from Apollo. A central taller figure, Zeus, adjudicates. What is successful in the composition is the axial central figure who is also the moral axis – with whom, clearly, the judgement rests. Yet across that central vertical, a violent struggle takes place, the diagonal lines of the tripod legs representing the to and fro of the argument. The struggle is thought-provoking:

Fig. 13 The east pediment and east frieze of the Siphnian Treasury, Delphi, *c.* 525 BC, as arranged in Delphi museum. *Above*: pediment, Heracles attempts to steal the tripod of Apollo; *below left*: frieze, seated gods; *below right*: scene from Trojan War.

How can Heracles challenge the god Apollo in his own sanctuary? However, the viewer can rest assured that justice will prevail since Zeus is clearly in charge.

This miniature pedimental sculpture is carved in a somewhat experimental way that has never been copied; perhaps it was found to be a clumsy experiment. The lower half of each figure is carved in deep relief: the upper half is 'freestanding' in that the background slab has been cut deeply away. Another experiment has been to abandon exact symmetry. Although the central group of three figures is symmetrical, the rest of the figures and their horses are arranged in a more relaxed way: they face in random directions, not mirroring their opposite number, which would be the usual presentation of a pediment. As this pediment is only 0.74m high, while the frieze below it is 0.64m high, it may be that the designer decided to treat it like another frieze, where characters would be facing naturally in different directions. The result is a bit messy, and again has not been copied.

Frieze

This sophisticated archaic work already shows the full range of tricks which frieze-designers can use for the ribbon format.

Below the east pediment (Fig. 13), the viewer would also be rewarded by a highly original stretch of frieze showing, to the left, seated gods in animated conversation. The architectural nature of this carving is reflected in the repeated line of seats and in the flute-like folds of the draperies. The originality of the design is to take social interaction as a topic for narrative rather than battle or a procession. The talking gods are then juxtaposed with a battle scene from the Trojan War, to the right, thought to be the

Fig. 14 The north frieze of Siphnian treasury, Delphi, *c.* 525 BC. *Below*: Gigantomachy: Themis in her chariot drawn by lions; giants; Apollo and Artemis (far right); *above*: leaf-and-dart moulding and small bead-and-reel.

topic of the divine discussion. This parallelism worked very well as narrative; but the asymmetrical arrangement was another experiment which would not be repeated.

Each side of the building has a different topic: the north frieze has an especially strong narrative theme – the Battle of Gods and Giants (Fig. 14). The story leads on from episode to episode, using various visual devices to link the sections and exciting detail to keep the eye following. As appropriate, Apollo and his twin sister Artemis are seen moving purposefully upwards, while, elsewhere, Themis, Athene, Aphrodite and other gods also form episodes, overlapping to create depth and continuity. A lion creates excitement with its feathery mane and fierce bite. Fallen bodies can make horizontal links on the lower level, while glances and other interactions carry the eye along the top level of the frieze. The north frieze is the side seen from the Sacred Way: as the viewer walked on up, he would find gods steadily keeping pace with him, while doomed giants head downhill (Fig. 11).

The tiny building demonstrates what can be done with Ionic style, though making no use of the usual trademark volute capitals. The idea of the narrative frieze and sculpted pediments may in fact be a response to Doric decoration, since neither of these features is typical of Ionic in its homeland. Metopes from an earlier Delphic treasury-type building (known as the Sikyonian but currently without sure attribution) show very strong narrative which may have aroused a competitive response.

The Athenian Treasury

As visitors continued on up, rounding the first bend of the Sacred Way, they were next confronted with the Athenian Treasury (Fig. 15), which scores by its commanding position at the turning point. To those coming up, it presents a three-quarter angle, showing off both front and side views, and for those descending, it gains in drama too.

The little triangular forecourt in front of the treasury may have been used to display war-trophies (possibly from Marathon); metal grilles once protected whatever was kept in the interior; one purpose of a treasury was to display the prestigious loot.

The Athenian Treasury (6.6 × 9.7 metres) is a simple Doric cella with a distyle in antis porch, raised on a high platform without proper steps. The fine Doric frieze is sculpted (unusually) on all four sides; the tiny pediment also contained sculpture, and there were dramatic acroteria – horse-riding Amazons. Though the building is of conventional Doric design, the amount of sculpture and the material suggest conscious rivalry with the Siphnian masterpiece down the way. Of the three sorts of marble composing the Siphnian treasury, Parian was the finest, used only for the figurative sculpture. But the Athenian treasury extravagantly uses Parian throughout: this building is intended as an Athenian showpiece. Though the reconstructed building is now inevitably battered-looking, it was originally fitted with very fine joints and perfectly smooth white walls, which would have stood out well against the rugged background of rock and terracing.

Fig. 15 Athenian treasury, Delphi, *c.* 506–480?

Frieze

The frieze, with its 30 metopes, contains two separate series that closely mirror each other. Each has a hero battling monsters, Heracles and Theseus – in many cases the same monster. Heracles was the hero par excellence of all the Greeks. Theseus, mythical king of Athens, was paradoxically credited with the founding of its democracy. (He was supposed to have introduced synoikism – the combining of the scattered villages of Attica into one cohesive city state or polis. After doing this, he laid down his kingship in favour of the people (Plutarch, *Life of Theseus* 24).) As an unknown young man travelling to Athens from his birthplace Troizen, Theseus famously cleared the area of brigands such as Procrustes and Skiron. Arrived at Athens, he proved his identity to his father Aegeus, king of Athens. He soon went to Crete for his greatest exploit, the killing of the Minotaur; and his greatest shame – the abandoning of Ariadne. On the treasury metopes he tackles a boar, a bull, an Amazon, all Heraclean exploits. Theseus is also seen standing in quiet companionship with Athene in the first and most conspicuous of the metopes, linking him firmly with Athens.

The series showing Theseus was placed on the prominent south side of the building, facing the ascending viewer. To see the Heracles metopes, one would have to leave the path and circle the building. While Heracles mirrors Theseus and adds sculptural richness, he is subordinated in position on this Athenian building while the 'democratic king' stands forth boldly. Some fragments of sculpture from the tiny pediments do survive: chariots and a frontal Athene from the east pediment, and a fight from the west. The two heroes together may have flanked Athene on the east.

Fig. 16 shows one of the best preserved metopes – Heracles captures the Keryneian Hind. Theseus and Heracles are shown as similar figures, but Heracles is distinguished by his lion-skin scarf, neatly knotted round his neck. The Keryneian hind, with its golden horns, belonged to Artemis, so had to be captured carefully and sent back undamaged. The hero bends over the beast almost lovingly: similarly, Theseus bends over the Amazon whom he is subduing on another metope. In our example (Fig. 16), the hero's finely carved features and well-modelled torso demonstrate the care put into this all-marble showcase building. This quality and dynamism of carving looks forward to the fifth-century work we shall see in the Heracles metopes at Olympia (cf. Heracles and the Bull).

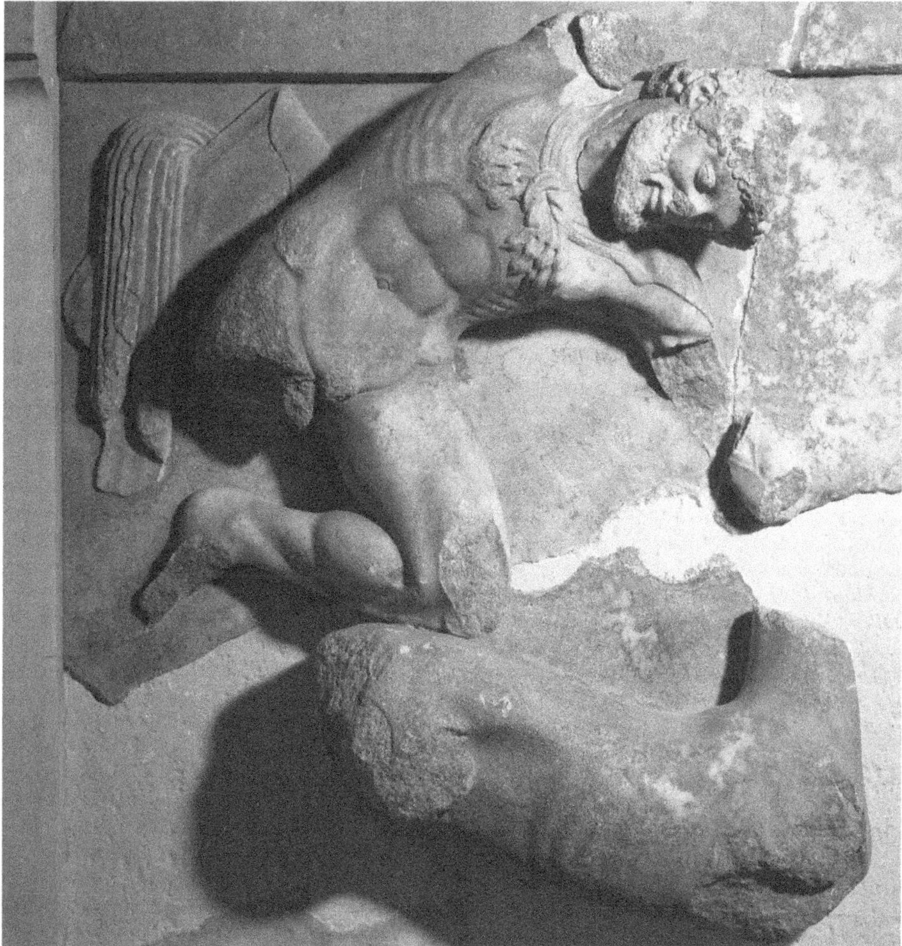

Fig. 16 Metope from the Athenian treasury: Heracles capturing the Keryneian hind.

Date

The second-century AD writer, Pausanias believed that this treasury was built with spoils taken at the victory of Marathon in 490 (Pausanias 10.11.4); some scholars accept a post-490 date, while others have suspected the building must be earlier because of the still-archaic sculptural style (e.g. Dinsmoor 1975, p. 117). There is also a strong suggestion that the treasury may commemorate an earlier event of significance equal to Marathon – and, in a way, closely connected – the foundation of the Athenian democracy in 507 BC. This date fits the sculptural style better; the idea could be supported by the subject matter of the metopes (though it would be equally appropriate for Marathon).

Parian marble may give another clue. While clearly this fine material could in theory have been used at any time, by the period following Marathon the Athenians were beginning to develop their own marble quarries at Mount Pentelikon. This beautiful local stone was used for the great temple begun in Athens to celebrate Marathon after 490 and was usually the material of choice from that time on in Athens. But there was another Athenian building in Delphi already incorporating Parian marble – the entrance front of the temple of Apollo, built by a prominent Athenian family, the Alkmaionids.

This aristocratic family was in exile at Delphi during the Peisistratid tyranny. When it was decided to rebuild the temple of Apollo that had been destroyed by fire back in 548 BC, they turned this necessity to their own advantage. They contracted to get the new temple built with funds that had been collected from many cities for the purpose. However, of their own free will, they paid more to replace limestone with Parian marble for the façade structure and its sculpture. This was clearly an astute move since from that time on, the grateful oracle constantly urged the Spartans to put a stop to the Peisistratid tyranny of Athens – and incidentally to the exile of their opponents, the Alkmaionids. By 510, the Spartans had helped the Athenians to expel the Peisistratids; as a result, a democracy was established in Athens, and Hippias, the hated Peisistratid tyrant departed for Persia (Herodotus, *Histories*, 2.180; 5.62/3). These events demonstrate the importance of 'the favour of Apollo', but also of the high value placed on buildings and the details of their construction.

The precedent of the Alkmaionid façade could for a short time have established Parian marble as – in a sense – a 'democratic', an Athenian and a 'fortunate' material, entirely appropriate for a treasury which might have acted as a thank-offering to Apollo and his favourable oracle for the new democracy. The treasury in Parian marble could then almost be seen as a tiny pendant to the temple. It echoes it in its Doric style, in being of the same material, in being situated close below it, and with the same orientation, and in being an Athenian offering. These echoes have often been noted (Neer 2004; Scott 2009), and they can easily be read as a subtle hint that Athens and Apollo are on the same team.

The surviving acroterion is interesting: a slim clothed rider on a fine prancing horse, now lacking its head, but matching the Amazons in the metopes; probably one of a series of four on the corners, if not the apex too. Both Heracles and Theseus pursued and dominated Amazons as seen in the treasury metopes: they were picturesque, they were female, and they were worth beating. As a subject for acroteria on a small but showy building, mythical Amazons could be a good choice. They are eye-catching with their prancing horses, they are almost airborne as acroteria should be, and they are attractively female (but not the property of any man). However, after the Persian wars, Amazons tended to stand in iconographically for Persians, especially at Athens where they could specifically represent the Persian attack on the Acropolis made in 480. For example, they are seen in this role in the west Parthenon metopes, in heavy conflict. One might query why a serious enemy would be placed on the top of a patriotic building as an architectural flourish. Prior to the Persian wars, they could be seen as fair game and simply the most exotic form of prey to be hunted: both brave heroes proved their prowess by catching them or conquering them. To have taint-free Amazons prominently in the iconographic scheme would therefore suggest an earlier date for the treasury, as, post-Marathon, their presence would have graver implication.

Further reflections on date

The date of the treasury remains controversial. The points that argue for a later date, (post-490), are:

- Pausanias states the treasury was built 'from the spoils of the landing of Datis at Marathon', that is, from the victory at Marathon, 490 BC (Paus: 10.11 4).
- He says this probably on the basis of an inscription that he saw on the plinth south of the treasury, where an exhibit of 10 life-size bronze statues was installed, after Marathon.
- The 'Marathon plinth' has been found to rest upon a one-foot ledge of stone protruding from the treasury suggesting the two are integral.

Against these points:

- Pausanias is sometimes wrong.
- The inscription can refer specifically to the plinth with its (vanished) display, and not to the building.
- The one-foot ledge has been found to continue round to the west wall of the treasury, so, it seems to not be an integral part of the plinth after all (Ralf den Hoff, 2009).
- The sculptures with Archaic smiles, shell curls and bulging eyes do not look post-490.
- Paros sided with Persia against Athens at Marathon. It seems unlikely that Athens would want its marble after 490, especially for a memorial of Marathon.

In other words, the plinth and display may well have been added, post-Marathon, to the treasury that was already so proudly proclaiming the Athenian aretē (excellence) at Delphi. If this is correct, the dedication of the treasury is connected with the events that established democracy at Athens, and would date back to *c.* 507, a date which would fit the sculpture-style far better.

A further complication is the suggestion that the Marathon display on the plinth, and the numerous group of Marathon images near the entrance, were one and the same (Barringer 2008, p. 162 n. 61). It certainly seems unlikely that there were duplicate major sets of images celebrating the same event in the same sanctuary. In other words, the images could have been moved from the treasury plinth to the entrance, at some later time, for a variety of reasons. Chief among them would be the urge to competition with the other cities' statue groups, and then perhaps greater availability of space.

The polygonal wall and the Athenian Stoa

Continuing up the Sacred Way on the second leg, a high, solid wall soon appears on the left (Fig. 17). This is the terrace wall, stabilising the huge artificial terrace essential for the very large temple of Apollo. It is built with polygonal blocks as an anti-earthquake measure. Though rather counter to the usual Greek aesthetic of clear angles and geometric form, there is much use of this polygonal feature at Delphi and it has clearly worked well. The joints still fit perfectly, but with random shapes which are planned not to slip apart as easily as rectangular blocks.

Along the same stretch of path, against the polygonal terrace wall, is the Athenian **Stoa**. This was a long, open, roofed platform, fronted by a colonnade of seven widely spaced

Fig. 17 The Athenian stoa (mid-fifth century) and polygonal wall supporting temple terrace, Delphi.

slim Ionic monolithic columns. The wide spacing indicates a wooden superstructure, lighter than stone. This covered platform was intended to display spoils of war, including parts of captured ships. It was once thought that the display was of spoils taken from the Persians, but a careful reading of the extant dedicatory inscription suggests that the stoa was built in about 450 BC, and that the spoils were taken in the First Peloponnesian War, and were probably added to as occasion arose. The inscription lacks detail out of tact: the 'enemies' were not Persians but other Greeks (Walsh 1986).

This monument, running right under the temple terrace, continued the suggestion of Athens's special connection with Delphi. In terms of sanctuary planning, Walsh points out the typical pairing of a smaller building in Ionic style in the shadow of a larger Doric one. Additionally, slender Ionic served the purpose of maximum visibility for the display inside the colonnade.

Politically, the use of Ionic style could also reflect the growing rift between Athens and Sparta by mid-century. The older Athenian treasury was just down the path with its Doric form and brave mainland heroes in the metopes. The new building was both a development in architecture, as the exterior Ionic columns were a novelty, and a sign of Athens's increasing identification with Ionian allies.

The archaic Sphinx of the Naxians (565 BC), now in the museum, once stood on its high Ionic column, just under the polygonal wall supporting the temple terrace (Fig. 17). It serves to represent the wonderful variety of the offerings that once adorned the site.

Fig. 18 The archaic Sphinx of the Naxians on an archaic Ionic capital, Delphi Museum.

The visitor now walks the full length of the temple below the temple-terrace, before rounding the next bend and arriving at the steps up to the temple. Above to the right was another war memorial with an upbeat message – the triple bronze serpent surmounted by a golden victory tripod, commemorating the important battle of Plataea against the Persians. The names of the many allied Greek cities who fought were inscribed on the serpent's body, recording a rare cooperation against a common enemy. (The remains of this triple serpent are now in Istanbul.)

As we have advanced along the Sacred Way, we have seen war celebrated in various ways. Intercity conflict does not seem to have embarrassed the Greeks much, and might seem almost like an extension of athletic competition. Yet within the context of a Panhellenic shrine, all Greeks must be thought of as meeting in neutral territory under the influence of the god. This attitude is reflected in the enforced peace which accompanied some religious festivals, notably the Olympic games and the Eleusinian mysteries. While the common enemy, Persia, can be proudly named and triumphed over, Greeks themselves should ultimately stick together, despite quarrels. What a shrine like Delphi or Olympia offers is one form of social cohesion, where, outside of any particular polis, common Greekness is celebrated.

The temple of Apollo

The visitor is now about to negotiate the steep steps leading to the temple forecourt. Pausanias gives a strange prehistory of the temple of Apollo:

> They say that the most ancient temple of Apollo was made of laurel, and that branches were brought from the laurel grove at Tempe. This temple would have been designed in the form of a hut. Next, the people of Delphi say the temple was made by bees out of beeswax and feathers … as for the story about how they plaited a shrine out of feather-grass when it was still green, I shall not even start on it. The story that the third temple was made of bronze is no surprise … the shrine of Athene of the Bronze House survives at Sparta to our times … so a bronze temple for Apollo would not be unlikely. (Pausanias 10.5.5)

This list may hint at pre-stone building methods. We get onto more secure ground with the archaic temple, burnt down in 548 BC. The temple of Apollo whose ruins can be seen today (Fig. 9) is the fourth-century temple built after the landslide of 373. But it preserves the layout and even the style of the late archaic temple completed by the Athenian Alkmaionids. This brief list indicates how many vicissitudes of accident (and perhaps fashion) a temple could go through. Delphi, being subject to earthquakes, was particularly vulnerable.

The temple building and its altar

At the entrance to the temple is a small forecourt bounded on one side by the temple steps and neat ramp and on the other by the altar of the Chians, clearly a prestigious offering which earned for its donor polis an important privilege: priority in consulting the oracle (promanteia). 8.60 metres × 5 metres × 4 metres in height, it was small in proportion to the temple, but the placement is effective. An inscription records the gift and the privilege. This altar was first built by the Chians to align with the late archaic Alkmaionid temple, and was rebuilt by them after the landslide, not quite aligning with the new fourth-century temple.

The rectangular block of the altar is clad with dramatic black limestone in pseudisodomic formation (alternation of high and low courses). It is made elegant by the addition of a creamy marble cornice on top and a similar marble band at its foot. On the inner side of the e-shaped altar were steps for the celebrant to climb up for duty. On the outer side, the altar rose directly from the slope of the Sacred Way and the ascending visitor would skirt its dark, smooth wall. This was the chief altar of Delphi. Attendees at sacrifices must have jostled for position on the temple terrace, or below on the various stretches of the Sacred Way (Fig. 19).

Fig. 19 Reconstruction drawing of the temple area, showing top of Sacred Way, with altar of the Chians, temple forecourt, fourth-century Apollo temple, etc.

In this forecourt, we may imagine the young hero Ion in Euripides's play of that name, sweeping the floor and scaring off the birds, in his role as temple servant (see Chapter 15); or the Pythia looking over the parapet at the view before entering the temple for her day's duty (cf. Aeschylus: *Eumenides* 1 ff). Here we may imagine the queues of people wishing to consult the oracle (there is not much space), and a temple servant like Ion instructing them as to the procedure, checking their credentials and receiving their offerings.

Dark limestone makes up the platform steps and forecourt, creating a somewhat gloomy or awesome atmosphere. The style of the Doric columns visible today is heavy, with a wide echinus; these columns may well be the archaic ones re-used, or copied (Dinsmoor, 1975, p. 217). The **hexastyle** layout is still elongated in the archaic manner with fifteen columns down the flanks, but there is a practical reason for this. It is to accommodate an extra **adyton** or inner chamber for the oracle. This fourth-century building seems to have copied its predecessor. There is now no visible trace of the oracular chamber in the foundations; though every visitor hopes to see it, it remains a mystery; it was possibly just the adyton rather than an underground chamber. The cella originally contained a stone called the Omphalos (navel) to mark the central point of the world. There was also a laurel tree, a statue of Apollo, and, oddly, the grave of Dionysus.

Prominent in the temple area was a famous feature: three inscriptions embodying Delphic wisdom. Two are well-known sayings: 'Nothing in excess' and 'Know thyself'. The third was totally cryptic even to the Greeks – a letter E.

The visitor can still walk all round the temple. On the downhill side, the dark limestone platform is built much higher as the ground falls away, and there is a gap here in the masonry for the exit of the sacred stream Cassiotis which once flowed right under the temple.

Architectural sculpture

The late archaic temple built by the Alkmaionids between 530 and 510 had a landmark marble front, as discussed above. Some of the archaic pediment sculptures can be seen in the museum. The entrance-front central motif seems to be the arrival of Apollo by chariot, with a frontal line-up of gods each side of him (Fig. 20). As can be seen, this method of representation results in a very small god. This disadvantage will be re-thought by subsequent pediment designers. At the corners of the composition are fantastic lions

Fig. 20 Reconstruction drawing of the east pediment of the archaic temple of Apollo, Delphi, *c.* 515 BC.

eating animal victims, so the bestial image of divine power is still represented (as seen on Corfu: Fig. 7), though a more humanist vision of deity is now taking centre place.

The back pediment probably featured a limestone battle between gods and giants. Athene, rushing in profile to her giant-slaying task, and some fragments of giants can be seen in the museum. Zeus's chariot was possibly the centrepiece, paralleling Apollo's on the front pediment. However, this is mainly an action scene, executed in profile, whereas the front is confrontational and static.

The Lesche of the Knidians

Looking further up the slope (Fig. 10) between the temple and the cliffs, away from the main route, the ancient visitor would have seen the Lesche or club-house of the Knidians.

This was a simple stoa-like recreational building, decorated inside with very famous mural paintings by Polygnotos. The influence of this artist from the first half of the fifth century was felt throughout every form of Greek art. He introduced the idea of depicting contemplation rather than action. He also designed figures among landscape features, arranged up and down the full height of a wall rather than in the frieze-like arrangement familiar from pots or sculpture. Pausanias describes in great detail painted scenes from after the Fall of Troy, the Descent to the Underworld and other topics of a sad or thoughtful nature. The building was intended, according to Pausanias, for those who wanted to discuss 'old times and serious questions' (Pausanias 10.25.1). The paintings, with their moral challenges about war and justice, were certainly conducive to such talk.

The theatre, stadium and hippodrome

The last 'leg' of the path now zigzags back on level ground, between the temple and the theatre. The theatre, being cupped in shape, is successfully accommodated to the terrain and is the only competition space within the temenos. The stone seating seen today was completed in the second century BC, monumentalising the earlier, less formal seating arrangement which took advantage of natural topography. There are 35 rows of seats with an audience capacity of 5,000. The first competitions held at Delphi were musical, Apollo being patron of music and art: sports were added later.

Continuing up from the theatre, visitors now leave the main temenos through a break in the peribolos wall, and ascend by a steep winding path through rocks and pine trees. They will be surprised to find a complete stone-built stadium, 177.5 metres in length, fitted into a terraced area high above the sanctuary, round a shoulder of the mountain. Stone tiers of seating for 6,500 spectators are ranged on both sides of the running track, and high stone piers mark the starting places for the runners. Before this stadium was made in the third century, foot races had been held down in the valley. The hippodrome for chariot racing remained down on the spacious and flat valley floor at Crisa: this was more suitable for the management of the horses. The site is not identified.

The famous bronze charioteer of Delphi (478/4 BC), damaged by earthquake, was found buried under the Sacred Way: burial on-site was one way of dealing with spoiled offerings. Originally, he formed only a part of a large statue-group of four beautiful bronze race-horses, a chariot and small groom. As he stood calmly and solemnly on his chariot by the path between the theatre and the temple, his long-fluted charioteer's dress must have taken on an architectural look, matching him deliberately with the adjacent Doric colonnade – two kinds of offering to the god. The charioteer has traditionally been linked with Polyzalos, Tyrant of Gela in Sicily, because of the inscription excavated in its close vicinity, however, the link between sculpture and dedication has now been proved problematic (Adornato 2008). Nevertheless, the Sicilian inscription demonstrates the connectedness across the Greek world, and the role of Panhellenic sanctuaries in providing the locus for western display (Shepherd 2000). Adornato reminds us that Apollo, as Delphic god and promoter of colonies, 'is closely linked to the earliest Greek foundations in southern Italy and Sicily (Adornato 2008, p. 40). Whoever the dedicator of the charioteer itself, the very fine sculpture illustrates that chariot-racing (as at Olympia) was the most spectacular and elite event at Delphi. Another vanished chariot-group from nearby is described by Pausanias: 'The driver is Cyrene: Battos is in the chariot with Libya crowning him with a wreath' (Pausanias 10.15.3). Cyrene was a Greek colony in Africa, and Battos was its original **oikist**. Probably the group celebrated the successful city, rather than a sports victory.

The many, many dedications at Delphi have just been touched on here, enough to suggest how crowded the site would have been, how varied and spectacular the offerings, and how the wider Greek world was represented. Each offering would have been inscribed with the identification of the giver; a stroll around would have been like a trip round much of the Greek world in a microcosm.

Plutarch, writing in the second century AD, laughed about the 'sacred guides' of his day who insisted on reading out every single inscription, however dull (Plutarch: *Pythian Responses* 2). However, especially when the inscriptions were fairly recent, they would have held interest and relevance to many.

Athene Pronaia (Marmaria)

A second smaller sanctuary is found below the main road, between the spring and the sanctuary of Apollo. It too is steeply terraced, and contains several archaic and later temples including that of Athene Pronaia, treasuries (including that of Massilia – Marseilles) and other buildings, many unidentified.

The tholos

A **tholos** is the architectural star turn of this sanctuary (Fig. 21), dated approximately 375 BC. It is a photogenic building, its pure white marble standing out dramatically against the backdrop of valley and mountain, as it must have been planned to do.

Fig. 21 Sanctuary of Athene Pronaia, Delphi: tholos, *c.* 375 BC.

A tholos is circular – a shape used sparingly in Greek architecture, always attracting attention. From Mycenean times, impressive underground tholoi still could be seen with their stone beehive vaults (Pausanias 2.16.5). A sense of mystery attaches to the circular plan, with associations of death, or the sacred hearth. The purpose of the tholos at Delphi is unknown, perhaps a shrine or treasury. Pausanias does not note any round building in his description here. We know the architect – Theodorus of Phocaia – because Vitruvius records that he wrote a book about it, indicating that its design was of special interest.

Exterior

On a circular plinth (13.5 metres in diameter), an exterior Doric colonnade of 20 columns supported the normal Doric entablature. The columns are rather slimmer and placed closer together than they would be on a rectangular temple. This spacing avoids uncomfortable gaps on the profile of the building. The white marble cella wall is finished at the foot with a finely carved moulding of leaves, underlined by a strip of black limestone.

The metope frieze of the outer entablature was carved in deep relief. A smaller metope frieze in shallow relief circled the exterior cella wall, either below or above the roof of the colonnade. Examples from both sets are shown in the site museum.

A decorative gutter (sima) of foliage punctuated by lionhead waterspouts crowned the architrave and the metope frieze. On a rectangular temple, the lateral sima enlivens the otherwise plain flanks: on a circular tholos, flank and façade are all one, giving extra emphasis to the entablature – which in a sense replaces the pediment (Fig. 22).

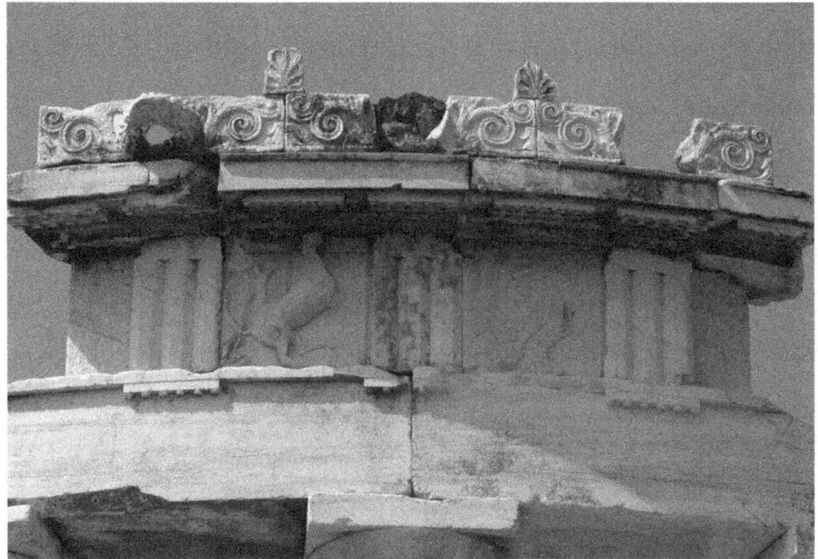

Fig. 22 Delphi: details of tholos

The roof – a flattened cone – may have been in one unbroken section, or in two clear steps with the lower section roofing only the colonnade. As remnants of two simas have been found (one smaller than the other), either both sections of roof were edged with a decorative sima; or the higher sima demarcated the position of the cella wall, but without a step in the roofline. The smaller scale of the higher sima would have given a sensitive perspective effect from below, (whatever the actual arrangement of the roofing). If the roof was stepped, there would have been a small vertical drum between the two levels; this could even have accommodated the smaller metope frieze and the smaller sima as a full second entablature, using the existing elements in the showiest way possible. (The restored drawing of the Philippeion, an Ionic tholos at Olympia will give some idea of its appearance: Fig. 37.) A decorative acroterion crowned the apex: its practical purpose was to strengthen the central meeting point of the radiating roof beams. Eight radiating ridges with elaborate ridge tiles supported upright palmettes, and perhaps small, coloured acroterial sculptures.

This unusually decorative roof would have been very clearly seen from above and at close quarters, since the main road between the two sanctuaries runs just above the tholos where it stands on the lower terrace of Athene Pronaia, giving the traveller a most unusual viewpoint.

Interior

Inside the cella was a ring-colonnade of ten columns, either half-columns, or full columns just touching the wall in order to maximise the central space. Their placement corresponded to every alternate column of the outer ring, and they stood raised on a limestone bench running all round the wall: this made them shorter, more slender and space-saving. The capitals were Corinthian, like the one at Bassae (see Fig. 84). The use of a decorative new style, Corinthian, is thus confirmed as an interior feature in Greek architecture.

The building was of white marble, but used black limestone for colour contrast. The decorative strip circling the base of the exterior cella walls was black, as was the interior bench. The paving of the cella floor was black with a white disk in the centre. These colour effects would have served to emphasise the circularity of the form.

The gymnasium

Adjacent to this sanctuary area were a gymnasium and other sports facilities, on more terraces. On an upper level was a long covered track (xystos) for bad-weather training. Directly below were the **palaistra** with a peristyle court and separate rooms opening off two sides of it. Next to that was a circular plunge pool. This was fed with cold mountain water, which ran into basins from bronze lionhead spouts fixed in the terrace wall, and then flowed into the pool. Later the Romans added a heated bath complex.

Votive offerings and monuments at Delphi

Though the Sacred Way still guides the visitor through the temenos upwards to the temple and beyond, what is now missing from a visit to Delphi, as with any ancient sanctuary today, is the proliferation of votive offerings, statues and monuments of all sorts. (A few have been mentioned.) Those dedicated by individuals mostly commemorated athletic victories, but state dedications were predominantly monuments to military victories. Treasuries could also be thank-offerings for victories – implying an influx of funds – ten per cent was expected by the god. Treasuries or major war monuments could be placed defiantly opposite your defeated enemies' monument, especially when that former victory was over you! In the crowded conditions at Delphi, this kind of juxtaposition was common, for example, the treasury of Syracuse was placed right opposite that of the Athenians (after 413 BC), after the Syracusans defeated the Athenian expedition against them.

Other dedications can be seen in the museum in a variety of types and materials: archaic chryselephantine gods, exquisite ivory miniatures, down to the humble moulded terracotta votive offerings. The life-size archaic silver bull, with its golden mane and hooves must once have been an amazing sight; still impressive today, in its glass case, though squashed and pieced together.

'Cleobis and Biton' are twin archaic kouroi dating from *c.* 580 BC. They are chunky youths with archaic smiles, archaic clenched fists, unusual little boots, and a certain naive radiance in their broad faces. A story attaches to them, told by Herodotus (*Histories* 1.31). Cleobis and Biton were sons of a priestess of Argive Hera. When she lacked transport for the journey to the temple, her sons took the place of oxen, yoking themselves to her chariot. The grateful mother prayed for the greatest blessing of all for these devoted sons: they died in their sleep then and there. Though the story fits the statues nicely, they might have been originally intended as Castor and Pollux, the heavenly twins, commonly worshipped together: however, that is not such an exciting story for a guide to tell.

These few statues, randomly preserved from the multitudes once crowding the sanctuary, give an idea of the variety and richness of offerings, and the great interest they added to a visit to the complete site.

Conclusion

Delphi, home of the oracle, includes the experience of the whole landscape: the twin peaks of Parnassos, the Castalian Spring in its rocky gorge, the mingled sun and storm of the valley, Marmaria (the lower sanctuary), and the Corycian cave of the nymphs high on the untracked mountain. When Dionysus took over the shrine for the winter session, Bacchants roamed far and wide under the influence of the god – Bacchants who were normally you and your neighbours.

Sophocles, poetically contemplating the source of the divine word, imagines it as emanating not from the Pythia herself but from all of the various elements of the place: 'Rock-face of Delphi speaking the word of god … manifest voice ringing clear from snow-bound Parnassos … power of prophecy from the central heart of earth' (Sophocles, *Oedipus the King* 462–81).

Despite suspicions of collaboration with the Persian enemy and the occasional evidence of bribery, the shrine and oracle of Delphi held immense prestige in the Greek world for over a thousand years. The last oracle is recorded as an epitaph for a great institution: the young pagan emperor Julian in the fourth century AD, who tried to fight Christianity and revive the old religion, received this answer to his inquiry about the state of the shrine:

> Go tell the king, the well-wrought house is fallen
> No shrine has Phoebus now, no prophetic laurel,
> No speaking spring; quenched is the chattering water.

(Cedrenus, cited in *Works of the Emperor Julian*, Loeb edn, vol. III, p. lvii)

CHAPTER 6
OLYMPIA

Olympia was a Panhellenic site, like Delphi, of enormous prestige. Still renowned for its games until today, in its heyday, it was a religious site of year-round activity in honour, mainly, of Zeus. Like Delphi it had an oracle and it was served by two prophetic families, the Iamidae and the Klytidae who interpreted the sacrifices. Its great fame however was due to the games, first in importance of the four quadrennial sports events held in mainland Greece for all Greeks.

The Olympic games traditionally date from 776 BC. The ancient Greeks used this year as the start of their dating system, indicating the importance of the games. The cult of Zeus is thought to have been established on the site at least as early as the tenth century, developing by gradual stages into a Panhellenic athletic festival. And the start has been dated even earlier, in the late eleventh century BC (Kyrieleis 2003), based around the prehistoric tumulus that would later be named the tomb of Pelops.

The site of Olympia is unusual for Greece – as different as possible from Delphi – open and flat, green and lush, low-lying between slow, strong rivers and mounded, wooded hills. Today there are vivid blossoming trees and wildflowers, meadow-like grass, a tranquil atmosphere. The air is soft and pleasant, the view of the sky vast. There is no formal planning, no axial line-up, but a relaxed, spacious layout of the various amenities.

In antiquity, the sanctuary was a great deal fuller than it is today, since statues, altars and monuments crowded wherever they could find a free spot; and complete buildings take up more visual space than do ruins. But still, the open sky and the low hills would have ensured the same spacious feeling. Zeus, the king of gods and sky-god, was often worshipped in broad-level open sites like this one, though he typically had mountaintop shrines too.

Though located apparently in the middle of nowhere, the sanctuary was really very accessible for visitors, as its ancient success proves. Olympia is about 30 kilometres from the coast and lies in a rolling landscape of shallow valleys. Two rivers, Alpheios and its tributary Kladeos, border the site – and on occasion flood it, increasing its fertility. On the north boundary is a richly wooded sacred hill, Kronion, or the Hill of Kronos (Zeus's father).

The central sacred area or temenos of Olympia was known as the Altis (this word is a version of *alsos,* Greek for 'grove'). The sanctuary still has the character of a grove, with wild olive, oaks, pines, planes and poplars; Pausanias mentions the plane trees of the Altis, the poplars for firewood and the wild olive for the victors' garlands. In the earliest days when the sacred Altis was just a natural grove, worshippers probably hung their offerings from the branches of trees. The developed Altis contained the main altar of Zeus, two

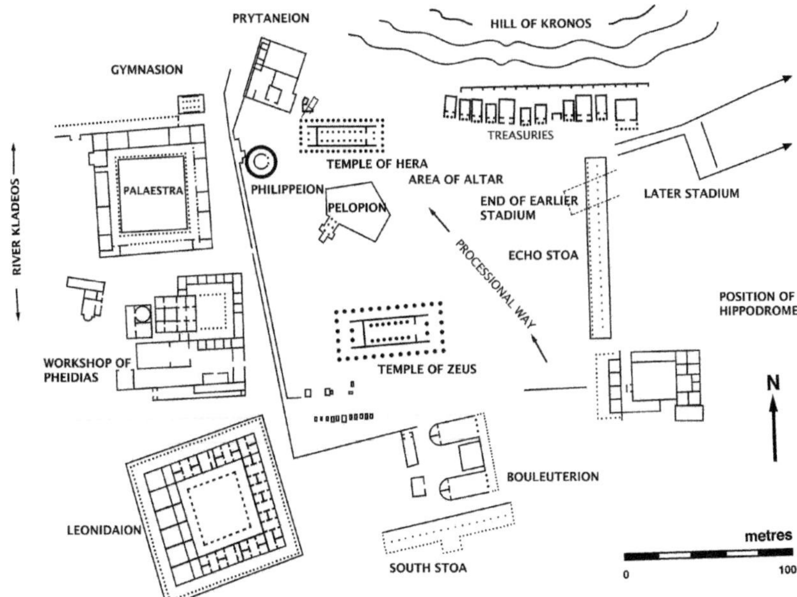

Fig. 23 Site plan, Olympia.

main temples, two hero shrines, a large variety of other dedications, altars, etc. At some time, a wall was built enclosing the Altis and marking it off from the outer area (Fig. 23).

Surrounding the Altis were other permanent features vital to the running of the sanctuary and the festivals: to east and west, sports facilities, to north and south, administrative buildings. Beyond this built-up area was plenty of open space for the temporary necessities of the festival: care of horses, stabling and pasture, visitor campsites, food outlets, water-sellers and so on.

The games took place every four years in August. There was a guest house for the select few, but mainly the visitors had to camp. The balmy climate of Olympia must at that season have been oppressively hot and humid – harsh for the athletes – but campers were probably assured of acceptable sleeping conditions. Camping at Olympia is sometimes said to have been unpleasant, particularly because good drinking water was in short supply. For those who disliked the outdoor life, there would be compensation for discomfort in the sight of superb naked athletes and the drama of high-level competition. But not every camper was uncomfortable, and competition was not only on the racecourse. The assembling of Greeks from every level of society and from all over the Greek world offered an important opportunity for social display. Plutarch gives the example of two politically ambitious Athenians competing as campers: 'When (Themistocles) went to Olympia … he tried to rival Cimon in the dinners he gave and in the magnificence of his furniture and the tents in which he entertained his visitors' (Plutarch, *Life of Themistocles* 5). Clearly camping at Olympia could reach very high standards indeed. Many rich men would be present, competing especially in chariot events; their entourage and equipment would be expected to add to the glittering spectacle. Examples would be Theron of Akragas and Hieron of Syracuse who both won horse events in 476 BC and paid for Pindaric odes in their own honour.

The Olympic games were the oldest and foremost of the main four on the athletic circuit – Olympic, Pythian (Delphi), Nemean, Isthmian. A well-off young man of the sixth or fifth century might do the circuit of all four games and devote much leisure to training seriously. Euripides makes his mythical character Hippolytus say, anachronistically: 'I would wish to come first in the Panhellenic competitions, and to be second in politics …' (Euripides, *Hippolytus* 1016–19). Hippolytus is the illegitimate son of King Theseus and can never be king; he tailors his ambitions to those of a private gentleman who would bring honour to his city if he were successful, and would receive honour in return – in the form of statues, poems, free dinners and probably cash. The celebrity acquired by an athlete could also be used to gain advancement in politics: for example, an Athenian, Cylon, attempted a political coup in the late seventh century on the strength of his Olympic victory (Herodotus, *Histories* 5.70). Alcibiades, a well-born Athenian 'celebrity' figure of the later fifth century, made an enormous impression with seven teams of racing chariots at Olympia, scooping up at least three top wins. For this, he was acclaimed and wooed by other cities with rich gifts, including a 'magnificently decorated tent' and food and wine to enable the lavish entertainment clearly expected of a man in his position at the games (Plutarch, *Life of Alcibiades* 12). Understandably, the role of athlete changed and became increasingly professionalised in later centuries.

Manning a sanctuary

Modern Olympia serves just one purpose – tourism. In ancient days, it must have been much the same, since the sanctuary served no one community but the whole of the Greek world. Obviously, the activity intensified greatly for the four-yearly festival, but the sanctuary was running all the time. For example, Pausanias on his visit tells of sacred guides who show him the sights and explain them. In addition to the governing committee, a huge staff would have been necessary at all levels to manage such a major shrine on a daily basis: officials to deal with distinguished visitors, staff for crowd control, priests and lesser acolytes to see to all the practical details of the sacrifices, groundsmen to keep up the sports facilities, medical attendants – especially for sports injuries, masseurs and bathing attendants, caretakers to maintain the whole site. For the festival, valuable horses would have to be accommodated, would need to be fed and cared for over some days, even weeks, might have to be recuperated from a sea voyage or long journey. Pausanias tells us there were woodsmen who cut poplar wood especially for the sacred fire of sacrifices (Pausanias 3.13.3), and others who had the hereditary task of caring for the great gold-and-ivory statue of Zeus:

> Pheidias's descendants, who are called the polishers and who were granted by Elis the office of cleaning dust and dirt from Zeus' statue, offer sacrifice at the altar of Athene the Worker, before they begin their polishing. (Pausanias 5.14.5)

There were over 60 altars, not associated with temples. Pausanias tirelessly lists them all – 'in the same order in which the Eleans sacrificed' which they did 'once a month'. These sacrifices were 'in antique style … they burn frankincense with honey cakes on the altars, and lay olive-branches on them and pour wine.' They were staffed by a 'priest (elected for the month), prophets, and wine-carriers, a sacred guide and a flute-player and the woodman' (who would have supplied wood and lit the fires) (Pausanias 5.15.10). These details give an idea of the ceaseless religious activity which would have gone on in a major shrine.

As the shrine grew more complex in later years, with its hotel, the Leonidaion, built in the fourth century, and, much later, the club-house built by the Emperor Nero, there would have been more and more staff required. Altogether, Olympia was a going concern for more than a thousand years, constantly changing and growing, and always successful.

Control of the sanctuary

The site was managed by Elis, a small polis situated some 30 kilometres away. This city, not particularly distinguished in other ways, had the major role in running the site for most of its history. Another city, Pisa, closer to Olympia, historically vied with Elis for control of the shrine, since it was a source of enormous income as well as prestige. In 471 BC Elis finally wiped Pisa off the map – its site is not even known – and won uncontested control of the sanctuary. According to Pausanias, the funds for building the temple of Zeus came from the profits of this war between Elis and Pisa.

Olympia flourished after the Persian wars. A major Panhellenic sanctuary, Olympia was remote from that theatre of war and was particularly accessible to the west. Elis was not implicated in any politics yet did send a small force to fight. In contrast, Delphi, somewhat more accessible to the east, a shrine of equal or greater fame (because of its oracle), had not been seen as supportive to the Greek cause, and was suspected of inclining too much towards Persia. Olympia seized the double advantage of increased funding and a clean political reputation to honour Zeus with a new temple.

The Sacred Way

A Sacred Way should lead worshippers from the entrance to the altar. At Olympia, the Sacred Way seems to be just a natural route between monuments. Pausanias refers to the processional entrance, but as this could be a Roman addition, it might even be that the entrance and the sacred route have been changed over the years; no route is now clearly demarcated. In this respect, Olympia is a complete contrast to Delphi where the Sacred Way is almost sculpted into the landscape, and with its three 'legs' is clearly defined by the buildings lining its steep ascent.

The temple of Hera

Of the two large temples at Olympia, the oldest is an early archaic building [illegible] dedicated to Hera. In a sanctuary of Zeus, this is a little puzzling, though it is [illegible] that the temple was not the most vital element in worship: the altar was. Worship of Zeus was centred on his open-air 'ash altar' (described below) and continued to be so after his fine new temple was built.

Pausanias tells us that in this temple the cult statues he saw were an enthroned Hera and, next to her, a standing Zeus with beard and helmet (Pausanias 5.17.1). If true, this could suggest that the temple was once shared by Zeus and his consort.

The building

The temple of Hera is interesting because, though currently dated at about 580 BC, it was built in an already outdated seventh-century way, using mud brick for the walls on a base of stone, and a superstructure of wood with a roof of terracotta tiles and a wooden colonnade. Still visible today (Fig. 24) is the limestone platform with two steps only and neat masonry of the cella to a height of one metre, the orthostates upon which the perishable materials were constructed.

The proportions are archaic. The front was hexastyle but the sides were elongated with sixteen columns; these were widely spaced too, which indicates a lighter architrave of wood rather than stone. However, already the corner columns were more closely placed

Fig. 24 Temple of Hera, Olympia, *c.* 580 BC.

ıan the others – this variation could suggest a Doric triglyph/metope frieze above, as contraction of column spacing solved a design problem at the corners.

The few standing stone columns (some monolithic) are a non-matching set in a stocky Doric style. We know from Pausanias that they were added one by one, over time, by different donor cities, to replace the original wooden ones, the first stone addition being not long after the building of the temple. When Pausanias wrote his book in 173 AD, just one wooden column still remained – in the back porch. The fact that each city made no attempt to match their offering to the rest suggests that there was a desire for the individual offering to be seen as such. This idea is reinforced by the fact that some columns are cut to receive a dedication tablet.

This antiquity of construction seems strange for a major temple in a major sanctuary. Very many temples were accidentally destroyed and, in the process of replacement, were also updated. It may be that the temple of Hera, though a bit outdated even when first built, acquired, as time passed, a special sacredness of nostalgia. It was 750 years old when Pausanias observed its single wooden column – a venerable column that would have 'seen so much'!

In the Olympia museum are the remnants of a vertical terracotta disk two metres across, heavily patterned with concentric geometric borders. This was the pedimental decoration or acroterion of the Heraion: there would have been one at each end of the temple. Similar patterned disks (though not so large) have been found in sanctuaries near Sparta – suggesting that this is a specially Peloponnesian design feature.

Inside the cella was an unusual arrangement. In order to avoid putting too much stress on the mud-brick cella walls, the outside columns were lined up with those of the interior colonnade, the object being for two sets of columns to carry each of the beams that supported the inner ceiling and heavy tile roof. Originally, each alternate interior column was attached to the cella wall by a little 'spur wall' creating a series of alcoves.

Contents

The temple of Hera eventually became something of a museum for precious artworks. While the cult statues of a throned Hera and standing Zeus were early archaic, or (as Pausanias puts it) 'simplistic', there were many more sophisticated and elaborate sculptures and objects of gold and ivory on display. The marble Hermes of Praxiteles (possibly an ancient copy) now in the museum was excavated from one of the alcoves; and there was also the famous archaic chest of Kypselos, made of cedar-wood and inlaid with gold and ivory, decorated with a whole compendium of myths – described at great length by Pausanias, who loves a story. The first scene was the chariot race of Oinomaos and Pelops: the foundation myth of Olympia. Pelops was seen racing in his chariot with his bride-to-be, Hippodameia, and their chariot horses were growing wings, so they are divinely powered (Paus 5.17.7). This is a story we will meet again.

Fig. 25 Olympia: Archaic head, possibly of Hera.

Based on Pausanias's description of the 'simplistic' group of Zeus and Hera, a female stone head in the Delphi museum, excavated near the temple, has been identified as Hera's (Fig. 25). It is early archaic, quite large and wears a tiara, as Hera would. However, it has been pointed out that Pausanias categorises all the statues from this temple as chryselephantine, which the 'Hera head' is not (Arafat 1995). While this head could well be from a sphinx, it is equally possible that Pausanias wrote carelessly, meaning that *most* of the statues were chryselephantine. In this case, the archaic head may be that of Hera. (Amid the mass of detail that the periegete gives us so unstintingly, a few inaccuracies are not surprising.)

The temple of Zeus: 471–457 BC

By the second quarter of the fifth century it must have become evident that an archaic mud-brick temple, an ash altar and an earth stadium in a natural hollow of the ground were hardly impressive, no matter how prestigious the games or the festival. With increased funds from the conquest of Pisa, the Eleans could enhance their acquisition appropriately. The building of the temple of Zeus thus fitted the needs of the Elean managers of Olympia at this time, and must also have chimed with the general triumphal mood of Greece as a whole after the defeat of Persia. Although the struggle was not completely over, mainland Greece seemed secure, thanks to the co-operative effort of most of the city states and its distance from the war zones. The final stages of the war took place either by sea or on the eastern borders of the Mediterranean. With funding and security at Olympia, the way was now clear to build a temple suitable for the king of the gods in his major sanctuary. In particular, this temple would need to surpass that of Delphi.

The building

The new temple (Paus. 5.10.2–5) was clearly planned as the monumental centre of a prestigious shrine (Fig. 26). It is situated almost parallel to that of Hera (Fig. 24), at a comfortable distance so that both temples roughly face the important ash altar, as well as the rising sun. There were no factors to limit the design and it seems few restraints on expense. The temple of Zeus is enormous (27.68 × 64.12 metres) and its size still impresses today, even now that the columns are felled and, except for the high platform and one re-erected column, scarcely one stone remains on another. Zeus, the sky-god, is huge and this is apparent even from the ruins of his house.

The temple is of course Doric, the mainland style. Sometimes it is called the 'classic' Doric temple – or even, disparagingly, the 'bog standard' Doric temple. The temple is – as Pausanias puts it – built of 'local stone' and designed by a 'local man' called Libon. Despite criticisms of its 'dullness', it should be seen as superbly fitting for its purpose: to impress, to provide an up-to-date architectural focal point for a major sanctuary, to express the character of Zeus, king of the gods.

If the temple of Zeus is standard Doric, it may be because in fact it sets the standard (Fig. 26). Its 'formula' of 6 columns to the front and 6 × 2 + 1 to the flanks results in a pleasing classical proportion (Fig. 27). A glance back at the elongated late archaic temple at Delphi will show that this classical layout seems up to date and smart in comparison.

The proportions of the new temple were carefully worked out to form a rational system of relationships: for example, the distance between each column centre and the next was half the height of a column. A similarly proportionate system has made the Parthenon famous as a model of Greek rationality and harmony. The collapsed state of the temple of Zeus makes it impossible now to detect this virtue of proportion, yet if the building were complete the eye would perceive it unconsciously and be pleased.

The temple is set upon the usual three-stepped platform: the format of a Doric temple remains the same, whatever the size. Because of the resulting great height of each step, a ramp is inserted leading up to the entrance on the east. The platform is built of the same local limestone as the rest, and is fairly intact to this day. Its immense, close-fitting blocks have survived disastrous earthquakes which toppled everything else.

The 'local material' used is **shelly limestone**, a coarse-grained stone which cannot take very fine detail and weathers poorly. When the temple was complete, the rather rough shelly surface would have been finished off with marble-dust **stucco**, making a

Fig. 26 Reconstruction view of Olympia showing the temple of Zeus and the earth altar, by Friedrich Adler from Ernst Curtius and Friedrich Adler, *Olympia*, vol. 2 (Berlin, 1896).

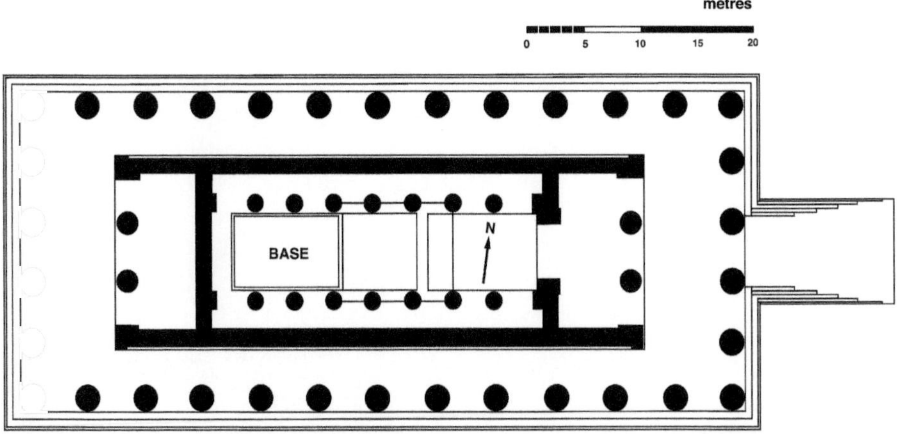

Fig. 27 Ground plan, temple of Zeus, Olympia, 470–458/7 BC.

Fig. 28 Reconstruction of the east front, temple of Zeus, Olympia.

smooth marble-like protective surface. The whole building was constructed of this stone, except for the gutters, lionhead waterspouts, roof tiles and sculptures – all these were of imported Parian marble.

The architrave, frieze and pediments were classical Doric (Fig. 28). The column capitals have the compact, neat mid-fifth-century profile, very different from those of the temple of Hera, which mainly have the wide flat archaic style. The sturdy column shafts contributed to the massive effect of the building; and they themselves were massive enough to visually support an entablature of heavy proportions. The outer metopes were plain; the pediments were furnished with particularly spectacular sculpture. The central acroteria were gilded bronze Victories, the outer ones were gilded bronze tripods: tripods were athletic prizes in Homer, so military and athletic victory is teamed on the roof decoration.

The spacing of the corner columns of the outer colonnade was slightly reduced (see pp. 61 and 103). The porches and the corridor (**pteroma**) of the outer colonnade were particularly spacious and would have provided a raised promenade area. The porches were distyle in antis, the back porch (opisthodomos) being a 'dummy', purely for symmetry, but providing a pleasant, shady, elevated area for the visitor (Fig. 27).

It was this prominently placed back porch, facing towards the palaistra, which Herodotus picked as the perfect platform for a public reading from his new book: *The Histories*. Here, the unknown visitor from Halicarnassus could attract enough attention to establish his immediate fame as a Greek writer, demonstrating what a lively, alert crowd attended the games, and how the Olympic season hosted a greater range of cultural happenings than purely athletics (Lucian *Herodotus* 1).

Within both porches there was a surprise, since the inner metopes were sculpted (Fig. 29).

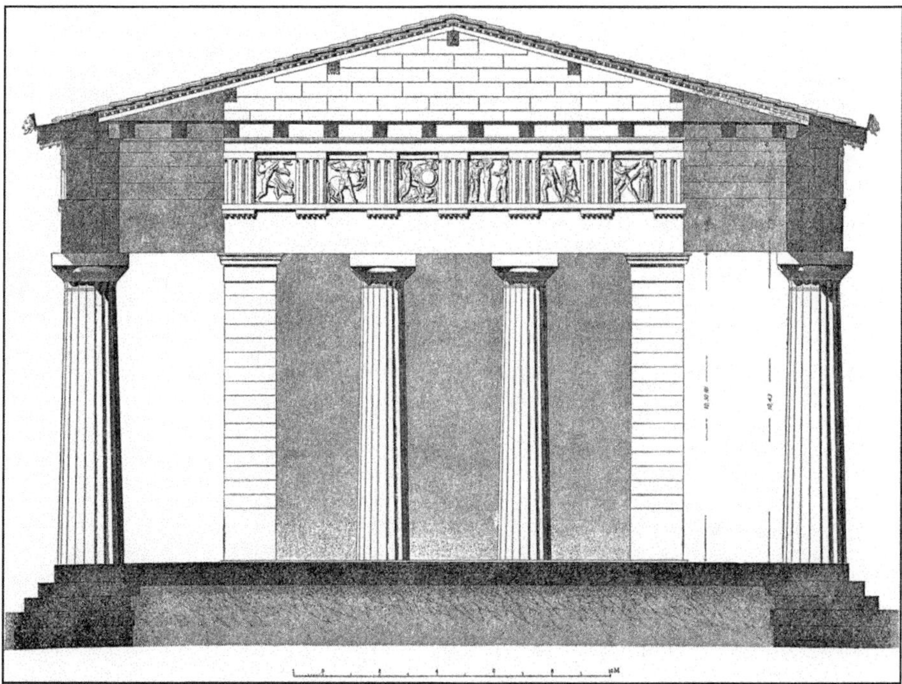

Fig. 29 Reconstruction of the inner porch, temple of Zeus, Olympia, showing the Heracles metopes.

The cella and the statue of Zeus

All this exterior spaciousness left a comparatively small cella (Fig. 30). It had a central 'nave' divided from the side 'aisles' by two colonnades, each of seven small-scale double-decker columns separated by an entablature. This two-storey arrangement enables an economical use of space, as the columns can be slimmer.

It is not known whether there was a statue originally – possibly the archaic standing Zeus was brought over from the temple of Hera. In any case, at some time following 432 BC, some 20 years after the completion of the temple, the interior was slightly adapted to accommodate a colossal new statue of Zeus. Either originally or at that time, the upper storey of each double colonnade was made to carry a viewing gallery which could be reached by a winding wooden stair inserted each side of the entrance (Paus. 5.10.10).

Pausanias writes at great length and in loving detail about Pheidias's statue. Had he not done this, the evidence for this renowned masterpiece would be meagre. With his help, the wonderful, colourful work can still be imagined (Pausanias: 5.11.1–11). The detail of the description suggests that Pausanias is writing from his own experience, and that he had access to the naos floor, and probably to the viewing gallery he mentions, for a view of the statue. It must be remembered that he was writing in the second century

Fig. 30 Cross-section of the temple of Zeus, Olympia, showing the colossal statue of Zeus.

AD, 600 years after the dedication of the temple, but still in the pagan world. The rules of access might have been relaxed in the intervening years, but given the conservatism of religion, they may not. The statue itself was closely protected by a solid marble barrier as well as a marble pool.

The enthroned Zeus was about twelve metres high, and his implied size was greater: if he ever stood up he would raise the roof. He was crowned with wild olive, like Olympic victors. His flesh was ivory while the large expanse of his golden robe was 'wrought with animals and lily-flowers'. In one hand was a Victory (**Nike**), a sizeable statue in itself, and in the other a sceptre, 'flowering' with precious metals and topped with Zeus's eagle.

Every part of the throne, and even of the footstool, was adorned with mythical characters and beasts, while the gold finish was varied with ebony, ivory and coloured gems. The god himself appeared to be made of solid gold and ivory, though in fact these materials were a veneer pieced together on a core of carved wood. This use of gold and ivory (chryselephantine) was an ancient technique whose other-worldly effect was perfect for representing divinity.

Pheidias, designer of the statue, must have felt that the massiveness and comparative plainness of the temple were an appropriate foil for this daring project. How easily the ornate colossus could have become ridiculous – but instead it was judged 'to add something to established religion, so closely did the majesty of the work match the deity himself' (Quintilian, *Institutio Oratoria* 12.10.7–9). This majestic Zeus could truly be seen as the king of heaven, moving away from the naughty Zeus of myth to embody ideas of power and justice.

The statue plinth is known from Pausanias to have been black **Eleusinian limestone**, and it can still be seen today in the ruins, taking up the entire width between the two 'nave' colonnades. In front of the statue, Pheidias had an innovative feature inserted, also still visible: a large shallow pool, also of black limestone and with a raised rim of white Pentelic marble. Since the pool was as wide as the plinth, an adjustment had to be made to fit the pool rim to the column feet (a clue that Pheidias's input was something of an afterthought to the original temple design). The dark pool was filled with olive oil. Pausanias tells us that the oil was to counteract the humid atmosphere's effect on the statue, partly ivory, on a basis of wood – two organic and unstable materials. Probably the hereditary 'polishers' used the oil on the statue to stabilise it, and perhaps poured it into the wooden core as well. Whatever the practicalities, the aesthetic effect of the pool would have been great. Any filtered sunlight or lamplight would have created a vast mysterious mirror of oily darkness in which the glittering gold and glimmering ivory would be reflected in calm or in movement.

The plinth and the pool together took up two-thirds of the space within the 'nave'. This was acceptable, since the main purpose of any temple was to house the statue. (Even if there was – as sometimes – no statue, a temple was still by implication the house of the god.) The space was further limited by fencing in the central nave with decorated low screens between the columns, both to the front and the sides; partly coloured in blue, these screens also had sections painted with myths, often repeating the stories sculpted on the temple (Pausanias: 5.11.1–11). This barrier cut down access to the precious statue, but serious tourists could probably get nearer to it via the side aisles and also get a good view from the gallery, as Pausanias did. From his detailed description it is clear that a close view repaid the effort.

On the black stone plinth of the statue, another scene was worked in attached gold or gilded figures. This represented the birth of Aphrodite from the sea, with many attendant gods to welcome her; the divine assembly was framed at each end by the rising chariot of the Sun, the sinking steed of the Moon. Aphrodite was the city goddess of Elis: this may explain her presence on the plinth: she is also commonly considered as Zeus's daughter. For Elis itself, Pheidias made a full-size chryselephantine Aphrodite (Palagia 2000). It is in any case an upbeat, joyful theme for a base: bases quite often show birth scenes. (The cosmic element of the sun and moon will also be seen on the Parthenos base in Athens.)

Pheidias's workshop and the statue of Zeus

Just outside the temenos area (Fig. 23), to the south-west of the temple, a substantial structure has been identified as an ancient workshop (later built up into an Orthodox church on top of the ancient stone courses). Several finds from the foundations suggest that this was the sculpture workshop of Pheidias, as attested by Pausanias (5.15.1). Many terracotta moulds were excavated here in which the folds of the golden robe of Zeus and his Nike could have been formed, and also moulds to make coloured glass 'gems'. With them was another treasured piece of evidence – a plain black mug of the same period with the rough inscription: 'I belong to Pheidias.' Some have thought this find too good to be true. Yet it has at least been identified as ancient together with its scratched lettering (Snodgrass, Sather classical lectures, 1987). These items, now in the museum, support the interpretation of the building.

The interesting thing about this workshop is that it reproduces the dimensions of the nave area where the Zeus was to be placed. The inference is that the statue was planned precisely for its available space: height, width and depth – possibly even the same lighting might have been reproduced in the workshop. The sculptor had exactly calculated the overwhelming effect of the enormous enthroned god in his temple. As a matter of fact, sculpture workshops were probably routine on sanctuary construction sites. But since the Zeus of Olympia has often been criticised for its 'overcrowded' proportions within the cella, this workshop offers a specific answer to the criticism.

Pausanias finishes his description of the Zeus with this tribute:

> I know the recorded dimensions of height and width of the Zeus at Olympia, but I shall not recommend those who measured them since the dimensions claimed by them fall a long way short of the impression this statue has created in those who see it … (Pausanias 5.11.9)

Pausanias could have added that it was the careful calculations of the designer, Pheidias, which manipulated this deliberate effect of great size. Instead he tells us that Zeus himself commended the work with a thunderbolt, in answer to Pheidias's prayer.

The statue was eventually taken to Constantinople where it may have influenced the representation of Christ in the development of Byzantine Christian art; it was accidentally destroyed by fire in the fifth century AD. It has left a few material traces of its existence: the finds from the workshop of Pheidias displayed in the museum, the black limestone base and black pool floor, still to be seen in the denuded cella. Ancient coins still give an idea of the face and general design of the enthroned Zeus.

Architectural sculpture

Like the gold-and-ivory statue of Zeus, the pedimental sculpture of the temple of Zeus represents a major financial investment. Reducing the enterprise to these crude terms, we should enquire what goals would justify all this expense. The new temple of Zeus, by its location, quality and size was making a declaration of significance which would reflect upon the whole sanctuary, the games, and their precedence in the Panhellenic festival world. Delphi, the rival sanctuary, already had its large-size oracular temple with impressive pediments. The temple of Apollo at Delphi must have been a competitive trigger to the Olympic managers. The temple at Delphi had contrasting pediments: a frontal line-up of divine persons (bracketed by beasts) in Parian marble, and on the back, a fight-scene – a Gigantomachy. Turning to the new Olympic pediments, we find a similar pattern, but a far more impressive presentation.

The east pediment

The east pediment features a frontal line-up, surrounding the god of the temple (Fig. 28). The plain and solemn 'severe style' of the carving fits the heavy Doric architecture perfectly. All five central figures are as straight as the columns above which they stand, and even the fluting of the columns is echoed in the folds of the women's long dresses. This relationship with the building can now only be seen in a reconstruction: the actual sculptures are in the Olympia Museum.

There are several major improvements on the Delphic scheme, helped by the move from late archaic to early classical style. The archaic beasts have been dropped in favour of a unified theme. The central god, Zeus, is not smaller – at Delphi, Apollo was smaller, due to his elevated position in a chariot – but is appropriately larger than all other characters and fits well in the apex: this may have an important psychological effect on the viewer, as we shall see. The supporting cast are not just standing frontally as separate statues, but are now a dramatic group, with psychological awareness of each other, bound together in an intense retelling of the myth. Each figure is not just characterised as young, old, male female, etc., but also interprets its own part in the story with appropriate body-language. The viewer at Olympia is not just confronted, but is also drawn in; by being encouraged to puzzle out the meaning of each figure, he or she is challenged to interpret and to respond for himself – or herself, since this story is not only of a victory but also of a marriage. Zeus is present as the one who judges – but it is left to the viewer to contemplate the judgement.

The subject of the sculpture on the east pediment is 'the preparation for the chariot race between Pelops and Oinomaos' as Pausanias usefully tells us. The story of Pelops's chariot race is also the story of how he won his bride, Hippodameia. She was a princess whose wicked father, Oinomaos, was king of Pisa. He was reluctant to let her marry, and any suitor of hers had to win her in a chariot race against him; the penalty for losing was immediate death. Already thirteen suitors were decorating Pisa with their severed heads when handsome Pelops arrived. This time Hippodameia fell in love. From here, the story has several versions. The nice version is the one we have seen on the chest of Kypselos – Pelops had magic winged horses given to him by Poseidon who had been his lover, as Pindar tells us (Pindar: *Ol.* 1). Other later versions involve the bribery of Oinomaos's charioteer Myrtilos, sabotage of his master's chariot's lynchpins by replacing them with wax, and, finally, destruction of the complicit charioteer, who managed to curse the house of Pelops before he died.

Mythology is a ragbag from which artists can pick the version that suits their purpose best. Cheating was utterly forbidden at the games and some argue that the pediment represents a warning to athletes not to cheat; but, vital as this issue was, it would make a poor theme for the most important sculpted area in the sanctuary. What we actually see is the king of the gods amid the preparation for a race on which a great deal will hang – the life and fame of Pelops, the fate of Hippodameia whose father is wronging her by preventing her marriage. As spectators, we can only hope that the best man will win – as in any athletic competition – and he will, if the gods favour him. Zeus, the god of Justice, is thought (although his head is missing) to incline towards Pelops whom we may trust is the chosen and destined winner. In fact, Pelops stands to win the greatest athletic prize ever, as he takes up the risky challenge. He will gain a wife and a kingdom: athletes of the day will win lasting fame and honour in their cities.

The figure of Oinomaos, hand on hip, looks overconfident as he explains the cruel terms of the race. His wife, Sterope, holds her hands in a grieving or thoughtful posture. Hippodameia stands at the ready because she will ride in the chariot with Pelops. Hippodameia should be imagined as beautiful. Thirteen suitors have already died for her. Admittedly her future husband will gain a kingdom, but she must be desirable in herself. Looking good on the pediment, she makes her own gesture of desire as she lifts her veil (a recognised sign indicating willingness for marriage).

This story was the foundation myth of Olympia; Pelops, the winner, gave his name to the Peloponnese and was the founder of the Olympic games, especially the chariot race.

More sanctuary themes are found further along the pediment. The famous rivers, probably the first ancestors of all other river-god statues, are lying in the extremities

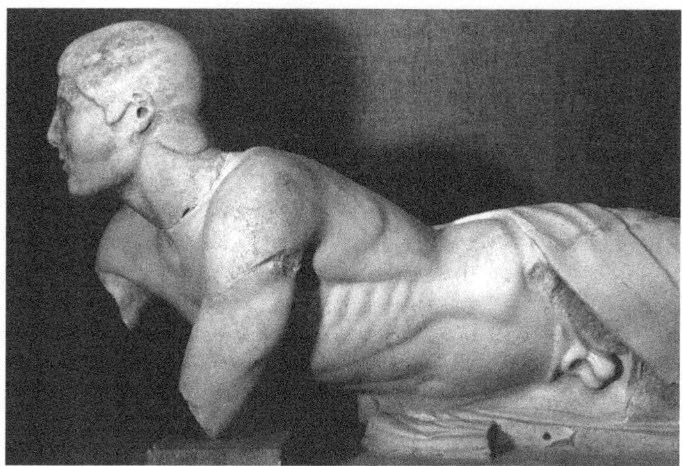

Fig. 31 River god, Kladeos, from the east pediment, right side, detail, Olympia museum.

of the triangular field, where diminishing figures are needed. They are characterised as slow-flowing Alpheios on the left and its livelier tributary, Kladeos, on the right (Fig. 31). Another geographical reference may be the young boy crouching: he is sometimes identified as Arcas, the boy-hero of neighbouring Arcadia.

Last but not least are the two groups of horses. Animals are popular on pediments because they bring a desirable variety of organic form, especially useful for creating horizontals and carrying the eye pleasantly along the pediment slope. The four-horse teams introduce a note of physical power: horses were the sports cars of antiquity. Here the viewer will look up into the mass of legs and appreciate the display of fine horseflesh, seen unusually from below. The promise of power and speed varies the stillness of the composition as a whole; in fact this chariot race will be a kind of metaphor for the human catastrophe to come, but also for the daring and achievement of the victor. Horses are very relevant to the Olympic setting, and these ones face the hippodrome area.

The role of sculpture

The mere presence of sculpture, but especially if of impressive quality, was a political claim to importance. Sculpture on a temple was capable of pulling together messages, not only about the building, but also relating to the whole sanctuary. We shall see that the temple of Zeus sculptural programme interprets the sanctuary as a whole.

Taking the sanctuary on its simplest level, as a venue for athletic competition, there is reference in the sculpture to many of the competitions: chariot racing on the front, wrestling on the back, and, in the metopes, many forms and approaches to competition. These references spin out to the various sports locations of the sanctuary. There is the foundation myth of Pelops and Hippodameia: the hero and heroine are brought to life, and as we shall see are also visited and honoured in adjacent shrines at the heart of the sanctuary. Men and athletes can look up at the hero Pelops and emulate his courage: girls can be inspired by the sturdy figure of Hippodameia: her prize was marriage, and the girls' games at Olympia in honour of Hera, the Heraia, which she founded are also rites of passage marking transitions towards marriage. Politically, Pelops represents and justifies Elis – who, by eliminating Oinomaos's city of Pisa, has taken charge of the games. At the same time, we are aware that the one ultimately in control is Zeus, both on the pediment and off. As we examine the tableau, we wonder about the judgement and justice of Zeus. Whatever particular backstory actually was intended by the sculptors here, they have introduced an intriguing note of tension and expectancy. This is particularly conveyed by one or two onlookers within the scene who, like a tragic chorus, act as a vehicle for the viewer's emotions and questions. The splendid young river god (Fig. 31), tributary Kladeos, looks up eagerly, ready to see some action. Filling the corner position, his taut figure is clean and architectural. Nearer the centre, in the rising triangle of the pediment, sits the old seer, Iamos (Fig. 32). He too is cleanly sculpted, to express both age and thought, as he turns with a sharp gesture of attention and a troubled look on his face. He and his counterpart on the left represent two prophetic families attached to Olympia

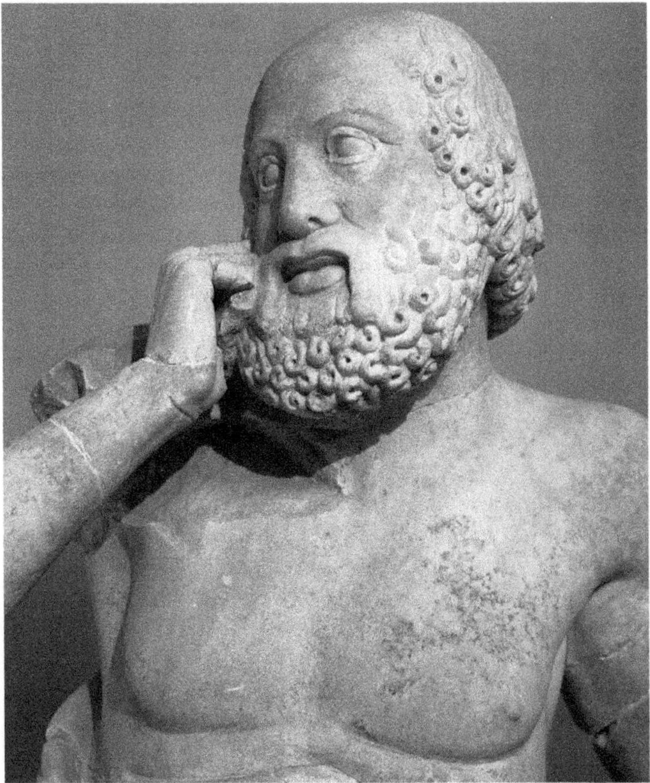

Fig. 32 Old Seer Iamos from the east pediment, right side, detail, Olympia museum.

from time immemorial, the Iamidai and the Klutidai – a reference to the real shrine and a topical device to create questioning in the viewer – What should be thought? What and who is Zeus? – The son of Pelops will be Atreus who served up the cooked children of his brother, Thyestes, and brought down a curse and plenty of murder, as told in Aeschylus's tragedy, *Oresteia*. If this questioning mood sounds unconvincingly modern, it is to be found in the *Agamemnon* of Aeschylus, especially where the puzzled chorus cry out:

> Zeus – whoever is he? – if
> he answers kindly to the name
> then this I call him – Zeus.
> I have nothing to compare
> weighing in the balance all,
> only Zeus ...
>
> (Aeschylus, *Agamemnon* 160–5)

Aeschylus wrote this in 458 BC, at just about the time when the temple of Zeus was being finished. What the sculpture offers as comfort to the viewer is a noble and worthy Zeus-figure at the axial point of the scene, probably conceived as invisible or as a statue, since no character directly reacts to him. Although the story itself arouses discomfort, the nobility and strength of the half-unveiled Zeus figure, and its strong, pivotal position, act as the repetition of the name of Zeus does for Aeschylus's Chorus: it is something to lean on.

The west pediment

As at Delphi, the front is calm while the back pediment features a fight (Fig. 33). At Delphi, the grand archaic figures told a story, but did not combine or touch. The Olympia sculptors have reversed the gods – Zeus is on the front pediment, Apollo on the back – the still point of a squirming world. Around Apollo are men, women and horse-bodies, entangled in close contact and violently active. The composition is highly structured and complex. In places, it does not quite work, understandably because it is so experimental.

Fig. 33 West pediment sculptures, temple of Zeus, Olympia museum.

The scene is the battle of Centaurs and Lapiths. Centaurs are half-man, half-horse, their lower half representing the animal nature in man. Centaurs can be noble and wise, but often they fail to live up to the Greek ideal of self-control. In this myth, the Greek Lapith hero Peirithous gives a wedding feast for his bride, Deidameia, supported by his best friend, Theseus. At the feast, the Centaurs succumb to drink, and grope the women and young boys. Lapiths fight them off without weapons.

This popular scene may well have reference to the Persians and their recent attack on Greece. (Persians were famed for their horsemanship, so were compared to centaurs.) However, it can have wider reference. The pediment faces the palaistra area where wrestling and boxing took place – this connection chalks up a positive view of fighting, suitable for an athletics venue. Animal elements can be seen as entirely bad, or as sheer energy in need of control. The fight can be political/historical – or psychological, applicable to everyone – or ascetic, referring to the rigorous physical training undergone by athletes, who must avoid all those pitfalls of drink and other indulgences which have tripped up the centaurs. Or it can be just a fight.

The way in which the groups of fighters on the west pediment are entangled provides an exciting natural-looking scene. However, the design is very carefully worked out so that the sculptures form two exactly balanced groups, one each side of central Apollo

Fig. 34 Apollo with centaur, west pediment, Olympia museum.

who stands (like Zeus on the east) isolated as a pure vertical at the apex (Fig. 34). Apollo himself, with his archaic hairdo, is perhaps a statue, a **kouros** – but a kouros come to life. His vertical central figure keys the pediment into the architecture of the façade as a whole; and (more visibly involved than Zeus), he stretches out a horizontal arm to bring order, structurally parallel to the architrave and base. The pediment contains both order and disorder, since the chaotic groups fit the pediment neatly, and exactly balance to left and right. The scene simultaneously presents strife and harmony: strife between the opposing forces of civilisation and animal energy; harmony in response to the unseen god. Apollo is of course the son of Zeus, so acts as an extension of the power of Zeus.

This group has plenty to offer in the way of role models for the viewer. The young men are all handsome and they protect their womenfolk bravely, against fierce strong aggressors. The women, whose bodies are being attacked, fight back with strength and serenity. Women, in this sanctuary, are fighters, and racers, and they make choices about their own destiny.

The metopes

A further set of sculptures is found on the metopes within the porches – the Labours of Heracles (Figs. 35 and 36). Heracles, another son of Zeus, was an interesting choice for the position half in and half out of the temple, since he is the mortal who became a god. Heracles is often represented as slightly comic, devoted to food and drink, slightly animalistic in his lion-skin garment: here he is a purer, nobler figure, genuinely moving in his strong, quiet, patience. As he won immortality through suffering and struggle, he is a wonderful role model for the athletes who will win a brief immortality in victory. On the metopes, Heracles demonstrates a variety of wrestling moves and feats of strength. He also shows that he can suffer and endure, he can use thought and skill, and even (in the cleansing of the Augean stables) technology.

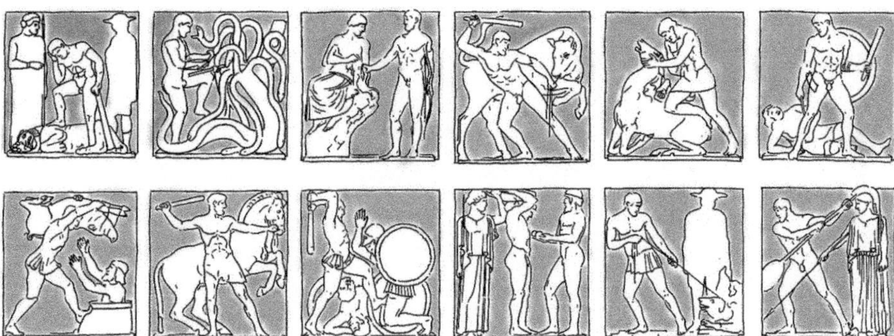

Fig. 35 Reconstruction drawing of the Heracles metope series, temple of Zeus, Olympia.

Heracles also traditionally founded the foot race at Olympia in 776 BC. (In the typical way of myth, there are two important foundation stories, but room is made for both.) Many incidents chosen for the labours take place around the Peloponnese, and also perhaps in visitors' own homelands. The hero also descends to Hades to capture Cerberus, the guard dog, and receives the golden fruit of immortality; these feats give him an appropriate universality.

The twelve Labours of Heracles neatly fit the two sets of six metopes (Fig. 35). Arranged as they are at opposite ends of the huge temple, it is interesting to speculate how far the ancient viewer would have been able to view them as a unity. Looking at the restored drawing we can perceive a sort of pattern. Metope 1 of the series includes Athene and Hermes, metope 3 also has Athene; metope 10 has Athene with Atlas, Hermes reappears

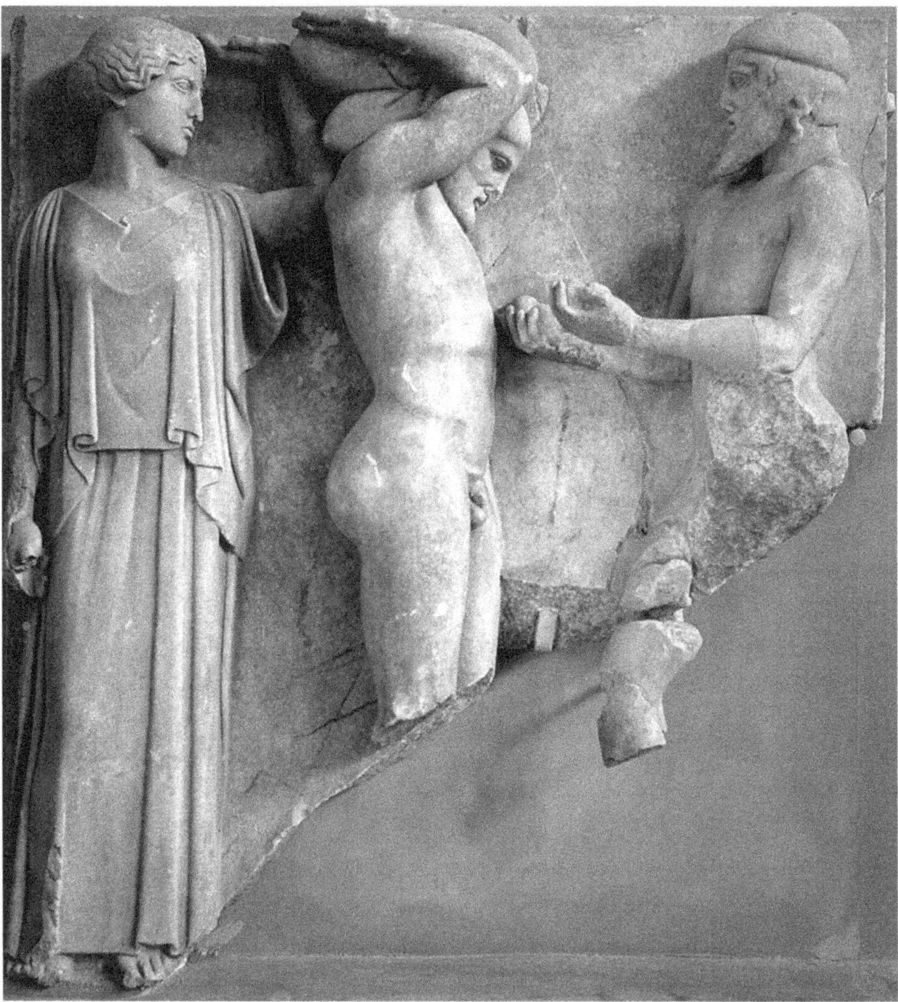

Fig. 36 Heracles metope: Heracles, Athene, Atlas and the apples of the Hesperides: Olympia museum.

in 11, and 12 also includes Athene. Of course, Heracles is in every panel. Athene, facing inwards, is the start figure and the finish, bracketing the series. She is the goddess who helps heroes as well as being the daughter of Zeus. The series begins and ends in a similar way, and the designer, it seems, has expected the viewer to remember this over some few minutes while strolling from one end to another.

The series also plays with a variety of poses. In scenes of battling with monsters, Heracles stands in action poses, mainly using diagonals. However, in scenes including gods, there is an emphasis on the vertical. When associating with gods, Heracles himself stands vertically and the scene is a peaceful one. Viewed in combination with the architecture, these scenes take on extra resonance, since the building includes the major verticals of the columns and the smaller triple verticals of the triglyphs, which divide the scenes. Two scenes contain three figures, namely scenes 1 and 10. Scene 10, viewed in architectural context, resembles a triglyph, with its two upright immortals and the rigid Heracles between them (Fig. 36). In scene 1, by contrast, Heracles is bowed between the two upright divinities. Here he has just killed the Nemean lion, and is famously exhausted by his first task – but by scene 10, he has matured enough to bear up the heavens. When these two scenes are compared, it seems that with maturity, the hero has become a part of sacred architecture, along with gods. If this suggestion is correct, it seems that the designer was indeed confident of the ability of the ancient viewer to make the link by memory without the aid of diagrams and notes. (see Barringer 2005 for discussion and extensive bibliography)

Heracles and Olympia

As mentioned above, Heracles was a founder of Olympia, just as Pelops was. Heracles established the foot race: according to Pindar, it was also he who brought the olive tree from the Danube (surprisingly) to grow in the Altis, and give its shoots for the olive crowns for the victors. The poet imagines that the valley 'had not put forth its radiant forest' and there was no shade, till the hero remembered trees he had seen in the land of the Hyperboreans, and 'longing came upon him' to create grateful shade for his athletic sanctuary (Pindar, *Ol*, 3.2/3). This poetic idea reflects the real delight created by the leafy Altis in the fertile and well-watered valley of Olympia, in a country otherwise often tending to be harsh and dry.

The ash altar of Olympian Zeus

This was a very different sort of monument from the sophisticated temple, but it must have been the true religious heart of the Altis (Fig. 23).

Pausanias tells us that it lay 'at the same distance from the Pelopeion and the temple of Hera, but further forward than either of them' (Pausanias 5.13.8). We would know nothing of it without his *Guide* as it has completely disappeared. The fifth-century temple of Zeus was obviously built in relation to this important altar, but as usual without any formal lining up. Both temples faced it at an angle so it seems to have been acceptable for a temple to face its altar at an angle, rather than symmetrically as might be expected.

The altar was built from sacrificial ash – reputedly started off by Heracles and so very ancient and sacred (Fig. 26). It was cone-shaped, stepped and circular; the outer circumference, marked by stones, was 125 feet according to Pausanias, and in his time the top reached 22 feet in height. At each sacrifice, the part to be burnt (rather than the part eaten by worshippers) was taken up to the top; and the ashes obtained were saved for the nineteenth day of the Greek month Elaphios, then mixed with Alpheios water and daubed over the altar, increasing its size a little every year. The height and bulk of the altar, composed entirely of pulverised sacrifices, was thus a tangible record of the antiquity of the cult. Girls and women were allowed to climb the stone steps to the first level, but only men could go up to the top.

Hera had her own ash altar near her temple, and so did Earth herself.

The Pelopeion

Two more monuments are important for the meaning of the sanctuary, even though one has scanty remains and the other has vanished. The Pelopeion was a hero shrine of great antiquity. What could be seen was just a low grassy grave mound: in the fifth century (perhaps in association with the building of the temple) this was made more monumental with a surrounding wall in an odd five-sided shape, and a classical propylon. Inside were trees, statues and a mound. Although modern opinion has varied as to whether this 'grave' really had any contents, it is now thought to contain a genuine Bronze Age burial (Kyrieleis 2003). The connection with Pelops supplies a foundation hero for Olympia and the mound is perhaps the oldest thing at Olympia. Pausanias says that Pelops 'was worshipped more than any other hero at Olympia, just as much as Zeus was worshipped more than any other god' (Pausanias 5.13.1). Pindar imagined him blessed with 'the gifts of Aphrodite' (sexual appeal) which won him the favour of Poseidon – and then of Hippodameia: 'Now Pelops, reclining at the Alpheios crossing, shares the sacrifices, … his tomb is bustling, near the populous altar (of Zeus)' (Pindar *Ol.*1.90 f.). The quiet but heroic warrior figure already seen on the pediment of the temple of Zeus brought this ancient, buried, foundation hero to life and provided a good role model for the male visitor.

The Hippodameion

The other hero shrine was for the bride of Pelops – Hippodameia. No trace of this remains, but Pausanias describes it as 'a walled enclosure of a quarter of an acre which women enter once a year to perform rites in honour of Hippodameia and to offer her sacrifice' (Pausanias 6.20.7).

Plenty of other activities were associated with Hippodameia. As at Athens, a **peplos** was woven every four years for presentation to the goddess: here, it was for Hera. Sixteen married women were chosen for the task. They in turn chose sixteen girls to compete in the Heraia – women's games for Hera, distinct from the Olympic games for men. These included girls' foot races for three age groups, run in the same stadium as for men – but one-sixth less in length: 'they run with their hair loose, tunic above the knee, and the right breast and shoulder bare'. Girl-winners of races got crowns of olive, a share of Hera's sacrificial ox and the right to dedicate a painted portrait. These games were said to be founded by Hippodameia herself. Although they took place at a separate time from the men's competitions, they could have been an intrinsic part of the games at Olympia from the beginning (Pausanias 5.14.1–4). We know that Spartan girls did athletics. These Peloponnesian girls were not specified as Spartan, but it seems unlikely that any girls would run a serious race without any training at all – probably sporting activities were a normal part of their education. The Sixteen also arranged dances for Hippodameia; another sixteen women were chosen to 'serve' the Sixteen; altogether many females would have had a chance to be involved, at some time, in some way, in the Heraia. All this suggests much more organised activity for women than is often supposed.

The vanished shrine of Hippodameia was extensive and had more of a presence than we might have guessed. The young figure of Hippodameia on the east front of the temple gathers up some real feminine interests, not only the myth and the tomb. It is a focus for girls and women who are interested in marriage, even perhaps an inspiration for some self-motivation. Hippodameia was thwarted in her efforts to move normally from girlhood to marriage, by her perverse and cruel father. Hippodameia (Horsetamer-woman) was active enough to promote her own destiny: she went in the chariot with Pelops, perhaps choosing him as husband. In some versions of the myth, she even took a hand in the defeat of her father. She then founded the Heraia in thanks for her marriage, Hera being goddess of marriage. By partaking in the games, girls would be promoting their own growth from child to adult, a move sometimes considered problematic for either sex by the ancient Greeks. On the pediment, Hippodameia is lifting her dress at the shoulder, a gesture indicating readiness for marriage. The female career is thus catered for at Olympia, and in a more proactive way than we might have expected.

Oinomaos's pillar

To complete the trio, even wicked King Oinomaos had his memorial. Preserved under a low shelter was a stump of a wooden pillar – now vanished. A poem on a bronze plaque informed the ancient tourist that this was the remnant of Oinomaos's palace, struck by Zeus's lightning! So, the little monument neatly recorded both an ancient king and the justice of Zeus (Pausanias 5. 20. 6).

Treasuries

Here at Olympia, as at Delphi, there were treasuries, mostly archaic, dating from 580 BC onwards. West to east, the treasuries were dedicated by: Sicyon, Syracuse, Byzantion, Sybaris, Cyrene, Selinus, Metapontum, Megara and Gela (Pausanias 6. 19. 1–15). Of these cities, all but two were colonies. They stood together in an uneven line of eleven, on a raised terrace at the base of the Hill of Kronos (Fig. 23). In the sixth century, the terrace would have been a good viewing station for the stadium, which was then inside the Altis. However, as the sanctuary developed, more room was required within it, and the stadium was moved eastwards to just outside the Altis. The terrace remains a good vantage point for architectural display. At Delphi, treasuries were dotted and interspersed throughout the sanctuary in a seemingly random way, sometimes challenging each other, sometimes jostling for a dramatic site. At Olympia, the treasuries were lined up in orderly fashion, and could have been compared and appreciated all at once.

The treasuries were largely Doric, and each one was distinctive; they tended to exemplify the individual characteristics of their own local building styles, and often were made of materials imported from the home city. For example, the largest, that from Gela in Sicily, had a characteristic terracotta cladding, ornately painted in geometric patterns of black, red and white, which had to be made and brought from the homeland in Sicily – or possibly was constructed at Olympia by Sicilian craftsmen. The system of terracotta cladding was originally intended to protect wooden or mud-brick structures from the weather. This treasury was stone-built, suggesting that the cladding had a special decorative and stylistic purpose as 'branding'. Another treasury, owned by the mainland city of Megara, had a small stone pediment, featuring the Battle of Gods and Giants. Treasuries were somewhat larger than a double garage, with a porch and an inner room. Probably open to view from outside, they held offerings. As at Delphi, each treasury was like a stall at an international fair, advertising the value and uniqueness of its own polis or city state.

Among Olympian treasuries, there was a very strong presence from the colonies: Syracuse, Selinus, and Gela in Sicily; Croton, Sybaris and Metapontum in Magna Graecia (Southern Italy); Byzantion from the East (Istanbul); Cyrene from the Mediterranean coast of Africa; Sikyon from Northern Peloponnese, not so far from Olympia and even nearer to Delphi across the gulf, where there was another treasury of Sicyon; and Megara in Attica (itself a founder of colonies – Megara Hyblaea in Sicily, and Byzantium and Calcedon in the East) with a treasury at Delphi also. These cities competed of course. Partaking in the games was a useful and high-profile way of being part of the Greek polis community in a neutral Panhellenic context; this also gave an opportunity for all sorts of non-athletic interaction on every level, between individual cities. The treasuries themselves were also a form of competition with each other.

Overall it was clearly important for colonies to have this permanent architectural presence at the major Greek gathering place, Olympia; they put in considerable effort and expense to achieve it.

The Nike of Paionios

One of the many statues once crowding the Altis was so monumental as almost to compete with the buildings. A huge winged Victory (Nike) descends upon a ten-metre pyramidal column, topped by the beak of a ship. The artistic point of the sculpture is to make a mass of marble appear to land with feather-lightness from the air, while spread wings and billowing garments swirl upward in the windy wake of the goddess. An eagle under her feet may be a courtesy nod to Zeus, since the monument was directly opposite his temple, and the goddess herself reminds us of the golden Nike held by the chryselephantine Zeus.

Victory was naturally a theme at Olympia. The Nike of Paionios recorded the victory of the Messenians and Naupactians over the Spartans (420 BC). Its inscription continues: 'Paionios made this and was victorious … in winning the commission for the temple acroteria', adding the concept of artistic contest to the other forms: military and athletic.

Of the hundreds of statues which Pausanias tells us once crowded Olympia, sadly few are left. These are well displayed in the Olympia site museum. Of life-size marble, there is this Nike and the Hermes of Praxiteles, and all the sculptures from the temple, happily preserved by the flood mud of Alpheios and Kladeos. Almost everything else has fallen prey to chance, to the sophisticated Roman collector, or to the unsophisticated melter of bronze or recycler of marble.

The Philippeion

As at Delphi, outsiders could gain prestige by making showy offerings at a famous Panhellenic shrine. One such building would have been very noticeable, tucked just within the Altis area, behind the Heraion and Pelopeion and almost against the boundary. It has even been suggested that the temenos wall was diverted here to make space for it. The Philippeion was a tholos of stone and marble in Ionic style (Fig. 37), started sometime after 338 BC, by Philip of Macedon to mark his final victory over the Greeks at the Battle of Chaeronea, and possibly completed before his death in 336 BC.

The outer colonnade of eighteen columns was Ionic, and supported a plain 3-stepped frieze topped by dentils. The roof was marble, probably in two steps, and conical, crowned by a bronze poppyhead. Pausanias tells us it was built of brick and marble. In fact, it had marble columns and a marble dado base to the cella wall: above that was limestone, stuccoed and painted to imitate brick. The cella, lit from its door and possibly by two windows, was decorated inside with nine engaged Corinthian columns, one corresponding to each alternate exterior column space.

The building might count as a treasury – a cross between a temple and a storehouse. Yet it is placed, not among the treasuries, but on the edge of the temple area. And the statues it housed represented no god of the sanctuary, but were full-height family portrait

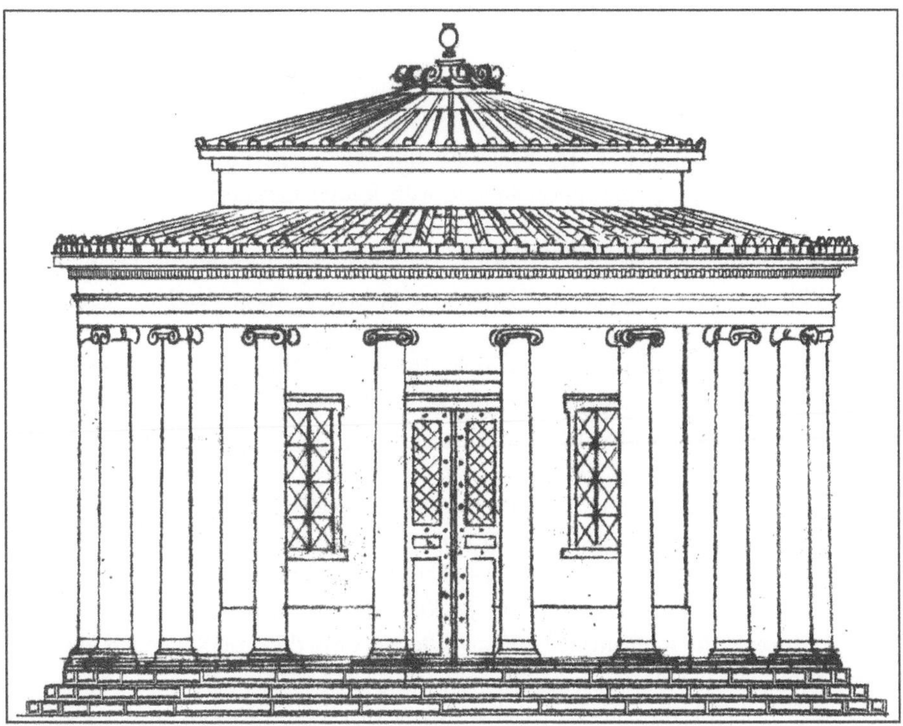

Fig. 37 Reconstruction drawing of the Philippeion, Olympia, shown with a stepped roof.

sculptures of Philip, his parents, his queen Olympias and their son, the young Alexander the Great, all grouped on a crescent-shaped plinth and sculpted by Leochares, a highly regarded Greek sculptor (Pausanias 5.20.9–10).

The presence of this monument shows the power of Macedon at the time. As said above, non-Greeks could make offerings at Panhellenic shrines – for example, Croesus, the king of Lydia had loved to enrich Delphi – but this particular offering would seem to make certain claims. The statues were probably of polished and gilded marble, giving a similar effect to the nearby chryselephantine Zeus of Pheidias. Votive statues of winning athletes were marble or bronze, girl victors dedicated paintings only: in the hierarchy of materials, gold was for divinity. Possibly even more offensive to some was the use of Ionic style and the combination of an Attic frieze with dentils: did this amount to a claim to be 'spiritually' Athenian? (Rhodes 1995, p. 162) The Macedonians were not considered by the Greeks to be really Greeks (although they claimed they were), and anyway Philip was an invader and occupier of Greece. The choice of a round building in the refined Ionic style made sure of catching attention in a mainly Doric mainland site. Additionally, this Olympic tholos, more exotic than its Doric competitor at Delphi, evened up the architectural score between the sites.

Pausanias tells us that the statues were chryselephantine, just like the statue of Zeus. However, recent examination of the statue plinth has shown that they probably had to be marble; but gilded marble would appear very much like chryselephantine and would give a similar impression. It could probably be created more quickly too (Schultz, 2009). It seems, again from the plinth, that the central statue of the group was larger than the rest, so, that one would be Philip, (if achieved during his lifetime,) with a smaller flanking Alexander as his battle assistant and heir. The whole group of five would have echoed the central group of the East pediment of the nearby Temple of Zeus – two men and two women bracketing the central dominant male. Schultz points out that if this striking building were achieved in the short space of two years (prior to Philip's death in 336) it would appear almost magical to the Olympic visitor. 'One of the fundamental components of the Philippeion's impact was that the monument materialised almost overnight in the middle of the Altis for every Greek to see.' (Ibid. p. 133) (In this way, it would be the very opposite of the patchy-looking Heraion (*c.* 580) whose impact was drawn from its obvious antiquity.) With this monument, a step has been taken towards the idea of the divine ruler.

The experience of entering the Philippeion, as Schultz and others have argued, would be similar to that of two other circular statue arrangements, the Argive monument at Delphi and the Achaian monument at Olympia. Both these depend on the viewer's standpoint among the life-size and lifelike statues – which outnumber the viewer, and must overawe him/her by their heroic superiority. The Argive statues necessarily surrounded the viewer on both sides in the passage along the Sacred Way at Delphi, and the monument at Olympia invited the viewer into the gathering of Homeric kings, armed and drawing lots for a duel with Hector: Nestor being separately based from the others (Paus 5.25.8). This type of experience would be greatly heightened in the roofed and enclosed setting of the Philippeion where the viewer would be confronted by the gilded figures *and* cut off from everything else. All this would make it easier to digest the proposition that these royal figures were somehow more than human.

There is another possible inspiration for Philip's display of sculpture, and it further illustrates the close-knit nature of the Greek world and its visual ideas. In the late fifth century BC, the Athenians built a small temple on the sacred island of Delos (427 BC), squeezed in between existing buildings. This Temple of the Athenians was **amphiprostyle**, hexastyle, with large acroteria and a rich interior. Through the six porch columns and the four slender piers of the front could be seen a semicircular plinth taking up most of the interior space. It supported seven chryselephantine statues, including a central Apollo flanked by his mother Leto and his sister Artemis. The interior was further enriched with carved marble tympana – indoor pediments. Unusually, there was no ceiling, the inner space rising to the pitched rafters, which were interspersed with decorative coffering (Dinsmoor, p. 183–4).

Although Philip conquered the Thebans and Athenians at Chaeronea and was obviously seen as a huge threat to Greek freedom, his purpose, in the words of Lapatin, was less 'to claim victory over conquered Greeks, but to unite them behind him for the eastern campaign [against Persia]' (Lapatin 2001, p. 117). He therefore took steps to appear generally Philhellene, and reasonable with regard to Athens because of their useful sea power. Philip already had 'ties' with Olympia – as an Olympic victor in the horse-race (356 BC), and he also claimed to be a descendant of Heracles and Pelops, founders of the games. By the dedication of the Philippeion, he strategically slotted himself into the Greek cultural and devotional scene, in their foremost sanctuary to the king of the gods, while adopting flattering Athenian undertones.

The Echo Stoa and the stadium

This mid-fourth-century stoa ran 100 metres from north to south, separating the Altis from the stadium area (Fig. 23). It had a double corridor, divided by an Ionic interior colonnade; the exterior was Doric. Paintings decorated its back wall and an echo gave it its name. Stoas in general provided a civilised place to meet, and also to set out stalls and do business, all in the welcome shade. This stoa was well-placed to provide a useful multipurpose amenity bordering the Altis. It also gave definition to the different areas, the Altis and the sports area.

The original archaic stadium was within the Altis itself, in full view of the treasuries. It was moved several times in the sanctuary area, and finally found a place just outside and to the east of the Altis, where there is ample room. It was and still is mainly an earth construction, as Pausanias describes, taking advantage of natural contours of the ground. It accommodated 45,000 spectators and was 212.5 metres long, 28.5 metres wide.

On the central south side there were stone seats for the presidents of the games and opposite this point on the other side was a 'white stone altar on which a married woman sits, the priestess of Demeter'. Pausanias adds surprisingly: 'Virgin girls of course are not barred from watching' (Pausanias 6.20.8–9), although elsewhere we learn that married women were barred on pain of death except for the priestess herself, who was married. Pausanias, writing in the second century AD, may be misleading us about the classical era: as athletes competed in the nude, there would be reason to ban women from attending. On the other hand, the presence of virgins could well have been part of the marriage preparation that also seems to be a theme of the sanctuary.

The stadium is still reached through a long masonry passage that was once a barrel-vaulted tunnel called the Hidden Entrance. Through this, the judges and athletes could make a dramatic appearance. In front of the treasuries and leading to the Hidden Entrance is the row of thirteen plinths for the Zanes: these were bronze statues of Zeus, paid for by fines exacted from athletes found cheating.

Later, there was a separate course for chariot racing and horse events, the hippodrome.

Other buildings

The early-fifth-century **Prytaneion** just within the Altis was a useful building for officials and VIP hospitality. It contained a sacred hearth and an eternal flame.

Just outside the Altis, many other functional buildings were gradually added. The palaistra (third century) and gymnasium (second century) would have been appreciated for their shady colonnades; before they were built, the activities they housed – boxing, wrestling, etc., would have been carried on in some more informal setting, perhaps on roughly the same sites. Colonnades provided shade for philosophical discussion as well as athletic activity. Other amenities such as baths would have been equally appreciated: Greek-style baths were built in the early fifth century; the rivers offered washing places in earlier times. The Leonidaion, donated in the late fourth century BC by Leonidas of Naxos, was a generous addition to the comfort of their stay for superior guests. It was a 'hotel' built in a square around a garden courtyard and containing numerous bedrooms, rather like a modern motel.

The **Bouleuterion** or council chamber just outside the Altis was a double building of archaic horseshoe plan. One of the two linked sections was an authentically archaic council house – the other was a fifth-century reproduction in archaic style! Interestingly, the up-to-date style was not always considered appropriate. Between the two was the important statue of Zeus Horkeios ('of oaths') where athletes swore to follow the Olympic rules.

Conclusion

The sanctuary of Olympia operated successfully for over a thousand years. It continued to be developed well into Roman times (though here we have mainly looked at buildings up to the late fifth century BC). The site was extraordinarily well-chosen for access and attractiveness, as is proved by the success and fame of the games. It must also have been extremely well-run considering the huge numbers attending and competing. Visitors today still find the site seductively pleasant – some echo of the senior Greek games festival still lingers on in a lasting holiday mood.

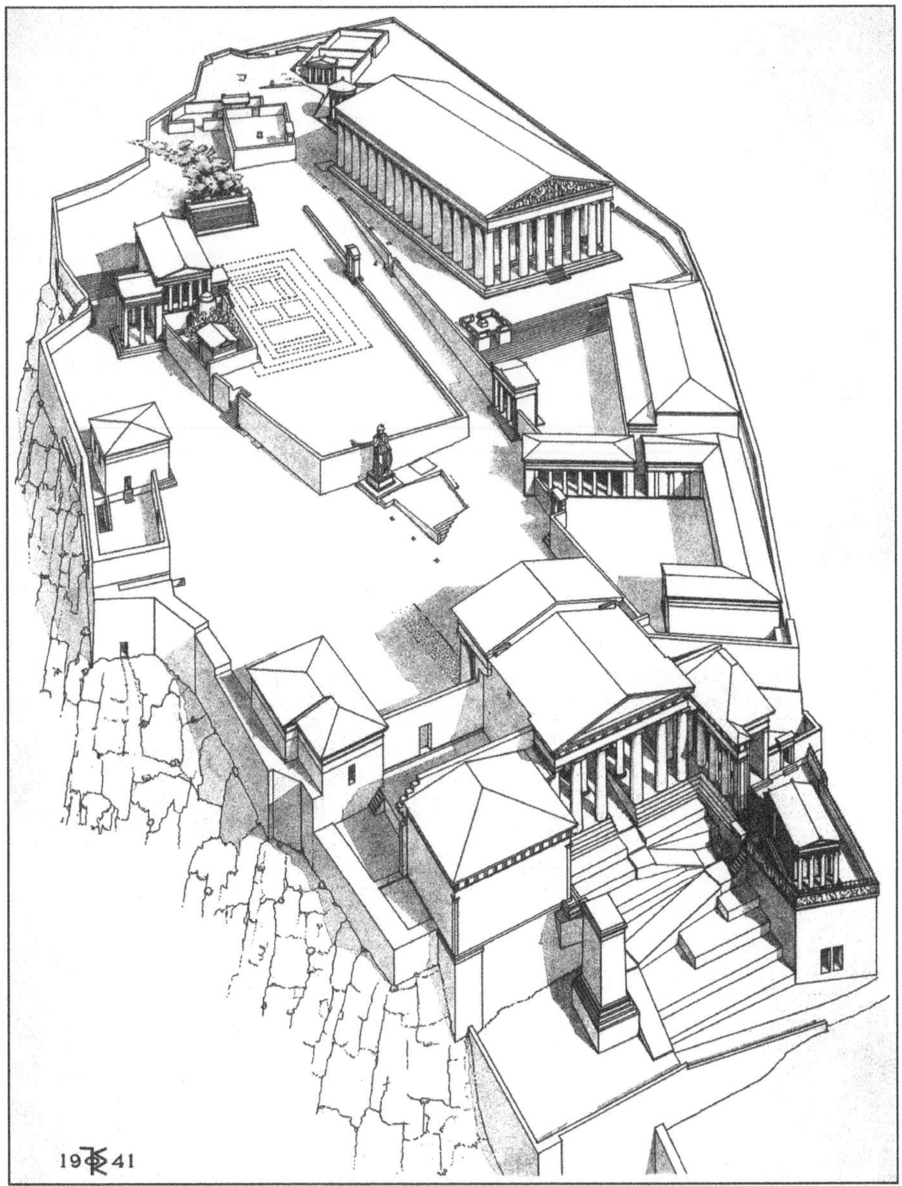

Fig. 38 Reconstruction view of the Athenian Acropolis from the west; clockwise from front: Propylaia, House of the Arrhephoroi, Erechtheion, ruins of 'old Athene temple', Parthenon, Khalkotheke, sanctuary of Artemis Brauronia, sanctuary of Athene Nike.

CHAPTER 7
THE ATHENIAN ACROPOLIS: HISTORICAL BACKGROUND

The buildings of the Athenian Acropolis form a remarkable ensemble. Unlike the other sites we have looked at, they were built as a continuous project, completed in less than 50 years. They can be seen as the product of a single inspiration, to celebrate Athens and to give glory to Athene, and to express the life of Athens at a particular time in her history. The stylistic approach is coherent, although each building is unique. And this architectural achievement has amazed people in its own time, and been treasured in subsequent eras.

The historian Thucydides famously stated that the Acropolis buildings would give subsequent ages a false picture of the power of Athens – they exaggerated its true power: 'If Athens were to be left in ruins, the visible evidence would make it seem to have been twice as powerful as it really was' (Thucydides *History* 1.10.2). This statement seems to suggest that the purpose was achieved. To gain a fuller understanding of this achievement, some historical background is worth pursuing.

The Acropolis is, even today, a startling city-centre feature rising abruptly to a height of well over 100 metres from street level (see Frontispiece). It is a natural limestone outcrop with steep cliffs on all sides but the west; its sloping summit has to some extent been squared off with infill and terracing; its upper sides have been clad with sheer fortress-like walls. In the lower slopes are found natural caves, many adapted as shrines. There are also springs and fountains at this level, approachable from above: this vital feature led to its early adoption as a defensible habitation. The top of the rock is an elongated sloping plateau, measuring very roughly 270 × 156 metres.

In Mycenaean times, the Acropolis seems to have had an unremarkable history. Towards the end of the period, around 1300–1200 BC, it acquired a palace complete with substantial terracing, and was encircled by Cyclopean walls, including a propylon on the western slope.

Following the collapse of the Mycenaean 'palace civilisation', the Athenians lived in an undistinguished way around and sometimes on this natural fortress for centuries. Their subsequent rise to prominence was reflected in the buildings that eventually came to adorn it. Two distinct periods are represented in architecture: the archaic and the classical. They are sharply divided by the year 480/79 in which invading Persians systematically destroyed what was already built, leaving the site – in a sense – cleared for future development.

This is the site and the opportunity that Pericles later exploited so successfully (Figs. 38 and 39).

The archaic era: From tyranny to democracy

During the sixth century, the Acropolis was developed with many buildings and votive sculptures. After the destruction of the site by the Persians in 480/79, damaged sculptures were buried in pits. Excavation has brought these to light, demonstrating the richness of the archaic Acropolis. However, it has proved difficult to assign the architectural fragments to particular buildings or locations. Constant redevelopment of the sanctuary has obliterated precise traces of the past.

Politically the sixth century was also one of change. There were class struggles and vigorous attempts to establish an equitable legal system. In 540, Peisistratus seized power as tyrant (unconstitutional ruler) and was succeeded by his son in 527. The Peisistratid dynasty did many things to enhance the life and the culture of the city, but Hippias, the son, eventually became very unpopular and in 510 he was ousted with the military help of Sparta.

By 507, a democracy was organised in Athens. Democracy was 'the rule of all the citizens' – which in practice meant all Athenian males of qualifying age and status (not, of course, foreigners, slaves or women). With this proviso, the citizens of Athens had a remarkable degree of access to the processes of government. Most officials were chosen by lot annually. The boule (deliberative council) was a revolving group of 500, chosen by lot; their meeting place was in the **Agora**. The ekklesia (full assembly) was for every qualifying male to attend; there he could voice his opinion if he wished and could give his vote as a matter of duty. This assembly met on a hill called the Pnyx which overlooked the Agora and faced the Acropolis.

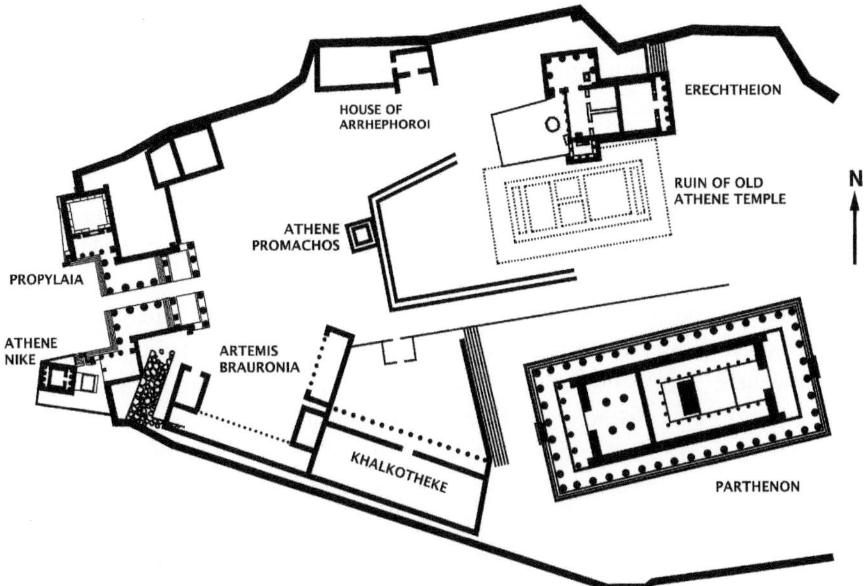

Fig. 39 Ground plan of the Acropolis, second half of fifth century.

The Athenians rejoiced at this change from the rule of one man, however enlightened and benign. They reckoned a system where every citizen had his own voice in government (isegoria) – and had equality before the law (isonomia) – a civic possession of infinite value.

Archaic buildings on the Acropolis: 'Bluebeard' and the 'old Athene temple'

The Peisistratids are often credited with important building programmes on the Acropolis, but it is uncertain which, if any, they really undertook. In the period 570–550 there was a great deal of activity, clustering around the introduction of the quadrennial festival, the Greater Panathenaia, in 566/5. During these years, dozens of statues were offered by individuals, the western access ramp was enlarged, and a sizeable limestone temple was built whose pediments (now in the Acropolis Museum) featured ferocious lions and a strange 'Bluebeard' figure. It is not known where this temple stood, whether on the Mycenaean terracing or possibly on the site later used for the Parthenon.

Towards the end of the sixth century another limestone temple was built on the Acropolis whose foundations can be clearly seen today. It took up some of the space once occupied by the Mycenaean palace, and was sited on its ancient terracing for impressive effect. This temple was built to house the ancient cult statue of Athene Polias (protectress of the city), and must have replaced whatever temple already did that important job, whether the 'Bluebeard' or a yet older one. Again, it is not known whether the Peisistratids were the patrons of this grand late archaic building, or whether it was built to celebrate the new democracy – or even was adopted half-built and completed by the democracy. Some of the marble pedimental sculpture can be seen in the Acropolis Museum: Athene dispatches giants; possibly Zeus arrives in his chariot. A similar Gigantomachy was probably on the west end of the Alkmaeonid temple at Delphi; it seems the two Athenian-influenced temples should be related to each other, but it is still unclear which is earlier.

The fifth century: From the burning of Sardis to the building of the Parthenon

War and the threat of war with Persia dominated the first half of the fifth century BC for the Greek city states generally. Athens in particular was a target for the Persians right from the beginning. This was because of her special relationship with the Ionian Greek city states and island states which bordered the Persian empire along the eastern Mediterranean coastline (see Map 1). Persia's enormous and expanding empire already included a vast interior land mass, ending at the coast.

Traditionally and mythically the Ionian city states were offshoots of Athens. When the Ionian cities felt increasingly threatened by Persia, it made sense for them to approach the Athenians, who were persuaded to play an unwise and dangerous game; they joined the Ionians in a military expedition to the Persian interior, and in 499/8 they captured and burnt Sardis. Herodotus (*Histories* 5.104) tells how the roofs of that city were all flammable thatch; accidentally, the temple of Cybele was destroyed. This insult explains why the Persians were later so very particular to destroy every temple on the Acropolis.

Persia's ambitions apparently included the absorption of the whole of Greece. The invasion of the mainland began with the famous landing at Marathon in 490, under the guidance of old Hippias, the exiled Peisistratid tyrant. Had it been successful, Hippias would have become the puppet king and Athens would have lost her treasured new democracy along with her freedom.

The battle of Marathon was the 'miraculous' event in which the terrifying invading power was defeated by a citizen army less than half the size. The casualty figures recorded by the Greeks were: 6,400 Persians slain on the field of battle to only 192 Athenians. Heroes and gods were observed to fight for the Athenians: Pan, Theseus and Heracles were all present. On the field of battle a mound was raised in Homeric style for the burial of the slain heroes. The victory was the iconic event of the new Athenian democracy. In commemoration, a great new marble temple was begun on the south side of the Acropolis – the 'pre-Parthenon'.

Salamis

Not everyone believed that lasting victory was achieved. Sure enough, the Persians were planning a return – which happened in 480/79. The invaders reached Attica, encamped on the Areopagos, penetrated the Acropolis and deliberately threw down or burnt everything which they found up there, the huge Mycenaean fortification wall, the dedicated statues and the temples, including the partly built pre-Parthenon temple.

But the Persians were destroying an abandoned city. After Marathon, Themistocles had persuaded the Athenians to build up their fleet, as he believed that sea power was the way to withstand Persia. When it was known that the Persians were actually on their way back to Greece, the Athenians sent to Delphi for advice: they were told: 'Seek safety in the wooden walls.' A few diehards interpreted this as the wooden planking forming part of the Acropolis gateway. They stayed to defend the Acropolis and were slaughtered as they took refuge in the 'old temple'. But most were convinced by Themistocles that the 'wooden walls' were the new ships, standing ready for an emergency such as this. The priestess of Athene Polias backed him, pointing out that the sacred snake had already deserted the Acropolis, a powerful omen.

The whole population of Athens (apart from those few diehards) evacuated the city, carrying with them the sacred image of Athene Polias. It certainly was a bold strategy: the women and children were placed in safety in Troezen and Salamis. The men manned the ships at Salamis, visible from the Acropolis. Proactive Themistocles even manipulated the battle, tricking the Persians into attacking in a space far too narrow for their large ships to manoeuvre in. They were trapped and became sitting targets for the battle-rams of the more versatile Athenian triremes. Once again, Pan was seen to fight for the Athenians. The battle was a triumph for democracy against tyranny and barbarism.

Insofar as a city is 'men not walls', Athens was gloriously safe. However, the built city, Athens, especially the Acropolis with all its memorials of history, was now a wreck. All the temples, all the beautiful statues dedicated to Athene were broken and spoilt. Also, although the Persians had been beaten back, they were a great power, angry, shamed and hostile. They might return.

The Delian League

Athens, glorious victor of Salamis, then made an offer to the rest of the Greeks (478/7 BC). Any city state which felt itself too small to build up a navy of its own could contribute yearly ship money to Athens. Athens would use it to build and maintain a naval force sufficient to protect them all. This would mainly be of interest to city states and island states bordering the Persian territory and in the Eastern Mediterranean. It was an offer that small and vulnerable cities could scarcely afford to refuse: its effect was to give Athens almost imperial power.

The money raised would be kept on the sacred island of Delos, hence the name of the scheme. By 454, the leader, Pericles, had transferred these funds to Athens. The Delian League worked very well in that Athens did successfully police the Ionian Sea, until the Persians finally agreed on a truce or treaty in 449. It also meant that Athens now had enormous resources. Following the truce, Pericles saw fit to propose the rebuilding of the Acropolis sanctuary.

The oath of Plataea

It is said that the Greeks – or perhaps just the Athenians – swore an oath during the war with Persia known as the oath of Plataea, in which they promised 'not to rebuild any of the temples burnt and ruined by the Persian, but to leave them as a testimony to future generations of the impiety of the barbarian'. This oath is recorded by two rather later ancient writers (Diodorus and Lycurgus) and it is not known for certain whether it is authentic. Plutarch makes no reference to it when discussing Pericles's plans for a Panhellenic conference on the rebuilding of the sanctuaries throughout Greece, and it may be that the oath was invented later to explain the fact of the delay in rebuilding.

For whatever reason, it seems that the Acropolis, ruined by the Persians, was left unrestored for 30 years without any significant new architectural projects, although the Athenians must have tidied up sufficiently to be able to carry on the cult activity, and to shelter their precious Athene Polias, and probably an Athene Nike (Victory) as well. It is quite possible that part of the large temple sited towards the north (whose stone foundations are still visible next to the Erechtheion) was repaired, or shored up, to contain the Athene Polias statue and other treasures. What else was done within the sanctuary is unclear.

The defensive walls around the city were rebuilt straightaway – swiftly and haphazardly, with whatever material was to hand. Even parts of damaged sculptures and inscriptions were reused simply as useful and available stone material.

On the Acropolis, the north wall was rebuilt in an unusual way: architectural elements were used, but not haphazardly. Column drums and triglyphs were arranged, each in a line, in a correct relationship to each other (Fig. 79). This wall is the one clearly seen from the Agora, the main public space of the city. This deliberate display of salvaged temple parts was highly visible, and tellingly reminded everybody of 'the impiety of the barbarians'.

Pericles

Pericles was a leader of the 'popular' party who held outstanding influence in the Athenian democracy increasingly from about 461 till his death in 429. It was he who proposed the re-modelling of the ruined Acropolis with buildings which would reflect Athens's own pride in herself and her new position among the Greek city states. For this purpose, he moved the funds of the Delian League from Delos to Athens. Despite criticism from various quarters he pushed ahead with a major scheme which did in fact give both pleasure and widespread employment to the citizens, and ever since has reflected fame upon Athens, just as Pericles hoped.

When the buildings of the Acropolis sanctuary were half completed, alliance between the Greek city states broke down due to the increasing power of Athens and resulting aggression from Sparta. These two cities were the major leaders in Greece, Sparta being supreme in the 'Dorian' mainland, Athens having her Ionian allies and her sea power. The resulting war – the Peloponnesian War, 431–404 BC – was especially horrible, as it was Greeks against Greeks. It lasted on and off for the rest of the fifth century and weakened both sides permanently. Pericles was the leader of Athens during the first part of the war but soon died. His Acropolis building programme seems to have been carried out more or less in its entirety, being continued after his death, despite the terrible conditions such as plague and disastrous defeats.

Something of Pericles' vision of Athens is glimpsed in his Funeral Speech for the fallen in 431–430, the first year of the war with Sparta, as recorded by Thucydides. In this speech, Pericles is represented as praising Athens for her open and equal society. He contrasts Athens with her Dorian opponents, rejoicing that Athens is a well-rounded society in which aesthetics and qualities of the intellect can be valued without any loss of physical courage. Of course, Sparta was well known as a military state in which citizens were under constant surveillance, and the restrictive constitution was purely aimed at preserving the status quo.

Pericles claimed that in contrast: 'We (Athenians) choose to face danger in a relaxed way rather than with a painful regime, and to trust more in our naturally courageous character than in state regulations ...We love beauty yet are not extravagant, and we love wisdom yet are not soft' (Thucydides, *History* 2.39).

The sturdy Doric style prevalent in mainland Greece represents the manly character which Pericles here claims for his citizens: yet the elegant Ionic style originating from the east Mediterranean represents those cultural values which Athens also embraced. On the Acropolis, these two styles will be seen combined in a perfect blend, mirroring the perfect city.

CHAPTER 8
THE PARTHENON

The Parthenon was the first of the great Periclean structures: the 'flagship' of the whole programme (Fig. 40). The Parthenon is unique, yet appears to be 'the classic Greek temple'. Its fame puts it frequently before the public eye. Familiarity creates acceptance: yet, almost everything about the Parthenon is different, and the competitiveness expressed by Greek buildings should lead us to anticipate this.

Two names are commonly put forward as architects of this temple – Iktinos and Kallikrates (Barletta 2005, for discussion and bibliography). Kallikrates is named as architect of the Athene Nike temple, which included the restoration of the ancient buttress (Shear 1963). Iktinos was also named by Pausanias as the architect of the temple at Bassae. It will be seen in Chapter 15 that Bassae was a temple of ideas, and in some ways a continuation of Parthenon themes. The contribution of the two men is sometimes conceived as divided into the more practical and the more imaginative. The logistics of getting the Parthenon built were daunting indeed and needed practical genius. The design was refined and new in dozens of ways, and it had to work. It is speculated that Kallikrates was the practical genius, while Iktinos began to expand the boundaries of Doric. However, if Kallikrates was also the designer of the Ionic Nike temple, then he should be seen as gifted in both areas. As so often, information is scant and it is the buildings themselves which speak most clearly. Additionally, the Parthenon metopes, frieze and pediments and other decoration, together with the great statue of Athene were a unique ensemble on a huge scale. Pheidias is named by Plutarch as sculptor of the chryselephantine Athene Parthenos and overall director of the Acropolis project (Plutarch: *Life of Pericles*, 13.4).

The platform

A foundation for a great temple on the south side of the Acropolis plateau was prepared shortly after 490, to commemorate Marathon. The rock itself was stable and strong, but a huge amount of preparation had to be done in order to lift a flat building-surface to the highest part of the rock profile. This had entailed building a massive retaining wall parallel to the southern edge of the hill, and then infilling back to the desired level. (It is possible that older foundations of an archaic temple underlie the Marathon platform, but this is uncertain.)

Despite the Persian damage done to the partly built pre-Parthenon temple in 480/79, the foundation platform was still perfectly good and could be used again. But, by 447,

Fig. 40 Reconstruction view of the Parthenon from the west.

its proportion was not acceptable, being too long and too narrow. To create the classical effect, as seen at Olympia, the platform had to be made wider, and a small amount of the length had to be wasted.

Expanding the temple footprint to the north not only modernised the proportions but also allowed the temple to be seen from the Agora. The modification was simple: only normal foundations were required because the rocky ground was already high enough on this side.

The Doric Parthenon

The Parthenon is overwhelmingly a Doric temple, though with Ionic influences and details. At a quick glance, it resembles the temple of Zeus at Olympia, but there are very many differences (Fig. 41).

The Parthenon had a lower pediment with a flatter angle, so despite its slightly larger footprint, the overall height was much the same. The flattened pediment appears more elegant and less dominant.

The standard three steps of the new Parthenon platform are, like those of the temple of Zeus, too large to ascend by stepping. Where the Olympia temple has a ramp, the Parthenon designers opted for intermediate steps – a neater solution.

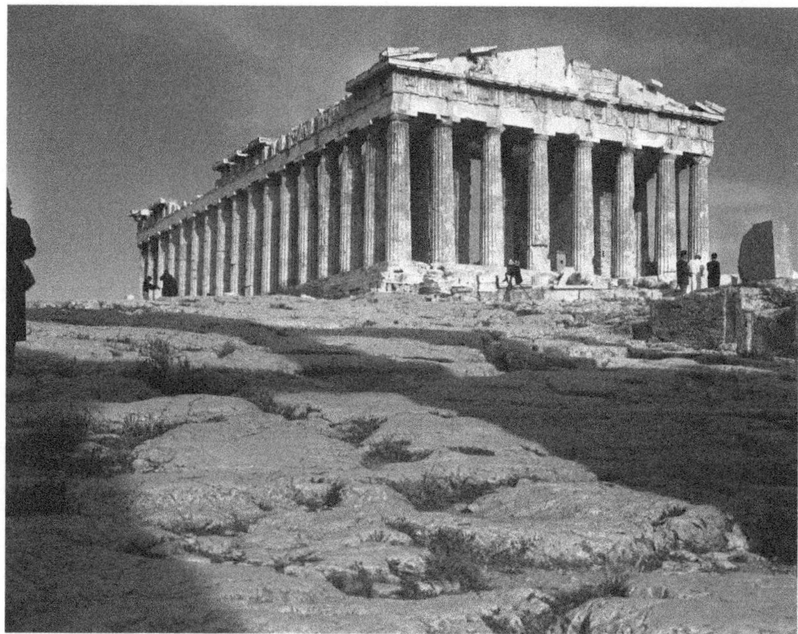

Fig. 41 View of the Parthenon from the west.

The temple of Zeus is hexastyle, the Parthenon is octostyle. This is unusual for Doric, but not unique. (The early archaic temple of Artemis at Corcyra was octostyle and so was a late archaic temple at Selinus.) It should be noted that a frontage of eight columns does not necessarily create a larger temple than one with six. The Parthenon is slightly larger but the columns are more slender: Zeus's more massive columns each take up more room (Fig. 41).

The temple of Zeus was built of shelly limestone with stucco coating, and its sculpture carved from Parian marble. While this worked very well, the Parthenon being built entirely of Pentelic marble achieved a finer finish and an increased elegance.

The Parthenon is 30.88 × 69.5 metres; the temple of Zeus is 27.7 × 64.1 metres. It is clear from these measurements that the comparatively small increase in footprint is deliberately competitive. Both temples are colossal and impressive on a very similar scale. Considering that the Parthenon's pre-built foundation would have allowed for a longer temple, while it was actually decided to create a broader but shorter temple, it is clear that the uppermost ideas in the designers' minds were first to achieve an up-to-date classical proportion, and secondly to cap the size of the rival temple at Olympia. The Parthenon does create an effect of enormous size. Its position on the crest of a hill, and in a relatively small-scale site, increases this effect. The temple of Zeus used more massive detailed proportions, such as the heavy columns, the more imposing pediment. Its low-lying and spacious site worked towards an effect of strength, weight and solidity. In contrast, the slimly styled Parthenon, first viewed against the sky, appears airy and weightless.

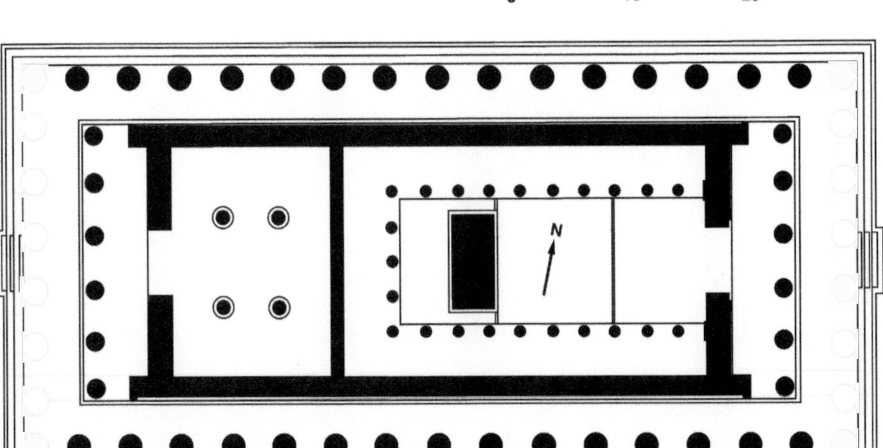

Fig. 42 Ground plan of the Parthenon.

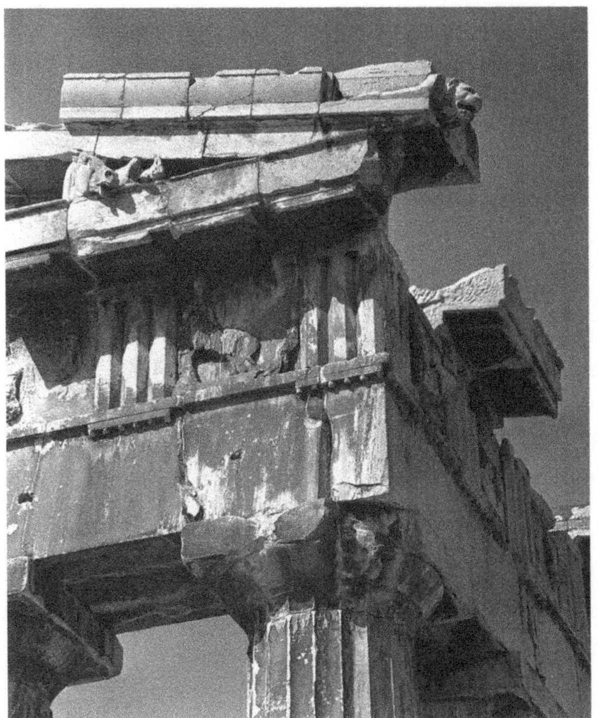

Fig. 43 North-east corner of the Parthenon entablature.

To achieve an up-to-date classical ground plan, the Parthenon uses a version of the 'Zeus formula': double the number of façade columns plus one more results in 8 × 17 columns (Fig. 42).

The Parthenon column style is, of course, high classical (Fig. 43): the round echinus is shallow, taut and compact; the square abacus fits neatly upon it, just overlapping the architrave edge above. The shaft appears straight, but is gently tapered with a subtle entasis. The column base is almost the same diameter as the echinus.

The slim columns were (as far as possible) reclaimed material from the hundreds of drums already prepared for the pre-Parthenon temple. The sensible economy resulted in a design triumph. The columns as used on the new Parthenon were to be one drum taller. Since many of the old drums were reused, their dimensions were fixed, and so by adding one more to the height, they became in effect slimmer. The slimness then required an octostyle façade to fill up the dimensions of the new footprint. This airy colonnade of elegantly styled, slender, classical columns is one of the beauties of the temple. The easy workability of the local Pentelic marble also helped: at Olympia, the designers had to work within the limitations of shelly limestone.

The entablature has the standard Doric arrangement of smooth architrave, with triglyph and metope frieze above. All 92 metopes are carved in deep relief and both pediments have sculptured compositions of many free-standing over-life-size marble figures (discussed below).

Porches

The inner porches of the Parthenon are hexastyle prostyle (Fig. 42). Most Doric temples have their inner porches distyle in antis, for example the large-scale temple of Zeus at Olympia. The benefit of this for Zeus was a large spacious area to give importance to the temple door, to display the porch sculpture, to be enjoyed as a viewing platform. In the Parthenon, the porches are unusually shallow, and the priority has been given not to space but to a multiplicity of columns. The prostyle porch columns are scaled smaller than those of the outer colonnade, and are raised on two steps.

The prostyle porches housed great cedar-wood double doors, 10 metres high, one pair in the east, another in the west. The likelihood of chryselephantine decoration on these doors is discussed by Pope and Schulz (2014). Gold and ivory were repeated on the statue. From temple inventories, the doors are known to have included gold rams' heads, gorgon heads and ornate golden studs. The small gorgoneia would have been a good preface to the great Athene Parthenos statue within, since she had a prominent gorgon head on her **aegis**. Doors could feature narrative panels (for example the chryselephantine doors of the temple of Athene in Syracuse may have done so ("argumenta" could mean stories: Cic. *Verr.* 2.4.124)), but here it may have seemed more fitting to have only abstract motifs and ornament, since the temple was already so loaded with narratives. With decorative restraint, the doors could prepare for but not upstage the inner vision of Athene. In fact, when the doors were shut, they could substitute for her; when open and folded back, they would not be seen, but the statue would appear.

Strong wooden grilles closed the inner porch by joining the six porch columns, and then joining the end columns to the antae. This protective system was normal (cf. the temple of Athene Nike), and created security for any treasure stored inside.

Interior

Inside, the Parthenon was divided into two unequal non-communicating chambers. The eastern chamber, facing the rising sun, was the cella intended for the statue of the goddess. The western chamber, sometimes called the 'Parthenon' (maiden's chamber), or opisthodomos, was a 'strong-room' for storing treasure. Each chamber had its own porch entrance.

The eastern chamber, or cella, unusually had two windows flanking the splendid door, bringing in more light. It had the now usual double colonnade of two-storey Doric columns, with the difference that behind the statue plinth, the colonnade returned on itself, creating a U-shape (cf. Fig. 76). To give access to the attic, a wooden staircase was inserted in the thickness of the cella wall, next to the window towards the north side, encroaching on the window space.

The cella was unusually wide – this was achieved by making the exterior colonnade unusually narrow. This scheme was the opposite to that of Zeus at Olympia where the cella was narrow, the outer colonnade spacious. Pheidias himself, sculptor of the Parthenos statue, friend of Pericles and, according to Plutarch, artistic director of the whole Acropolis programme, was presumably present at the planning stage: it seems likely that he requested extra interior space to surround his projected Athene statue. The effect would be the opposite of that later achieved by his oversized Zeus – a noble goddess standing at ease in a spacious interior, bathed in light.

Roof and acroteria

The roof was tiled in marble. Lionhead waterspouts and the usual palmette antefixes enriched the long sides. The ceilings would have been all coffered, wooden on the inside and marble along the colonnades and porches, since this was fairly standard on a grand building.

Most temples had acroteria, but we are not often lucky enough to know what they were. Current scholarship suggests that the Parthenon had central floral decorations, up to 4 metres high. Surviving fragments suggest a filigree design of scrolling tendrils (Palagia 2005, pp. 253–4). The lateral acroteria may have been flying Nikai. They have been reconstructed as daringly flying over the edge of the cornice (Korres 1994b, Fig. 8). This conjecture is based on careful examination of the stonework that supported them. We would expect that the finishing flourishes on the Parthenon would be of no ordinary sort.

Refinements

'**Refinements**' is the term for all the many ways in which a Greek temple can deliberately avoid straight lines, right angles and mathematical regularity. Refinements are typical of Doric style and are not generally found in Ionic style. As well as tapering and entasis of columns, there are curvatures of surface and many variations on the expected regularity. Tapering and entasis can already be found in archaic temples such as the temple of Apollo at Corinth and can be rather obvious, even crude. Here on the Parthenon, in its most developed form, the use of the system is so subtle it is almost imperceptible:

- Starting with the stylobate or platform on which the columns rest, the overall surface is very gently convex, as are the lower steps. This upward curve is mirrored in the architrave and cornices of the pediment.
- The architraves, cornices and steps are not actually cut to a curve; they are jointed at imperceptible angles so that an overall faint curve is achieved. This still meant that the jointing of every single stone had to be considered and worked to ensure a tight fit and perfect finish.
- All columns are tilted slightly inwards; the corner columns tilt slightly inwards at an adjusted angle to blend with both façade and flank. Famously the columns have been calculated to meet if projected a mile into the air.
- The columns are not only tilted and tapered with a curve (entasis); the flutes are flatter and wider at the base and gradually narrow and increase in depth till sharper arrises create more shadows at the top.
- The corner columns are very slightly thicker than the others. Vitruvius tells us this is to counteract the optical effects of light, which 'eats' into the profile of the silhouetted corner column. However, a thicker column would also subtly suggest more strength just where psychologically needed, on the corner.
- The corner columns were not only slightly thicker but were also placed slightly closer to their neighbour, reducing the **intercolumniation**. This too would add to the impression of strength and would be pleasing. This is known as corner-contraction.
- The 'triglyph problem' comes into play here. Vitruvius criticises the Doric order because of this intrinsic difficulty. A Doric frieze must end with a triglyph on the corner. However, as triglyphs are also supposed to be centred over columns and intercolumniations, there is a logical problem. So a little juggling has to take place, moving the end-column in slightly and spreading the triglyph-metope arrangement until the triglyph reaches the corner (Fig. 43). Visually this works very well. It too is part of corner-contraction.

What these refinements mean in terms of construction is a separate calculation and adjustment for every column, according to its place in the building, and for every apparently straight line in the whole building. The extra cost of shaving all the marble surfaces to the exact desired fit must have been considerable. What were the gains?

Drainage has been put forward as an advantage of a sloping floor, and this is clearly a sensible point. However, it does not account for the rest of the system. Looking at the size of the Parthenon, it is clear that such a huge building based on rigid geometry could easily become mechanical and therefore ungainly and ugly. Aesthetic concerns must have been the main factor in this expensive effort.

Visually, because of entasis, the columns seem to react to the weight placed upon them, like toned muscles. An almost organic effect is achieved by the refinements, as though the building were a living entity. There is also a kind of false perspective: the tapering and inclination suggest a greater height without mass. Such optical effects enhance a style of building so dependent on columns.

The Greek word for the outer colonnade of a temple is pteron – 'wing'. One desirable effect of an open colonnade is that the building feels light – the roof almost seems to be floating. The Parthenon, placed on a rocky height, appears with its subtle curvature to have just alighted, or to be poised for flight. It appears strong but not heavy, live weight, not dead weight.

As mentioned above, refinements are an integral feature of Doric style and certainly contradict any impression that Doric is crude or mechanical. The Parthenon is the most extreme example of the use of 'refinements'; this is not only due to the ambition of the project but also is a function of its huge size, the unprecedented number of columns, and the need to achieve the elegance appropriate to a goddess.

The Ionic Parthenon

Many things about the Parthenon are Ionic. To begin with, the all-marble building was common in Ionia but not on the Greek mainland. The mainland precedent for an all-marble building was the Siphnian Treasury of imported island marble and also the Athenians's own treasury at Delphi. A building the size of the Parthenon could scarcely have been built in imported marble because of the enormous expense. Luckily for Athens, there was beautiful and plentiful marble available from Mount Pentelicon, only about fifteen kilometres away.

Looking again at the temple of Hera at Samos (Fig. 5) one can see that a characteristic of a full-blown Ionic temple was the 'forest of columns' effect. Columns were slender and lofty, typically eight or more across the façade. Behind those might be eight more, creating a dipteral or even tripteral formation. Additionally there might be an inner porch, two or three more columns deep.

The Parthenon, while remaining absolutely within the parameters of Doric style, has manipulated the possibilities of Doric to create this 'forest' effect. Columns proliferate, especially at the short ends where the hexastyle prostyle porch is combined with the octostyle front (Fig. 42). All the columns in their slenderness are 'influenced' by Ionic proportion; a mass of heavy Doric could not have been so appealing.

While the exterior frieze is Doric in keeping with the colonnade, the continuous frieze running around the cella wall exterior is of course Ionic (Fig. 44). Zeus at Olympia had the Heracles metopes in the porches. The Parthenon extends this idea by extravagantly continuing the frieze down the sides of the temple. Above the frieze ran a plain Doric hawksbeak moulding, painted with a colourful pattern: a piece of this with the pattern plainly visible is in the British Museum. Below the frieze were the guttae and mutules that properly belong under a triglyph frieze. This might be a clue that a triglyph frieze was originally intended. But equally it may be yet another ingenious way of mixing the two orders – a Doric-Ionic or 'Attic' frieze. There is an aesthetic gain too. Owing to the high location of the frieze the line of sight has to pass the lower border to reach the frieze (Barletta, 2009): but the neat guttae and mutules do not detract from the refined masterpiece of carving above. (The florid mouldings running above and below the Siphnian frieze could be criticised for overbalancing the refined sculpture.) Also, looking at the two friezes together in Fig. 44, the uniformity of the guttae, etc., running underneath both friezes makes for a neat, unified effect, despite the two very disparate lines of sculpture. With the Parthenon's 'overload' of sculpture, this restraint is welcome; and it also emphasises that the different levels of sculpture do form a single programme.

A further good reason for an Ionic frieze may have been precedent. The ruined 'old Athene temple' may have had an Ionic porch frieze. If so, the Parthenon would preserve

Fig. 44 Parthenon frieze, metopes and west pediment.

this memory, while also going one better, since a continuous frieze in the corridor surrounding a Doric cella was new. Mouldings in the inner porch above the doors seem to make provision for yet another Ionic frieze, not executed. Since the temple is already so well-furnished with sculpture, it is tempting to think of this as an 'unseen frieze' – it is left to the viewer's imagination.

In the Parthenon chamber or opisthodomos, four slender space-saving Ionic columns supported the ceiling (Fig. 42). Double-storey Doric columns could have been used, as in the cella, but since the room probably housed the treasure of the Delian League, there was a wry appropriateness in using Ionic.

It has been suggested that the four columns of the chamber were Corinthian, because Corinthian capitals are four-sided in design, and fit better in an interior where they are seen from all sides (Pedersen 1989). The slender shafts of a Corinthian column are similar to Ionic. However, this suggestion seems unnecessary. It is uncertain whether the style even existed at this date. More to the point, the adjacent Propylaia will mix Doric and Ionic colonnades, as a feature clearly meant to match the Parthenon style.

Parthenon sculpture

The metopes, 447–442 BC

The metopes all featured battles. On the north side: scenes from the Fall of Troy (Ilioupersis); west: Athenians fighting Amazons (Amazonomachy); south: Lapiths and Centaurs (Centauromachy); east: Gods fighting Giants (Gigantomachy). This last topic revived a pediment theme from the 'old Athene temple'. The great feats of Athene in the Gigantomachy were also woven each year into her presentation peplos; probably they were the focus of the Panathenaic ritual, so this theme was very appropriate for the entrance front.

The metopes were, as usual, the earliest of the sculptures; due to construction methods, they had to be inserted into position between triglyphs, above the architrave of the outer colonnade, before the building could be continued. There were 92 carved metopes on the Parthenon, an unprecedented number. The metopes which remain intact are almost all from the south side – the least frequented side, being away from both the entrances and the processional north walk. One theory suggests that their somewhat severe style indicates that they predated the Parthenon and were prepared for an earlier temple on the same site (Carpenter 1970). It would naturally be the case however, that as the necessarily large team of sculptors embarked on the work, the style also developed and evolved.

The south metopes featured a Centauromachy (Battle of Lapiths and Centaurs). There were 32 south metopes in all, of which a handful is well preserved. The evidence for all the vanished compositions is found in the work of the artist known as Jacques Carrey, who made sketches of the Parthenon sculpture in 1674, shortly before much of it was destroyed by an explosion in 1687. These show the metopes we have and also a more varied central section whose subject is still controversial but was most likely an episode in the same story (see Schwab 2005, and for bibliography). The sculptural style is not unlike that of the temple of Zeus: clean-cut, unfussy, rather severe. However even non-experts can detect that different hands have been at work. In some of the scenes, it is also possible to detect new stylistic tendencies which will be developed as the temple progresses: a softness of facial type and fluidity of drapery, to be seen in full glory on the pediments.

The carving uses varying depths of relief, with some limbs completely in the round, standing away from the background. They even partially protrude from the surface of the architecture and catch the light, lending drama to the action and liveliness to the face of the temple. This can be seen well in Fig. 45, an old photo which shows the first metope on the left, south side, when it was still in situ. And it illustrates the role played by strong sunshine and shadow in bringing the metopes to life, reminding us how the **chiaroscuro** would have been constantly changing throughout the day. The angle of the photo emphasises the combination of solid geometry with organic, lively form. Here we see the mutules above, with their curious, 'petrified' forms, and the 'box' formed by the angled triglyphs, the ledge below, and the shallower frame above. The apparently living figures inhabit this box.

This first scene is one where the struggle is in balance, not clear who will win. The Lapith is gripped by the centaur, whose head overlaps the top frame, pushing the group forward into human space and out of architectural space, while his flailing back arm, holding the remains of a weapon, seems hampered by the box. Meanwhile, the athletic Lapith with flexed leg and head is actively pushing the centaur back into the stone frame.

Fig. 45 South-west metope in situ: Lapith and Centaur.

He has stabbed the horse in the lower belly with an iron spit (missing), but his own head is trapped in a stranglehold. Who will succumb first? The monster could still be shoved off balance as his front legs paw the air, or may collapse from his wound, before he can strangle the youth; the Lapith's pushing head is foregrounded and we see his face clearly, while the centaur's is obscured by his own shoulder, and retreats into a back plane.

The figure style and action are extremely realistic. The perfectly formed Lapith is in a convincing head-locked pose (considering his opponent is a centaur!) Where the two bodies collide off-centre, there is some crowding with the falling garment, the detail of the boy's face and ribcage, his hand pulling at the centaur's arm, the two opposing knees and so on. However, the clear lines of the centaur with his smooth, shapely horse-body filling the rest of the composition make it easy to look at. The facial type of this centaur is human. Indeed, it has been speculated as a portrait of Pheidias (Brommer 1967). Others in the series have the bestial masks that were also seen at Olympia.

Of course, this metope, and all of them, would have been made more distinct by clear colouring, figures probably standing out against a red background in a sequence interrupted by blue triglyphs. What is new here is a degree of realism and liveliness that interacts strangely with the formal architecture, almost like a cast of cartoon characters playing against a serious background. Where previous temples carried sculpture as formal decoration, this one appears to be inhabited by stone characters with a life of their own. At the same time, the figures are an integral part of the building, being 'stone of its stone', and emerging from an essential architectural member – the metope. This group is carefully composed within the confines of the field, nudging closer to the left to give the impression of the Lapith's disadvantage, although he can use the edge to push back with his braced foot. It is also carefully composed in terms of depth. The slender Lapith is very nearly in the round, his leg standing away from the stone field so light passes behind it. The bulky centaur's solid rump and (now broken) leg is almost overhanging at the front, while his legs on the further side are only just emerging from the stone background.

The designers of the south metopes had to invent multiple combinations of man and horse-body in various wrestling grips. The whole series would have built up an effect of simultaneous cartoon-like movement along the regular geometrically framed strip. A glance at the great length of a Parthenon flank colonnade with its seventeen columns makes very clear that some visual relief would be thought desirable. The sometimes criticised decision to 'overload' with sculpture has definitely an aesthetic purpose to it after all.

Another metope, seen in Fig. 43, though in poor condition, illustrates similar points. The first metope to be seen by the visitor rounding the corner to the east front, it concludes the Gigantomachy series on the right. It shows the triumphant rising of the chariot of Helios at the end of the battle. Immediately above it, on the extreme right of the pediment, is the outermost head of the four horses of Selene, the setting Moon, as they approach the horizon and the day dawns. This exquisite head catches the light as it overlaps the **geison** or floor of the pediment. The pedimental team sinks to the right while the winged metopal team rises from underneath it, towards the left. According to M Korres, this metope had another horse fronting the extant one, overhanging the metope floor in its flight, while the head above momentarily rests on its ledge. Above both these was the right-hand acroterion, also restored by Korres as projecting some way beyond the strict corner of the temple (Lawrence 1996, Fig. 166, Schwab 2005, p. 161). This grouping of the sculpture levels shows a finely coordinated design and conception, daringly executed (in the case of the flying Nike acroterion), all with the physical characteristic of transgressing the strict outlines of the building. In this way, the very perfect and refined temple is 'overtaken' by its own sculpture, apparently bursting with its own life over its own boundaries.

The frieze, 442–438 BC

The metopes were unusual for their number, the Ionic frieze for its length (160 metres long × 1 metre high). With the frieze, the Parthenon sculptors seem to have found their unique style. To the layperson, the frieze would appear to have been carved by a single hand: only experts detect differences. Many aspects are remarkable, including continuity of narrative, variation in pace and incident, drama achieved with a very shallow depth of carving, and overall naturalism and grace. Quite apart from any Ionic associations, an excellent reason for replacing metopes with a continuous frieze can be found. The staccato effect of so many metopes, each one self-contained and mostly expressing struggle, could have become wearisome if re-duplicated. The frieze is the diametric opposite of struggle: it expresses cooperation. In the frieze, the citizen body appears united, expressed visually by similarity of type and mood, and the overlapping style. Old and young, woman and man, man and animal, are all intent on one purpose; as one city they worship Athene.

The Parthenon frieze was glimpsed through columns, giving a stop-start effect as the viewer walked forward at ground level outside the temple (Fig. 44). It is uncertain how clearly it could have been seen, but the white marble floor would certainly have thrown up reflected light and the marble ceiling would have added downward light. The limiting factors for viewing would not have been illumination so much as the great height and the sharp viewing angle. Today much of the frieze is on show in the British Museum and can be closely examined. Originally, extra clarity would have been added by the painted colour-contrast background, and the painted details of faces and clothes.

The carving style of the frieze contrasts with the metopes, and makes a pleasant change for the eye as well as the mind. The metopes had distinct, athletic figures, combined in mainly violent poses, two or three at a time, modelled in very deep relief: the frieze is carved in very shallow relief, the figures lightly 'sketched', some almost fading into the stone; slight shadows create elaborate and changing textures. While the metopes were closer to free-standing sculpture, the frieze is nearer to painting or drawing. Nevertheless, it takes advantage of its stoniness. In Fig. 46 we see the corner nearest to the visitor's entrance point. Instead of disguising the structure of the corner, it is emphasised. The marshall on the west face turns back to summon the commencing procession, and marks the corner by his clear upright stance. On the north face, two modest youthful figures, the younger with his obvious naked behind, also draw the eye

Fig. 46 North-west corner of the Parthenon frieze.

to the structure. The corners of the frieze employ these upright accents like 'brackets' to finish the design in a controlled and architectonic way. This particular corner is the natural start-point for the arriving visitor, although the action has started already on the south-west corner, where the frieze takes off in two directions west and south.

An essential trick is the manipulation of scale. As in metopes, the dimensions of the field must be considered. The frieze is a metre high and must be filled by a variety of figures. Men are as tall as horses, but mounted men are the same height. When it comes to the seated gods, their heads too fit neatly within the border. If they stood up, they would not fit the frieze. Such devices remind us that – however lifelike the frieze – we are actually looking at a building, a stone structure, a temple (Fig. 46).

The movement of the frieze is orchestrated according to the anticipated movement of the viewer. The west end (which is – from a worship point of view – the back) is where a viewer might be expected to pause as he takes in his first close-up view of the temple – and here the frieze-procession also is beginning to gather itself together (Fig. 46); young men prepare to mount their horses. The long sides are where the visitor might be expected to walk faster to reach the front of the temple – here in the frieze-procession, the cavalry is seen to gallop (Fig. 47), and some high-speed competitive games are included, involving chariots. There is controversy about the reason for so many horsemen in the frieze, since they fit no known context exactly: looking at the work itself, the thrill of thundering cavalry riding by, in stone, seems to suggest one answer. The sequence of mounted riders is beautiful and exciting; it enlivens the long sides of the temple. It keeps the viewer on the move towards the goal at the east. Beautifully calibrated high-lights and shadows (made by under-cutting) create the lively scene, yet the total depth of carving is minimal (Fig. 47).

As the viewer approaches the liturgical front and the proximity to Athene Parthenos herself, he will become more worshipful. Boys are seen carefully carrying ritual water-pots and animals are led to sacrifice.

Rounding the corner to the east front (Fig. 48), finally the procession slows to a standstill. Maidens and elders (Fig. 48) are a prelude to the central scene (Fig. 49). This section is arranged in a more architectonic style than the rest. The maidens, who walk so sedately that their robes are not displaced, are like fluted columns, walking delicately in a

Fig. 47 Horsemen on the Parthenon frieze.

Fig. 48 Parthenon east frieze: marshalls and maidens.

living colonnade. The seated gods, in their organised ranks of six-a-side, frame both the real portal and the mysterious sculpted central ritual (Fig. 50). Here, the stools provide insistent horizontals and verticals. There is a sense of calm and revelation as the frieze grows more formal. Here, the visitor has arrived at the entrance to Athene's house and the realm of the gods.

The realm of the gods, however, intersects with the mortal realm of the Athenian Acropolis. For a start, the visitor himself is accepted into the sculptural presence of the newborn Athene among her peers, chief of whom is Zeus her father – on the pediment (see below). We have seen that the east metopes display the triumph of the gods against their only challengers, the giants. On the frieze, the designers have complemented the

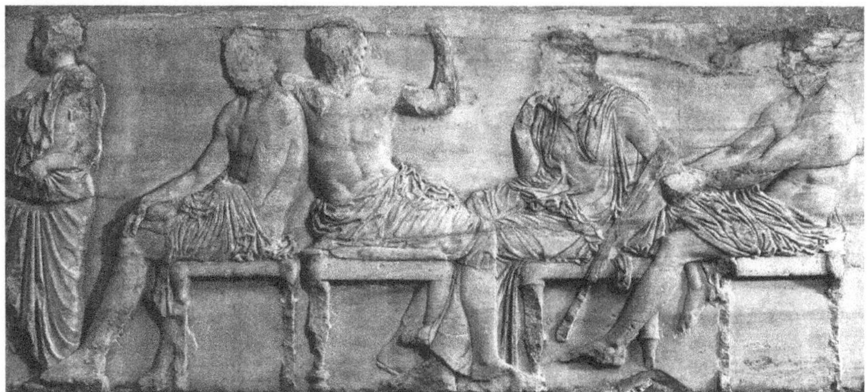

Fig. 49 Parthenon east frieze: seated gods, left side.

Fig. 50 Parthenon east frieze: Peplos episode.

city by showing all the Olympian gods sitting at ease among the Athenians at their great festival. The symmetrical rows (Fig. 49) bracket the small human episode in the middle (Fig. 50). The more formal arrangement proclaims that here is the climax of the frieze, as appropriate for the entrance to the temple.

The central episode is pictorially undistinguished, but for all that, is clearly of great significance and is the focal point of the entire frieze (Fig. 50). Two adults, a man and a woman, back to back, greet children. The representation is naturalistic with informal poses. The man bends gently towards a child, who lifts his face responsively; a folded cloth is handed between the two. The gender of the child is not clear, but is probably male. The woman welcomes two older girls who carry items. It seems likely that the adults are the priestess of Athene Polias and the priest of Poseidon-Erechtheus. The girls could be arrhephoroi, as there were two of them. The child might be a temple helper, a boy appropriately helping the priest. Other interpretations are of course possible. Broadly speaking, it is accepted that this is a scene from the 'peplos ceremony' – the handing over or presentation of the new peplos for Athene. This event was the climax of the liturgical year in Athens and was prepared for, starting nine months ahead, by the woman and girl weavers and helpers on the Acropolis. The peplos was woven with a special design – it always represented the Battle of Gods and Giants. Here it may be remembered that this was the topic of the metopes, exactly on the stretch of entablature outside the frieze. The modest little representation at the centre of the frieze is enigmatic to us, but would presumably have been clear as day to the original viewer. Neils identifies it as a moment towards the close of the ceremony, from which the viewer would gain a sense of satisfaction that all had been accomplished appropriately and the city would be secure for another year in the favour of Athene and her father, Zeus (Neils 2001, p. 67–70, 166ff).

The patterned composition using repeated stools and conversing gods with level heads is a clear quotation from the Siphnian Treasury (Fig. 13) where two facing groups of gods to the left of the composition discuss the battle scene to the right. Why would the Parthenon designers borrow like this? Is it plagiarism? In the Greek spirit of competition and vying for excellence, conscious emulation is both a tribute to the past and a bid for superiority. If Ionic style is to be used, then it should improve on the best of previous examples. This sculptural competitiveness does illustrate another point. Designers and sculptors were peripatetic. They travelled to where work was. Drawn from a variety of cities, they would not only interact with each other, but would acquire invaluable detailed knowledge of the sculptural repertoire, having worked at Delphi, Olympia and other centres.

The fifth-century designers have added classical naturalism to their archaic model, and they have improved the layout by making it symmetrical; they must have objected to the rather odd Siphnian arrangement of two adjacent scenes. A comparison with the archaic work seems openly invited. Each Parthenon god is characterised naturalistically. The gods in Fig. 49 are (from left) Hermes the messenger, looking towards the approaching procession, Dionysus leaning on him as though at a symposium, Demeter grieving for Persephone, and Ares who kicks his leg restlessly (as he does on the Siphnian frieze). The new style of representation is indistinguishable from the idealised humans in the procession. Gods and men are at one.

Fig. 51 The west pediment of the Parthenon: seventeenth-century drawing by Jacques Carrey. Above: left side; opposite: right side.

The Parthenon gods appear to turn their backs to the central episode, but the designers were forced to decide whether the gods should be carved to face the approaching procession of Athenians, or turn their backs in order to watch the central ceremony. It clearly seemed more important that they should turn towards the representatives of the city. A persuasive explanation has been made for a 'perspective' reading where the gods are understood to be in a semicircle, and aware of events on all sides (Neils 1999). This parallels 'perspective' effects that have been identified in some of the cavalry sections on the flank walls, where overlapping riders should be understood as drawn up in formal ranks. Certainly, we should not think that the gods are indifferent to the ceremony.

To sum up, the Parthenon frieze has directionality and unity. It begins, gathers pace, pauses and reaches its destination at the east portal of the temple. This is also what worshippers do – and as they reach the main portal, there is a display of gods, both inside and out. Gods fight giants on the metopes, gods are seated on the frieze, the pediment gives us a scene on Olympos, and the open doors will reveal the colossal chryselephantine Athene within. Gods also congregate on the base of the statue to collaborate at the creation of Pandora.

The pediments, 438–432 BC

We are told the subjects of the pediments by Pausanias. This is lucky because what remains is not enough to identify the themes. He says: 'Everything on the (east) pediment has to do with the birth of Athene; the far side (west) shows Poseidon's contest with Athene

over the land' (Pausanias 1.24.5). In each case, the central motif is now missing, while the extremities survive. The seventeenth-century AD drawing by Jacques Carrey, and ancient copies of individual figures, show us what the complete west pediment was like (Figs. 51a, b).

West pediment

The west pediment (first to be seen by the visitor approaching the temple) shows the two gods competing to give their name to Athens. Each may have created a gift – Athene an olive tree, Poseidon a salt-spring. A recent suggestion is they have competed in an **apobates** race, perhaps ending in a tie (Schultz 2004). The contestants are visually well-balanced, Poseidon appearing dominant while the eventual winner is Athene; muscular Poseidon stands in front, while slender Athene compensated visually with many glittering bronze accessories (Pelagia 2005, p. 245). These divine figures fill the apex (although what the space between them may have held, whether olive tree or Zeus's decisive thunderbolt, is unknown). Behind each god appear their rearing horses, their chariot and their charioteer. Poseidon's is Amphitrite, his sea-goddess wife: Athene's may be Nike. Beyond these are smaller figures, thought to be ancient kings and heroes of Attica, and in the corners are river gods of Athens. Athene, to the viewer's left, is backed by King Cecrops with coiled snake beside him, and one of his daughters, the snake element referring to the autochthony theme. Beyond them is thought to be reclining river-god Ilissos, accommodating himself to the corner position. The nymph to the far right is perhaps the local spring, Callirhoe. So, as at Olympia where rivers set the geographical scene, these figures would reveal the scene as Athens, in fact, the Acropolis.

The centre section with the divine contest is explosive: the two gods pull apart in dynamic poses, and in a chiastic arrangement that doubles the amount of movement. The rearing horses each side of the gods convey the power of the central event; they are the chariot horses of the two gods, but they also act as a visual metaphor for the divine conflict.

This pediment is particularly crowded with about 29 figures in all. The contest between two major gods is being judged or witnessed by representatives of Athens from the most ancient times. Clearly, for a democratic or valid judgement to be made, a crowd is required. But a crowd on a pediment needs to read well from a distance. Here the huge divine protagonists take up their own space in the successful chiastic or 'crossing' pose (so successful in fact that it will become a 'classic'). The rest of the characters are smaller in scale. Rather surprisingly, the crowd includes women and children. The characters sit or loll against each other, very informally, even affectionately. There is a relaxed family atmosphere in the crowd that contrasts with the dynamic centre, but they pay attention to the events. In the words of Castriota (1992 p. 148), these people are not 'passive witnesses ... their poses are varied and responsive to the contest.' This pediment is of course the largest area of sculpture that confronts the visitor as he/she enters the sanctuary, (although it is the architectural back). As was discussed with the east pediment at Olympia, it would seem that an upbeat message would be desirable and appropriate. The Parthenon west pediment is exciting and intriguing, with plenty of active characters whose informal gestures even seem to include the viewer in the event depicted. Even without certainty of the detailed story, the scene conveys that the contest is being decided, and Athenians are witnesses, or even voters. Athene will be the ultimate choice as name-patron, and this is of course a cause for rejoicing in the Athenian viewer. Palagia (2005) concludes that the aim of the pediment is to show 'the reconciliation of Athene and Poseidon, who join forces to protect Athens'. Despite the agonistic nature of the scene shown, this seems like a satisfactory overall reading of both the artwork and its location as the first message to be seen on the temple.

Several earlier commentaries on this scene look to later ancient literature for an interpretation. Later elaborations of the myth (e.g. Varro, quoted by St Augustine, *City of God* XVIII, 9) represent Poseidon as a poor loser who punishes Athens with a flood and then has to be dissuaded from destroying Attica. This was done by punishing the women with curtailment of their rights and pleasures – because they voted for Athene as patroness. (See Castriota 1992 pp. 146–151 for extended discussion and bibliography, Blundell 1998, Palagia 1998, Barringer 2008). The myths invoked for these interpretations not only post-date the fifth century, but also introduce an unnecessary complexity. A pediment should be easily understood by a viewer of its own period, and the intended meaning should be underscored by the sculpture style and content. The idea behind it should be appropriate too. A negative or punitive factor aimed at women, or an invocation of dangerous hostility from Poseidon, here seem unlikely, as the purpose of the pediment is to honour Athene as patroness of Athens, and to honour Poseidon also. The 'poor loser' interpretation would throw a dismal light on both gods, and on the watching crowd. Poseidon, as said above, is a proud and dominant figure: the sculpture does homage to his prowess, while still acknowledging Athene as winner. To borrow the words of Castriota, the sculptors have used the 'highly suggestive qualities of scale and sculptural placement' to express the lasting glory of the two clashing gods at the climax of their 'quarrel over the land'.

We are also well aware that fifth-century Athenian women were deeply involved in many ways with the public worship of Athene, and the Pan-Athenaia itself (Lefkowitz 1996). They are an essential part of the city and feature positively in Acropolis sculpture. Below the west pediment is the series of metopes featuring the Amazonomachy. This display of transgressive females is sometimes thought to support the supposed theme of suppression of women in the pediment. However, it should be remembered that Amazons are not normal women – they are exotic mythological characters. In the metopes, they act out their attack on the Acropolis from the Areopagos in the days of Theseus, a myth which may have been invented mainly to carry the meaning of the real-life Persian attack which took place on the same spot: to reject Amazons is to reject the Persian enemy. These intractable female warriors are entirely to be differentiated from the ancient Athenian women who cluster comfortably on the pediment, and who dwell in male/female families, lovingly nurturing their children.

The composition has been criticised for its inconsistency of scale. However, we have already noted the convention used on the Parthenon frieze, that gods are larger. If this is borne in mind, there is no inconsistency. The lesser deities, heroes, kings and rivers are able comfortably to crowd the further reaches of the pediment, giving the desired effect. In addition, there is sensitivity in the size-reduction, which respects the triangular pediment form and even acts as a pseudo-perspective, foregrounding gods and presenting the Athenian onlookers as backers and supporters.

East pediment

In contrast, the east pediment, (the entrance front), is more static and confrontational, though it too contains a narrative – the birth of Athene. We know this from Pausanias, and we also have limited evidence in Jacques Carrey's drawing where the central group is already missing.

Athene was born fully grown and ready-armed from the head of her father Zeus. It is now thought that the moment depicted in the pediment is that just after the birth; not the violent action of Hephaistos as he releases Athene from the head of Zeus with his axe, but a few moments later when the newborn goddess is displayed calmly in her glory beside her father. Zeus will give her the aegis, so the power that she wields to make Athens victorious is securely underwritten by the king of the gods. At this moment, it is appropriate that Athene is surrounded by her divine peers. Their presence validates her full godhead which protects Athens.

The east pediment is peopled entirely by Olympians and the scale is more consistent than on the west (Fig. 52). The impressive outer figures from each end are well-preserved, many being on display in the British Museum.

The stubborn problem with the composition is the vanished central group. Plenty has been written about it (see Palagia 2005). Zeus (an essential character) has been proposed in profile or in three-quarter view, seated or standing, in a number of combinations. The idea of a birth narrative would lend itself to the profile solution, an arrangement

Fig. 52 The east pediment of the Parthenon: left side; plaster cast.

supported by a Roman-era carved wellhead in Madrid, known as the Madrid puteal. However, this once influential piece of evidence has now been discounted on grounds of date (Palagia 1998). It may also be discounted on grounds of appropriateness. A well-head has a frieze-like field, and the figures are strung around it with no focal point. A pedimental composition tends to symmetry. Vase-paintings also depict the birth, usually with a seated Zeus in profile, Hephaistos with his axe and Athene flying up like a tiny fairy. But, on a temple, Zeus should not be shown at a moment of weakness and Athene should have her true stature. Zeus should not be shown at a lower level, or out of scale with the other gods, or sidelined. Although this is Athene's temple, Zeus, as king of the gods, if present should be central. From the figure style of the surviving figures of the east pediment, we can conceive the central figures as noble, generously draped, full of convincing life. They would be Zeus, flanked by Athene and probably Hera. Hephaistos may have been present as the 'midwife' to the birth of Athene. The other surviving gods seem very much at home, in relaxed, or sometimes excited, poses. The central triad may have been a little more formal as the anchor of the composition, and because of the importance of the birth.

Zeus could perhaps have been large, frontal and throned, serving as a rehearsal for the colossal chryselephantine Zeus of Olympia: but it is more likely he was standing, at ease, as he stands on the east pediment at Olympia. The newborn Athene would have her first epiphany next to her father. (Her greatest glory is reserved for inside the temple where she appears as the colossal golden Athene Parthenos.) The male Zeus would be the tallest, fitting into the apex, as at Olympia. With symmetry, height, bulk and balance, we have already seen how successful a dominant Zeus can be in a pediment. In the assembly of gods on this pediment, his axial figure would have given out a welcome message of power, good order and stability to the city of Athens, and to the viewer.

It will be seen that the preserved figures balance each other visually in a symmetry of opposites – for example the reclining male nude to the viewer's left is balanced by a reclining draped female to the right (Aphrodite). Each side has a close group of three figures: reclining, seated, standing and so on. The poses are relaxed, but the sequence is precise. For the viewer, there is an endless invitation to identify, compare and contrast, letting the eye rove from side to side, finding more correspondences: clearly this invitation is deliberate and intended.

The problem of the extreme corners is solved in a completely new way. Beyond the reclining full-size figure at each end are the horses of Helios and Selene, sun and moon. It is understood that the pediment floor is the horizon, behind which the heavenly bodies can rise and set. We see little enough of the two charioteers, and their horses are represented only by the eager heads of one set, the panting heads of the other. The presence of rising sun and setting moon sets the time of the scene – dawn – on Athene's birthday: they also set the pace – the movement of heavenly bodies is slow. And they suggest that the scene is set on Olympus.

In both pediments, all figures are carved in the round and are completed on the back almost as much as the front. It seems quite possible that they were put on display on the ground before they were ever raised to the pediments, and would then have been appreciated from all sides. Plutarch reports that: 'The rumour was put about that Pheidias arranged intrigues for Pericles with free-born Athenian women, when they came on the pretext of looking at works of art' (Plutarch, *Life of Pericles* 13). Plutarch gives no credence to the accusation but it must be plausible that respectable Athenians had the interest to visit and inspect the sculpture as such, before it was installed on the temple. When in situ, the over-life-size pieces were stabilised with iron bars fixed in the tympanum at the back and bedded in the stone shelf under the largest statues.

The statue of Athene Parthenos

The sculptural programme was completed by the colossal gold-and-ivory Athene Parthenos inside the cella.

We have noted earlier that the temple interior was made extra spacious while exterior colonnade space was lost (Fig. 42): this arrangement can only have been for the benefit of the statue. There were also the two eastern windows high up in the east wall, flanking the door, an unusual feature in a temple: so the interior was deliberately made both light and spacious. These windows would have directed their light down the side aisles, so the entire cella would have been light-filled, with no shadowy areas. In front of the statue was a shallow rectangular marble-lined pool of water. Pausanias tells us this was to counteract the effect of dryness on the statue, which was of course wooden under its coating of ivory and gold. The pool must have increased the available light by reflection, like a mirror. In sunlit or lamplit conditions, wonderful effects of rippling light, reflecting gleaming gold and shimmering ivory, would have played all over the cella, and over the statue itself, especially if the water were stirred. It is not known whether this pool was the first of its kind, or was added in response to the dark oily pool made for Pheidias's Zeus at Olympia.

The Athene Parthenos was made by Pheidias, almost certainly before he made his Zeus of Olympia. The chryselephantine technique was already an old one, but the colossal size was new; the statue was 11.54 metres in height. The Pheidian style can be guessed at from the figures of the Erechtheion caryatids. Athene would have stood like them, upright with one leg relaxed, in modest feminine draperies, but also with aegis and helmet, shield and spear. In her right hand, she carried a two-metre golden Victory, supported on a pillar. An ancient marble replica gives a general idea of the long-vanished colossus (Fig. 53). (The colossal chryselephantine Athene, despite its enormous expense, was so desirable, that subsequently many cities acquired such a statue, starting of course with Olympia (Lapatin 2001).)

Pausanias describes for us the elaborate iconography of the figure. The triple-crested golden helmet of the goddess was bristling with griffins and a sphinx; she wore her aegis with a central Gorgon's head in ivory: her shield sheltered a sacred snake. Three of the themes were already on the temple exterior: on the shield's outer side was carved an Amazonomachy, inside was painted a Gigantomachy, and on her golden sandals was a Centauromachy (Pausanias 1.24.5–7). Victory (Nike) of course was a major

Fig. 53 Athene Varvakeion, an ancient small marble replica of Athene Parthenos. National Archaeological Museum, Athens.

Acropolis motif. This Athene was the biggest and most glorious of all her many artistic manifestations on or off the Acropolis.

The base of the Parthenos

Grand statues often had grand sculptured bases. We have noted the base of Zeus at Olympia which featured the birth of Aphrodite in gold figures on a dark limestone ground. Athene Parthenos had a creation story on its base – the Creation of Pandora, executed in gold figures on the marble base (Pausanias 1.24.5). The marble cladding of the base was probably white: a wide, white limestone core is preserved. The evidence of small size copies suggests a long row of calm standing figures representing the creation and adornment of the first woman, Pandora – 'she who receives all the gifts'. Each god gives something wonderful: Hephaistos creates her from clay, and Athene gives adornment and womanly craft skills. Other gods and goddesses give their own attributes. The newly created maiden is divinely beautiful and perfect in every way. So far, the story on the base replicates on the human level, the perfections of the colossal golden goddess above, rearing over 11 metres up to the temple roof. At each end was a cosmic motif: Helios rose on the left, and Selene set on the right, echoing the scheme on the east pediment at the birth of the goddess.

However, the story of Pandora has prompted some scholars to detect misogyny here. Pandora had her famous box of troubles which she disobediently opened. Or in another version of the story told by notoriously pessimistic Hesiod, Pandora was in herself the punishment to mankind. (However, the poet goes on to say that an even worse punishment for man is to have no wife at all.) In his poetic presentation of the 'beautiful evil', woman, she does appear irresistible: sweet, lovely and modest, crowned with flowers and with the grace of Aphrodite, clothed in silvery raiment and embroidered veil made by Athene, and crowned also with worked gold by Hephaistos (Hesiod: *Theogony*, 570–589, and *Works and Days*, 60–82).

To present the first and ideal woman as a mortal parallel to the great goddess seems a sufficient motif for this statue base. Pheidias is claimed to have taken Homer's noble description of Zeus from the *Iliad* as inspiration for his Olympian statue – but the passage cited carries on uncomfortably with Zeus's dishonourable promise to Thetis and his sneaky deception of his wife Hera (*Iliad*: 1.528–530; Dio Chrysostom, *Oration* 12.25–6). The visual inspiration is opportunistic in that case, and may also be in this. Pandora, standing calmly and sweetly, surrounded by a line-up of 20 gift-giving gods, is most likely intended as a very positive image (Hurwit 1995, Lapatin 2005).

Interpretation of Parthenon sculptures

The wealth of studies written about the meaning of the Parthenon sculptures may leave little still to say. Nevertheless, after looking at the various components individually here, there should be an attempt to draw some kind of conclusion about the totality of the programme.

Remembering the enormous effort and expense which went into making the sculptures, one would expect that they are intended to glorify Athens, and to celebrate her victories and her goddess, Athene. Given the historical point in time of its conception, the temple should express thanks for the city's hard-won and almost miraculous safety, and joy for its freedom. The message should be perennial in expression rather than topical, for it is built to endure. There could even be – as in Greek tragedy, which was expected to 'make the city better' – a didactic note as well as a triumphal one.

There are three levels of sculpture, seen by the viewer at different moments, at different distances. At times, parts of all three levels could be seen at once. Fig. 44 shows the sculpture that first greets a visitor. Overall, the metopes show episodes of conflict, the frieze shows the city at worship, while the pediments reveal the gods, on Olympus (east) and on the Acropolis (west).

Katharine Schwab (2005, p. 168) comments that the scenes of conflict may not only refer to outside forces, although it is gratifying for the Athenian viewer to link mythological battles with the recent victories. The gods themselves once battled with giants to secure cosmic peace. However, a democratic society is based on permanent struggle. Sophocles has a strange phrase in his play *Antigone* (which itself is about the struggle for what values should prevail in a city): in his famous chorus on Man and his marvels, he lists the 'city-protecting passions' ('astunomous orgas': *Antigone* 355–6). The same idea is repeated in a chorus of *Oedipus the King*: 'I pray that god will never put an end to the struggle that benefits the city' ('to kalos d'ekhon/ polei palaisma': *Oedipus the King* 880–881). The south side metopes could be a commentary on the idea expressed by these phrases, as Lapiths fiercely resist the internal attack of semi-bestial Centaurs, their guests. Schwab identifies reference to 'not just a foreign enemy (from the distant or recent past), but also a psychological or political enemy within … an internal conflict in which civilizing behavior … is relentlessly confronted by animal-like behavior'. The struggle is hard and endless, and can refer to every level, political, personal, etc. It normalises the idea that a good city needs vigilance and effort. Similarly, on the west and north, something has gone wrong with external relationships and must be corrected; on the east, the gods show the way.

The staccato metopes give way to the flowing lines of the inner frieze and the vision of the harmonious city. The two areas are not separate but linked. The hard battles on the exterior secure the unity on the interior. The frieze's overlapping style expresses this cooperation, and in fact a new sculpture style seems to be born here – from severe-style we move to the 'loveable style'. Pollitt (1972) uses several aspects of Pericles's funeral speech (as recorded by Thucydides, Bk 2) to interpret the frieze, and this seems an excellent place to look, as the nearest we could get to Pericles's thoughts on Athens. The speech emphasises the combination of beauty with courage, and urges his hearers to contemplate the city till they 'become lovers of Athens'. Viewers of the frieze would note at least a general approximation to the Panathenaic procession, especially culminating in the familiar peplos ceremony, but also comprising the groups of young people, boys, young men and maidens, and the handsome middle-aged marshalls. The nude and semi-nude young men are certainly idealised, not just in their beauty and heroic nudity, but in their grace and charm of gesture. The horses too are very fine and their spirited behaviour adds an edge to the scene – which might otherwise get too sweet. The fiery horses show off the control exerted by the riders, especially in the apobates scenes where feats of daring are done. The admirable marshalls punctuate the procession, allowing the viewer to understand it is going well and to plan. The youths and maidens show off the Athenians to themselves at that most interesting phase of life, one that is very commonly treated in tragedy. Will the young Hippolytus or the young Antigone take the right direction in life? Here on the frieze, it can be hoped that they will.

Finally, the sculptures reveal the glorious life of the gods. Incorporated with the physicality of the temple itself, they appear on the east metopes, then at home on Olympos at the birth of Athene, and on the west, in competition for patronage of the city. They also appear on the east frieze where the idea of ritual **theoxenia** (hospitality to gods) is a fascinating one to apply. Disguised gods sometimes received human hospitality in epic. But **theoxenia** as part of real-life worship involved the ritual setting out of seats and laden tables for the gods, who could then be imagined as receiving lavish hospitality on the spot. This is discussed by Jenifer Neils as a backstory to the seated gods surrounding the peplos episode, and she points out that appropriate handsome seating was stored in the Parthenon back-chamber (Neils 2001 p. 198–200). If empty seats were set out like this during real-life worship, then the frieze would reflect real life, yet make the invisible visible: the viewer would see the hidden 'reality' of gods as happens in epic when the hero's eyes are opened. As the humans on the frieze do not seem to see the seated gods, it is left to the viewer him/herself to take the hero's role and receive the revelation (cf. *Odyssey* 16.157ff).

There is widespread agreement among commentators that the frieze broadly represents the Panathenaic procession. However, there are many variations of this idea and other theories too, since the images do not exactly fit what is known about the Panathenaia. Much work has been done on the varieties and formations of the ranks of horsemen, the identities of the mature male figures, and so on. The figures are clearly idealised in their nudity and their perfection, whether they stand for contemporary, historical or even mythical Athenians. Interesting suggestions, not necessarily found plausible, are the equation of the males in the procession with the 192 who fell at Marathon (Boardman 1999); another is the complete reinterpretation of the peplos episode as a preparation for the human sacrifice of Erechtheus's daughter (Connelly 2014). Many detailed and persuasive readings combine contemporary with mythical identifications, or pick out particular historical features of costume, pose, etc. (also see Jenkins 2005, Neils 2005 with bibliography, Neils and Schultz 2012).

Do the pediments relate to the 'city theme'? Athene's birth from her beloved father Zeus, and her reception of the aegis, ensures the well-being of Athens. Her competition with Poseidon shows the city is worth winning, and the 'ancestors' crowding round bring the event to Athens's backyard in a most gratifying way.

Seen bunched together, the different levels of sculpture around the temple can be viewed as linked and interdependent (e.g. Fig. 44). The Athene Parthenos, inside the temple, gathers up several of the Parthenon themes. However, her 11-metre glorious grandeur and beauty would be the greatest theme, and the focus of adoration for her. It is often pointed out that she was not the cult statue: the venerable, ancient, (maybe shapeless) olive-wood Athene Polias was the object of ritual worship. Yet Athene Parthenos could be seen as a visual aid, an epiphany of what Athene Polias stood for, the glory of the goddess. In the following age of chryselephantine colossi, this may have become a pattern, for example, chryselephantine Argive Hera and her ancient pearwood counterpart at Argos (Pausanias 2.17.4–5)

It may be objected that the above comments are rather broad-brush – which they are. They are an attempt to trace impressions which an Athenian might be supposed to have received on a perambulation of the temple. JJ Pollitt (1972) concludes that he or she would feel they had 'seen an exalted picture of themselves', without particularly searching for a more detailed or obscure underlying explanation of the whole. There was plenty to catch the eye and simply enjoy in the highly original topics and masterly carving.

Did the Parthenon serve any practical purpose?

Cults and festivals were an important element in the social cohesion of a polis. The great temple of Athene Parthenos was a visual symbol for the Athenians, gloriously reminding them at all times of their greatness and unity. However, it is often pointed out that the Panatheniac worship and offerings actually centred on the altar of Athene and the image of Athene Polias, both situated on the north side of the Acropolis; Athene Parthenos was not a cult image in the sense that Athene Polias was. It has therefore sometimes been questioned whether the Parthenon really was a temple at all.

The statue of Athene Parthenos was plated with a great deal of removable gold and it was not thought inappropriate for Athens to 'borrow' this gold in times of national necessity – so long as it was replaced. Inscriptions also record the large amounts of gold and silver objects kept in both chambers of the building, probably for use in rituals. These were secured not only by great lockable wooden doors, but also by bronze or wooden grilles across the porches.

In Aristophanes's comedy *Lysistrata*, in a bid to put an end to war, the women barricade themselves into the Acropolis sanctuary; their plan is to trade sex for peace. It soon becomes clear that by taking possession of the sanctuary (*Lysistrata* 486–97) they have also gained control of the war chest or city exchequer. Where could this have been kept? Some valuable goods, including armour, must have been kept in the Chalkotheke or bronze-store, situated between the Parthenon and the shrine of Artemis Brauronia (Fig. 39). But judging from the large amount of gold and silver objects stored in the temple, it seems that the Parthenon itself may have had a role also as a treasury.

However, the Parthenon was a temple, referred to as such by for example Pausanias (Paus 1.24.5). In sheer size, it has the importance of a temple, it affirms the identity of the deity, and it goes to enormous lengths in characterising Athene and making her seem to be vividly present in her city sanctuary. In fact, the more astonishing the image of the goddess, the more she would seem to be present in almost living form (even though not being the 'cult-image', and even though its maker was known and still living). This may be why Pausanias's famously brief description of the temple refers only to the goddess's life story, seen in the pediments, and her 'portrait', the Athene Parthenos statue. In this regard, the Parthenon carries on the task of the previous Acropolis temples. They had graphically shown the power of the divine with the archaic pedimental Athene as giant-killer, and in the still earlier forms of lions overpowering bulls. Now the flashing beauty of Pheidias's Parthenos gorgeously displayed that same power. The Periclean Acropolis was the successor to the vanished Archaic acropolis, and even to the Mycenean one.

Conclusion

The Parthenon was the first building in Pericles's re-creation of the Acropolis sanctuary. In many ways it is the iconic building of his programme. Its existence is a testament of his vision, which was to ignore expense and to have something built which would fully express the greatness and supremacy of Athens.

The verdict of Plutarch, written in the second century AD, still seems more than valid:

> The buildings went up, as remarkable in sheer size as they were matchless in form and grace, since the workmen strove to excel in the beauty of their workmanship … For in its beauty, each (building) immediately seemed antique, yet to this day remains in perfect bloom, and fresh, as though brand new. (Plutarch, *Life of Pericles* 13)

CHAPTER 9
THE PROPYLAIA

Before Pericles

Since late Mycenaean times, there had been a stone-built propylon or fortified gateway on the west side of the Acropolis, the only side that gave moderately easy access. The western slope offered the best approach to peaceful visitors and also most needed defending from attackers.

The Mycenaean propylon would have been something like those still to be seen at Mycenae and Tiryns. It was turned at an angle to the direct ascent, and channelled visitors (or attackers) into a corridor or forecourt before they could arrive at the gate itself. The propylon had formed a defensive unit with the Cyclopean wall surrounding the whole Acropolis.

The Cyclopean wall continued as the fortification wall of the Acropolis right up to the Persian sack of the city. The Mycenaean propylon, however, was replaced, shortly after Marathon (490 BC), with a more up-to-date Doric propylon of marble, limestone, stucco and timber. The few diehards who remained to man the Acropolis against the Persians relied on this gate for protection – identifying it as the 'wooden walls' of the Delphic prophecy. It suffered in the sack along with most of the Cyclopean wall.

A broad approach ramp dated from the expansion of the Panathenaia in 566 BC: a bigger procession would have been enabled by the great ramp of beaten earth whose archaic stone substructure can still be seen under the present access road.

For a yet grander Acropolis, a new gateway was needed. To match the new Parthenon temple, the gateway needed to surpass all others.

The Periclean Propylaia

The **Propylaia** ('gateways') was the second of the great Periclean Acropolis buildings; the name of the architect, Mnesicles, is known from inscriptions and from literature.

As soon as the Parthenon was finished in 438, work started on the Propylaia and continued until 432 when the pressures of the Peloponnesian War with Sparta became too great for building work to carry on. Whether or not the design was ever fully completed is a moot point which will be discussed below. However, even as it stood, the building was clearly considered an architectural triumph.

The Propylaia went way beyond what was functionally necessary, and clearly was intended to make a grand statement (Fig. 38). From the approach route and from afar, the white marble structure appears toweringly high (Figs. 57 and 77), and, from below, appears more massive than it really is. This is the result of clever use of topography. The entrance area rises around the approaching visitor like the seating area of a Greek theatre, but, as in a theatre, there is less substance behind it than appears. The real measurements are large, the central section of the building being about 20 metres wide; yet approaching viewers lose all sense of scale as they are gradually enclosed by a total environment of white marble and the outer world is left behind.

Like the Bronze Age propylon, the new Propylaia engulfed the visitor, but there was nothing military about the new building. Fine marble replaced the Cyclopean boulders, columned wings spread out invitingly, a smooth ramp made ascent easy. Bypassing the stairway to the Athene Nike shrine on the right (see next section), and looking ahead, the viewer would recognise the familiar form of a Doric 'temple' front with its obligatory three steps (plus one), and the smaller stoas rising up on each side, also with steps. The design appeared symmetrical as was expected in a Greek monumental building, but topography dictated that some sleight of hand was needed to get this effect.

The Propylaia is a bewildering building. Even the visitor actually standing in front of it will find it hard to take in more than a general impression. Essentially, the obstacle to comprehension is also the obstacle which Mnesicles the architect brilliantly overcame: the fact that the building must incorporate many levels and fit an awkward site, while remaining visually impressive.

The vast expensive structure, no longer military, still served the basic purpose of letting people in or keeping them out. In Aristophanes's comedy *Lysistrata* (performed 411 BC), the rebellious women of Athens are supposed to seize the Acropolis and barricade it. So, the sanctuary could be easily closed off; the Propylaia was both a physical and a psychological division between the outside world and the sanctuary.

Ground plan and cross-section

Careful study of the ground plan (Fig. 54) will show that the essential core element of the Propylaia is the cross-wall pierced by five lockable doors, graduated in size. To the west of this is a Doric hexastyle prostyle porch linked to the cross-wall by the colonnaded wide corridor; through the doors, to the east, is another similar porch giving onto the Acropolis. On the west, the building is elaborated in a unique way with wings or small stoas at right angles to the central section. Extra drama is added to the structure by these columned wings, set high up on each side to north and south (Fig. 57).

The cross-section drawing (Fig. 56) shows how the ramp rises smoothly between the wings and two paved flanking passages and emerges through the east porch onto the sanctuary plateau. To reach the same desired level, the paved flanking passages use the four entrance steps on the west and five inner steps on the east.

To accommodate the ascent at roof height, the eastern part of the roof has been stepped up, just at the point of the cross-wall and the five steps.

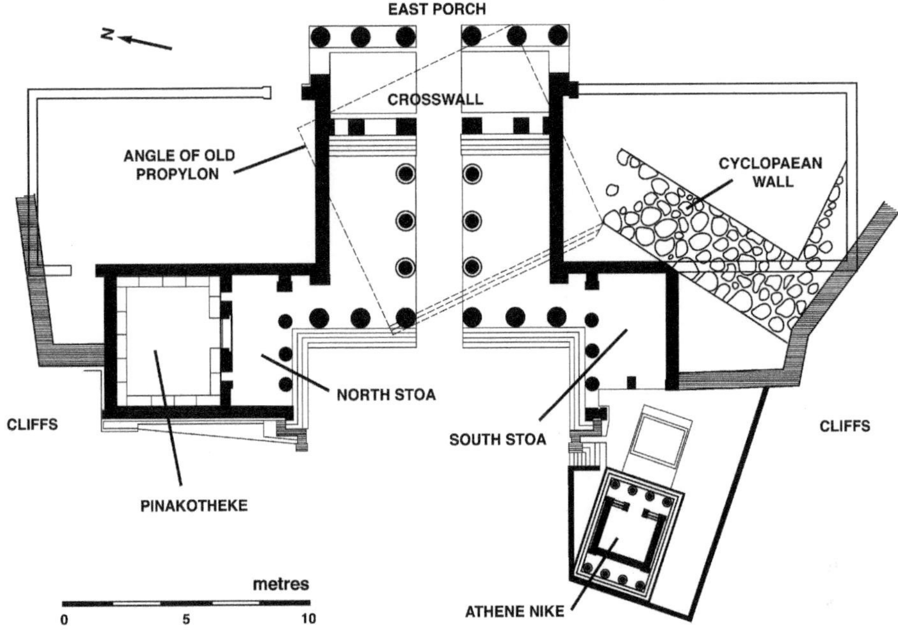

Fig. 54 Ground plan of the Propylaia including the Nike sanctuary.

Fig. 55 Reconstruction view of the Parthenon seen through the east porch of the Propylaia (the cross-wall and Ionic columns have been removed for clarity).

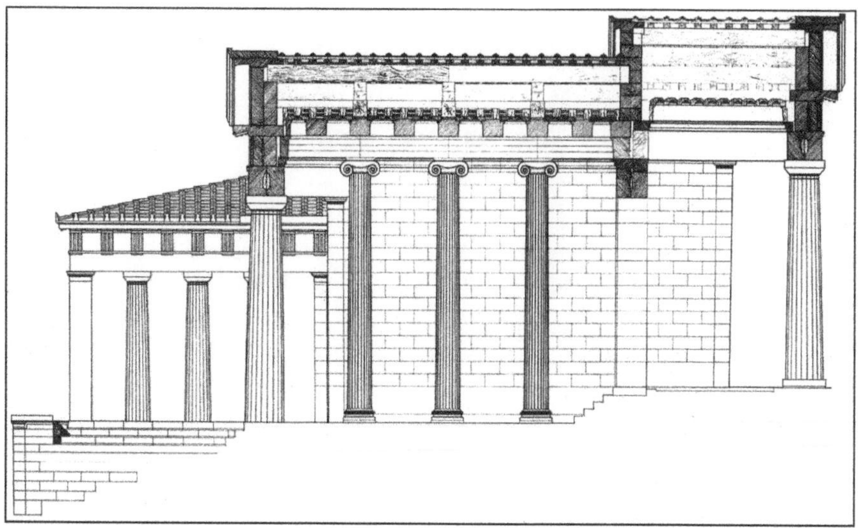

Fig. 56 Cross-section reconstruction of the Propylaia.

The central section

As visitors ascended the steep stretch of the Panathenaic Way, they saw the gateway above at a sharp angle. Today, the rock and marble path zigzags up: originally there was a straight ramp (perhaps stepped on each side). Ahead is a fairly conventional 'temple-style' Doric hexastyle porch, raised on four steps (Fig. 38). The visitor reaching the four entrance steps then enters the building through a shallow porch giving onto a 'corridor' about as wide as the porch. The corridor is divided into three 'aisles' by two rows of three lofty yet slim Ionic columns. The floor of the central aisle is sunk down and is a continuation of the sloping ramp, intended for animal access. The raised side sections are paved with marble and are level, for pedestrians.

This 'corridor' ended at the cross-wall with its five graduated doors. The ramp rose smoothly through the large central door. The paved side sections ended in a flight of five steps to reach the two sets of side doors. Beyond the doors, visitors emerged into the east porch at the sanctuary ground level – which however continues to rise steeply. Ahead, to the right and higher up, is the Parthenon. To the left was Pheidias's twelve-metre bronze Athene, raising her spear. Visitors emerged from shadow into the bright upper air of the sanctuary and were faced with a glittering sacred space – the city having vanished far below. It would have been rather like an ascent to Olympus, home of the gods (Fig. 55).

The north and south wings

The wings were an unusual feature, adding significantly to the impression of size and grandeur. Each wing (Figs. 57 and 60) is fronted by a three-columned stoa or open

Fig. 57 The Propylaia seen from the west.

colonnade whose floor is continuous with the paved floor of the central building. Each stoa is fronted by four steps, continuous with the four approach steps of the central section: but, as the sloping ramp falls away so sharply, the stoa steps give onto a sheer drop and are purely decorative. The resulting marble 'cliff' on each side is highlighted by a course of dark Eleusinian limestone forming the bottom step of the four. Vertical smooth white ashlar masonry below adds to the impression of Olympian size.

From the approach ramp, the wings appear symmetrical, but behind the identical three-columned Doric stoas they are adapted for different purposes (Fig. 54). The north stoa is slightly shallower and forms the entrance porch to a spacious room with off-centre door and two windows. The off-centre door suggests that the room was intended for dining: couches would typically be arranged round the walls of a **symposium** room asymmetrically, and this one could have accommodated seventeen couches. Sanctuaries regularly included formal dining facilities, and provided an opportunity for high-level hospitality. But the room is usually known as the Pinakotheke or Art Gallery because Pausanias describes for us the sizeable collection of important panel paintings which he saw there, including 'old masters' by Polygnotos. In a space used for entertaining VIPs, impressive decoration would be appropriate.

The design of the south wing (Figs. 54 and 60), while appearing symmetrical from the ramp, was modified to provide an easy way into the adjacent sanctuary of Athene Nike. The stoa itself provided shade and rest for visitors after their steep climb. Where the north stoa is completed with the west wall closing off the stoa and the dining room, the south stoa has an open entrance to the Nike sanctuary, and in fact is slightly shortened; this irregularity is visually masked by an anta marking the corner. The roofs of the two wings were **hipped** (i.e. sloping on all sides: see Fig. 38), while the more important central section was pitched and pedimented like a temple.

Ionic spacing

The ground plan (Fig. 54) also shows that on the west and east façades the Doric porch columns are not evenly spaced. The building had to cater for the Panathenaic procession with its 100 sacrificial cattle that had to emerge onto the Acropolis without crowding or jostling, since the calm behaviour of the animals was of importance for the success of the sacrifice. So Mnesicles adopted an Ionic solution: he widened the central intercolumniation, thus creating a more open access (Fig. 58).

An Ionic colonnade can easily vary its spacing in terms of its entablature, since an undivided frieze is extendable. However, with a Doric divided frieze (as here) there could be a problem because triglyphs must be centred above and between columns. Mnesicles found a solution: he increased the gap by one metope and one triglyph, keeping a symmetrical pattern but widening the entrance. The larger gap exactly aligns with the wider central doorway. Ionic influence here asserts itself in a very practical solution to a practical problem.

Fig. 58 The Propylaia seen from the east.

Decoration

It seems that no sculpture was planned for the Propylaia. Metope carvings would have to have been put in place at an early stage of building, so their absence is clearly intentional. If acroteria were planned they do not seem to have ever been put in place. The Propylaia was left deliberately plain in order to offset the abundance of sculpture on the three main Acropolis temples and to differentiate its function.

Despite the general restraint of the design, there are some innovative decorative details. One trendsetting idea is the use of dark limestone strips to contrast with the creamy Pentelic marble. Dark limestone is used for the bottom step of the four wing steps, and also for the top step of the five on the east end of the passage. Linking these dark accents, the corridors have fine large orthostate slabs of the same dark stone forming a long dado (emphasising the directionality of the passage). Thus, the theme of colour contrast is carried right through the building (Fig. 57).

This use of dark stone must be innovative because the whole Propylaia design is innovative and challenging. The stone is used to define the unusual spaces, to emphasise their connections and to underline where the building ends. Firstly, on each side wing, the dark bottom step of the four steps visually reduces the number to the conventional three steps; it also draws a line under the little Doric stoas as a whole and rounds off the design, separating it from the substructure.

The same horizontal accent carries all through the side passages in the form of the dark orthostates, till it touches the top step of the five final steps. That dark top step, level with the top of the orthostate panels, puts a frame under the view of the sanctuary that now begins to greet the approaching visitor. Of course, it also links each side of the passage, so that there is a 'box' of dark stone, used in different ways, all around the complex interior. In the long white passageway, the dark dado may have made a welcome change, and would have been a good background for anything placed in front of it, such as free-standing sculpture (just visible on right of Fig. 57).

We have seen this dark stone used before. It clad the Altar of the Chians at Delphi, and later it was used decoratively in the Tholos at Marmaria, Delphi. It was a fine-grained dark marble from a quarry near Eleusis, in Attica, and was greatly exploited in the Eleusis sanctuary, before emerging to be used sparingly but strikingly in some very specialised buildings (Shoe 1949). On the Periclean Acropolis, we shall see it again on the Erechtheion and the Athene Nike temple, and it also already formed the base of Pheidias's bronze Athene Promachos statue (456 BC), giving visual weight to balance the great size of the sculpture.

The Doric columns are matched in style to those of the Parthenon itself. The Ionic columns, higher and slimmer than the Doric, have plain bases with a double **torus** linked by a **scotia**. The capitals too are restrained with just an **egg-and-dart** decoration linking the volutes, and a small honeysuckle in the corners. Possibly these give a clue to the style of the vanished opisthodomos columns in the Parthenon.

Pausanias praised the ceiling of the Propylaia: 'The Propylaia has a ceiling of white marble which in the size and beauty of the stones remains supreme even to my time' (Pausanias

1.22.4). Pausanias must have been impressed by the immense length of the marble beams which spanned the corridors, almost six metres each side. The coffering between the beams was painted with colourful patterns and enlivened with gold stars on blue.

Refinements received special attention. The stylobate was not curved – probably because the middle section was removed for the central four-metre-wide ramp. But the pediments did curve in the expected way, exactly as on the Parthenon. The Doric columns also matched the Parthenon in tapering, entasis and inward inclination.

Iron beams

Normally Greek architecture is held together by gravity and the accurate fit of the structural elements. A small amount of dowelling and metal clamps is added as a precaution, because of the risk of earthquakes. In the Propylaia, the weight of the six-metre marble beams spanning the corridors from side to side seems to have worried the architect so much that he opted to use some reinforcement. Slim iron rods are imbedded in the tops of the marble architraves of the two Ionic colonnades which support the beams (Fig. 56). They were placed in parallel pairs to take the weight of the marble cross-beams, not above the columns (which already act as supports) but in the gaps between them where intermediate beams rest. The weight of these beams and the ceiling coffers was so great that this reinforcement seemed a good precaution to the architect. It is now thought that the marble structure was in fact sufficient, but this apparent anxiety reminds us of the experimental nature of the building and the daring of the designer at the time.

Propylaia and Parthenon

The Propylaia is on the same axis as the Parthenon, increasing the sense of a 'match' between them. In order to create this alignment, the previous smaller propylon had had to be completely demolished as it had turned more to the south, at an oblique angle to the ascent (Fig. 54). This deliberate change of direction resulted in several superb improvements. The new angle, facing square on to the broad Panathenaic Way, was far more triumphal in effect. From it were seen the sea and Salamis, site of the great victory; directly ahead and clearly visible would have been the defensive long walls linking Athens to her harbours on the coast about five kilometres away. In the other direction, the match with the Parthenon, both in angle and in style, resulted in a very grand scheme since the two massive structures now appeared as a unity. The natural topography added to the grandeur since the Parthenon was so much higher up than the Propylaia, and, from a distant view would appear as a higher storey of the already split-level gateway (Fig. 77).

On emerging from the inner doors, viewers were faced with the Parthenon ahead and to their right. This view was the most perfect possible – the three-quarter angle, showing all the features of the architecture at one glance. It was a comfortable distance away, and dramatically higher up. No other view of the temple as an individual structure is quite so good or so impressive (Fig. 55).

In architectural style, the Propylaia matched the Parthenon, with variations. The Doric columns were styled similarly, though in three sizes. The largest were on the west porch, the smallest were on the wings, the east porch columns matched those of the temple, which they face. There was the same mix of Doric with Ionic as in the Parthenon, and for the same reason, namely that Ionic columns could be much higher in proportion to the space needed for their bases.

This planned axial coordination between buildings was an innovative and influential idea. By it, the sanctuary itself gained a new kind of unity. In addition, it created a powerful sight line, linking the sanctuary with other significant elements of the polis – its defences and harbours. By this link between harbours and temple, through the gateway, Athene's protection was invoked over polis and territory (**chora**), and her character as victory goddess was proclaimed.

Unfinished work?

There is one mystery about the Propylaia: it appears unfinished. The features commonly cited to prove its unfinished state are these:

- The presence of many **lifting bosses** (small knobs of stone used in the process of construction which were normally removed afterwards), especially on the two flanking walls (Fig. 58). These can be seen as tiny dots on the wall to the left of the photo.
- Non-removal of the **finishing layer** (extra stone protective surface removed at the last stage) around the columns in the corridor floor (Fig. 59).

Fig. 59 Ionic column base in Propylaia, with 'finishing layer' still present.

- Indications in the stonework around the flank walls of the east porch that two large rooms (Fig. 54) might have been planned to north and south; that is, antae and provision for beams.

And yet even after work ceased on the gateway in 432 BC, two more main buildings of extensive workmanship were started and completed on the Acropolis. Since there were plenty of skilled workmen available on-site at a later date, why were they not asked to do the minimal task of removing the bosses and the finishing layer?

Had the two large rooms been constructed as projected by some scholars they would have overlapped the neighbouring shrine of Artemis Brauronia to the south and even risked projecting over the edge of the Acropolis itself. Were such rooms really required, and if built, might they not have overbalanced the whole Propylaia aesthetic by their enormous size? On the western side, the building seems Olympian in scale. This effect is achieved by the use of the natural slope, the addition of wings, the height from city level and (on a clear day) the vast panorama of coast, sea and islands. From within the sanctuary, the eastern porch (as built) looks quite small, dwarfed by the rising ground and the display of wonders within (Fig. 58).

A further point of great interest is the surviving remnant of the Mycenaean wall (Fig. 58, extreme left). This part of the wall once abutted the Mycenaean propylon. Now the eighteen-metre stretch of impressive Cyclopean boulders remains as a memorial to the ancient fortress of Athenian kings. Not only does the ancient masonry touch the Propylaia, but the classical masonry has been cut away or bevelled to allow the venerable wall 'built by giants' to merge with the smooth white ashlar surface of the classical building. It is noticeable that the Propylaia bosses are mainly left on the walls abutting the Cyclopean masonry. They tactfully provide a texture that accords well with the treasured ancient fabric; besides, they have a decorative quality that nicely relieves an expanse of featureless wall (Fig. 58).

We will later see how the ashlar facing of the Nike bastion is broken open to reveal the rough Cyclopean masonry and bedrock within: the perfection of the classical masonry is deliberately interrupted to allow the deep past to show through. In contrast, it may be that the lifting bosses were eventually left unfinished on purpose to imply the very opposite of the past – the bosses may imply a process which is not over yet; the masons' work is in touch with the future as well as the past. The Propylaia, interpreted in this way, would not only mark the transition between the lower city and the sanctuary: it would mark a transition between past, present and future.

Above all, it is a glorious building which granted the Athenian citizen a godlike experience and an Olympian approach to the sacred upper city.

CHAPTER 10
THE SANCTUARY OF ATHENE NIKE

The temple of Athene Nike – Athene joined with Victory – is the first of all the Acropolis buildings to greet the visitor (Fig. 60). Its platform is located outside the gateway and the remnant of Mycenaean circuit wall; strictly speaking, it is separate from the Acropolis sanctuary (Fig. 38). Considering that 50 years earlier the citadel had been completely sacked, there was amazing bravado in exposing this tiny, exquisite shrine on an eminence, outside any fortified wall. The positioning was itself a claim to complete victory. A sculpted marble balustrade surrounded the platform, whose only practical purpose was to stop visitors toppling off. Sparta famously boasted that her powerful city needed no walls: Athens made her walls into artworks.

The bastion

In Mycenaean times this rocky outpost of the Acropolis was a natural bastion, projecting out to the right of the propylon, and enhanced with Cyclopean masonry. It could have been additional protection for the gate when the rock was basically a fortress.

By the mid-sixth century BC the old bastion was already being used as a sanctuary for the worship of Athene Nike; the archaic image was a seated (or possibly standing) Athene holding a helmet for protection and a pomegranate for prosperity. During the Persian sack in 480/79, this sacred image was safely evacuated along with Athene Polias. On its return, it seems the image was protected by some kind of simple shelter on the site, for the continuation of worship.

A programme of Acropolis renewal would need to include this shrine, considering the obvious value placed on the image. Equally important was the location: first fruits for the goddess, first impressions on the visitor. This area had to fit in with the overall Acropolis scheme in design and in excellence. It is also understandable that, as the smallest of the projects, it should be left for completion nearly to the last, especially as it seems it was able to function as a shrine in the interim.

The date and the priestess document

Around 450–445 BC, the same period as the inception of the Parthenon, a decree was passed providing the appointment of a priestess:

> For Athene Nike a priestess who shall be appointed by lot from all Athenian women … Payment to the priestess shall be 50 drachmai plus the legs and hides from public sacrifices … (IG13 35)

Fig. 60 The temple and buttress of Athene Nike from the western approach ramp.

This apparently new office of priestess, chosen by lot from all classes, makes a nice democratic contrast with that of the traditional priestess of Athene Polias who had to be chosen from the Eteoboutadai family of ancient royal descent. Both offices were for life.

The same marble inscription which made provision for a priestess also records that Kallikrates was given responsibility for planning the sanctuary. The decree authorises doors to the sanctuary, a temple, and a marble altar 'as Kallikrates shall specify …'. However, at this early date, attention may only have been paid to the temporary shrine, and the structural work needing to be done on the crumbling bastion. Meanwhile the Parthenon and Propylaia were built. Not until 424/3 was a further decree recorded on the same piece of marble, confirming the payment to the priestess; this seems to suggest that only now is the sanctuary in business and the temple finished (IG13 36). The later finish date accords with the style of the architectural sculpture. Also, between the finishing of the Propylaia and the start of the Nike temple, an expensive war with Sparta had begun – the Peloponnesian War. These two events – other building work and war – easily explain any delay in starting the Nike project.

Some scholars suggest that the Ionic style of the Nike temple is a result of the Peloponnesian War and indicates that Athens was distancing herself from the Dorian Greeks, now the enemy, and allying herself more obviously with Ionia. This suggestion seems disappointing in that the style of the building could not then be seen as fully part of the Periclean vision, but more as an afterthought. The same would be true of the final temple, the Ionic Erechtheion. The decree shows clearly that the Nike temple was part of the initial thinking; as will be seen later, there are many positive reasons that can be suggested for the Ionic style being intended from the start.

The Nike buttress

Kallikrates, in partnership with Iktinos, is recorded as one of the builders of the Parthenon. He was also in charge of building a third Long Wall, joining Athens to the coast – a large engineering work. It seems the talents of Kallikrates lay in the area of practical engineering and that the huge and important jobs of preparing foundations and buttressing, planning for the movement of materials, etc., would have been his domain. However, if he designed the Nike temple itself, he was a fine and thoughtful architect also. In any case, there was urgent need for the skills of Kallikrates in preparing and renewing the crumbling old Nike buttress and raising its level to fit seamlessly with the Propylaia.

The sanctuary needed an entrance from the exterior part of the Propylaia, since there was no access from the Acropolis sanctuary. There are actually two entrances – which might suggest a flow of crowds – to avoid a bottleneck. A marble stair, cut into the north face of the buttress, rises from the ramp or main approach to the Propylaia. As the stair

Fig. 61 Reconstruction drawing of the sanctuary of Athene Nike.

reaches the level of the balustrade, the balustrade turns to follow it and a sculptured Nike is seen to climb with the visitor (Fig. 61). (This may have functioned as a pictorial 'Way in' sign.) Visitors could then leave by the false porch of the Propylaia and find themselves back en route at the level of the main entrance hall (Fig. 54). Equally, the level Propylaia entrance must have functioned as a processional route between the two sanctuaries since, from the hundred or so cows led up to be sacrificed at the Panathenaia, the most beautiful was selected for Athene Nike and conducted to her shrine. (Parke, 1977, p. 48)

The new temple replaced an older, simpler shrine consisting at least of an altar and a cult statue protected by a small building. Two blocks from the original statue base were re-used in the foundations of the new altar, demonstrating the importance of continuity in religious sites. Continuity is also found in the buttress itself (Fig. 60). The high mass of bedrock and Mycenaean masonry was squared off with poros and new limestone cladding, resulting in a neat, white, angled buttress, getting narrower towards the west front.

On the west front face, a little above the level of the path, are two tall rectangular 'windows', opening on a rough double niche in the Mycenaean masonry. This may have been a shrine or shelf for offerings. Round to the north side, where the ramp rises, a polygonal gap is left in the cladding, through which the original wall of the buttress can be seen. The contrast of white, **dressed stone** with the Cyclopean boulders and bedrock within is striking. At the foot of the bastion, the limestone blocks splay out slightly at each course; they are left rougher and they are interrupted here and there by the bedrock itself. At the top, the white limestone is finished with a cornice of whiter, smoother Pentelic marble. The bastion, which in effect is a massive plinth for the temple, suggests the spirit of Athens rising gradually upwards from its essential primitive roots in the earth to the refinement of the Ionic structure above.

The temple

The Ionic **tetrastyle** amphiprostyle temple stands on a neat three-stepped platform abutting the north-western corner of its precinct (Fig. 62), making it as visible as possible from below. It is tiny – 5.4 × 8 metres – with columns four metres high. As with the other Acropolis temples, the first view is of the back (Fig. 60). The western four-columned porch is purely decorative, containing a blank wall with a plain anta at each corner. The eastern porch (Figs. 61 and 62) reveals a tiny open cella, once protected by three bronze grilles fixed between the antae and the two plain slim rectangular pillars; this arrangement would have left the statue inside permanently visible. Two more grilles joined the antae to the porch corner columns.

The building is carefully detailed. The Ionic capitals are a half-size version of those in the Propylaia except that the corner volutes protrude at 45 degrees. Linking the rather wide volutes is an egg-and-dart moulding, while tiny honeysuckles fill the angles. The capitals spread very slightly further than the bases. The bases have a **reeded** torus above, and a rather spreading concave scotia below. The monolithic shafts are tapered but

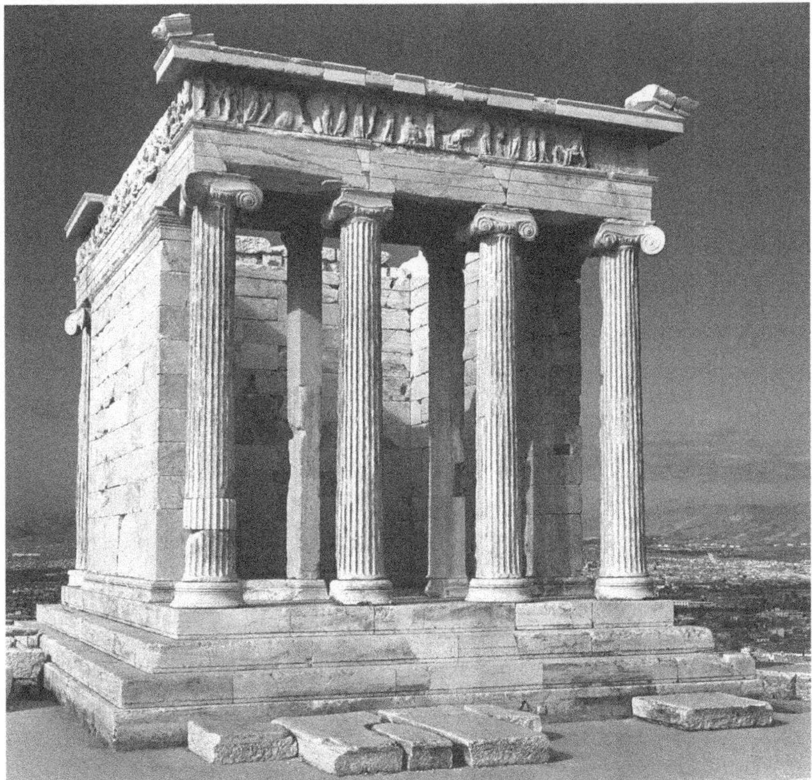

Fig. 62 The temple of Athene Nike seen from the east.

without entasis. As is typical of Ionic columns, they flare out slightly, very close to the lower extremities of the rounded flutes. Further details serve to unify the building:

- The reeded moulding and flared scotia of the column bases are mirrored by a moulding at the base of the cella exterior walls, running all round the building. The anta capitals have a simple moulding at the top, similarly carried all around.
- The architrave has the traditional triple-stepped horizontal division: a sharply angled moulding runs along its top, supporting the sculpted ribbon-frieze above. Such details are unobtrusive but they help bind the building together visually.
- The inner porch architrave repeats the triple division. The inner porch rectangular pillars are joined to the sidewalls by a strip of the same base-moulding at floor level, while the central entrance opening is left clear.
- The lowest course of cella masonry (orthostates) is just over double the height of the courses above: and the upper course height visually relates to the ashlar masonry of the supporting buttress.
- The western façade is finished at the sides with plain dummy antae matching those on the east. All antae are thickened on the flank walls.

- The steps have the typical Ionic groove, undercutting each **riser**. Each riser slopes slightly forward and each tread slopes slightly outward.

The designers of this temple had to tackle the problem of visual competition with the adjacent Propylaia. They have adopted various strategies, typical of Acropolis design. The most obvious problem is size. How can a temple the size of a double garage achieve significance when placed next to the majestic Propylaia? One answer (also used by the designer of the Erechtheion), was to go for a contrasting effect, aiming at small and exquisite alongside large, plain and noble. The Ionic style is perfect for the small and exquisite. In fact, the temple of Athene Nike has more than its Ionic share of decoration (Fig. 61), since it seems to have included sculptured pediments as well as the all-round Ionic sculptured frieze which brings interest to otherwise blank sidewalls. There were very showy acroteria too. This profusion of sculpture mimics that on the Parthenon itself. In addition, edging the buttress was the unique carved balustrade (which would have faced outward); its wet-look drapery style extends that of the Parthenon pediment yet further (Fig. 63).

Fig. 63 Nike adjusting her sandal, relief sculpture, from the balustrade of the temple of Athene Nike.

To pursue the idea of contrast, the Nike temple is set at a slight angle to the Propylaia (Figs. 38 and 54). This means that when looked at from the west, the smallest of the temples is distinguished from all the others by its angle. The Erechtheion, Parthenon and Propylaia are all set on the same axis as each other.

The Ionic Nike temple borrows the sculpted pediment from the Doric tradition. It has other Doric borrowings too. Tiny as the cella is, its wall thickness tapers on the flank walls, narrowing towards the top like the old mud-brick walls – a Doric feature. This inclination would exaggerate the already sharp perspective of the initial view from below. The slight inward taper of the flank walls is continued in the flank surfaces of the antae. However, the front and back walls and antae do not taper (presumably saving extra work as they are masked by columns).

The columns at both front and back incline slightly inwards, in the Doric way; and, though slender, they are stockier than expected for Ionic. They have borrowed a touch of Doric sturdiness from their close neighbour, the Propylaia, so as not to appear flimsy by comparison. There is no curvature of the stylobate – this suggests that the need for curvature is a function of size: a tiny temple has no need of a corrective optical illusion.

Within the precinct, to the east, was the altar, as specified in the decree.

The sculptural programme

The sculptural programme of the temple links it securely with the Parthenon itself. The pediments, though obviously small (0.55m high), were (it is thought) sculpted with a Gigantomachy to the east, an Amazonomachy to the west. The pairing creates a parallel between Athens and Olympos, a bold comparison already noted on the east and west Parthenon metopes; moving the theme to pedimental level here has made it even more overt.

The marble pedimental figures were attached to the tympanum with pins, suggesting that the tympanum was of a contrasting material, maybe dark limestone, with the white figures creating a cameo effect.

Both pediments were crowned by gilded bronze acroteria, probably created by a technique of wrapping the bronze-sculpted core with heavy gold foil (Schulz, 2001). There were single Nikai at the corners and multiple figures on the apexes, one possibly incorporating a Bellerophon mounted on Pegasus and slaying the Chimaera. The Nikai perfectly suited the dedication and also echoed the larger golden one carried in the hand of Athene Parthenos, while the hero Bellerophon would provide a picturesque exemplum of victory.

These acroteria, judging from the size of the existing base slabs, were oversized (Schulz, 2001). The temple building was very small but it stood upon a high plinth or buttress, a position which lent it significance beyond its real dimensions. It seems that the size of the acroteria was adjusted to be more proportionate to the entire construction, rather than to the diminutive temple. Along with the rest of the Nike sculpture programme, these acroteria greeted the visitor from some way off: they needed the importance of size and brilliance to do this job well.

The sculptured continuous frieze ran around all four sides of the cella; the precise topics are still under debate. The gods gather on the east, again repeating a Parthenon theme. The battered friezes on the other three sides may show contemporary Athenians at war, as the costumes suggest Greek-on-Greek and Greek-on-Persian battles. If so the thematic boldness of the Parthenon frieze is repeated.

The balustrade

The sculpted balustrade was the special glory of the Nike sanctuary (Figs. 61 and 63). Rising from the smooth Pentelic cornice which crowns the limestone bastion was a solid marble balustrade, topped with a decorative metal grille of some sort. This barrier would allow visitors to see the view safely – and implies that they were expected to linger and look. The structure surrounded the sanctuary platform on three sides, finishing to the north at the entrance steps, and to the south probably level with the temple front. At the steps, the balustrade turns with them and stops. There were 24 slabs in all, three of which incorporated a corner; two corners were right angles while the north-west corner fitted the obtuse angle of the platform.

The subject of the carved reliefs is winged Nikai attendant upon Athene. About 50 Nikai are ranged in varied poses and each side has its own seated Athene. Some Nikai bring arms to build a trophy, marking victory on the battlefield. Others lead bulls to sacrifice. If contemporary Athenian battles really were celebrated on the frieze of the temple just above, this further element of the programme would be an appropriate reference to the fallen, rather like a modern war memorial. The joyous Nikai raise trophies, while the companionable presence of a seated Athene softens the idea of battle.

This carved balustrade was installed *c.* 410 BC, slightly later than the temple. In style, this carving has moved yet a step further than the Parthenon pediments: the flowing drapery is even more body-moulding and deliberately graceful (Fig. 63). Being about one metre in height, the parapet almost duplicates the format of the Parthenon frieze but exceeds it in richness and fluidity. Altogether, the Nike sanctuary with its Doric-influenced Ionic architecture and consciously beautiful sculpture makes a nice foretaste to the main Acropolis sanctuary.

CHAPTER 11
THE ERECHTHEION

The Erechtheion, constructed from 421 to 405 BC, was the last, but by no means the least, of the important buildings to be completed on the Acropolis. It is the most unusual architecturally, and in some ways it carried the greatest weight of meaning for the Athenians. As the Acropolis was the religious and historical heart of Athens, so the section of it occupied by the Erechtheion was really the ancient heart of the Acropolis (Figs. 38 and 39).

The citadel, as we have seen, in late Mycenaean times had a defensible propylon or gate, Cyclopean walls, and, towards the northern edge, a Mycenaean palace, smaller than but similar to those of Mycenae and Tiryns. Visible traces are left of this palace in the terracing which still surrounds the ruins of the 'old temple'.

To the joy of Athenians, this very palace seemed to be mentioned by Homer as the 'strong-built house of Erechtheus' that Athene entered (*Odyssey* 7.81). This mention puts the ancient king firmly back into the Age of Heroes; archaeologically, it accords with the thinking that Mycenaean palaces included domestic shrines. It also suggests that the patron goddess Athene had dwelt on her hill for a very long time, and was even conceivably already present in the ancient palace in the form of the long-revered wooden statue, Athene Polias.

Myth

While the palace is clearly historical, its famous occupant is rather less so. A kaleidoscope of inconsistent myths clusters about Erechtheus's identity – which on examination seems to merge into other identities, such as Erichthonios and even Poseidon. Poseidon and Erechtheus were worshipped together on one altar in the Erechtheion. The name of Erechtheus is important because it represents just about the earliest 'history' of Athens which could be imagined. The Greeks believed generally that, in earliest times, tribes known as Dorians had swept into mainland Greece and, settling there, had become the mainland Greek nation as they knew it. However, this had not happened in Attica. The Athenians considered themselves to be the aboriginal tribe of their own territory. They had not come from anywhere: they themselves were ancestors of the Ionian group of Greeks who had moved away and colonised the eastern Mediterranean. This Athenian belief in a special relationship with their own soil – known as autochthony – was of extraordinary significance to them and is expressed in the following rather strange myth.

Athene was hotly pursued by the amorous Hephaistos on the Acropolis. Being a virgin goddess, she rejected him. As she moved smartly out of his way, his seed fell on her leg. She wiped it off with a woollen rag that she then dropped on the ground. But the seed of a god was not wasted and immediately grew up into a child, Erichthonios/Erechtheus. He is frequently illustrated on vases, as Ge, the Earth, waist-deep in earth, hands the new baby up to Athene. Athene had pity on the child and arranged for his upbringing. He became the king and ancestor of the Athenians, and one of his grandchildren was Ion, founder of the Ionian race.

Homer in the Iliad – or just possibly an enthusiastic Athenian literary editor of the sixth century BC – seems familiar with the story of Erechtheus and Athene, referring to:

> Athens, the well-built citadel,
> nation of great-hearted Erechtheus whom once Athene,
> daughter of Zeus, cared for – yet it was the fruitful earth bore him –
> and she set him down in her own rich temple.
>
> (Homer, *Iliad* 2.546–9)

The myths about Erechtheus and the early kings crowd around this site on the north side of the Acropolis, making the soil itself meaningful and sacred. Cecrops, another of the earliest kings, was buried there, and a sacred snake in an underground crypt was their living representative.

Ion also is a significant character, since he links the ancient royalty of Attica with the Ionian allies of Athens in the Greek struggle to maintain independence against the Persians. During the fifth century, Athens moved on from simple kinship with the Ionians, first becoming their champion, then empire builder over them; always, the link was of great importance.

Interest in 'roots'

The shrines clustered in the patch of earth just to the north of the 'old temple' were many, and all had intimate mythical connections with the beginnings of Athens, her founders, gods and ancient royal family.

Two plays of Euripides, written about this time, suggest that there was quite a ferment of interest in these myths, probably because of the activity on the site and the public expenditure on the new presentation of these treasured cult areas. One play entitled *Erechtheus* deals with the dilemma of the ancient king and his wife Praxitheia who are called upon to sacrifice one of their daughters for the sake of the city. Praxitheia goes on to become the first priestess of Athene Polias, a role still extant in the fifth century BC, and still a hereditary post of women from the Eteoboutadai family, descendants of the ancient kings. All this ties the royal family and the city goddess together.

Another play by Euripides, *Ion*, tells the story of Creusa, daughter of Erechtheus, who was raped by Apollo on the Long Rocks under the Acropolis and there gave birth to

Ion, the ancestor of the Ionian race. (This explains a cult of Apollo known as Patroios ('ancestral'), with a temple in the Agora, and a sacred cave in the Long Rocks.) This story too highlights the royal family, its palace, its daughters, and its mythical links with the Ionian race.

These plays of Euripides presented the mythical characters onstage as living suffering people with whom Athenians could fully identify, as they wrestled with the human problems of the rape-victim, the childless couple, the foster child. Euripides intriguingly helped his audience 'get to know' these ancestors who were also 'neighbours', once dwelling on the familiar rock.

The style

One of the first choices to be made in planning a temple (along with site and material) would be the architectural order – whether Doric, Ionic, or the new 'mix'. The Erechtheion is Ionic and myth may have influenced this choice.

Just for once – in their 'finest hour' – the Greeks as a whole had grouped together successfully, against the Persian foe. But the alliance between 'Dorian' Sparta and 'Ionian' Athens, the two major Greek powers, had definitely cooled by the second half of the fifth century. In fact, they were soon actually at war. It would be understandable if the Doric/Ionic combination of the earliest Periclean buildings yielded to a more insular Ionic. But quite apart from the military and political hostility current at the time of building, it should be no surprise that the Ionic style was chosen for the Erechtheion site with all its time-honoured associations of autochthony and ancestry.

Herodotus – who was himself originally from an Asian/Dorian city, Halicarnassus – generally refers to Athens as Ionian, and tells a little story about this Ionian identity:

> When Cleomenes (King of Sparta) went up to the Acropolis … he approached Athene's shrine to say a prayer. The priestess (of Athene Polias), rising from her throne, before he could get through the door, cried: 'Spartan stranger, go back. Do not enter the holy place. It is not lawful for Dorians to enter.'
>
> Herodotus, *Histories* 5.72

This kind of sensitivity makes it possible that the Ionic style of the Erechtheion would have been included in the initial planning of Pericles's carefully balanced programme, and not just as a response to the Peloponnesian War.

The building

The building is so unusual that many points need discussion and explanation. Aesthetically, opinion is divided, some critics viewing it as a triumph while for others it is a product of compromise and incompetence. What is certain is that the quality of workmanship, finish and elaboration exceeds, if that were possible, the other magnificent buildings already created on the Acropolis. It is also clear that a building was necessary in this area of the sanctuary for Athene Polias, and that some form of monumentalisation was necessary to tidy up the multiplicity of sacred spots and smaller shrines which had long existed there. The Erechtheion was a solution which combined these aims, and which held its own aesthetically in the overall plan of the sanctuary.

The site: What was there before the Erechtheion?

Looking at the ground plan (Fig. 39), it can be seen that adjacent to the Erechtheion on the south is a large area of ruined foundations. As was mentioned in Chapter 7, these are the remains of the 'old temple' of Athene Polias, built in the late sixth century. This temple was aligned with the main altar to its east and therefore was a sensible setting for the Panathenaic sacrifices. The visible foundations show an unusual interior layout, with a double non-communicating cella. While the eastern cella had a double interior colonnade, the western was subdivided into three compartments. This arrangement would be replicated in the new Erechtheion, which suggests that the various cults of that

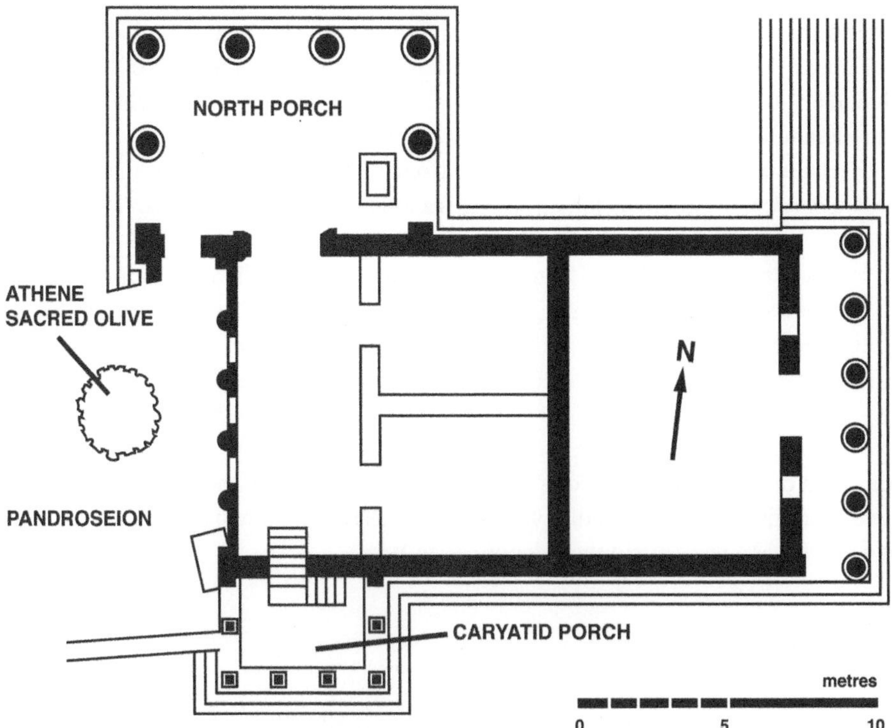

Fig. 64 Ground plan of the Erechtheion.

temple were long-standing and revered. It also implies that the Erechtheion is specifically the replacement for the 'old temple'.

The 'old temple' of Athene Polias had been grand for its time. Though it was mainly of limestone, many individual parts of its entablature were island marble. The marble pedimental sculpture, featuring a Gigantomachy, was over life-size (an Athene and a giant are in the Museum). It was carved free-standing and stood against a tympanum of limestone. This major temple was badly damaged by the Persians when they sacked the Acropolis in 480/79. The Athenians on their return, having kept the sacred Athene Polias safely with them, must now have housed her either in a remnant of the ruined temple itself, or in some adequate 'temporary' shelter on the site. This situation would have continued from 479 BC until the dedication of the new Erechtheion in 405. The foundations of the 'old temple' are now visible though they may have once been covered over or left open as a memorial to the sacking of the sanctuary by the Persians. In fact, it is unclear how much of the ruined temple was still standing, even when the Erechtheion was built. Clearly, the old temple could in theory have been built up again, just as before. However, this might have been forbidden by the controversial oath of Plataea.

Even without any oath, there were good aesthetic reasons for leaving the old foundations and moving on. Since the Parthenon was to be built as massive as it was, there was little visual space left between it and the 'old temple'. And once the Parthenon had been built, nothing further could be achieved in the line of Doric temples. Also, a rebuilding of the now old-fashioned archaic temple would still leave the problem of the adjacent multiple shrines unsolved, especially now that the aesthetic stakes had been raised so high by the Acropolis team under Pheidias. All significant new building had to reach at least a similar standard of design.

The building

Like all major Acropolis buildings, the Erechtheion is constructed of Pentelic marble. It consists basically of a hexastyle prostyle Ionic temple, similar to, but considerably larger than, the temple of Athene Nike. Inside, it has two cellas that were on different levels, east and west. Additionally, it has two very unusual side-porches, north and south (described below). Like the Propylaia, this building has had to be designed on a difficult site in terms of ground levels, and the designer has solved some unique problems with great ingenuity (Fig. 64).

It is often said that the Erechtheion is built on sloping ground, but that is not quite true. The temple straddles an abrupt drop in levels, probably the remains of ancient terracing around the Mycenaean palace (Figs. 65 and 67). The south and east façades appear to stand on the higher ground (Fig. 66). However, from the north and west, it is clear that the building is double height and has its foundation on the lower ground level (Fig. 67). Outside access to the lower level from the main Acropolis

Fig. 65a Restoration drawing of the east elevation of the Erechtheion.

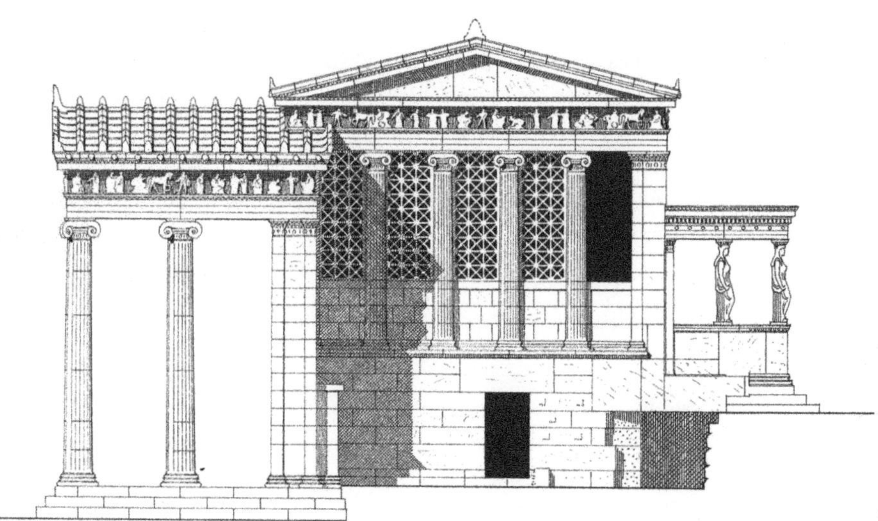

Fig. 65b Restoration drawing of the west elevation of the Erechtheion.

plateau is by a steep flight of steps to the east, and by a roundabout route from the west (Fig. 39).

The complex continues on the lower level towards the west with the sanctuary of Pandrosos, once an enclosed garden with an Ionic stoa surrounding it and a tiny temple building. This garden gave access to the tomb of Cecrops tucked under the south-west corner of the Erechtheion. It also contained Athene's sacred olive tree and an altar to Zeus Herkeios or 'of the Courtyard' (a feature typically found in Athenian houses) (Fig. 67).

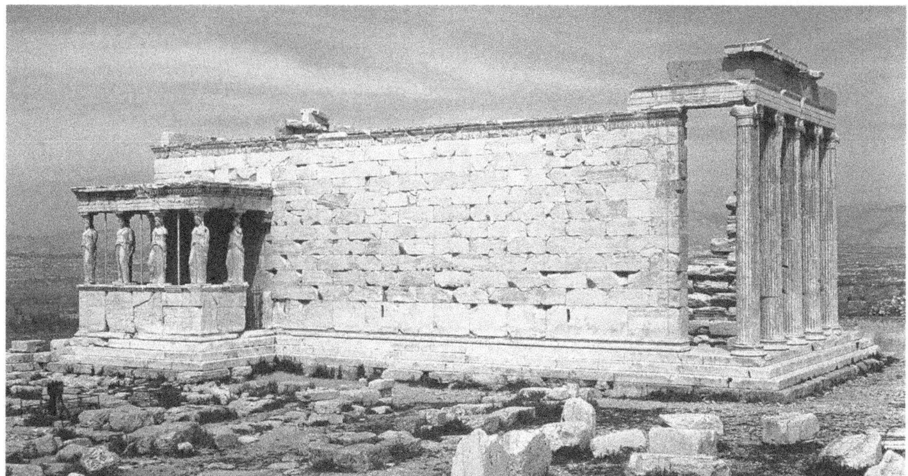

Fig. 66 Erechtheion: from the south.

Fig. 67 The Erechtheion from the west, showing the foundation wall of the 'old temple' and the Parthenon.

The east porch

The east porch is the most acceptable for those who demand a conventional, symmetrical temple front (Fig. 65). It would have faced the main altar of Athene and perhaps been the backdrop for the giving of the Panathenaic peplos, since the east cella is thought to have been the new home of Athene Polias. The basic decorative scheme of the temple starts from here and runs around the whole building, gathering other features on its way.

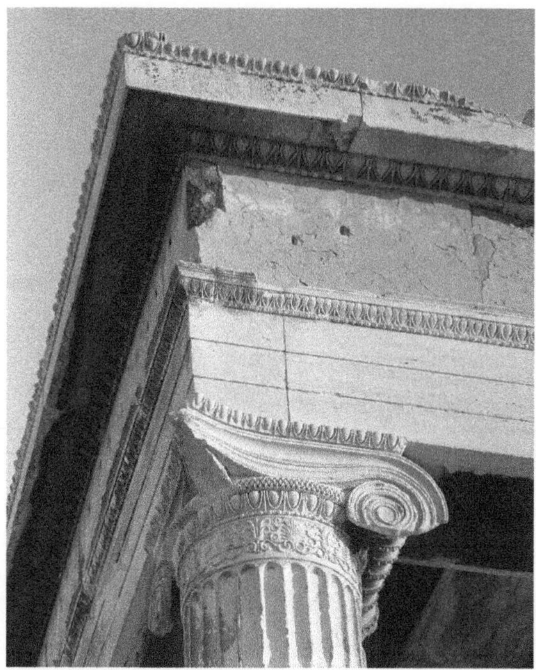

Fig. 68 Detail of the entablature from the north porch of the Erechtheion.

The six slender Ionic columns, 6.6 metres in height, stand on a three-stepped platform whose steps are not undercut. They taper elegantly without entasis, as is normal for Ionic columns. However, they do lean very slightly towards the cella: a Doric but not Ionic trait. The capitals are very fine with multiple outlines to the volutes; a fine lotus-and-palmette ornament running around the neck under the capitals, topped by a tiny beading, an egg-and-dart and a small guilloche (cf. Fig. 68). The corner columns have their corner volutes at a 45-degree angle so that volutes can be seen from both front and flank. This means that the inner side of each corner capital correspondingly has two scrolled sections.

The frieze

The east porch columns supported an Ionic entablature and pediment (Fig. 65a). The entablature consists of a triple-stepped architrave below a continuous Ionic frieze. The frieze is composed of a dark Eleusis limestone strip as background: to it were once pinned the figures of the frieze, carved separately in white marble to create a cameo effect. Although some figures are preserved, the subject of the frieze is not known; it may perhaps have included myths of the ancient kings. This striking and unusual decoration continued all around the building at the same height – except for a height variation on the north porch.

Both the frieze and the pediment cornices above were outlined by small leaf-and-dart mouldings; they were unobtrusive but gave a neat yet rich finish (cf. Fig. 68). Attention to detail is one of the characteristics of this very expensive building.

The lotus-and-palmette border

The antae inside the east porch have a very beautiful lotus-and-palmette (anthemion) flat capital. This is continued as a border at the same height all around the main cella, with a break only on the west end between the antae. The exquisitely carved anthemion is topped by smaller mouldings, an egg-and-dart and a leaf-and-dart, each underlined by much smaller bead-and-reels (Fig. 69).

On the porches, the antae border runs inside the porch, while the architrave and frieze run outside. On the two long flank walls of the temple, the dark limestone frieze, the three-stepped architrave and the anthemion border all run together, piled up in an unusual and very showy ensemble.

There is another subtlety of the design which is easily missed in the rich mix. On the antae, the lotus-and-palmette capital has an intensified version of the pattern: the elements are placed more closely and are enriched. Although this variation is not easy to detect, it results in an apparent strengthening of the corner elements. Like corner-contraction, it adds a feeling of extra stability to the corners. The effect is visually satisfying, although of course this is just an effective optical illusion.

Although most of these mouldings are in themselves routine, the effect of piling so many together, and then joining them with the frieze, creates a richness that was

Fig. 69 Mouldings from the Erechtheion, north porch. *From top*: leaf-and-dart, bead-and-reel, egg-and-dart, bead-and-reel, lotus-and-palmette (anthemion).

obviously considered desirable for the purpose. On this temple, the rich mouldings are set off by large expanses of completely featureless marble wall (Fig. 66).

At the feet of the antae is a reeded double torus moulding which also continues around the whole building, just above the triple-stepped platform. All these prominent continuous features do much to bind the diverse parts of the building together visually.

The north porch

The north porch has its own surprises (Fig. 70). It was the main entrance to the lower cella. Rather than appear as the mere back door to the basement, it receives extra architectural importance from many features. To begin with, it is built on a scale appropriate for heroes or gods, and is disproportionately large to the building it enters.

Unlike the south porch, it was pedimented and had its own pitched roof, almost like a mini-temple (Figs. 65, a, b). The reconstruction shows that it would have carried its full complement of antefixes and even acroteria. The columns supported the same three-

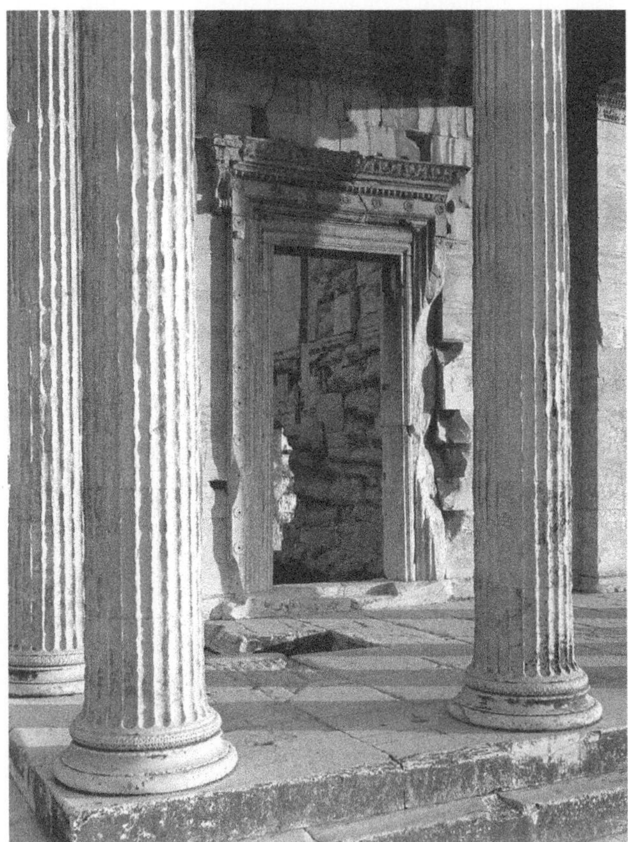

Fig. 70 Erechtheion, detail of the north porch with hole in the pavement.

stepped architrave and the dark limestone frieze – all on a slightly larger scale to accord with the greater height of the building here. As on the east porch, the anthemion border separates from the frieze and runs along the back wall of the porch, connecting the two antae, which are decoratively enhanced, as described above (Fig. 69).

The six Ionic columns stand prostyle, four abreast and one behind on each flank (Fig. 64). They are 7.6 metres in height, and even more ornate than the east porch columns. Like those of the east they have a slight taper, but they also have a nearly imperceptible entasis (borrowed from Doric style). The capitals (Fig. 68) are even finer than those on the east, and they were originally enlivened with gilding and paint; coloured glass 'gems' of red and yellow, green and blue were inserted into the 'eyes' of the guilloches. (This colour and glass could still be seen in the eighteenth century AD.) Gold wire was inserted into the grooves of the spirals, and gold tassels hung from each central 'eye'. The bases are ornate with another guilloche design on the upper torus, each one very slightly different; these designs echo those on the capitals above (Fig. 71).

The ceiling of this porch (still intact) was the grandest on the whole Acropolis. Its coffers are triple-stepped and each coffer once contained a central gilded bronze star. Each marble beam dividing the coffers is outlined with an egg-and-dart design, carved instead of just painted as would be more usual.

The door to the lower cella was bordered with multiple fine mouldings, and spaced rosettes on the broad outer border. The lintel was very ornate with egg-and-dart and an anthemion above, between two scrolls (volutes) decorated with **acanthus**. Like the porch itself, the door was scaled so huge as to be fit for heroes or gods: it was nearly five metres high and very slightly tapered, adding to the impression of size by false

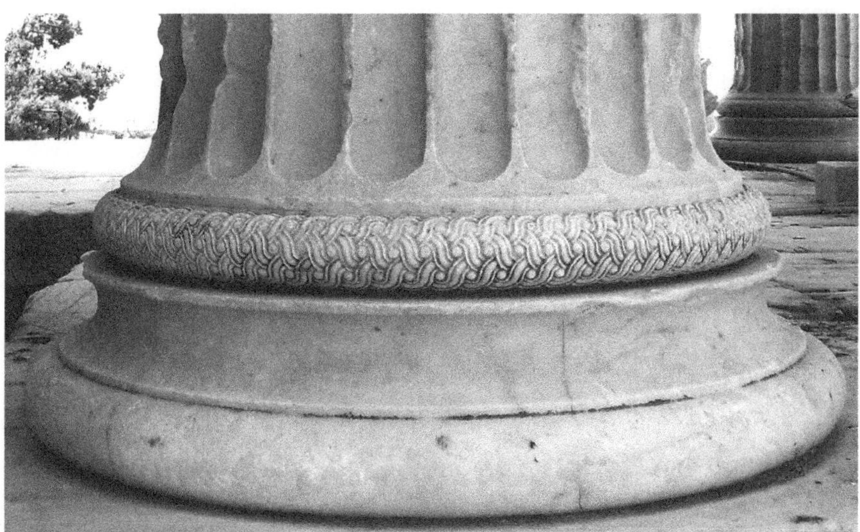

Fig. 71 Column base from the Erechtheion: guilloche moulding on top torus; plain scotia and lower torus.

perspective (Fig. 70). The sides of the porch were defined by prominent antae, linked by the anthemion border. All this grandeur indicates the importance to Athens of the cult objects that lay within.

The porch was itself a sort of shrine, since to the left was a hole in the floor, through which a natural fissure could be seen in the rock (Fig. 70). So sacred was this spot, touched by a god (Zeus's thunderbolt or Poseidon's trident), that a corresponding square hole was left in the roof giving clear access between sky and fissure. Somewhere under the paved floor was a crypt where lived the sacred snake or snakes cared for by the priestess of Athene Polias. (Snakes were a not unusual feature of Greek shrines as they were thought to provide a link with the underworld.) Here in the Erechtheion there was an added significance as the earth-born Erichthonios was snake-legged. Athene Parthenos also sheltered a snake within her shield – as Pausanias tells us laconically: '... probably Erichthonios' (1.24.7) (Fig. 53).

An oddity of the porch is that it actually oversteps the cella on the north-west corner, far enough to allow for a small door giving onto the open-air precinct of Pandrosos (Fig. 64). This apparent mistake must have been carefully considered. It would have been so easy to provide a separate door in the precinct wall to enter from outside: but the intra-porch entrance binds the precinct in a more integrated way to the temple.

The west end

The eastern prostyle porch is 'normal', but the western end is 'different' (Figs. 65b and 67). There is no porch, and the four columns, while matching those of the east in style and nearly in height, are embedded in the western wall on the upper level. The end columns are replaced by two piers: below this at ground level is a solid wall with an unobtrusive entrance to the west cella. It is thought that there were originally bronze grilles between the four upper-storey columns and the left-hand pier, and an open space between the last column and the corner pier on the right. (The west end has been tampered with over time.) A pediment above helped to normalise the west façade and this was very important for the distant panorama of the Acropolis as a whole. Under the pediment, the dark limestone frieze and the architrave ran right across. However, the anthemion decoration on the west stopped at the anta.

The south porch

The south porch starts from the west corner of the south wall, extending for only a few metres, leaving the rest of the south wall plain (Fig. 66). The porch protrudes southward from the main rectangle with the result that it trespasses onto the visible archaic foundations of the 'old temple', and rests upon their terracing. A small entrance was tucked into the northeast corner of the base, and another led from inside the lower cella.

Fig. 72 Erechtheion, Caryatid porch from the south.

This porch is a unique feature. It takes the form of a high plinth or platform on which stand six over-life-size marble maidens as columns (caryatids) supporting a flat roof with a decorative architrave and cornice (Figs. 66 and 72). The mouldings vary from those on the rest of the building:

- Just under the feet of the maidens, the platform or plinth is topped by a cornice carved with an egg-and-dart moulding; the torus and three-steps treatment from the rest of the temple continues around the base.
- The maidens are crowned by architectural egg-and-dart crowns in the place of column capitals, mirroring the moulding found under their feet.
- The maidens carry a three-stepped architrave carved with widely spaced rosettes; above them is a continuous frieze of Ionic dentils outlined by tiny egg-and-darts above and below, and topped by a plain protruding cornice.
- Since the porch is not the full height of the building, space is left for the anthemion or lotus-and-palmette decoration to continue uninterrupted, as a unifying feature around the top of the cella wall, under the architrave and the continuous dark limestone frieze.

The six maidens themselves stand prostyle in a row of four, with one more behind each corner: their positions correspond to those of the columns in the north porch. The maidens are almost identical but have slight variations of drapery and hairstyle. Each rests her weight on the outer leg, while appearing to begin a forward step with the bent leg. The pose is thus a mixture of static and forward moving. It also divides the left- and right-hand groups by leg position. In their hands, it is thought that they once held **phialai** (shallow offering dishes), possibly designed with lobes like the rosettes above. The sculpture is in the Pheidian style of the Parthenon: a graceful yet solid figure style and flowing, body-moulding drapery. The multiplicity of folds catches the strong sunlight in varied ways, especially because of the left- and right-hand stances, the variety giving an illusion of movement among the figures; they seem to move as the viewer moves.

The maidens are suited to their role as columns by a sturdy upright stance, by a strengthening of the neck area with their flowing locks, by the replacement of what might have been baskets on their heads by the architectural member with egg-and-dart decoration, and by a tendency of the skirt surrounding the straight leg to revert to the fluting of an Ionic column – a visual pun.

We know that caryatids were used in Delphi on two of the finest archaic Ionic treasuries. There may have been archaic caryatids on the Acropolis too: caryatids were a lavish feature of Ionic style.

Vitruvius gives the name caryatid to this type of figure and tells a little history to explain it – the people of Carya collaborated with the Persians in the war so their women became slaves as punishment. However, the ancient term for these figures was simply **kore** – maiden. The archaic caryatids of Delphi obviously predate the Persian War; and to link a story of guilt and treachery with the Erechtheion maidens would seem a sad lapse in appropriateness. These high-classical maidens are also sometimes said to replace the many archaic **korai** or girl statues which once crowded the Acropolis sanctuary but were destroyed by the Persians. However, it may be more interesting and fruitful to look at the specific meaning of the Erechtheion itself.

Given that the shrine of Pandrosos actually adjoins the temple, and that daughters figure so profusely in the various myths about Erechtheus and the other kings, it should surely be no surprise that maidens populate and support the south porch, which covers the 'tomb' of King Cecrops. If the maidens carried phialai in their vanished hands, they were equally able to make offerings at the ancestral tomb or to Athene Polias. There is also something about this unique loggia or viewing porch suggestive of the balcony of a palatial dwelling house. One could imagine that from its vantage point, the priestess with her young girl attendants might watch over crowds and ceremonies; alongside them would be the priest of Poseidon (who also had to be a member of the Eteoboutadai family); for onlookers from below, living figures on the porch would move among stone maidens in an intriguing way. The priest and priestess of the double temple, both being descendants of ancient king/priests, were a visible blood-link with Athenian myth-history. The maidens themselves, though high classical in dress and form, have their hair in the archaic fashion with prominent locks and ringlets, recalling maidens of olden time.

To the west of the complex was probably situated the House of the Arrhephoroi where girl and women weavers (creators of the ceremonial peplos) were housed. So, the maiden theme would continue along the whole north side of the rock (Fig. 39).

Rather similar columnar maidens are found on the Parthenon, on the important east frieze (Fig. 48). Their sedate and maidenly profile-walk on the frieze is replicated by the profile view of the porch maidens, who seem about to join the Panathenaic procession with ready handheld offerings and forward-leaning pose. The slow and eternal advance of the Erechtheion korai across the sacred space between the two temples can be seen as linking the Erechtheion with the Parthenon in one unified act of worship to Athene. Cleverly, the frontal view of the Erechtheion maidens is more dominated by the upright weight-bearing leg with its column-like flutings, whereas the more dynamic side view suggests a forward movement, thus uniting the two Athene temples across the ruins of a third.

Inside the temple

Internally the temple is split-level and had a double cella (Fig. 64). The eastern section was probably single-storey height (entered only from the east), and the west was double-storey. There was no internal access between the two levels. The eastern cella interior floor seems to have been infilled to the upper level height, while the separate western cella floor was on the lower ground level. The western cella seems to have imitated the unusual triple layout of the 'old temple' western cella, while the eastern one replaced the old eastern cella, both still observable from the ruins. However, the exact internal arrangements of the Erechtheion are still debated, as subsequent use of the building has destroyed most of the evidence.

Inside the building, there was quite a lot to take in, according to Pausanias:

> As you go in there are altars: Poseidon's, where they also sacrifice to Erechtheus … and one for the hero Boutes, and a third for Hephaistos. On the walls are paintings of the Boutadai family, and, the building being double, some sea-water inside a well. This is not so very surprising… . But the extraordinary thing about this well is that when the wind blows south it makes a sound of waves. The mark of a trident is in the rock. They say that these things appeared as evidence for Poseidon in his struggle for the land. (Pausanias 1.26.5)

Most importantly there was the olive-wood image of the city goddess – Athene Polias: 'Rumour says it fell from heaven. I shall not go into whether this is so or not' (Pausanias 1.26.6). The heavenly origin suggests that the statue could have been **aniconic** (non-representational). Or it could have been so old that it retained little of its original form. There were extremely ancient statues of stone or wood of this type, and the antiquity only increased the sacredness. It was this statue which received the gift of a new peplos or dress at every Panathenaia; most likely it was kept in the eastern cella, but this is not certain. The decorative peplos, woven by specially selected women and girls each year, always featured the Battle of Gods and Giants in which Athene had distinguished herself. There is discussion about how these textile works of art could have been displayed and stored: one suggestion is that the long plain stretch of south exterior wall next to the caryatids might have been used as a display area.

Athene Polias was lit by a wonderful golden lamp made by Callimachos which could burn for a year without refilling: 'above the lamp a bronze palm-tree goes up to the roof and draws up the smoke' (Pausanias 1.26.7). There was also an amazing collection of ancient art and contemporary memorabilia:

> A wooden Hermes, said to be the offering of Cecrops, hidden by myrtle branches
> A folding stool made by Daidalos
> Among the Persian spoils, the breastplate of Masistios, commander of cavalry at Plataea
> A Persian sword, said to have belonged to Mardonios. I know Maisistios was killed by the Athenian cavalry, but as Mardonios fought against Spartans and fell to a Spartan, the Athenians could hardly have obtained the sword then, and the Spartans would surely not have let them have it. (Pausanias 1.27.1)

Pausanias shows an analytical streak here as he thinks about the authenticity of the Persian spoils. But, as usual, he makes no mention of the architecture.

Was the building a triumph or a disaster?

Each viewer must give his or her own answer to this question.

The temple has been greatly criticised for its eccentric and almost haphazard design. But it should be pointed out that each aspect works well in itself and not all aspects can be seen at once. From east and south it appears a one-storey building. The north porch is impressive from close up, and from afar its height gives it a needed importance. The west view is harder to assess since it was once enclosed and bounded by the garden shrine of Pandrosos. Here too grew Athene's sacred olive tree whose twentieth-century replacement now masks the lower part of this façade. However, from a distance, the west columns and pediment took their place satisfactorily in the general Acropolis line-up of large Doric and small Ionic temple fronts (Fig. 77).

It may be that hostile criticism is simply based on expectation: this temple is different. However, while some scholars may hate it, architects have loved it – as a treasury of ideas. Ancient Greeks, who delighted to reduce anything and everything to component parts and then adore the perfect relation of the parts to the whole, may have found it refreshing to contemplate this eccentric but fresh assembly of perfect elements.

CHAPTER 12
THE HEPHAISTEION

The temple of Hephaistos gains importance from its strategic position, and also from its excellent state of repair. It gives the visitor a good experience of a temple, as its exterior is fairly complete, with porches and porch sculptures in situ. It is roofed over the cella, but the roof is not original, dating only from when the temple was used as a church.

The temple and precinct of Hephaistos stand on the small hill bounding the north-west side of the Athenian Agora (Fig. 78). The plan of the temple and the arrangement of the sculpture decoration are designed to give special emphasis to the east front, unlike the Acropolis buildings, which cater for all-round views. The modern path winds upward from the Agora, allowing the visitor both frontal and three-quarter views of the temple, as intended (Fig. 73).

Natural foliage makes the precinct a pleasant place to be. Round three sides of the temple, square sunken pots have been found, once planted with alternating pomegranate and myrtle bushes, an arrangement dating from the third century BC when formal landscaping became fashionable (Fig. 74).

It appears that no sanctuary existed here before the Hephaisteion, so building on this spot would have been no violation of the oath of Plataea. The purpose of the temple was to honour Hephaistos, god of armourers, for his help in defeating the Persians. Since metalworkers were not at the top of the social ladder, this thank-offering was also a nice democratic touch, acknowledging what the working **demos** (people) contributed to the city.

The temple was started in 449 but not finished until around 420, the cult statues being dedicated 420–415. It looks as though the commencement of the Hephaisteion was among the first architectural signs of confidence and recovery after the Persian War. Around this time, other improvements were being made to the city, both practical and pleasurable; the massive south wall of the Acropolis was built up, paid for by profits from the victories of Cimon, a successful general and a political rival of Pericles. Cimon himself paid for the construction of the defensive Long Walls running from Athens to her coastal port, Peiraeus; and he irrigated the sacred grove of the Academy, and had the Agora planted with plane trees to bring shade and refreshment to the civic space. But Cimon died in 449 and it is not known who promoted the new temple overlooking the Agora. In 447, it was Pericles who proposed the Acropolis renovation. Understandably, the Acropolis now took precedence in using resources, since it was the major city sanctuary, but it was also Pericles's own vision. This explains the long time taken to complete the Hephaisteion.

Fig. 73 The east front of the Hephaisteion from below.

The building

The Hephaisteion appears to be a standard classical Doric temple, although by now we should not really think that a standard form actually exists.

The building today still retains all its colonnades, the outer metope frieze (though damaged), both inner-porch friezes, and the pronaos (front porch) ceiling with its marble coffering (Fig. 73). The ancient marble-tiled roof and wooden coffered ceiling over the cella have been replaced by a medieval barrel vault (added when the temple was used as a church).

The temple stands on the usual three-stepped platform, but the lowest step is limestone, which now has the unfortunate effect of blending too well with the ground and visually reducing the height. The temple is hexastyle with a distyle in antis porch at each end. The flank columns follow the 'formula' of $6 \times 2 + 1$. The outer measurement is 13.7×31.7 metres. Inside is a single cella, with one entrance on the east front (although an entrance was later cut into the back wall). It seems that the foundations indicate a change of plan during construction. The original intention was for a more archaic layout – longer and narrower, but the proportion was changed, early on in construction, to the new classical 'look' as seen at Olympia and the Parthenon.

The temple is criticised for having a top-heavy entablature carried on rather slender columns. However, this proportion works well from below – the angle from which it is mostly seen – whether from the Agora or from the steep approach path. The architect must have carefully weighed up the advantages of an optical correction which only worked well from a limited viewpoint.

The porches are not equal in size. The ground plan (Fig. 74) shows that the east front porch is a whole columniation deeper than the rear porch:

- the front antae are set further back than usual, level with the third flank column
- the cella entrance lines up with the fifth flank column
- the rear antae are only just past the second flank column.
- the rear cella wall is level with the fourth flank column

What was gained by all this juggling of proportions? The viewer is most likely to see the temple almost frontally, as said before (Fig. 73). The spacious east porch and deeper inner porch offer interesting depths and shadows. Ionic influence, which so often heightens attention to the entrance, can be seen at work here, creating a sense of arrival and of mysterious inner space: yet this has been achieved entirely by Doric methods.

Ionic features

The Doric Hephaisteion adopts some overtly Ionic features, which seem deliberately to quote the ruined Acropolis buildings. Like the ruined pre-Parthenon temple, it is all

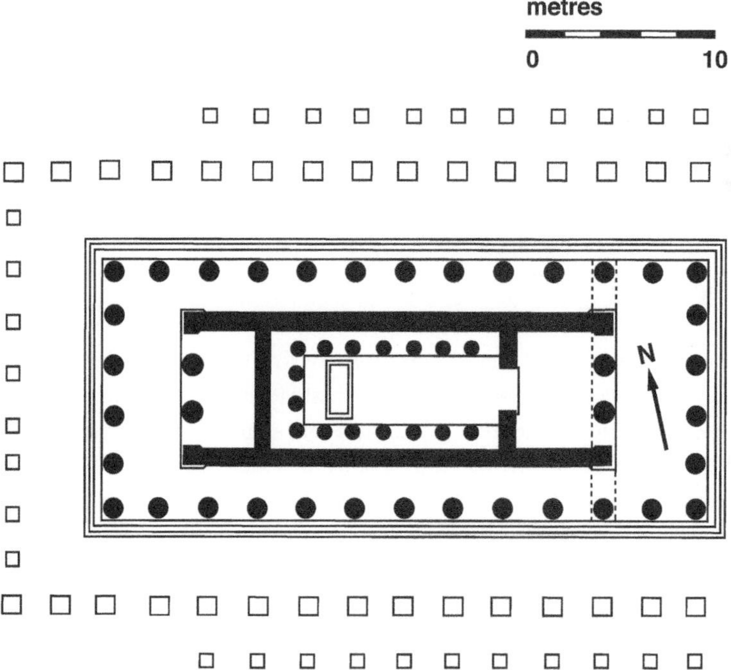

Fig. 74 Ground plan of the Hephaisteion.

marble (an Ionic feature) except for the lowest step. An Ionic moulding at the foot of the cella wall was also a quotation from the ruined pre-Parthenon.

The Hephaisteion has inner porch Ionic friezes. The 'old Athene temple' on the Acropolis, which was Doric, also probably mixed the orders in this way.

This sequence suggests that the Parthenon itself with its Ionic frieze was following a peculiarly Athenian tradition of mix and match, rather than being a surprising innovation.

Innovations

It is questioned whether the Parthenon influenced the Hephaisteion, or vice versa. The Hephaisteion's Ionic frieze could have been added in imitation of the Parthenon, however, the unusual alignment of the east porch antae with the third flank column could not. This alignment – not found on the Parthenon – adds to the emphasis and interest of the front porch because it enables the frieze to stretch from side to side of the colonnade, creating a rectangular 'box', surrounded by sculpture: outside on the front and sides, inside at the back (Figs. 73 and 74). The temple of Poseidon at Sounion, one of a group of contemporary Attic temples, had a rather similar arrangement of a carved Ionic frieze which actually went all round the interior of the front porch, forming a more complete 'sculpture box'. However, in the Hephaisteion back porch, the Ionic frieze runs only from anta to anta and the columns are (as was more usual) not aligned.

All the sculptures of the Hephaisteion are of Parian marble – unlike those of the Parthenon which are of Pentelic. Because the Parian had to be imported, it seems likely that all the marble was ordered prior to construction; the metopes were carved early on in the process as they had to be; but by the time the friezes were carved from the ready-prepared Parian pieces, cheaper 'home-grown' Pentelic had become standard for Athens.

The metopes

The east front metopes are all carved, and so are the first four on each flank, starting from the east corners (Fig. 73). This emphasises the east façade and the approach area.

The carved metopes of the front façade and side angles had to be placed in position during the construction of the colonnade since this was normal practice. The 'severe' style of the carving agrees with a mid-century date and is stylistically comparable with that of Olympia.

The metopes are shared between Theseus and Heracles. (In fact, the temple has traditionally been misidentified as the Theseion because of the Theseus metopes, but the real Theseion is now known to have been elsewhere.) These two heroes have shared an Athenian building before – the controversial treasury at Delphi. The pair goes well together: buddies, action heroes, monster-busters and friends of the downtrodden.

Heracles is arranged across the front, Theseus, less divine but more Athenian, has the first four slots down each flank. Heracles takes precedence although Theseus had a special prominence in Athens at this period: his gigantic bones had been recently brought 'home' to Athens by Cimon who had the good luck to 'discover' them while on military campaign in Skyros. Theseus, though an early king of Athens, had come to be seen as a champion of democracy. Heracles had been a hero of the previous Athenian regime – the Peisistratid tyranny – but Heracles could not be dispensed with. He was too precious a hero to lose, and was of course featured on the Temple of Zeus at Olympia. He was also a good hero for metopes because of the episodic character of his exploits.

There are no carved metopes on the west façade; this fact points the viewer's attention back to the east front.

The Ionic friezes

The inner porch Ionic friezes seem to have been added after a break of some years; the style is now soft, flowing and Parthenon-like. The east porch frieze shows a battle in the presence of six Olympians. These gods sit in two groups of three, framing the inner scene of warriors on which they are intent, as on the Siphnian frieze – but arranged symmetrically, as on the Parthenon frieze. However, here they face the central scene with another scene behind each group to left and right. They sit informally on rocks, turning naturalistically. The central subject of this frieze is still debated; probably the hero is Theseus fighting giants at Pallene (Harrison, 2005). The west porch has a Centauromachy, which also could imply the presence of Theseus. Both pediments contained sculpture and there exist some fine large Parian fragments, but not enough for the subjects to be identified. The acroteria also seem to have been sizeable marble-draped figures.

The internal colonnade

The initial plan for the modestly sized cella interior was for a simple room with fresco decoration on plastered walls. Some scholars believe that, inspired by the Parthenon, a double Doric colonnade was added for which there was actually very little space (Fig. 76). The columns would have returned behind the statues, as in the Parthenon, in a row of three or more. Those on the sides would have been so close to the walls that they would have appeared more like a series of niches than a free-standing colonnade. In fact, it is not certain whether this rather problematic colonnade could have existed at all. (Dinsmoor 1968, Delivorrias 1997) Admittedly there were internal columns in the temple of Aphaia on Aigina, and this temple was of very similar dimensions to the Hephaisteion. However, the Hephaisteion also had to accommodate a substantial bronze group, standing on a wide base of Eleusinian limestone, still partly in position.

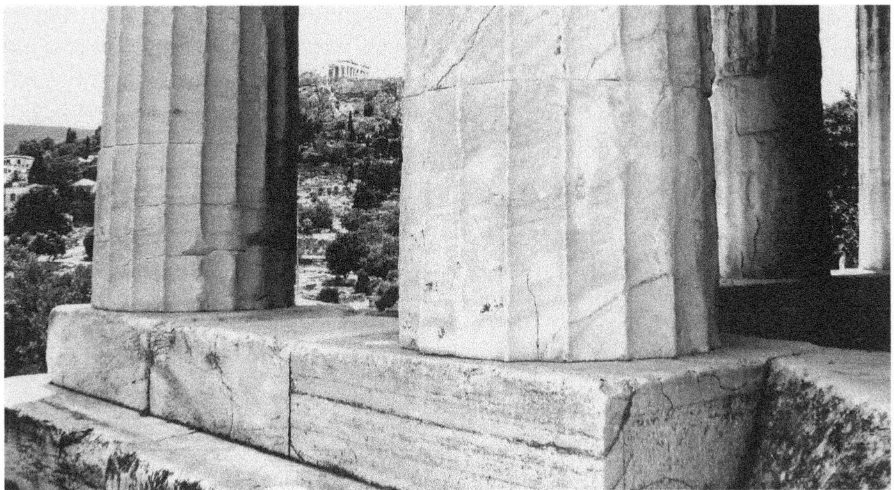

Fig. 75 Hephaisteion, view of Acropolis from the colonnade.

The cult statues

The cult statues (421–415) were joint offerings to Hephaistos and Athene in bronze by the sculptor Alcamenes. Large-scale bronze was more normally used for outdoor sculpture: its use here is a direct reference to the special domain of the smith god.

Fig. 76 shows a reconstruction of the cult statues in their setting. Athene is her tall gracious self with helmet and aegis: Hephaistos wears a workman's cap and workman's short tunic: he looks very much as Homer presents him in Book 18 of the *Iliad* where we see him in his workshop. Valerius Maximus (first century AD) tells us that 'the god's lameness was masked; he stands there displaying some trace of it unobtrusively beneath his garment.' To present a god in this down-to-earth way indicates a compliment to the artisans of Athens and a cheer for the democracy which played so great a part in winning the war.

These two gods together have special value for the Athenians. Hephaistos (who made the armour of Achilles) is the metalworking god or smith. Around this temple has been excavated plenty of evidence that this was the metalworkers' quarter where armour and weapons would have been produced. Clearly Hephaistos needed a special thank you from the Athenians for his help in defeating the Persians. Athene belongs here too – because she is everywhere in Athens, because she is the goddess of military strategy, and of victory; also, because she too is a craftsperson, patroness particularly of potters and weavers. Appropriately, the potters' quarter (Kerameikos) was behind the temple, adjacent to the armourers'. She is also the 'not really' consort of Hephaistos; he sits next to her on the Parthenon east frieze; he helps release her from the head of Zeus on the east pediment; he collaborates with her (as fellow craftsperson) at the Birth of Pandora on the pedestal of the Parthenos. As the metalworking god, Hephaistos is responsible for the success of the bronze sculpture by which gods (including himself) are revealed.

Fig. 76 Reconstruction of the interior of the Hephaisteion with cult statues of Athene and Hephaistos.

The two cult statues shared the large base of black Eleusinian limestone, still to be seen in situ. This was probably decorated with white marble or gilded relief figures dowelled on, just as on the Erechtheion frieze; dowel holes can still be seen.

It will be remembered that Hephaistos and Athene were the parents – although unconventionally – of Erechtheus/Ericthonius. The narrative frieze on the base is thought to have shown, not the conception, but the birth of the autochthonous child. The view from the colonnade links this temple by sight line with the Acropolis – especially the north side, birthplace of Erichthonius (Fig. 75).

Conclusion

It is often said that the reputation of the comparatively small temple of Hephaistos suffers from its proximity to the glories of the Acropolis. However, it should not be seen as a rival but as a complementary sanctuary. Together, the two sanctuaries sandwich the vital areas of civic and social activity in Athens.

CHAPTER 13
VIEWS AND THEIR MEANINGS: THE ACROPOLIS AND ITS SURROUNDINGS

At Delphi and Olympia, we have seen that buildings could be placed in conscious relationship to other buildings. This often happens where a new structure is added to a very ancient setting, or next to a significant pre-existing element; for example, the temple of Zeus at Olympia had to be placed in relation to the ancient ash altar of Zeus.

The Athenian Acropolis was, to a certain extent built on a cleared site. However, this is only partly true. There were landscape elements and topography; there were pre-existing shrines; there was myth-history; there were customs, altars, ceremonies, that all had to be considered. There was also the architecture itself to be set off at its best. Each building had to do maximum service, aesthetically as well as in a practical sense. The Acropolis buildings that we have looked at were incredibly expensive. They represent an enormous investment of time, skill and attention, as well as money. They were a terrific chance for Athens to make the most of a rare opportunity. The following sections will explore how the Acropolis buildings may relate to the wider landscape around, and also how the sanctuary rock with its buildings would appear when seen from the wider landscape.

The view from the west

The view from the west is the major view, looking towards the public entrance and the ceremonial gateway. The view from the west (Fig. 77) is also the one from which the entire Acropolis line-up fully makes visual sense. From every compass-point, something interesting can be seen rising over the Acropolis rim, even today; in the pristine state of the buildings, there would have been so much more. But only from the west do the buildings range themselves into a single unified composition. Not only do the four major façades (though architecturally the backs) appear from their individual best angle, but also, from a distant and level point west, all the buildings fall into a perfect relationship with each other. Even the somewhat questionable west view of the Erechtheion now makes sense. It 'reads' as three linked entities, the central part with columns and pediment appearing as a quite conventional temple above a precinct wall. The Parthenon is revealed as the glorious crown of the hill, being by far the largest and highest up. The Nike below it closes the view; by inclining to the left, it pulls attention back to the centre.

Fig. 77 View of the Acropolis from the Pnyx.

There the Propylaia, even at a distance, opens its powerful wings and repeats, on the lower level, the great theme of the Parthenon Doric front. Also, central and clearly visible would have been the twinkling spear of the twelve-metre bronze Athene Promachos (see Fig. 38).

What is this high western viewpoint from which the whole line-up makes sense? It is the Pnyx, the designated meeting place for the full democratic Assembly of Athenian citizens (Figs. 77 and 78). This low hill or ridge faces the Acropolis across lower ground, and is a short walk from the Agora. After the expulsion of the Peisistratid tyrant, Hippias, in 510 BC, meetings were at first held in the Agora; but by 500 BC, the Pnyx had been set up for the purpose. It became an obvious symbol of freedom, and of the democracy – under which Athens had repulsed the invader, Persia, and her own old tyrant, Hippias.

Whether the speakers faced the Acropolis, or whether the assembled citizen body faced the Acropolis (as each did at different phases) hardly mattered. What was important was the visual link between the two civic spaces, one housing the most democratic process of the city and the other the worship of the goddess, symbol, protectress and patroness of the city. The sense of visual satisfaction derived from the view underlines the purposefulness of this connection.

A sculptural focus for the western view was Pheidias's colossal bronze statue of Athene, sometimes known as Promachos (fighter in the front rank). On Panathenaic vases, Athene is shown ready to attack with her spear: whether the bronze Athene stood in attacking pose is not known (Hurwit 2004, pp. 80–84). However, her spear and helmet gave her a military connotation in reference to the Persian wars. According to Pausanias she was created from the spoils from Marathon (Pausanias 1.28.2). This monumental Athene greeted the visitor to the Acropolis at the entrance, and her base was aligned with the ruined Athene temple, and with the sight line towards Salamis. Equally, as Pausanias tells, she was visible from the sea at Sounion, off the Attic coast.

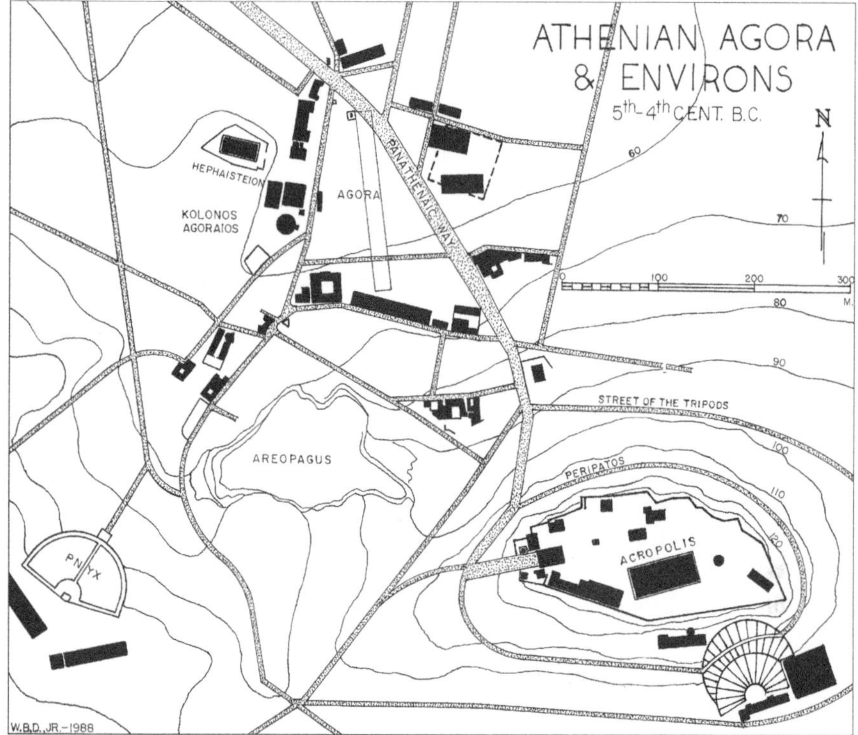

Fig. 78 The Acropolis and its environs.

In Sophocles's *Ajax*, the chorus of homesick sailors, trapped at Troy, imagine this view of home:

> Oh to be rounding the wave-washed wooded cliff
> below flat headland Sounion;
> there to greet holy Athens. (Sophocles: *Ajax* 1218–1224)

The glitter of Athene's spear would have marked out the Acropolis from afar, from Sounion and from Salamis, greeting the visitor or those returning home.

Looking west from the Acropolis

The westward view may be obtained either from the crowded Propylaea, or more conveniently from the western Nike buttress. Leaning on the Nike balustrade, the ancient viewer had a splendid view of the Pnyx; much closer at hand he would see the Areopagus; and in the distance, the sea and Salamis.

All these various elements are linked in the history and symbolism of Athenian victory. Salamis was the decisive sea-battle in the Persian war. Sea power was vital for

Athens in war and peace. The significance of the Pnyx is as the political gathering place of the demos, set up some time after the fall of the tyrants in 510 BC. The strange reddish rock to the right, the Hill of Ares (Areopagos), was said to be the site of the Amazons' encampment when, in the heroic age, they besieged and attacked the Acropolis, and were beaten back by Theseus. This victory is commemorated on the Nike pediment just at the back of the viewer who is looking west, and will be seen again on the west metopes of the Parthenon and on the shield of Athene Parthenos. All three times it will be paired with the Battle of Gods and Giants. Emphatically, attacks on Athens and on Olympus are paralleled.

Although it was King Theseus who defeated the Amazons, democracy still is in the picture, because Theseus is credited with founding Athenian democracy (see p. 41). The mythology has its important fifth-century parallel. The real-life Persians also encamped upon the Areopagos in 480/479 BC and from it attacked and sacked the Acropolis; ultimately, they were defeated by (in the Athenian view) the Athenian democracy. Apart from Marathon, the most defining contribution to Athenian victory was the sea-battle of Salamis, the site of which can be clearly seen from the Nike bastion. Ironically, the evacuated Athenians from their refuge on the island of Salamis could have actually seen the fires of their burning Acropolis: now, on that once desecrated site, pointedly and proudly rose the new monuments of victory. No wonder the Nike balustrade was carved with the most seductive, luxuriant series of 50-odd Nikai, honouring the dead, the victors and their patroness Athene Nike.

There are further links between the Pnyx, democracy, victory and the Parthenon. The west pediment of the Parthenon (Fig. 51) shows the contest between Athene and Poseidon for patronage of Athens. The two great central gods were flanked by rearing horses. As the pediment narrows, many smaller figures crowd in, both male and female. Those figures – who are ancient kings, heroes, princesses, local nymphs and rivers – are all there to represent Athens – they are there to vote. They choose Athene, and who could argue with that choice? The voters showed their wisdom in picking a victory-bringing patroness, and so give strong encouragement to the citizen body of the fifth century to exercise their right and duty of voting.

But there is also Poseidon. Two major gods, Athene and Poseidon, form the centrepiece of the pediment in their full creative power and as divine antagonists. The clash of gods makes an exciting pediment. It may be objected that it is odd to show a god as the loser as well as a goddess as the victor. However, we need not think of Poseidon as a loser: he will receive worship in the Erechtheion where he had his priest alongside the priestess of Athene Polias. It is true that he will not give his name to Athens – but on the pediment, his magnificent nude musculature is, if anything, more prominent than the slender draped figure of Athene; he is taller and bulkier, and his stretched leg overlaps that of Athene up to the knee (Fig. 51). The traditional superiority of male against female is visually maintained, but more particularly, the balance of sea power against land-power is asserted. It was by sea that the Athenians were victorious in the Persian wars: Athens owes victory to Poseidon as well as to the warrior Athene. Facing west to Salamis, it is clear the city cannot do without him. By this sculpture he receives honour and so does democracy – Athenian democracy and sea power go hand-in-hand – because the navy was manned by citizen oarsmen.

This is reading the Parthenon pediment according to the victory theme; but the gifts of Athene and Poseidon have equal relevance to peace. The benefits of Athene's olive tree are clear: the olive was an essential commodity in the ancient world as its oil was used for lighting, cooking and washing. Yet Athens was absolutely dependent for prosperity on her foreign trade, and this was of course carried on by sea. Athenian pots of Athenian oil and wine went all over the known world to be exchanged for other goods which, with her limited soil and climate, she could not produce. This peacetime collaboration of land and sea further explains the conjunction of deities on the pediment.

Looking south from the Acropolis

From the south wall, the viewer could look down on a range of shrines and sanctuaries. The most important was the sanctuary, temple and theatre of Dionysus (Fig. 78). Here the major drama festivals were staged with their attendant processions and civic ceremonies. Next to it was the Odeion, the covered concert hall built by Pericles. And clustered in the cliffs of the Acropolis rock itself were various shrines.

If the awakening male nude to the left of the east Parthenon pediment is Dionysus (Fig. 52), as usually interpreted, then he is looking over to his own theatre-sanctuary. If, however, as some suggest, he was actually Heracles, then *he* would be looking at his own shrine of Kynos Arges, also to be found a short distance from the wall.

The view from the south

The southern Acropolis wall was particularly well built up with smooth vertical masonry. From the theatre, the corner of the Parthenon could have been seen rearing up above it, unmistakably. That glimpse of Athene's temple underlined many a political point made on stage; wherever a stage-city was set, the real Athens was never far from the dramatist's mind, or the audience's; for example, when Antigone unknowingly sees distant Athens which will be the salvation of her father Oedipus, the actor would surely gesture towards the citadel:

> Father, miserable Oedipus, the towers that roof
> The city, so far as I can see, are still far off . . .
>
> (Sophocles, *Oedipus at Colonus* 14–17)

Looking east from the Acropolis

The Acropolis plateau rises gradually towards the east. From its furthest point, the drop is dramatic, the view mountainous. From the space in front of the Parthenon temple, rocky peaks can be seen to lift above the parapet, but otherwise, the world beyond the Acropolis is cut off, and this area would have been strictly an abode of gods only. In fact, it contained other sacred areas, perhaps without buildings, such as the altar of Zeus Polieus, protector of the city. This is reflected in the god-focused east front, where only gods are celebrated – except on the frieze where the Athenians bring their offerings in solemn procession, reflecting real-life ritual.

The view from the east

The eastern view of a temple should be the principal one, architecturally speaking. But because of the rising ground, nothing can be seen from below at this point but precipitous cliffs.

It was these cliffs, thought impregnable, which enterprising Persians scaled during the siege of the Acropolis in 480/79. In the natural rock, below the vertical buttressing, there is a large cave with a sanctuary sacred to Aglauros, one of the daughters of Erechtheus, linking the east cliff with the main family sites on the north. Pausanias tells us of further events in the life of Erichthonios when:

> Athene put Erichthonios into a chest and gave him to Aglauros and her sisters Herse and Pandrosos, ordering them not to meddle with the (contents). Pandrosos was obedient, but the other two opened the chest, saw Erichthonios (who was snake-legged) and went raving mad; they threw themselves from the sheer cliff of the Acropolis. (Pausanias I.18.2)

This east cliff would have been the site of their suicide. (Obedient Pandrosos had her shrine next to the Erechtheion.) In a variant story, Aglauros willingly sacrificed herself in obedience to a prophecy, leaping to save Athens, so her sacred cave would have inspired the ephebes, the young trainee warriors, whose base was situated nearby. Appropriately, it was at the sanctuary of self-sacrificing Aglauros that each cohort of new ephebes made their famous oath, marking the start of their service and dedication to the city.

The north cliff of the Acropolis

In the north Acropolis cliff-face are found other impressive caves including the Long Rocks, scene of Apollo's rape of Creusa, and sacred to him.

Also, somewhere on this side of the Acropolis is the site of a mysterious ceremony recorded by Pausanias which was carried out annually by women and girls responsible for the weaving of the ceremonial peplos. The House of the Arrhephoroi was on the summit of the north cliff, and below it was the remnant of a Mycenaean well-shaft, traversed by dangerous steps. ('Arrhephoros' means 'carrier of secret items'.) Pausanias records the ceremony like this:

> Two young girls dwell near the temple of Athene Polias – the Athenians call them Arrhephoroi; these girls live for a season next to the goddess, and when the festival comes around they perform ceremonies during the night as follows. They place on their heads what Athene's priestess gives them to carry, and neither she who gives it nor they who carry it know what it is. Within the city not far off is a precinct called Aphrodite in the Gardens containing a natural underground passage; this is where the girls go down. At the bottom, they leave what they were carrying, and they pick up something else and bring it back covered up. They are then sent away and other girls are brought to the Acropolis instead of them. (Pausanias 1.27.4)

This is the finale of the yearly cycle: the mysterious things carried recall the myth of Athene's care for the earth-born baby, Erichthonios, entrusted long ago to the royal princesses.

Looking north from the Acropolis

From the north side of the Acropolis (Fig. 79) the viewer could survey the Agora and the broad processional route linking the Acropolis to the city wall and Sacred Gate, starting-point of the Panathenaic procession. From the gate, the Panathenaic route crosses the Agora, passes the Eleusinion (a city outpost of the Eleusis sanctuary) and finally winds up between the Areopagus and the Acropolis till it reaches the foot of the straight ramp leading to the Propylaia (see Frontispiece).

Fig. 79 The north wall of the Acropolis showing column drums (left) and triglyphs (right).

The Sacred Gate and the adjacent Dipylon Gate lead out of the city, through the Kerameikos burial area just outside the walls, to Eleusis on the coast where the famous mystery cult was celebrated. Between the gates, a large fourth-century building, the Pompeion, housed the equipment and practical preparations for the Panathenaic procession. Here and in the Agora, many of the festival-related activities took place, such as feasting and competitions.

The view of the ramparts from the north

From the Agora, the view of the Acropolis is particularly intriguing. It was an important view since it was in the Agora that the daily public life of the city – social, commercial, legal and governmental – was largely lived.

From this angle, it is architecturally very satisfactory that the north porch of the Erechtheion is scaled so large – it shows up well above the ramparts, almost as a temple front in its own right (Fig. 79).

In the north wall under the Erechtheion, the rebuilt rampart incorporates architectural pieces salvaged from the Persian sack, arranged in a deliberate 'architectural' order. To the left, looking up, are unfluted column drums; to the right and higher up the cliff, is a short stretch of triglyph frieze. The column drums must come from the partly built pre-Parthenon temple – they are unfinished. The triglyphs are from the 'old Athene temple'.

This display of ruined elements was inserted into the north wall at some time after the Persian sack of 480/79. It is usually interpreted in the spirit of the oath of Plataea: 'I will not rebuild …'. But by the time the Acropolis had risen in greater beauty from the ashes, these fragments take on a more triumphant note. They can be read as a layer of history. Like the Mycenaean masonry and shrines visible under the bastion of Athene Nike, they speak of the past; and they carry the more glorious future aloft. In a sense, by crowning the mass of the rock itself with a suggestion of architectural form, columns topped by triglyphs as they would be on a temple, they convert the whole of the rock to a kind of 'natural temple' – above which the new glory of Athens can rise yet higher.

Furthermore, this is the sacred earth from which was born Erichthonius/Erechtheus, ancestor of the race, and where his sacred snake still lived. This precious ground is full of mysteries, at which the triglyph wall hints.

All this mystical history makes it very appropriate that there is also a clear sight line across the Agora between the Erechtheion and the Hephaisteion (Fig. 75 and Fig. 78). Hephaistos, who also receives worship in the Erechtheion, is honoured together with Athene in his own temple. We have seen that there is reference to Erichthonius under the bronze cult statues of his quasi-parents in the Hephaisteion. One may stand in the porch of Hephaistos's temple, looking out at the very spot on the Acropolis which originated the autochthonous race of Athens. The resulting sight line across the Agora neatly embraces the city, linking the house of the sturdy worker-god with the Acropolis and its more aristocratic associations.

CHAPTER 14
THE SANCTUARY OF APOLLO EPIKOURIOS AT BASSAE

High on its lonely ridge in the snowy mountains of Arcadia, the sanctuary of Apollo Epikourios at Bassae holds a special fascination for many (see Map 1). It sits alone, some distance from its founding city, Phigaleia. Despite its isolation, it is architecturally rich, and is the first building to incorporate all three of the Greek orders.

Once striking in its landscape setting (Fig. 80), today the temple can be seen only under a permanent covering or tent, which increases the gloom of its natural dark colouring. The restored structure now stands alone, although the foundations of other buildings can be seen scattering the hillside nearby. The almost complete frieze and some other sculptural fragments in late-fifth-century style are displayed in the British Museum.

Bassae carries on the architectural development we have seen on the Acropolis: in fact, Pausanias tells us it was designed by Iktinos, architect of the Parthenon, and it may well be a direct continuation of his work in Athens. Iktinos was pleased to push the rules in Athens; in Bassae they are pushed even further.

The temple is outwardly Doric, in a plain and rather unrefined style. The exterior suits its dedication to a soldier god, Apollo Epikourios, and suits its magnificent but bleak setting in bare mountain terrain. The building material is the sombre local limestone with a strange, fissured surface. Sculptural detail was carried out in marble. The tiled roof was also of marble, as we know from Pausanias. According to RF Rhodes (1995 n.3 p. 202) quoting FA Cooper, the harsh limestone was not stuccoed. There would have been a dramatic contrast between its extra rough finish and the smooth marble elements of the roof tiles, antefixes and sculptures: a combining of the roughness of the mountainside itself, and the smooth brightness of Apollo.

The building

There were six façade columns and fifteen to the flanks, an elongated, archaic proportion (Fig. 81). At 14.5 × 38.25 metres, the temple is not very large and refinements are minimal. There seems to be no upward curvature of the stylobate; if there is slight entasis of the Doric columns, it is almost imperceptible. On the two short ends, the columns are slightly thicker than those on the flanks: those on the flanks are spaced slightly more closely than those on the ends. Despite the late-fifth-century date, these are archaic traits.

Fig. 80 Temple of Apollo Epikourios at Bassae, from the north, *c.* 420 BC.

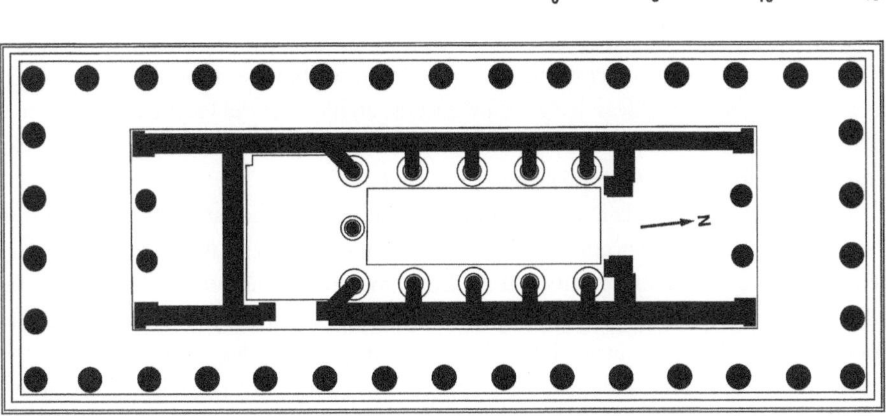

Fig. 81 Ground plan of the temple of Apollo Epikourios, Bassae.

The two porches in antis are deep, the door of the pronaos being almost on a level with the fifth column, and the opisthodomos slightly shallower.

There was apparently no sculpture on the exterior metopes; it is uncertain whether there was any on the pediments, since they are shallow.

Surprisingly, on the vertical face of the sloping cornices of the pediments was a beautiful carved anthemion: Doric temples routinely had painted patterns on cornices, but carved borders were an Ionic feature. This oddity hinted at the richness to be found on the interior. (A section of this carving can be seen today in the British Museum.)

Figural sculpture started on the inner porches. The porch metopes contained scenes depicting departures and arrivals: in the entrance porch, the return of Apollo in Spring from the land of the Hyperboreans; on the back porch, the departure of the Daughters of Leucippus, seized by the Dioskouroi. If these interpretations are correct, the theme of arrival and departure would be particularly relevant to the sun-god in his daily and yearly cycle: in this harsh landscape of long winters, the return of spring must be especially welcome. Arrival and departure are also of keen interest to the professional soldier, especially as ancient warfare was seasonal, ceasing for the winter.

So far, the temple mainly follows the Doric formula, but with a certain archaism. The fifth-century marble roof had some archaic features: figured antefixes, and flowering acroteria with central discs. These echo the archaic terracotta roof of the previous temple, as excavated fragments show (Kelly 1995). Another obvious oddity is the north/south orientation with the main entrance facing north. Inside are two interconnecting chambers, the cella and a further small adyton. (It is the existence of this adyton which has demanded the fifteen flank columns – as at Delphi.) From this small chamber, a side entrance opens onto the eastern colonnade. This means that despite the odd north/south orientation, the rising sun can still strike into the temple (Fig. 81).

The cella

In the cella are several surprises (Fig. 82). The interior colonnade is Ionic in two rows of five; each row is attached to its sidewall by short spur walls. It is now thought that this oddity preserves the archaic plan (Kelly 1995). (We have also seen spur walls in the archaic temple of Hera at Olympia.) However, no columns have quite looked like these before. The capitals are Ionic, with rather heavy and widely spreading capitals of a unique design, which shows volutes on three sides, instead of the usual two. The reconstruction shows why this was necessary, given the sharp angle of viewing. The shafts are not made up of real drums, but of shaped sections which tie into the cella walls (Fig. 83). From the front, they resemble complete columns, but from the side, the rounded fluted section merges with an unfluted straight spur wall. At the bottom, they swing out into large, rather flattened bases. (The swinging profile of these bases is an exaggerated version of the conventional type.) The bases are almost complete discs, interrupted only at the rear where the connecting spur joins the column to the wall. An advantage arises from the use of semi-engaged Ionic columns, even such strange ones as these. The tall thin proportion makes them 'space-savers', as they were in the Parthenon opisthodomos. Here there is an even greater need to save space, as this cella is quite small. The use of engaged 'columns' – instead of two free-standing colonnades – makes the tiny area spatially viable as well as interesting with its unusual deep alcoves.

These columns are Ionic in a Doric building, a combination already familiar from the Parthenon and Propylaia, but here their peculiar forms arouse an additional feeling of strangeness and disorientation. The ancient viewer, looking towards the adyton and the eastern side-doorway, would have been astonished to see a limestone shaft blocking the way between the cella and the adyton and, on it, in glimmering white marble and colourful paint, a completely new kind of capital. This was the first **Corinthian** capital

Fig. 82 Interior reconstruction of the temple of Apollo Epikourios looking towards the adyton, Bassae.

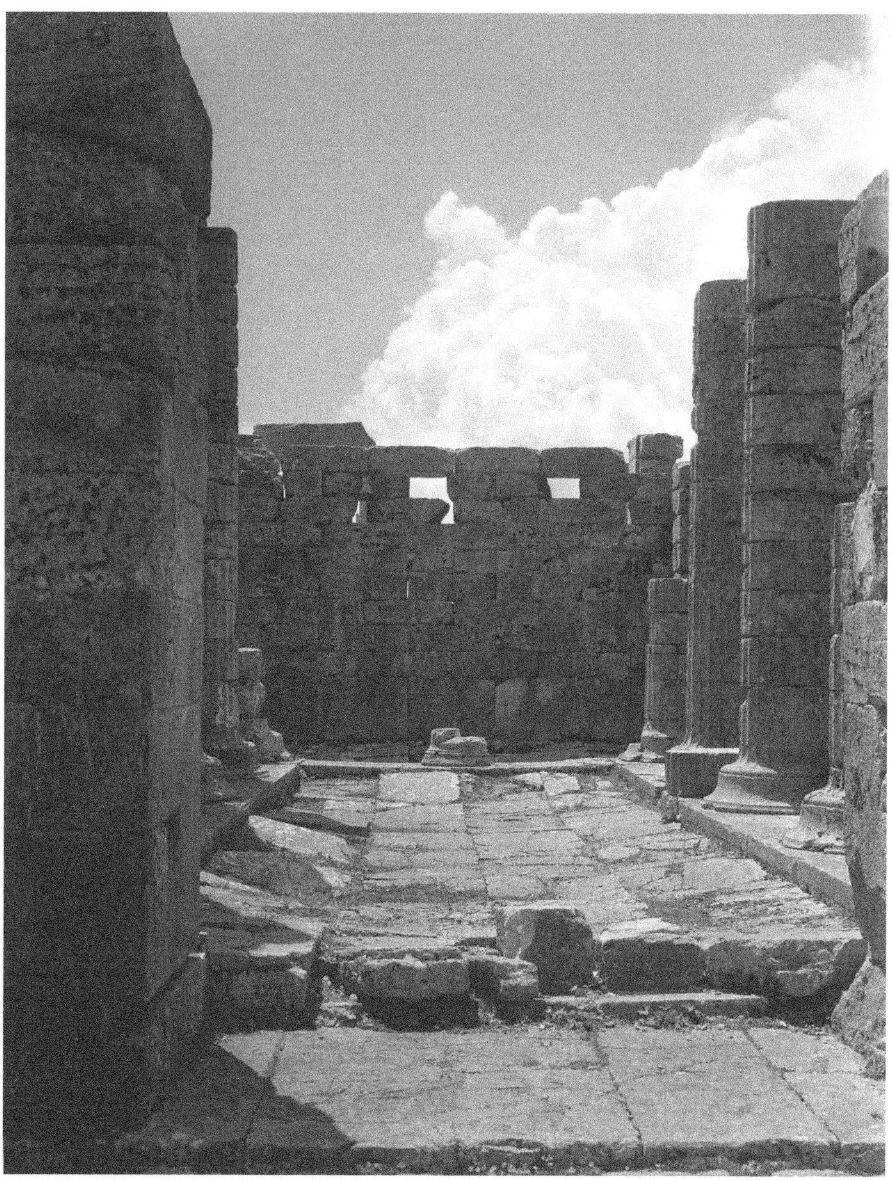

Fig. 83 View of interior of temple of Apollo Epikourios, Bassae, from the north.

that we know of, maybe the first in architecture (Fig. 84). Its particular suitability to the free-standing position is that the design of the four-sided capital works well from every direction.

The two Ionic end spur columns towards the south – which flank and frame the Corinthian central column – are set at an angle. This can best be understood by reference to the plan (Fig. 81). Opinions differ as to whether these too were Corinthian, but it seems unlikely and would spoil the impact of the unique newcomer. This special column would have appeared differently according to whether the eastern door was letting in light. When illuminated, the adyton would show the silhouetted column up as dark, but if the cella was the only lit area, the column would stand out clearly against the dark adyton.

Sadly, the new capital was mysteriously destroyed, leaving only fragments and a sketch that was made on the day of discovery in the early nineteenth century AD. But the slim pale base is still to be seen in situ (Fig. 83), contrasting suggestively with its gloomy surroundings and with the wide plate-like bases of the Ionic columns. Callimachos, the sculptor who created the elaborate, bronze lamp cover 'like a palm tree' in the Erechtheion, has been suggested as the probable designer of the elaborately decorative new capital.

This early version of the Corinthian capital design is used again very soon inside the Tholos at Marmaria, Delphi (cf. p. 55). Part of an example can be seen in the Delphi museum. It is a combination of a basket-shaped core, adorned with scrolls and leaves.

Fig. 84 Temple of Apollo Epikourios: Corinthian column restoration drawing.

At this stage of development, it is still fairly flat in conception. By the time of the later tholos at Epidauros (*c.* 360 BC) which has an interior colonnade of Corinthian columns, it has become more fully sculptural. The fourth-century temple of Athene Alea at Tegea, also in Arcadia, not far from Bassae, uses developed Corinthian columns for its engaged interior colonnade, with a smaller Ionic colonnade above. At first, the Corinthian style of column was preserved for rather specialised interior situations, possibly having a chthonic significance – which would also link with the idea of prophecy. Eventually its beautiful and versatile appearance made it the style of choice for any showy, luxury building (especially for the Romans).

The frieze

The engaged colonnade of five Ionic flanking columns each side and one central Corinthian column supported an interior entablature and frieze. As far as we know, this is a 'first', maybe induced by a factor as prosaic as the bad weather conditions outside, or maybe a natural step on from the semi-interior frieze of the Parthenon, or both. The frieze features an Amazonomachy and a Centauromachy. Apollo himself appears, with his twin sister Artemis, in a chariot drawn by deer. Together they pursue enemies round the walls – Lapiths fight Centaurs – Heracles is there too, taking the belt of the Queen of the Amazons (Fig. 85).

Opinions differ greatly about the frieze. Some critics find it heavy and provincial; to others it is rich and exciting. The figure style is stocky, perhaps. But the action is dynamic. Drapery is more than wind-blown – it writhes with a life of its own – or it

Fig. 85 Interior frieze, temple of Apollo Epikourios, from section above Corinthian column. Heracles takes the belt of the Amazon queen.

stretches taut between the sturdy thighs of fighting women. Each group is linked to the next by flailing limbs, cloaks or rearing horse-bodies.

Critics say that the frieze would have been invisible in the darkness of the interior: but it seems likely that oil lamps would have been suspended to illuminate it: a flickering light would have made the shadowed limbs and drapery seem to flutter and move. The relief is very deep, especially compared with the shallow Parthenon frieze. The composition is compact and crowded, lacking space but taking great advantage of depth. As Fig. 86 shows, there would be a strong **chiaroscuro** which would have been especially effective in artificial light. This frieze is harsher and harder than the Acropolis sculptures, but it seems appropriate to its mountain setting and its soldier deity. It would have made a powerful impression in the small-scale cella.

Not only does the frieze represent dynamic action, but also introduces a new quality of pathos and intensity. This can be seen throughout the frieze: for example, the body-language of a nobly scaled woman, trying to save her clinging child, shows her yearning strongly away from an attacking centaur: the deep shadows add to the tragic mood (Fig. 86).

Today, the Bassae frieze is beautifully displayed in the British Museum, in a purpose-built room that replicates the dimensions of the temple cella, and is lit in subdued

Fig. 86 Detail of Ionic frieze; temple of Apollo Epikourios: Centaur attacking Lapith woman with baby.

artificial light. Unusually, this frieze encloses the viewer, who is thus cut off from the outside world, and engulphed in the intense and hectic world of the sculptures.

Dating the temple

Scholars were puzzled by many factors when it came to dating the temple. The dullness of the exterior, its north-south orientation, its archaic proportion and its odd side door made some ask whether the temple itself was in truth archaic with an updated cella decor. But, it is now believed that this temple is simply based on its predecessors on the site. In fact, archaic foundations have been excavated just a few metres away from the temple, to a similar scale, with all the same oddities of layout: the length, the adyton, the eastern side-opening, the interior spur columns: these were executed with a stone wall-base, mud brick above and wooden columns. The fifth-century designer brilliantly reinterpreted these forms in marble, and combined tradition with modernity. (Kelly, 1995) This conclusion leaves Pausanias's start date of 430–429 BC perfectly persuasive, with sculpture probably completed by about 425 (although some have dated it as late as 390 on stylistic grounds).

Aesthetically, the cella creates a thrill of difference by contrast with the plain exterior. Why is it so wild? Is it because the remoteness allowed Iktinos a free hand for experiment? Or did the city committee ask for a cutting-edge design? This seems a bit unlikely – till we notice the fourth-century temple of Tegea, also in remote Arcadia, and even more experimental. Tegea was designed by the sculptor Skopas who ran with the idea of interior mixed-order columns, used a central eastern side door, and also introduced extreme emotion to Greek sculpture, building on what we have now seen in the Bassae frieze.

The statue

It is not clear whether there was a cult statue in the temple of Apollo. There may be some evidence of a statue base in the south-west corner of the adyton. In this case, the statue would have received the light of the rising sun, especially on its particular feast-day, guided by the careful placement of the eastern opening, but would not have been clearly visible from the cella, or the main entrance. Pausanias mentions a twelve-foot-high bronze statue of Apollo Epikourios, which was moved from Bassae to Megalopolis where he saw it displayed 'in front of the precinct . . . to help ornament the Great City' (Pausanias 8.30.3). This sounds like an exterior work rather than a cult statue, which would need to be inside the temple. There are some sculptural fragments of a large **acrolithic** (i.e. with only the hands, feet and face of stone) statue from the temple (now in the British Museum together with the frieze and the metope fragments), but they are thought to be Hellenistic or Roman and not original to the design. The central column in any case gave rise to the problem faced by the earliest temples with their central colonnades: it rather interfered with a satisfactory placement of a cult statue. To place the statue centrally either in front of, or behind, the column would be a pity, as the one would obscure the other. One intriguing suggestion is that the central column took the place of a statue, and its slender shaft and foliage-like capital represented the elegant long-haired god himself. Iphigeneia's dream in Euripides's *Iphigeneia in Tauris* could suggest this: 'One single pillar … was left/… From the capital/ streamed yellow locks, and, taking human voice, it spoke' (Eur: *Iph Taur.* 50–2).

Apollo Epikourios

'Apollo the Helper': according to Pausanias, Apollo received this title for his help in stopping the plague of 430 or 420. However, as the sanctuary itself is evidently far older than the present temple, other explanations have been sought for the name. *Epikouros* can have the specific meaning of 'mercenary soldier', and the tough mountain men traditionally added to their meagre living by following this profession. They might have adopted Apollo as their patron specifically for this activity, or simply as their helper and ally generally; and the name could be as old as the sanctuary. Many finds of votive offerings of specially made miniature bronze armour back a military view of the cult at Bassae. Apollo as concerned with soldiers is unexpected but not unique, and fits the needs of the people who worshipped him here.

Phigaleia was the polis which built the sanctuary. Even for the people of Phigaleia, the temple was remote and hard to reach; only a long hard trek from the city would bring the worshipper to the dramatic goal. Judging from the harshness of temperature even in spring, the winter must have made it largely unviable and snow-bound. The return of the sun-god from the land of the Hyperboreans would have been very welcome!

Pausanias tells us that Iktinos designed the temple (Pausanias 8.41.9). This information might seem a bit far-fetched – but the temple shows signs of similarity with the Parthenon. There is respect for tradition and precedent. There is willingness to experiment and to find new solutions to fit the specific brief. There is the mix of orders. (This is the first known building to include all three.) There is the Ionic frieze – and, intriguingly, it quotes the Parthenon sculpture: Heracles and the Amazon queen adopt the same chiastic pose as that of Athene and Poseidon on the west pediment (Figs. 51, 85). This section of the frieze was placed in the prime position, immediately above the Corinthian column. By referring to the former work, the quotation could act as a sort of signature.

Pericles had his enemies – and we know that they attacked him through Pheidias, engineering the sculptor's exile from Athens (and resulting incidentally in the commission for the great Zeus of Olympia). It may be that Iktinos too found it convenient to accept work far away from Athens. If so, we can see that for him too his exile did not cramp, but rather released, his creativity.

CHAPTER 15
THE AGE OF GREEK EXPANSION TO THE WEST: PAESTUM

This section will explore a whole colony, or at least its sacred buildings. Paestum is a wonderful site to visit because of its completeness. It is easy to assimilate, and it has an excellent museum.

Paestum is remarkably complete because it was abandoned in antiquity and then overgrown. Due to its marshiness at that time it became malarial and unhealthy and remained so throughout the Middle Ages. Thanks to these factors, it was left alone, and was not treated as a quarry for building stone as were so many ancient temples and other structures. As a result, it has three standing temples, each quite different, and all in a good state of preservation. Additionally, there are other ancient remains from the Greek era, not least the city walls. As well as these, there are structures from the Roman period, such as an arena, a paved road, and so on. The Romans luckily took on the temples as they were, so they remained in use for a long time, fairly unchanged.

Not only is there a satisfying degree of completeness in the site, but also the temples themselves are architecturally fascinating, innovative and original. They offer themselves as examples of western architecture, but remain unique as well.

What was a colony?

It is well known that the Greeks, from at least the eighth century BC onwards, were spreading out to other lands, eastward and westward, to settle there in groups usually called colonies. The Greek word for this is **apoikia** – 'a journey from home', or 'a home away from home'. The group of a colony always had a leader, called an **oikistes**, or **oikist**. This leader tended to be an aristocrat, or member of the ruling class, though their reason for embarking on the enterprise might even be an expulsion from the home city.

The colony, once founded, was not what is meant by the word in modern history. It was a new, autonomous settlement. Certainly, there would be a relationship with the mother-city, but there was no prescription for this. Probably in each case the relationship was different or slightly different, and may have been close, complex, difficult or indifferent. Another difference from a modern colony is the time-scale. Many Greek colonies were planted from very early dates, and developed in tandem with their mother cities. To put this in chronological context: when Poseidonia (Paestum), the first colony we will look at, was founded, as late as *c.* 600 BC, Athens had not yet built her Archaic temples, let alone her classical ones. And Olympia was still thinking about its earliest temple, the temple of Hera, *c.* 580 BC. Even the early Archaic temple of Artemis, Corfu, was still to come, also in *c.* 580. The colonies kept pace with the development of mainland architecture in their own way from the beginning.

Some colonies were successful; others made several attempts at relocating, or failed completely. It was an adventurous proceeding. With time, the advice and blessing of Delphi came to be considered extremely important. There were few guarantees, but a favourable oracle was the best one available. A particular concern would be finding a territory that could be made to work well in a hurry. Another would be the indigenous population. Would it be hostile, or prepared to accommodate newcomers; would it need to be conquered or expelled? A fine virgin land without other claimants would be the best situation.

Reasons for sending out a colony were nearly as many as there were examples. Some would have been a result of internal affairs, pressure for resources, overpopulation or desire for more land. Some may have been to create useful outposts or trading contacts for the benefit of the mother city. Some may have been provoked by a desire to get rid of certain unwanted political elements, who could be more use elsewhere than at home.

Land-hunger

The *Odyssey*, epic of travel and domesticity, reveals two kinds of yearning. There is the joy of adventure – and there is the longing for home. As the poem advances, the longing for home and for the recovery of identity becomes the dominant theme. Yet at the opening of the poem, the hero is introduced as one who "... saw the cities of many peoples, and learnt their ways" (*Odyssey* 1.2). He has an appetite for travel, and he is alert to differences in foreign laws and customs: difference is in itself valuable and interesting.

Reading the *Odyssey* with the colonising movement in mind highlights several emotive passages about land-hunger. When Odysseus stays the night on an uninhabited island opposite the Cyclopes's territory, he describes it as the ideal site for a colony. The land ...

> 'home of wild goats ... is capable of yielding any crop in due season. Along the shore are lush water meadows where the grapes would never fail; there is level land for ploughing, where they could be sure of a tall-standing crop at every harvest, because the subsoil is exceedingly rich. Also it has a safe harbor in which there is no need of moorings ... all your crew need do is beach their ship ... finally there is a stream of fresh water, running out of a cave.' (*Odyssey* 9.130)

Here is virgin land, begging for a group of colonists to exploit its potential. Meanwhile, the silly Cyclopes, who have no law, no development and no community life, dwell in full view of this asset but have no means or desire to claim it. The key to acquiring land is ships – which the Cyclopes have no skills to make.

In contrast, rocky Ithaka, Odysseus's ancestral kingdom, is a poor land, incapable of supporting horses. It does not even support cattle very well: they have to be kept on the mainland and brought over by ferry to be butchered. (*Odyssey* 20. 185) Telemachus says to Menelaus: 'In Ithaka there is no room for horses to run … it is pasture-land for goats and more attractive to my eyes than the sort of land where horses thrive.' (*Odyssey* 4. 605–10) Menelaus commends young Telemachus for his love of home, even though the boy is praising its poverty. Similarly, when Odysseus must explain to Calypso why he chooses to return home rather than stay with her, a goddess, this is his irreducible reason – the desire for home. Whatever else tiny Ithaka may be, it is home and stands for Odysseus's identity. Those in the real world who have opted, or been forced, to colonise will also want to quickly develop this particular quality, the sense of self, of community and home. They will work hard for success, and they will develop the pride of place that makes for identity. We shall see how two colonies, Poseidonia in South Italy and Akragas in Sicily, became physically distinctive by using architecture to reflect their prosperity.

Magna Graecia

Greeks, it seems, first went to Italy in order to trade. For example, they had a trading post on the island of Ischia (Pithekoussai), where other ethnic groups traded too; then later a Greek colony was started in Cumae, on the opposite mainland (near Naples). Greeks may have gone to the west coast of Italy seeking metals, which they could not get at home. A trading post was not, however, a colony. A colony was a developed and complete city planted in a new place, with autonomous laws and government, and the intention to be permanent. Greek cities soon began to send out many colonies to South Italy (Magna Graecia) and Sicily, as well as to the Eastern coasts of the Mediterranean, and even further afield.

Sybaris and Troizen

It seems to be agreed that Poseidonia was a colony of a colony – Sybaris in the 'instep of Italy's boot' (see Map 2). Sybaris had been founded in the first wave of Greek colonising to Italy in about 720 BC, and was, for a time, very successful. It also became proverbial for its luxurious way of life. All sorts of anecdotes circulated, such as the one about the absence of cocks in the city, as cockcrow would disturb the late sleep of the inhabitants, or the man who found a bed of rose petals gave him blisters. But maybe this reputation was malicious invention on the part of others. Sybaris was wealthy, yet had a turbulent history: its initial foundation involved harsh treatment of the indigenous peoples and destruction of their settlements, although the Sybarites later offered citizenship to them. K. Lomas (1993) describes the later attitude the moralising Romans had towards the rich cities of Magna Graecia: they would be expected to fail, due to their success and great wealth, leading to luxury and hubris (Ibid. pp. 14–17). Sybaris fits well into this pattern. Eventually, in 510 BC, Sybaris was destroyed, thanks to their aggressive politics and the consequent hostility from Greek neighbours. At that date, a second contingent of Sybarite exiles found refuge in the newer city, Poseidonia.

According to Aristotle, the settlers who founded Sybaris were a combination of Achaeans and Troizenians. This had led to trouble because, in his words:

> 'Groups of mixed origin tend towards faction, unless unanimity is achieved .... Therefore most cities that up to now have accepted joint settlers or additional settlers have split into factions; for example Achaeans settled at Sybaris jointly with Troezenians, and later, when the Achaean group had increased, they expelled the Troezenians.' (Aristotle *Politics* 5.1303a)

The ejected Troizenian section of population is thought to have gone to Poseidonia in about 600 BC, well before the fall of Sybaris in about 510 BC. This new land was on the west coast of Italy, about 50 miles south of Ischia and Cumae (near Naples). The name Poseidonia may well derive from the Troizenian origin of the new settlers, since Poseidon was an important figure in the coastal territory of Troizen in mainland Greece: he fought Athene for the honour of being patron of the land. (Pausanias 2.30.6). Strabo likewise says that Troezen was once called Poseidonia from its being sacred to Poseidon (Strabo 8. 6. 14). Although the contingent that eventually departed for the west coast of Italy, from Sybaris in the instep, were presumably born in Sybaris, their expulsion seemed to be based on their origins, so it would make sense for them to highlight this factor in naming their new foundation.

Paestum

So, Paestum was once **Poseidonia** – the land of Poseidon. Even today, it is easy to see it as the ideal and desirable site for a colony: a broad and fertile semi circle of coastal plain, dissected by a river, circled by low mountains, mild of climate yet well-watered. Although there is no obvious sign of an ancient port, there is more than one place for ships to beach safely, and the Greeks did not always feel the need to construct a harbour. The territory taken over by the Greek colonists actually ended at the Sele river, halfway up the plain. Immediately to the north were the Etruscans. To the east, deep in the mountains were the Lucanians, the tribes who were displaced by the colonists.

According to Strabo, the colonists landed somewhere on the coast where they made a defended outpost, and only later moved inland. It seems most likely that this first outpost was at Agropoli, a picturesque little promontory with a defensible high 'look-out' point protecting a natural harbour. On the high point or acropolis, a sanctuary was founded, probably dedicated to Poseidon, a suitable site for the god of the sea, looking over both sea and coast: Poseidon had brought them to that place and would hopefully protect them and grant future prosperity, and this seems to be the only place in Poseidonia where the god may have had a dedicated shrine. The sanctuary site is now covered over by a medieval castle, but ancient artefacts have been found including painted terracotta revetments, similar to those of the 'Basilica' in the city, proving the presence of Greeks of the early sixth century on that spot. This outpost marked the eventual southern boundary of the territory, just as the Heraion at Foce del Sele marked the northern boundary.

Outlining the Greek territory were various sanctuaries. The best known (because of its architectural sculptures) is the Heraion, the sanctuary of Argive Hera near the mouth of the river Sele. The site was once nearer the sea than it is today, so it marks both the northern boundary of the colony, and a possible river port. It could even have been Strabo's 'landing place'. At its peak, it was a large and busy sanctuary, linked to the city by road.

Another important sanctuary known now as Santa Venere, almost attached to the south side of the city, outside the wall, was probably dedicated to Aphrodite. Other smaller sanctuaries are found dotted around the plain and in the foothills. All these sanctuaries, dating from the early days of the new colony, established throughout the territory a sacred geography that marked the presence and ownership of the Greek colonists. Either in a second phase (according to Strabo), or more likely from the very beginning, the settlers developed Poseidonia itself, as a complete city.

The Greek city of Poseidonia lies a little way inland, and is about five miles south of the river Sele (Silaris) that formed the northern boundary of its chora or territory. The actual site for the city was chosen to take advantage of a lucky accident of geology: it takes up the area of a large natural platform of **travertine** stone or calcareous limestone, visible above the grassy plain. This platform provided a very stable basis for building on, and travertine also provided the main building material used for the monumental structures (Fig. 87).

Fig. 87 Part of city wall, sitting on travertine 'plate', Paestum

Paestum is now famous for its three well-preserved Greek temples, one being especially well-preserved. Today, they stand out boldly in the flat, grassy site, surrounded only by low vestiges of other buildings. Originally these were conspicuous urban sanctuaries, surrounded by lesser buildings, by religious and commercial activities, city crowds and housing. The temples roughly marked the extent of the city from one side to the other, two at the south and one to the north. Between them on the north-south axis lay the agora and civic structures, while stretching much further to the west and east were the residential areas. The city was walled from the beginning, with four large gateways on the compass points.

Starting a colony

From the beginning of the colony, defensive walls were built around the city: sacred areas were marked out within the walls, including space for future temples; space was also allocated to civic and residential purposes. Possibly the walls also enclosed parts that were not to be built on but could be safely devoted to food production, vegetables or livestock.

Homer describes how the perfect Phaeacian city was laid out: 'There the godlike (oikist)… laid out the walls of a new city, built houses, put up temples to the gods, and divided up the land for cultivation.' (*Odyssey* 6:2) This could be Poseidonia. A colony did not 'just grow' as a Greek mainland city might do, over time, and from scattered beginnings. It was in a sense an 'ideal city', initially planned and created as a whole (although of course it would be subject to change and vicissitudes as time went on). The imaginary 'colony' of Phaeacia gives a taste of the optimism, even glamour, attached to such a venture. Its fantasy luxury, its highly coloured architecture, and the blessing of the gods which causes the vegetable garden and orchard to be productive all the year round amaze the traveller Odysseus. The ground is fertile and well-watered: it is also highly cultivated and well-organised. The civilised Phaeacians have made optimum use of their asset. All of this may well reflect the sense of possibility and excitement in the real-life colonial enterprise.

Not all attempts at colonies were successful. For many reasons, a group might have to move on from their first choice of site. Virgil's Aeneas was forced by plague to move on from Crete after laying out plots for houses and temples, and making laws (*Aeneid* 3.135) and famously had several false starts before arriving at his destined place in Latium. Aeneas had advice from Delphi which was misinterpreted at the first effort. A real-life case was that of Battos, a man from Thera who was picked out by the Delphic oracle to found a colony at Cyrene in North Africa. He suffered many vicissitudes, but by finally obeying the oracle correctly, he was successful and was the first of a dynasty (Herodotus 4.150ff).

Some real-life Greeks of Phocaia in Asia Minor, forced from their city in 545 BC by Persian attacks, had almost more false starts than Aeneas. They first moved to Corsica where they already had a colony; however, they upset the local mainland peoples by practicing piracy and were sent packing. At one point the whole group even returned to their home area, and, according to Herodotus, many of them were so overwhelmed by homesickness that they braved the Persian danger and returned home (Herodotus 1.163–7). Eventually in *c.* 540 BC the main group found a peaceful refuge in Velia (Elea), 40 kilometres south of Poseidonia, and were able to make a successful colony, based on their skills of seafaring and trade rather than agriculture, as their territory was limited.

Poseidonia seems to have been successful from the first. Archaeology has not discovered any distinct signs of battle in the area, or any substantial prior settlements. There seems to have been an uneventful takeover of a sparsely occupied and promising site. Coexistence seems to have characterised the ongoing relationships with the indigenous neighbours, even those who must have been displaced and moved to the hills. There are indications that there was cooperation and even a certain pooling of cultures. When the indigenous tribe of Lucanians took back Paestum at the end of the fifth century BC, again it seems to have been more a firm takeover than a very violent conquest. The city continued to be used as before, in much the same way; hence the temples and other amenities remained in use, more or less as they were. Greek was still spoken, the bouleuterion was used, worship continued. When the Romans eventually took over in 273 BC, they kept the temples but remodelled or replaced most of the civic structures, adding a Roman-style arena, Forum, Curia, wide-paved roads, etc.

The city of Poseidonia is fortified by stone walls, built of large ashlar travertine blocks. The circuit of the walls originates from the foundation of the colony, but they have been built higher, repaired and enhanced over time by successive populations. The four stone gateways, roughly on the four compass points, still seem to be as originally planned. In between are a great many tunnel-like small entrances piercing the thick wall.

The city was bisected, from north to south, by the line of three major temples. Each temple faces the east, as is traditional, and their fronts are all roughly aligned with each other, even the one that stands at a distance. At the back (west) they are not aligned, being of different lengths. Some metres to the east of each temple front is a substantial stone-built altar, lined up with the façade of its temple, and about as wide, originally approached by steps. Beside these altars are various stone-lined pits (**bothroi**), ready to receive the rubbish left over from the sacrifices. Each of these three temple areas shows signs of earlier buildings, probably including small archaic temples, and they were probably in active use as sanctuaries from the first, with the intention to add monumental architecture as it became feasible. The first of the major temples was begun within a generation or two of the arrival of the colonists.

It should be remembered that a designated sanctuary (temenos) needed very little to be functional for worship. An altar could be arranged for the essential sacrifices, whether a monumental stone one, a portable one of some material like terracotta (see title page), or an earth altar. The worshippers in any case congregated in the open air. Votive offerings could be made, (and usually the sacred dumps yield votives that are older than the first stone buildings). A functioning temple or shrine to shelter a cult image could be thrown up fairly quickly: on a stone base, walls of mud brick could be raised, with a roof structure of timber and thatch. When destroyed, this building would leave its trace of stone foundations. Small stone foundations still visible in the sanctuary areas may have been such buildings. However, it would be an obvious aim of a new settlement to replace the perishable structures with permanent ones, as soon as prosperity allowed for the necessary funds, skills and manpower. A monumental stone temple was by no means a necessity but was a marker of worldly success, wealth and stability. It would be an enormous undertaking.

NB: One difficulty in discussing these buildings is the uncertainty about their dedications, and so, what to call them. As there is no literary evidence, only archaeology

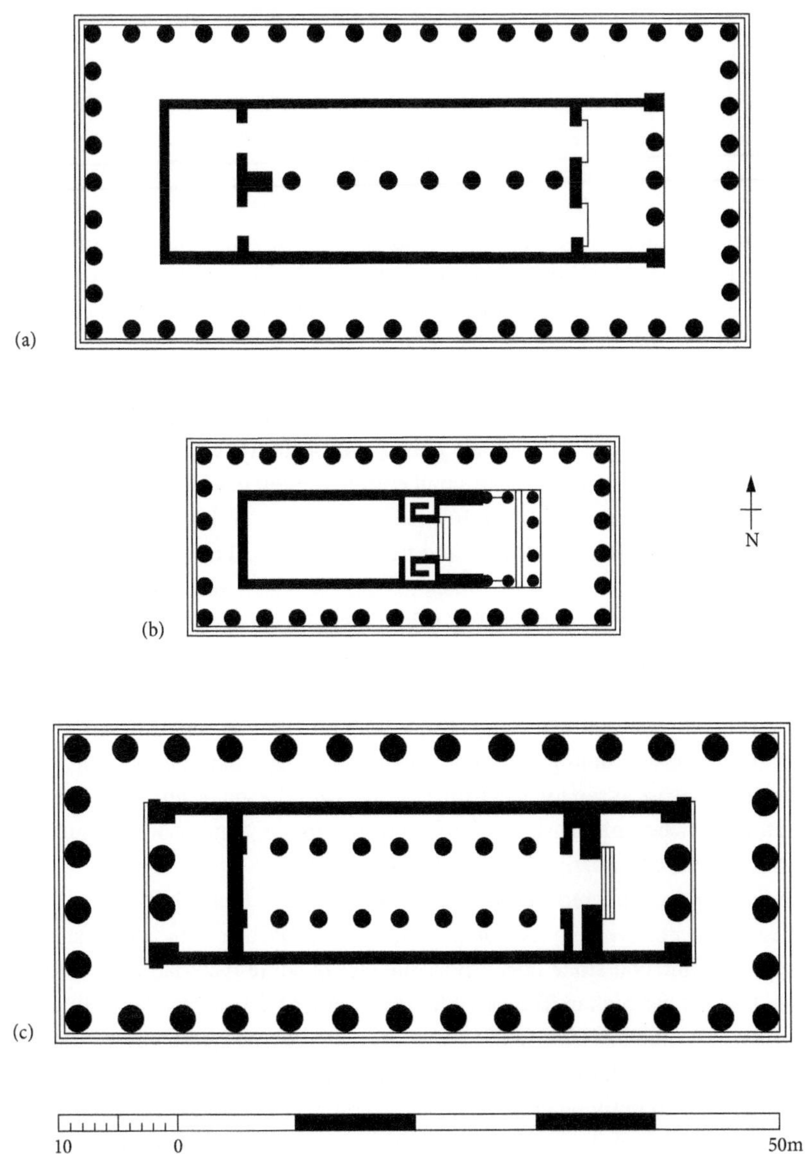

Fig. 88 Paestum ground plans, all drawn to same scale: (a) Hera I, 570 BC; (b) Athene, *c*. 510 BC; (c) Hera II, *c*. 460 BC.

can offer an answer, and this is not clear in every case. Meanwhile, mistaken names, invented by the first explorers in the eighteenth century AD, are still used, so they will be given here, alongside more correct ones.

Temple of Hera I

The earliest monumental temple lies in the south side of the city, not very far from the southern wall. It seems that it was certainly dedicated to Hera, as indicated by the abundant terracotta votive offerings excavated nearby (Figs. 89a,b). It is therefore now known as the temple of **Hera I**.

This first major temple was once known as the **Basilica** because, having entirely lost its pediments, it looked to the early-eighteenth-century explorers more like a civic building, a stoa or basilica, than a temple. This ambitious and showy building is an obvious sign of the success of the colony. It has been dated as early as 570 BC: its probable early date in the life of Poseidonia shows that the city soon felt itself to be both safe and prosperous: it had the resources and opportunity to monumentalise its worship of Hera, and the aesthetic freedom to create a unique temple (Fig. 90).

Hera I is the second largest of the three major temples, and in some ways, looks even larger than it is, because of its expansive horizontal proportions and comparatively low height, (exaggerated by the loss of the upper parts). It stands on a compact three-stepped plinth. The outline of each column has strong entasis and a 'baggy' echinus suggesting an early date in the sixth century (compare the temple of Hera at Olympia *c.* 580 BC). Each column leans very slightly inward, increasing the impression of settled stability.

This temple has nine columns across the front, a huge number, and unusual for being an odd number. This, combined with the equally huge number of eighteen columns down the flanks, produces a stoa-like look, and has even suggested to modern viewers that so large a space could not be roofed. Yet in fact, this temple (24.5 × 54.3 metres) is smaller than its neighbour, the more conventional 'Temple of Neptune'. The huge number of columns may serve several important purposes. As a monument, particularly in a new settlement, the extra-long colonnades are eloquent of success, of wealth, of self-sufficiency and confidence, of ownership of ample territory. As a functional place of worship, the large interior spaces probably had particular ritual uses, perhaps involving processions, at least of sacred personnel, if not the public. Here the external corridors are wide (almost two intercolumniations wide), and the cella is wide too, giving opportunity for ritual movement through the building, inside or out (See Fig. 88a). Pedley, commenting on the spaciousness of the ground plan concludes that the 'explanation of the twin naves in the cella must be liturgical'. He suggests there could have been a double cult of Zeus and Hera, or two guises of Hera (Pedley 1990, p. 54).

What remains of Hera I is the complete Doric colonnade, on three steps, with architrave and some of the frieze backers, inner porch and part of a central colonnade, all in travertine, but with some elements made of another softer stone, sandstone (Fig. 91).

Fig. 89 Three votive terracottas: a) Hera Kourotrophos, nursing a baby; b) Argive Hera with phiale and pomegranate; c) Athene with helmet and Gorgon shield, Paestum, Museo Archeologico.

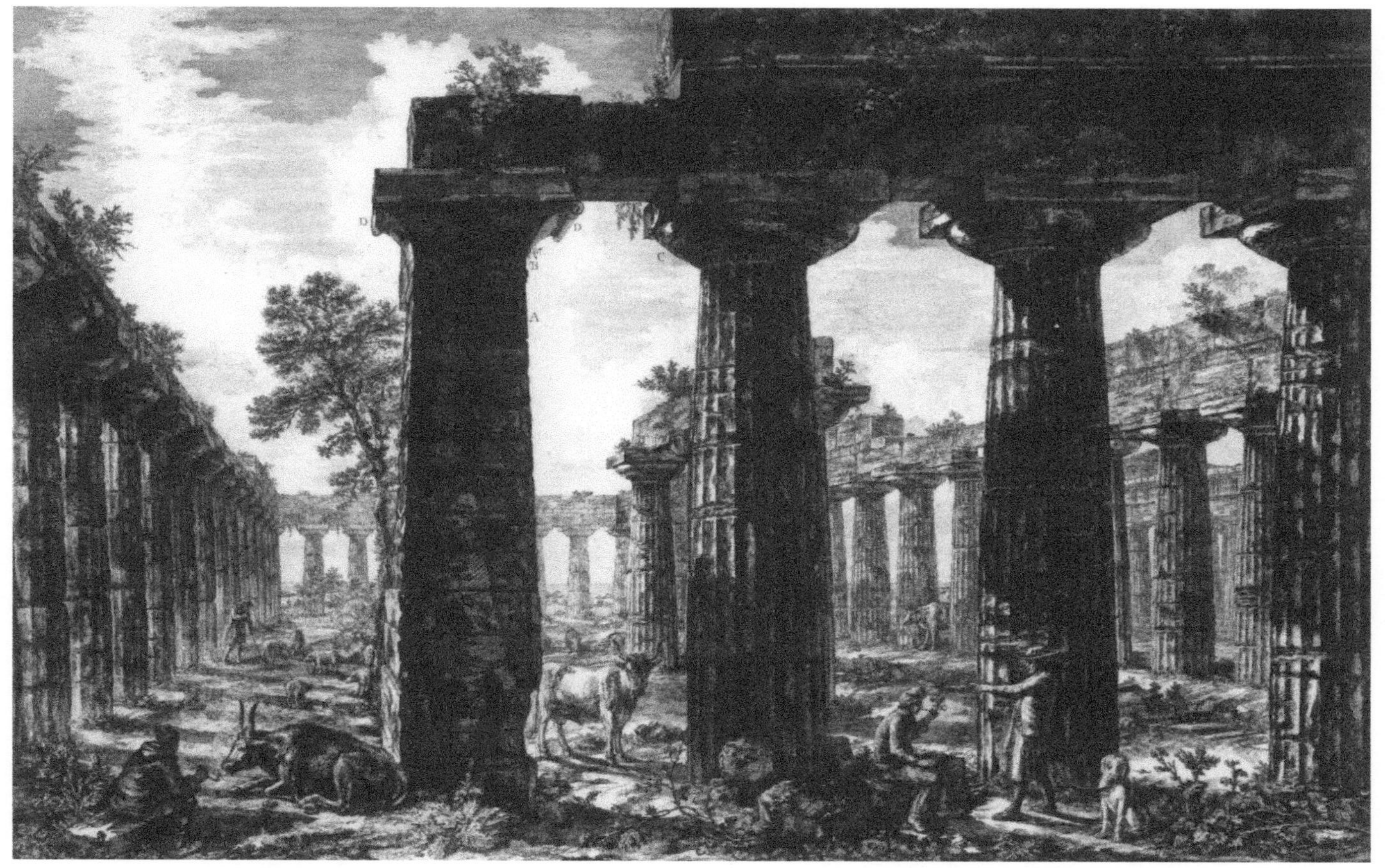

Fig. 90 Hera I: GB Piranesi: litho. Drawn mid-eighteenth century AD.

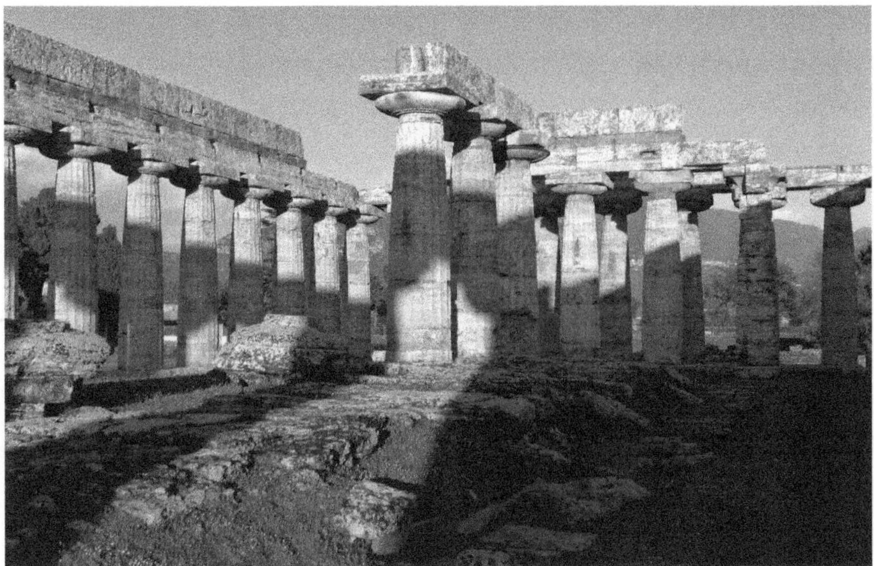

Fig. 91 Interior view of Hera I, looking towards east.

Above the frieze and architrave, the edge of the roof structure was originally masked with terracotta facings, brightly painted and patterned in cream, red and black. Along the flanks of the temple were terracotta revetments on which geometric and flower patterns alternated with small, open-mouthed, lionheaded mock spouts. The pediments, crowned with the even more elaborate terracotta sloping cornice with its regular florets standing up against the sky, and maybe finished with a patterned central disc, would have been striking indeed. (Samples of all these painted terracotta components can be seen in the Paestum Museum (Fig. 92).)

The building is clearly in Doric style, yet on closer inspection, the Doric pattern is varied in several ways, as follows:

The exterior

- The tops of the shafts and the capitals of the Doric columns have a very particular treatment. The flutes are topped with rounded forms, as in Ionic style, even though the edges of the flutes are sharp and not flattened (as they would be in Ionic). Above these, marking the junction between shaft and capital, most of the columns have a deep concave collar of carved leaves, and above that a raised anthemion band on the echinus (Fig. 93). These however vary between columns, and were perhaps left to each individual carver to finalise. All this special carving would have been brightly painted in reds and blues. Along the back of the temple (which faced a residential area) the treatments were even more varied and individual.
- Between the architrave and the frieze section above, a layer of soft sandstone is still to be seen. This was once carved with egg-and-dart and leaf mouldings, now weathered down, and a similar one was above the frieze, framing it.

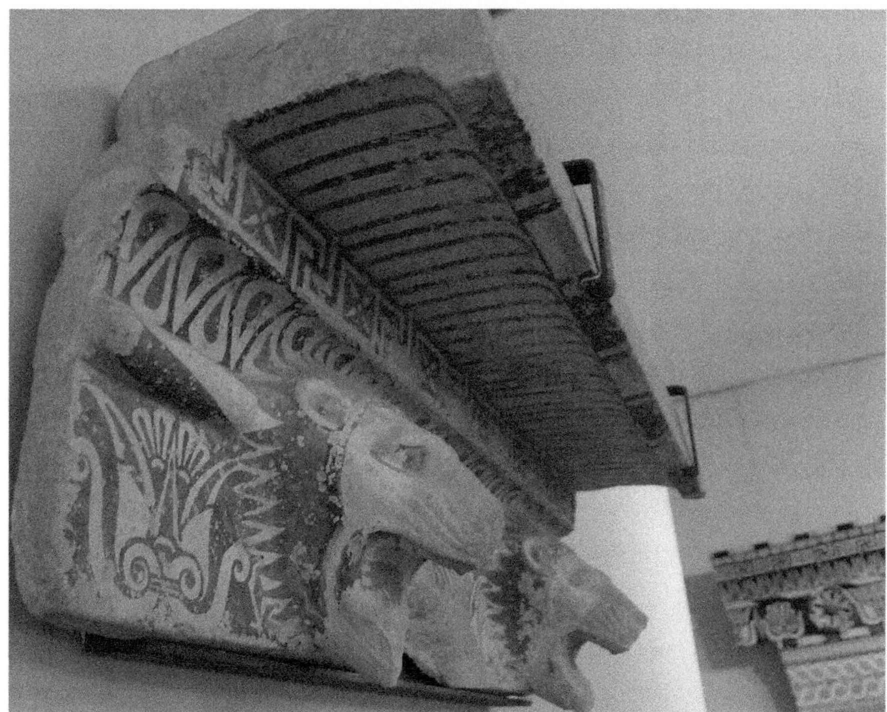

Fig. 92 Painted 'gutter' from temple of Hera I, Paestum, Museo Archeologico.

Fig. 93 Column capital from Hera I with carved anthemion.

The porch

- Within the front colonnade is a porch of three Doric columns in antis. The number three is unusual here because it creates two (or four) entrances instead of one central one into the porch space (Fig. 90).
- The wide porch of three massive columns is dramatic. It is made even more so by the form of the antae. Each anta is a tapering rectangular pillar, crowned with a 'capital'. The capital rises with a gentle expanding curve until it meets its abacus. Hanging from the top edge of the curve, to left and right, is a strange feature, a tiny pendant cylinder, like a skinny bolster (see Fig. 94). This curious pendant cylinder has also been found in fragments from Sybaris and Metapontum in South Italy, and in archaic sites in Corinth, Tiryns and Argos. Those from Sybaris are rather more scroll-like, though still small (Mertens (1993), Tafel 68; Williams (2003), p. 99). So, this little detail has a history and expresses an ancestry of buildings. We shall see it again in the extra-urban Heraion.
- Each anta has entasis and tapers like the columns; its abacus is also sized like those of the columns, so that the whole anta appears as a variant column. This correspondence creates harmony among the round and angled shapes, crowded into this eventful interior space. The tapering adds fictive height, as well as an elegant outline, and added even more drama within the darkened and crowded porch. (The now vanished cella walls also probably tapered, both within and without.)

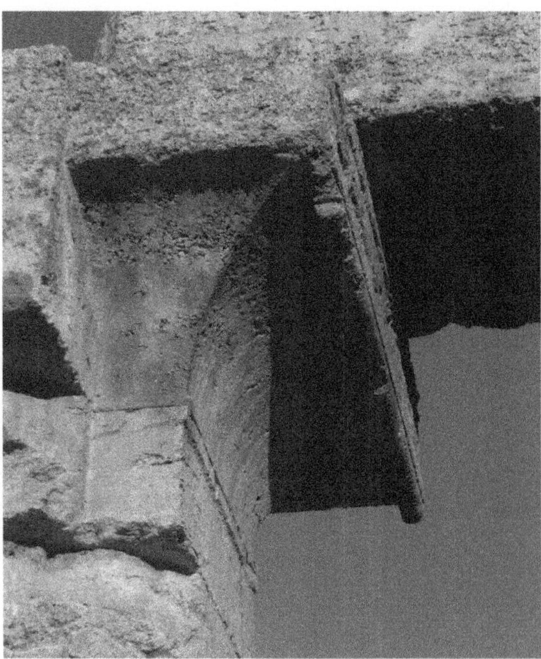

Fig. 94 Hera I: Porch anta capital with 'cylinder'.

- The entablature above the porch entrance now appears plain, but sandwiches another sandstone string course that was probably carved with leaves like the exterior sandstone stringing.
- From the inner porch area, two doorways lead into the cella (see Fig. 88, plan a).

The interior

- The wide corridor between the colonnade and the cella wall was apparently never paved but was floored with beaten earth. The cella interior with its steps and paving rose higher than the corridor. Each weight-bearing element – colonnades, cella walls – had deep stone foundations (Fig. 91).
- The large cella is divided into two wide aisles by a central row of 7 or 8 massive columns. These columns and those of the porch are all of equal size with those of the exterior colonnade. Normally the interior columns would be scaled down.
- The massive central columns do not stand upon the paved floor, but are imbedded in it. The buried level is not fluted – flutes were normally done after installation. Whether this shows a change of floor level or simply an idea for stabilising the columns is unclear.
- Corresponding to the porch, at the far end there was an adyton (originally planned as an opisthodomos). The adyton was closed to the back (the west), but was entered by two doors from the cella, answering to the two porch doors. As the cella itself was divided by the single central row of columns, the natural place for a cult statue (the centre) would be obscured. Therefore, in the final arrangement of the interior, it would seem that any cult statue had to be placed in the adyton. Another suggestion has two cult statues in the adyton, either Hera and Zeus, or Hera in two manifestations – maybe warlike and nurturing. If there were two cult statues in the adyton, they could still have been visible from outside if placed in line with the doorways, as in a niche. Statues that could be seen from outside could also see out, and this was desirable during ceremonies and sacrifices at the altars.

This early temple was built at a time when the Doric order could make many choices. Indeed, the Doric order could always make choices. But in the first half of the sixth century BC, there was much room for decisions about central aisles, numbers of columns, etc. Decorative choices such as collars of flowers on Doric capitals were perhaps more surprising and individual.

This first of the Paestan temples is clearly intended to make a strong statement. Huge and colourful, it has 'presence'. Individual in its size and design, it is a sign to the citizens themselves that their colony has 'taken'. It is a sign to visitors, whether Greek or other, that the Poseidonians are here to stay. Hand-carved and painted, with custom-made terracottas, the temple was a craftwork of huge value. The slightly handmade look of the stone flutings reminds us that every inch of the structure had to be quarried, moulded, sculpted, planned and executed by means of a coordinated team of trained craftsmen. As a gift to Hera, it should also attract favour from the powerful goddess whom it honours. Her particular nature would be suggested by the cult statue or statues within, and this would be to do with protection, nurturing, care of youth, fertility – of lands, of cattle and of women. This is made clear by the votive figurines found buried on the site, which probably reflect the cult statue(s).

Temple of Athene

The second temple, once known as the **Temple of Ceres,** was dedicated to Athene, as indicated by the deposits of terracotta votive offerings found nearby (Fig. 89c). This is the smallest, by far, of the three temples (14.5 × 32.9 metres). However, because of the proportional system of Greek architecture, it does not look small when viewed on its own. Situated towards the northern end of the city, it is sited on rising ground, artificially mounded to give extra height and importance (Fig. 95).

This temple was built towards 500 BC. It stands on three neat steps and has a Doric colonnade of 6 × 13 columns (Fig. 88b). Its damaged pediments are still partially in position, giving a fair idea of its original outline. This temple is poised between the archaic and the classical: the capitals are still quite spreading and the columns have obvious entasis; but the colonnade is classically proportioned. So far, the building has a regular Doric appearance. However, it soon begins to reveal its many extraordinary features (Figs. 96a and b).

The west façade is the better preserved in terms of its pediment. It can be seen that the **raking cornice** is extremely deep, and its protruding stone underside is coffered.

Fig. 95 View of Athene temple (*c.* 510 BC): from altar.

(a)

(b)

Fig. 96 Temple of Athene: a) Reconstruction of west façade; b) Reconstruction of inner porch, showing Ionic columns on rising steps. Drawing: F Krauss (by kind permission of the Archaeological Park of Paestum).

Each coffer once contained a central star, carved separately in sandstone, and inserted with a lead fixing. As this could only be seen by looking upwards, it may be intended as a symbolic sky and maybe the stars were even gilded and perhaps the coffers were blue. This deep roof overhang would have run all the way round the building. The vertical thickness of the stone edge, now very weathered, was once carved with an anthemion. All these elements would have been decorated in bright colour.

The usual horizontal cornice is not there: instead, the tympanum or triangular field of the pediment is more or less flush with the entablature. The normal horizontal cornice is where sculpture can stand, so no opportunity was left for that: instead, the flat triangle would have been stuccoed and decorated with colour. Between the pediment and the architrave was the Doric frieze of metopes and triglyphs. It can be seen from one remaining example that the triglyphs were sandstone and were simply inserted into slots cut in the travertine band of plain metopes (Fig. 95). Due to the erosion of the soft sandstone, they have mostly fallen out. This metope frieze was framed above and below by sandstone strings carved with Ionic egg-and-dart and small bead-and-reel mouldings – and a very rare design of snake-like curves (Fig. 97). Each of the three large designs was carved on its own sandstone string. (We shall see

Fig. 97 Temple of Athene: mouldings including wave moulding, Paestum, Museo Archeologico.

that the snake-like moulding links with the same pattern found on the right-hand anta from the early archaic set of sculptures at Foce del Sele. The same design can be seen at Delphi on a painted terracotta sima of Western origin dated 550 BC (Winter (1993) Delphi, Roof 29, S.182 Fig. 125).

The external Doric columns have a treatment around their capitals similar to that of Hera I. Above the flutes are leaves and garlands. These garlands were once coloured in red and blue, and even had gilded bronze **laminae** (thin plaques) interspersed with the leaves. In its pristine condition with its full load of colour, this temple front must have been a stunning sight. Moving to the flanks, another beautiful surprise awaits: the stone gutter is carved with stylish vegetable designs and sleek lion's head drainage spouts (Fig. 98). Lion's heads on this temple continue the theme from Hera I, and parallel those on the (roughly contemporary) second Heraion at Foce del Sele, where the heads are yet bigger and fiercer (see below). Urban Athene is both warrior and protector, as is Hera, in her extra-urban sanctuary at the edge of the chora.

Turning to the interior of the Athenaion, we find many unusual features:

- On approaching the temple through the front colonnade, the visitor was confronted by a deep Ionic porch on three rising steps. There were eight Ionic columns in all: four were in a row across the front, two were behind the flank pair, and two more engaged columns stood against the antae, or rather, they formed the antae. Each set of columns stood on a higher step, so the visitor would advance both deeper and higher to get into the cella (see Fig. 88b, Fig. 96b; Fig. 99 and Fig. 100). It could be that ideas of Ionic style were conveyed from the new neighbour, Velia (Elea), 40 kilometres south, whose origin was Phocaia, in Ionia, on the coast of Asia Minor. However, this link is not necessary, as visual ideas seem to have travelled freely across the Greek world.

Fig. 98 Temple of Athene: stone gutter with lion-head spouts, Paestum, Museo Archeologico.

- Between the porch and the cella was a brief passage. On each side of it were openings to small staircases, constructed inside purpose-built matching stone 'towers'; the steps could have been wooden (see Fig. 88b). These gave access to the attic level for purposes yet unknown. Such staircases were now typical of Western Greek temples (Miles 1998/99).
- The cella, as far as the vestiges show, was a neat rectangle without columns or any feature such as an adyton. A cult statue would have been displayed, maybe Athene as warrior, with her shield (cf. Fig. 89c).
- The box of the cella was non-aligned with the outer colonnade. As Pedley puts it: '... a common practice ... in Magna Graecia allowed the interior mass of the temple to float free of the surround and stress its own identity.' (Pedley, 1990, p. 54) Looking at the ground plan, it is remarkable that the actual cella entrance is lined up with the seventh exterior flank column, giving the cella only half the interior space: half the temple is taken up with the prostyle porch, the steps, and the inner porch and the narrow passage. This puts a very strong emphasis on the

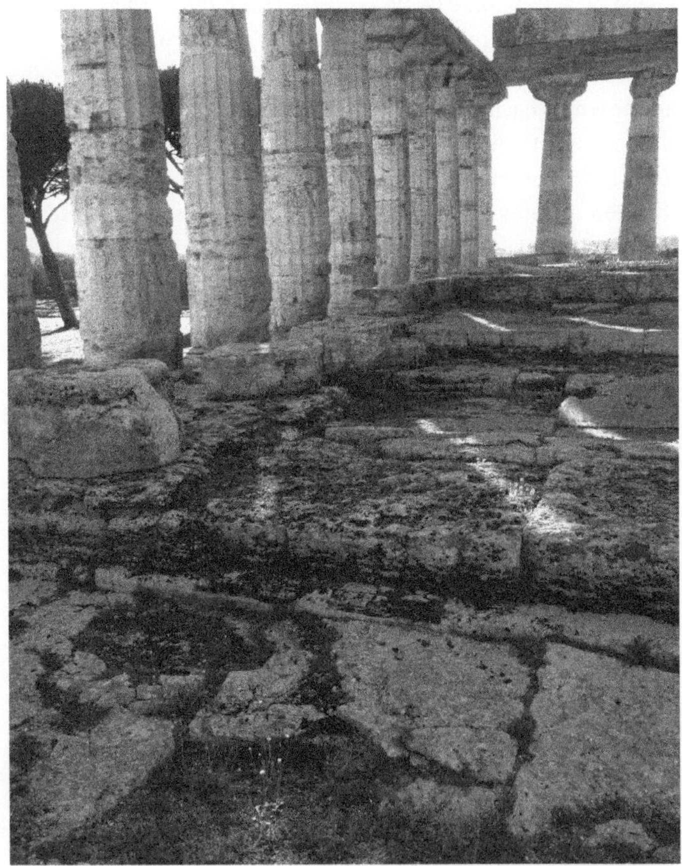

Fig. 99 Temple of Athene: looking at vestiges of inner porch.

Fig. 100 Ionic capital from inner porch, Paestum, Museo Archeologico.

approach, and gives a sense of a withheld and staged ascent to the sacred cult-image (Fig. 100).

So, at the early date of *c.* 500 BC, this temple anticipates the Parthenon and Propylaia of the Athenian Acropolis in mixing Doric and Ionic styles, just as the Doric temple at Assos in Asia Minor, of 540–530 did with its Ionic frieze. The 'rules' which existed were there to be broken or not, as the designer wished. If rules were followed, an impression was made: if they were not, a different impression was made. The play between the two styles was already a resource to be used at the will of the architect.

Temple 3

The dedication of the third temple

The third temple stands parallel to the first and quite close, inviting comparison. This, the grandest and largest of the three city temples was known from the eighteenth century as the **Temple of Neptune** (Fig. 101). It seemed to its first discoverers that this imposing building must be dedicated to Poseidon, namesake of the city; however, no archaeological finds suggest this. To this day it is not known to which god it really belongs. For convenience, it is currently known as **Hera II**, adjacent to – and updating – Hera I. A current suggestion that this might be an Apollo temple is based on signs of an interest in medical matters (Pedley, 1990 pp. 53–4). For example, a rectangular flat-topped sandstone block (or *cippus*) was found near the altars, inscribed: 'Cheiron's' = 'I am the *cippus* of Cheiron'. Cheiron was the wise and good centaur who instructed the young Asclepius, healer son of Apollo, as

Fig. 101 Hera II with Hera I in the background. GB Piranesi: etching, drawn in mid-eighteenth century AD. (Getty images)

well as the young Achilles, and was well-versed in medical matters. Apollo's ownership would also explain the slight extra length of the temple: 6 × 14 columns in the peristyle. Apollo's temples have this characteristic extra length at Delphi and Bassae.

Another suggested dedication is to Zeus. This would place his temple next to his wife Hera, an arrangement also found at Olympia, where the Archaic and the Severe Style temples are parallel neighbours. The building itself would be very fitting for the king of the gods, and, indeed, it is almost the twin of the temple of Zeus at Olympia, and almost as big. An archaic painted terracotta cult-style image of the enthroned Zeus was found buried nearby, and it could have been used in an earlier temple, possibly lying below the present one. Whatever cult statue there was (which may have had material value such as bronze or even chryselephantine, or marble which could be burnt for lime) has certainly disappeared without trace or rumour. So, it cannot yet be decided for sure which god was honoured here. Given the preponderance of Hera votives on the site, this may yet have been another Hera temple, since she was a highly honoured goddess in Poseidonia.

The exterior

The temple is dated to around 474 BC onwards. Its footprint is 24.26 × 59.98 metres. (For comparison, the temple of Zeus at Olympia is 27.68 × 64.12 metres.)

The outer colonnade consists of 6 × 14 columns placed on a neat three-step plinth (Fig. 88c). There is a plain architrave and a Doric triglyph and metope frieze with uncarved metopes. The pediment has the same neat shallow angle of the raking cornice seen in the great mid-fifth-century temples like Zeus at Olympia and the Parthenon. The Doric capitals also have the tight, straight fifth-century profile, pulling the huge columns elegantly in at the top. Each column top is 'girdled' with three plain grooves, which are echoed by four plain raised bands on the echinus. These exterior columns are 8.88 metres high; they have a 2.13-metre lower diameter, elegantly tapering to 1.5 metres by the top, with slight entasis. The travertine stone seems of finer grade than that of the other Paestum temples and has kept a finer finish; however, it would still have been coated with the usual stucco – in fact traces of this marble-like stucco can still be seen. Each exterior column has 24 flutes, (four more than normal) and the carving remains crisp. Though the columns are massive, the many flutings slim them, especially when strong sunlight catches the crisp outlines and the pale building appears radiant (Fig. 102).

The multiplicity of columns appears strong rather than heavy, since vertical lines give lightness and elegance. Overall there is a combination of vertical, horizontal, triangular, the emphasis being vertical: the flute-lines of columns are picked up by triglyphs. In the very restrained design, everything counts. Even the visual contribution of the horizontal line of guttae is surprisingly effective: in sunshine they mark the transition between architrave and frieze with sharp points of shadow.

Fig.102 Hera II view.

- 'Refinements' are used, which also lighten the mass: the stylobate and cornice curve gently up towards the centre, the columns lean gently inward. The corner measurements are slightly contracted, a trick that adds visual strength, though not actual strength.
- The tympanum of the pediment is now quite plain, but, when stuccoed it could well have been painted. The faces of the raking and horizontal cornices were probably painted and maybe even carved, but now are weathered flat.
- The slanting undersurfaces of the overhanging roof are smooth, while the underside of the horizontal cornice has **mutules** and holes as though to receive **guttae** (little stone pegs) – but they are empty.

The Interior

- Entering the temple, between exterior columns and cella the visitor is faced with the porch, which is distyle in antis (Fig. 103). Here the slightly tapering antae are restrained, gaining drama from their height and massive severity: this impression is increased by comparison with the more fanciful antae of Hera I.
- In the thickness of the wall that divides porch from cella, to the right and left are small chambers. On the right (entering) was a squared stone staircase. On the left, the chamber is now empty (see Fig. 88, plan c).
- Inside, the cella is divided into three aisles by two lofty double-storey colonnades that continue the vertical theme (see front cover picture). Each colonnade has seven columns with 20 flutes, smaller than the exterior ones, surmounted by seven even smaller with 16 flutes. This arrangement is familiar from mainland temples of the late sixth to fifth century BC (Aigina, Olympia, Parthenon).

Fig. 103 Hera II: distyle in antis porch.

The cella, now in broad sunlight, should be imagined instead as darkened, lit only by lamplight soaring into the darkness of the ceiling, or by dawn-light from the East creeping through the open porch; whatever light there was, being scarcely adequate for the huge spaces. To the worshipper in antiquity, entering the cella from the brightness of daylight, the interior would have gradually become apparent as his eyes adjusted to the dark: a slowly appearing vision, with columns like an avenue of tall trees leading to the cult statue.

When viewing the exterior, the viewer sees a 'forest of columns', an effect usually thought of as Ionic. Depending on where he stands, he sees the six façade columns, the two in antis, the two end flank columns glimpsed through the far corner of the colonnade, and possibly, the fourteen down the near flank.

As preserved today, this temple is purely abstract, without any representational feature. As a contrast to the other two temples, which are highly decorative and loaded with ornament, this one relies on proportion and purity of style. Seen glowing in sunshine, its crisp carving emphasised by light and shadow, it is an awesome sight. This temple showcases Doric style. Positioned next to the colourful and decorative temple of Hera I (the 'Basilica') it invites comparison. With a larger footprint, it is also taller. The impression is of Olympian size, of lightness, yet greatness. Originally the architectural features such as capitals, architrave, metopes and triglyphs, and both pediments, would all have been painted with red and blue designs or plain colour, enhancing the Doric accents, as was usual. Certainly, this colour would have given a different impression – yet today the temple succeeds by its abstract architecture alone and the perfection of its Doric proportion (Fig. 102).

Scholars have noted that the sixth-century tendency in the Greek West to inventiveness, to ornament, to mixing of styles, came to a halt in the fifth century. It has been observed that Western temples of the fifth century were more 'conformist', allying themselves to mainland norms. There may be many ways of looking at this phenomenon. It is true and remarkable that Paestum's temple of *c.* 470 is very similar to the contemporary temple of Zeus at Olympia. (Although of course it lacks the striking sculpture of Olympia, in most other ways it models for us today the lost appearance of Zeus's great mainland temple.) This similarity to mainland trends could reflect the Greek mood of solidarity that arose in response to Persian and Carthaginian hostility. It could also be a change in taste, a veering away from the archaic to a new classical taste, based on a pared down elegance, more minimal in decoration, more essential in its minimalism. The temple at Olympia carries the new Severe Style sculpture: the architecture corresponds. It is intriguing that the fifth-century temple at Paestum and its near-twin at Olympia are of approximately the same date. This suggests a commonality or interaction of designers in some way. We know from Pausanias that the temple of Zeus at Olympia was designed by 'a local architect, Libon of Elis'. How design news travelled, we don't exactly know. But as athletes from Paestum competed at Olympia, (and a Parmenides won the foot race in 468 BC), architects could certainly travel both ways, and so could ideas. The various areas of the Greek world were not cut off from each other – rather the contrary.

The Agora

The Agora of Poseidonia was planned out from the beginning as a space for civic activity, both political and commercial. It takes up intermediate space between the string of temples. Like the other areas, it was developed over time, but was useable from the start. Marked out by sandstone boundary stones (**horoi**), indicating a sort of sacredness, it contained significant items.

The hero shrine

In the Agora, an intriguing structure dated about 510 BC, was recently discovered under a grassy tumulus. It is a semi-subterranean chamber with pitched roof, the roof being doubled, stone underneath and outsize terracotta tiles above. The chamber was sealed, without any way of entry, so the excavators removed enough tiles from the roof to gain access. Inside were found a series of eight handsome archaic bronze vessels, (two **amphorae** and six **hydriae**), and an Athenian black-figure amphora (all now on show in the museum). The hydriae all feature heroic motifs, such as horses and lions. The painted amphora follows up this triumphal theme with the welcome of Heracles into Olympia, and, on the other side, a Dionysiac celebration. This amphora is very fine, and, as a sign of its value to the owner, has actually had its broken foot repaired in antiquity with lead. The vessels were filled with a black sticky substance, thought to be honey, suggestive of immortality and sweetness, a typical offering to the dead. Although there is no written clue to the meaning of all this, the structure seems to be a hero shrine and cenotaph, and most likely a hero shrine to the first oikist, or original leader of the colony, or else to the leader of the second contingent from Sybaris. Hidden from view, he would remain in spirit forever as a local divinity, a benign presence at the heart of the city he had promoted. (cf. Euripides: *Iphigeneia in Tauris* 650ff, where Iphigeneia plans just such an empty monument for Orestes, complete with honey.)

It was typical of colonies to have a cenotaph **heroon** in a prominent position, to commemorate the founder and give a mythic identity to the city. Some of these were at boundaries of the territory, to give protection, while others were in central political space, as here, in the agora. For example, Pindar remembers Battos, the oikist of the Greek city of Cyrene in Africa: now entombed in his city's agora, he was 'blest in life and worshipped by the people after death'. The poet then imagines similar 'sacred kings', who from the underworld will rejoice in their city's achievements when they hear celebratory song (Pind *Pyth* 5, 90). In a colony, the founder is not exactly invented – as a historical person, he might even be remembered by living persons at the time of creating the shrine – but he could perhaps also be 'reinvented'. Though the founding 'hero' could be seen as aristocratic, and probably was, there is no apparent problem with his supporting a democracy – as Theseus did at Athens.

Close to the hero shrine, the **bouleuterion** or citizen meeting place accommodating about 500 citizens, was constructed in the agora in roughly 480–470 BC. It may have once been walled, but was probably not roofed. With its circular tiers of stone seating, carved into the bedrock on which the city stands, it monumentalised the processes of democracy. (Previously, political activities must have been carried on in the agora, but without a dedicated physical structure.) Monumentalisation of the Greek approach to civic life at this date may reflect the pride in Greek freedom in the face of the Persian menace (and in the Greek West, the Carthaginian menace). The pure geometry of the concentric circular plan is comparable with the austerity of the neighbouring Doric temple of the same Severe Style era (possibly begun 474 BC).

So far, we have explored the three major temples of urban Poseidonia, whose construction roughly spanned the lifetime of the Greek city. We have also noted, very briefly, some other characteristic structures around them.

The Heraion at Foce del Sele

The territory of Poseidonia stretched to the river Silaris (Sele) in the North, to Agropoli in the South, and into the foothills to the East, marking out a large semicircle of land: in it were several sanctuaries, large and small, as well as many cemeteries. Sanctuaries large and small, outlining the territory (**chora**), were part of the concept of a colony. They would have been planned from the beginning and instituted as soon as possible.

A major extra-urban sanctuary, outstanding for its architectural sculptures, was the Argive Heraion which marked the border with the Etruscans, five miles north of the city at Foce del Sele, the mouth of the river Sele. Right across the border were powerful Etruscan settlements giving this site a particular importance.

This extra-urban sanctuary developed in phases, starting from the very beginnings of the colony in about 600 BC – keeping pace with the city itself. It was dedicated to the great goddess Argive Hera, who typically was honoured with grand extra-urban sanctuaries. The dedication to Hera is clearly revealed by the many and varied votive offerings found carefully buried on the site. Argive Hera links of course to mainland Argos and its great sanctuary of Hera: Troizen was in the Argolid, so here is another likely link to Poseidonia's origins. Jason and the Argonauts in the heroic age were said to be the founders (Strabo 6.1), when they wandered way off course on their return journey with the Golden Fleece. Hera was a protectress of Jason, among other heroes: Why should she not have guided the Argo to safe moorings in the marshy site by the river Sele between the mountains and the sea? And why would he not then have dedicated the site in gratitude to his patroness? This story lends the shrine a mythical Greek prehistory and ancestry, an antiquity of extra prestige, and a certain entitlement to the land.

The buildings of the Heraion of Foce del Sele

The first phase of this sanctuary (*c.* 600 BC) was marked by **stoas** and an **ash altar.** These offered shelter for worshippers and provision for the sacrifices and were quite sufficient for worship to take place. The site was clearly joined to the Northern gate of the city by a road – a processional way – indicating the close relationship of shrine to city.

The 'Treasury'

When the site was discovered in 1934, very important finds were made, but they have proved hard to interpret, and foundations of buildings still to be seen at ground level have proved ambiguous. An extensive and unique series of early archaic metopes were found, numbering 35 (some being fragments), possibly from as early as 570 BC. These were attributed to a rectangular foundation next to the large temple, first thought to be a treasury, and containing material in and beneath its foundations from about 570. This building was beautifully reproduced in the Paestum Museum, in order to display the metopes as a set, with their attached triglyphs. However, a new find of three more metopes upset the arrangement as now they had to be attributed to a bigger building. The 'treasury' in fact had no extant front wall, so it could be readily understood as having had greater length. However, later exploration revealed that the 'treasury' as seen was not such an old building after all, (fourth or third century BC), although given the find-spots of the metopes in that area, they could have been used on an older building and then re-used on the newer 'treasury', along with other archaic blocks. This still left the question of where

Fig. 104 Anta with 'cylinder', from 'treasury', Foce del Sele, Paestum, Museo Archeologico.

the metopes had started life. Adjacent to the 'treasury' was the large temple of Hera, dating to about 510 BC with its own set of metopes. More recent excavations near its foundations revealed that an earlier large temple had been started between the two visible buildings. Due to problems with these first foundations in a site that tends to be waterlogged, they were abandoned in favour of the larger Hera temple whose foundations are visible now, made with better provision for drainage (de la Geniere 1997; Barletta 1998). Associated with the early Archaic metopes are two decorative anta capitals (Fig. 104) which both display a version of the '**sofa**' design which we saw on Hera I at Paestum, as well as other patterns including the rare snake-like design which we saw on the Athenaion of Paestum. These antae would have stood at the front of their building, behind four prostyle columns.

The early archaic metopes

The **metopes** comprise an important and rare series of narratives. They form a major collection of architectural metopes of early date, depicting mythological topics, some forming narrative groups, others individual scenes. They have lent themselves to extensive study as to the sources of this large collection of designs (Van Keuren 1989). Did the sculptors have to look to images in other forms of art such as vase painting, and for the subjects, did they turn to poetry? Were the panels arranged in great themes, or were the topics simply popular stories? To what extent could such a series really have been planned as a whole at this early date? Or should the panels just be enjoyed separately, one by one? And, also, were these one of the very earliest examples of narrative architectural sculpture? And if so, why?

It is remarkable that the city temples, though spectacular, seem to lack all figurative elements, while the rural Heraion has not one but two extensive figural cycles. This distinction seems deliberate. It made a visit to the Heraion just that bit different from a visit to a city temple, repaying the extra effort of the mini-pilgrimage. It throws extra personality onto the border shrine that marks the extent of the chora to the north, and which hosted events and activities of particular meaning for the city and even perhaps for the wider non-Greek locality. The early archaic cycle especially, constructed so soon after the founding of the colony, was a huge statement of confidence, of identity and ongoing Greek presence in the place. It may be another manifestation of the mindset that asked for as many as 9 × 18 columns in the city Heraion of similar date.

The meaning of these metopes – now jumbled and damaged – would have been crystal clear to the ancient worshipper/visitor at the shrine. Viewed with their carved and painted detail, arranged in logical order as planned, the stories would have leapt to the eye of the viewer. Obscurities would be explained by detail, and recognition would have been aided by sequence. The scenes would have explained each other, and probably resolved themselves into cycles or groups. A visit would presumably include a circuit of the building and consideration of all the pictured themes, with an imaginative apprehension of the actions and fates of the characters.

These early panels are deeply carved, but some are carefully modelled while others remain quite flat in surface and are only carved in outline; this could represent a different style by another sculptor, or unfinished work. All the panels would certainly have been painted, with details added even where they were not carved. The difference in finish might also indicate that the work was discontinued, since the way they were discovered suggested they had not been put to use as planned, or else had been used and dismantled. The forms of the figures on the more finished metopes are very robust, clarified by crisp undercutting, so the image stands out sharply from the field. Within many of the figures, there is plenty of definition of muscles, knee-joints, tubular hair, features, etc. The figures are squat, strong, active. The flatter examples are similar in outline and undercutting, but lack the internal detail.

The compositions of many of these metopes are intricate. The Heracles killing the giant, for example, has the intricacy of a metal design, and this is not surprising as the visual schemes for many of these myths have been traced to the miniature repoussé designs used on archaic shield bands (Van Keuren 1989). Such designs would have been easy to access as the objects would very likely have been imported or seen by designers in their travels.

Though harsh and robust rather than charming, these carvings do not lack subtlety. The finely detailed panel of Heracles killing a giant (Alkyoneus) shows careful thought. The giant is in the archaic running–kneeling pose. This is modified by the natural tilt of the head backward, as Heracles pulls his hair hard from behind. The two figures combine as Heracles puts his foot firmly on the giant's leg. Though both figures are in archaic profile, Heracles's foot and the giant's foot are gently angled outward by the pressure of the contact. Additionally, Heracles is characterised as neater in presentation than the crude giant (Fig. 105a). Another expressive panel shows Sisyphos pushing his stone uphill with a winged demon on his back. The imaginative composition conveys the claustrophobia of Sisyphos's punishment, by having him crowded between a rock and a demon – who mirrors his pose but with a difference: the demon freely hovers above the sinner, Sisyphos, who is hunched over, trapped eternally at his task (Fig. 105b).

The soft sandstone panels still retain other narrative details. In the struggle for the tripod between Heracles and Apollo, the god wears a neat tunic, while the hero is skirted

Fig. 105 Metopes from early archaic frieze, 'treasury', Foce del Sele: a) Heracles and Alkyoneus, b) Sisyphos, Paestum, Museo Archeologico.

in a shaggy lion-skin and holds his knotty club. The twins, Apollo and Artemis, shoot their bows in unison very much as they do on the Siphnian treasury, Apollo with a short tunic in front and Artemis in a long skirt behind, visible between her twin's legs.

Some stories are contained in one panel, others stretch between two or three panels, as they do on the early Archaic 'Sikyonian' metopes at Delphi. Apollo and Heracles inhabit a single frame, while Apollo and Artemis shoot across a frame to rescue their mother Leto in the next panel. Two maidens (Leucippidai?) run away from the pursuing heroes (Dioskouri?) in the panel behind. One girl looks back at the pursuers while her sister looks ahead. One lifts her skirt to run, one waves her hand high in fear; both have pretty draped hair (Fig. 106). This attractive panel must have served as a model for the later series of dancers, with modifications to make it generic rather than narrative, and to update the style with late archaic drapery, elaborate folds and more elegant proportions.

Interestingly, every single one of the extant metopes from Foce del Sele (from both the early and late Archaic period) is a narrative scene, shown in profile. This is in contrast to the early metopes from Selinus in Sicily, where a confrontational frontal view is very frequent, even in story-scenes. (Cult statues of course, as evidenced by the votive figurines, would always have been frontal.) These Paestan metopes show a clear focus on storytelling, and a serious approach to representing a dramatic and telling action. It is for the viewer to study and respond to what he/she is being shown. Even the throned figure who is probably Zeus wielding a thunderbolt seems to be shown in profile and is directly threatening, not the viewer, but some misbehaviour in a following panel. Divine anger is a useful warning. Ajax's fate too (from the Trojan cycle) is salutary for the viewer, as the hero bows over his sword like a sad logo of **hubris**. His easy-to-recognise suicide shows where civic rebellion will lead. The gods will punish hubris, or any disorderly action: but, with care, all this can be avoided by the wise viewer.

Scenes from the Trojan cycle (however gory) link the sanctuary with the Greek epic past, and of course link the owners of the sanctuary with it too. The violent deeds of the House of Agamemnon take place at Argos, a look back at the old country, close to the old home. Such scenes with their strong familiarity emphasise historic identity. Most panels

Fig. 106 Metopes from early archaic frieze, 'treasury', Foce del Sele: a) youths pursuing girls; b) girls fleeing, Paestum, Museo Archeologico.

feature action, often violent: this encourages the viewer to boldness and success. Some reflect themes of travel and exploration – Odysseus (probably) rides a tortoise over the sea, Heracles captures the Kerkopes, (monkey-like creatures who were supposed to live on Ischia). Heracles himself also had links to Troizen, as it was claimed by Troizenians that there he entered the underworld to capture Cerberus (Pausanias 2.31.2). Orestes too had links, included in the Agamemnon story, since he was purified on a sacred stone in front of the Troizen temple where the purifiers' descendants still celebrated the event in Pausanias's time (Pausanias 2.31.7 & 11).

There is plenty of scholarly discussion about the iconographical scheme of these metopes and their planned placement on the building. It seems certain at least that the façade featured a series of six panels showing Heracles's adventures at the cave of Pholos. There, the well-behaved centaur Pholos (shown as more human) was a good host to the hero, but the other centaurs could not resist the smell of wine, and so a situation of good **xenia** turned to disaster (just as at the wedding of Peirithous), Heracles being the victor. Sadly, the bad behaviour of the centaurs caused the death of most of them. Here we have a hospitality scene with a heavy moral message, mixed with the additional themes of travel and adventure, and exotic creatures. The badly behaved centaurs live on the edges of the known world, and, though fascinating creatures, they are no match for the divinely strong Greek hero, the world-traveller, Heracles. These panels, though perhaps not the most visually elaborate, make a suitable meditation for the east façade of the temple, invoking Greek superiority and power to civilise other races.

If the deeds of Heracles metopes were arranged on the north side of the temple, as has been argued, this would be highly appropriate as a challenge to those beyond the border to comprehend the presence of the Greeks in the person of the travelling conqueror of beasts. This would leave the more diverse Greek stories of Troy, Agamemnon and others, facing the home front on the south, and signifying the domestic Greek traditions, as it were. Despite their often gory nature, they were the Greek national myth, and especially close to the hearts of folk from the Argolid, home of Agamemnon.

Heracles, who features in about half the metope scenes, is suitable for a temple of Hera – his name reflects hers, and appropriates her care for heroes. He is victorious in his struggles as he rids the world of monsters. As he moves through his various adventures, he is a marvellous role model for success. Though he meets with sadness and error at times in his life, he will ultimately become a god. (In fact, the hero shrine in the city Agora contained the vase-painting of the hero's reception into Mount Olympus.)

Attached to a shrine of Argive Hera, such epic, violent and heroic stories characterise the goddess herself as a powerful, warlike, protectress, associated with heroes. The sanctuary marked the boundary of the territory of Paestum and was marked out in the earliest period of the colony, when the colonists had everything to fight for and win. The sanctuary also marked almost the furthest point north in Italy, where Greeks had settled. Tales of travel reflected the lives of the bold colonists who had come this far, and intended to stay. On the other side of the river Sele began the territory of the powerful Etruscans. If it were thought that a warrior deity was needed to protect the border, the answer is that Hera was that warrior.

The later temple of Argive Hera

The later temple of Argive Hera, dating from about 510 BC, was very much bigger than the 'treasury' at 18.61 x 38.95 metres, and was roughly contemporary with the city Athenaion. It faced east, and faced its roughly aligned large stepped altar, with another altar to the north of it. It had eight façade columns and seventeen flank columns – the same number as the Parthenon and the Artemis temple at Corcyra. On the flanks, there was an impressive sandstone gutter, with emphatic mouldings and enormous fierce lion-head spouts, again reflecting the power of Hera (Fig. 107).

There was an inner porch of two Ionic columns in antis, introducing the Doric/Ionic mix yet again, similar to the Athenaion. Echoing the porch was an adyton. There were staircases each side of the cella entrance, now routine for temples in the West. This temple had its set of carved sandstone metopes in a Doric frieze, framed above and below by limestone cornices decorated with leaves. It is not known whether the later Heraion had sculpted metopes on all sides. A supposed complete set survives from the façade and a few more panels survive from the back of the temple. The back featured a battle, identified as an Amazonomachy with Heracles (Zancani Montuoro and Zanotti-Bianco, *Heraion alla Foce del Sele*, 1951, vol. 1, pl. 60), contrasting strongly with the peaceful action of citizen women on the front. (This could leave the flank friezes plain or painted, or just possibly they could have incorporated the earlier archaic metopes.)

The late archaic sandstone metopes from the façade are clearly a continuous series, all featuring the same scene: paired dancing maidens move to the right with raised heels and lifting arms, some flirting their skirts (Fig. 108a). They wear beautiful Ionic pleated chitons, and are 'deep-bosomed'. On the right, a single maiden looks back at the rest, like a chorus leader; by turning her head, she binds the series together as a whole scene, rather than individual images, or a decorative series (Fig. 108b). It has been suggested

Fig. 107 Temple of Hera, Foce del Sele: stone gutter with lion-head spouts, Paestum, Museo Archeologico.

(a)

(b)

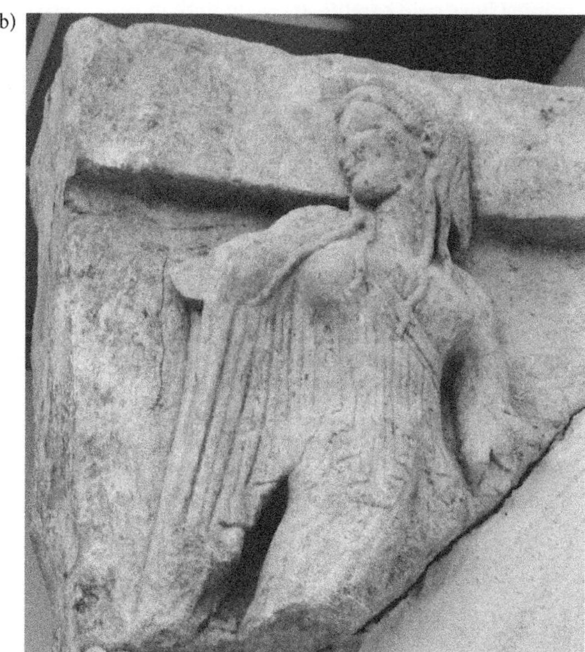

Fig. 108 Temple of Hera, Foce del Sele: metope: a) paired dancers. (By kind permission of Archaeological Park of Paestum) metope b) leader of the dancers, Paestum, Museo Archeologico.

that the maidens could be fleeing nymphs – Nereids for example – but these maidens make no gestures of fear. They move in unison, and their arm gestures are deliberate and level. Their skirts do not fly up, so their movement is measured, not frantic.

Sybaris itself had a continuous frieze of dancing maidens, now quite damaged, from a temple of Hera, *c.* 530; it seems not to be so expressive or thought out as the Sele one (Mertens, 1993, p. 567–569). The dancers seem to be shown in a simple chain with linked hands, and are accompanied by a single girl flute-player, whereas the Sele dancers overlap in pairs with complex drapery and varied poses. Nevertheless, the Sybaris example was surely known in Paestum, at least by reputation, and could prompt emulation. The style of the Hera II metopes has moved on from the earlier Sele set: proportions are less squat, faces are more natural, with shapely noses, mouths and eyes more modelled. Hair falls prettily, limbs are more slender, fabrics are differentiated, dresses are full and fashionable, their folds clinging to the limbs beneath. These later metopes consistently use an effective spatial trick: a raised frame at the top of the panel, overlapped by the heads. This has the effect of locating the heads in 'real' space, pushing the whole figure forwards and making them more vivid. Yet some of the tricks used in series two can already be found in series one. Both sets stand firmly on a ledge (like figures in vase-paintings on their painted borders). Both sets use strong undercutting and shadow, which means that not only limbs but skirts and sleeves stand out sharply in 3D. Both sets make use of overlapping to show figures acting in unison, and these pairs use an interesting mix of similar and variant in the poses. One early example (the running females) is so close to the later series, it seems the later sculptors must have paid careful attention to their predecessors' skills (Fig. 106).

Just as the first series of metopes (*c.* 570–560 BC) is grouped in themes and stories, particularly Heracles and the centaur Pholos (planned for the whole façade), here again is a single theme. It could be based on a particular story – but whether these are named characters or generic dancers, their action surely mirrors the real-life ceremonies carried out in the sanctuary in honour of Hera. Like the Parthenon frieze, the series both mirrors the worshipper and constitutes a permanent frozen worship of the goddess.

The Heraion

An extra-urban and border sanctuary like this must have had many functions. Its great importance to the polis is underlined by the magnificence and expense of both the earlier architectural sculpture and the later sculptured building which succeeded it. The sanctuary in its early phase must have been a self-conscious boundary marker. The dwellers beyond the Sele had to adjust to the new inhabitants south of the river, and the Heraion was there to emphasise that Greek Poseidonia was now a power to reckon with. At the same time, a sanctuary was not closed. Hera was there for all, and she could be a point of contact and meeting, perhaps a neutral zone. The size of the sacred area, its amenities in the form of porticos, altars with their ceremonies, the gradual addition of buildings, statues, and the opportunity for all – both Greeks and neighbours – to make offerings, would be inviting as well as impressive. Equally, the Heraion existed for the city. Its functions mirrored, expanded and added to those of the city Heraion (Hera I). Processions between the shrines would have bonded the two, and given opportunity for spectacle, for showing off what the city could do and offer, for involving those who processed and those who watched. It may well be that the extra-urban Heraion was also an amenity where women especially could contribute in ceremony and the often lengthy and complex preparation for ceremony. This would include weaving the sacred peplos, possibly training in choral singing and dancing, as well as taking part in the events themselves.

So, could this sanctuary have offered particular scope for women's activities? At the other side of the spacious site was a square building, dating from the beginning of the fourth century BC. Under this building were found large deposits of offerings, dating back from the sixth century, and onwards. Among these was a small marble Hera enthroned, holding a pomegranate (now in the museum). This was Argive Hera, as represented at Argos by Polycleitus in the same form but in colossal gold and ivory (Pausanias 2.17.4). In addition to the terracotta votives, there were, in particular, very many loom-weights. These may not even be offerings, but loom-weights that got left there during the work of weaving. This raises the attractive possibility that successive buildings on this site were the quarters of the girl and women weavers for the goddess's robe. Argive Hera regularly received a woven robe, as did other goddesses (cf. Pausanias 3.16.2, 6.24.10). (A terracotta relief from Sybaris shows a female divine figure wearing a robe with narrative bands (Cerchiai, 2002, p. 117).) We know about the new peplos made for Athene in Athens by resident arrhephoroi, and another for Hera at Olympia. Such sacred tasks, it seems, were much sought-after, and remembered as high spots of women's lives. Not only were these rites important and valuable to the city, safeguarding and prospering it; they also brought women together in a women-only environment, and were perhaps memorable life-stage experiences – like going to university is for us. Regular worship festivals were also a source of pleasure to women, a day out and an opportunity to dress up. In Euripides's *Electra*, the sympathetic Chorus of young women beg the miserable Electra to join in the festival for Argive Hera. It will 'take her out of herself', and if she has no nice outfit, they will lend her a dress and a gold necklace (Euripides: *Electra*, 190). The Chorus tell Electra: 'Great is the goddess' – she will be honoured by joyful worship.

Iphigeneia in Euripides's *Iphigeneia in Tauris* mourns that:

... in exile ...
without husband or child, city or friend,
I cannot sing and dance for Argive Hera,
or with my shuttle weave with many colours
designs of Attic Athene and the Titans
on the musical loom. (Euripides *Iph Taur* 219 f)

This is a cameo of a young woman's life – family and city, social life and female identity, are summed up by the partaking in civic/sacred rituals with her peers.

Argive Hera, relocated to Poseidonia, was a very powerful goddess in her own right. She was not the slightly comic, angry wife of Zeus, sometimes shown by Homer. She was the autonomous *kourotrophos*, protectress of youth, and warrior-protectress of the city. Hera *Hippia* cared for horses, Argive Hera carried a pomegranate to show how she promoted fertility. Hera as a goddess answered many needs of the new colony. She was a link with the distant homeland (now two stages removed.) She was a warrior and protectress in the new environment. As a goddess of fertility, she controlled crops and cattle that were the lifeline of the settlers. As a goddess of fertility, she had an interest in the other overwhelming need of the colony – the birth of new citizens. As goddess of marriage, cementing society, she would oversee the homes and families of Greek couples, and, importantly, of couples where the wife was indigenous. The shrine would be a meeting place where all could belong, Greeks and non-Greeks, and it could strengthen the wider community by the activities of joint worship. Compared with the urban Hera I, with which it was doubtless linked functionally, the much more spacious site and its amenities, not to mention the extra-urban situation, close to the border, yet in walking distance of the city, made it ideal for the purpose.

Summary

Strabo summarises the whole history of the colony like this:

> 'The city of Poseidonia, which is built about the middle of the gulf, is called Pæstum (Latin name). The Sybarites (when they founded the city) built the fortifications close upon the sea, but the inhabitants removed higher up. In after time the Leucani seized upon the city, but in their turn were deprived of it by the Romans. It is rendered unhealthy by a river which overflows the marshy districts in the neighbourhood ... The water of this river is reported to possess the singular property of petrifying any plant thrown into it, preserving at the same time both the colour and form.' (Strabo 5.4.13)

The river certainly watered the plain, but additionally it was sometimes uncontrolled, as the land conditions changed over time. It caused flooding and marshy conditions, created successive travertine plates with its 'petrifying property', and, at the very end of the inhabited life of the plain in antiquity, it caused malaria. The vestiges of population then took to the healthier hills, and the still-standing city temples became overgrown and forgotten till its rediscovery in the eighteenth century AD. Thanks to this forgetfulness, they were not plundered, and remain fairly intact today. In contrast, the Sele shrines have lost their above-ground stone, presumably to newer building, and they have lost any marble components which they ever had, to the burning for lime in lime kilns. The carved metopes however were preserved by their use as building fill.

We have now looked at the major surviving Greek buildings of Poseidonia, intra-urban and extra-urban, a neat and complete example of a wealthy and successful Greek colony. Poseidonia speaks to us only through its buildings, its layout, and the archaeological finds, and does not provide texts, inscriptions or literature, and is scarcely mentioned in ancient authors. Yet it is extra rich in the completeness of at least three generations of temple buildings, preserved quite by chance. (Other colonies could perhaps have provided equally rich architecture except for the same factor, in their case, destructive chance.) We have seen how the sanctuary buildings were made eloquent, first by their existence and then by their arrangement and décor, to speak of presence, of stability, of Greekness, of individuality. They put out a double statement of power and welcome. The summary given by Strabo of the colony's history seems to suggest it was rather uneventful, and simply got on with its business of creating a very successful self-sustaining city, surrounded by its own agricultural territory, and provided with a safe seaport. As a Greek city, it lasted about 200 years, through the sixth and fifth centuries BC, and was then absorbed peacefully, it seems, into the general flow of Italian history, along with other Greek cities in the west.

CHAPTER 16
THE TEMPLE OF OLYMPIAN ZEUS AT AKRAGAS, SICILY

Sicily

Sicily, marvellously fertile, with a long coastline, and positioned at a Mediterranean crossroads, was a sought-after possession in the ancient world. It was shared between three main elements: Carthaginians who set up coastal trading posts; the earlier inhabitants, Elymians, Sicans and Sicels, who tended to live (or were driven) inland; and Greeks who from the eighth century on were planting full colonies. Greek settlement began on the east coast and spread some way along the south and north coasts. Carthaginians were to the west of the island, controlling a harbour city at Panormus (Palermo) and settlements at Motya, and other points west. Notable settlements of the Elymians (a tribe supposed to be descended from wandering Trojans) were at Segesta, inland from the west coast, and Eryx, a rocky citadel famous for its sanctuary of Aphrodite. Carthage itself was just across the water in North Africa, surprisingly close. A look at the map will show how the geography of the island was an open invitation to all these peoples (see Map 2).

Greek colonisation in Sicily was in general a tremendous success story. The territory of Sicily was desirable for its great fertility (due in part to its volcanic soil), and many colonies became very rich indeed. Temple building was a sign of this wealth. It was a showy civilisation, given to conspicuous consumption, devoted to the arts and good living.

Akragas

Like Poseidonia, Akragas was the colony of a colony. It was founded in 582 BC by a group from Gela, led by two oikists, Aristonous and Pystilos (Thucydides 6.18). Akragas takes up territory on the south coast of Sicily between Selinus to the west, and Gela, its 'mother city', 75 kilometres to the east. Gela itself was a colony planted from Rhodes and Crete in 689 BC (see Map 2).

Akragas quickly became prosperous, due to good management of its splendidly fertile territory; and this success is reflected in its temple-building programme in the late sixth and fifth centuries BC. A comment of Diodorus on this topic is relevant, (even though he was writing in the first century BC about the latter part of the fifth century): he tells of their

> 'great prosperity, which I think would be relevant for me to describe. Their vineyards were outstanding in extent and beauty, and most of their territory was planted with olive-trees from which they gathered an abundant yield and sold it to Carthage ... The Agrigentines … gained fortunes of unbelievable size. Of this wealth, there remain among them many evidences' (Diodorus Siculus: 13.81.4–5)

The colossal temple of Olympian Zeus, among the many other smaller temples, was an exceptional one of these evidences.

This temple is interesting to study because of its bold difference from all other temples. In size, it rivals any of the colossal temples of both east and west. However, its design is what sets it apart. Its ruinous state is an obstacle to full understanding: the giant heap of masonry intrigues, but is slow to yield its secrets.

Akragas is built on two areas of high ground with a bowl of low ground between them, once containing most of the ancient city. To the north, the highest area includes the acropolis with a temple of Athene, and the Rock of Athene area containing some very early sanctuaries such as Demeter's rock shrine. To the south, a long ridge rises from west to east, keeping a view of the sea to one side and the heights of Akragas on the other. The temple of Zeus was built nearly at the base of this ridge, on level ground, while newer (fifth century) temples were dotted along the ridge, clearly seen from all prospects, and especially from the sea. The impression given to the visitor, even today, is of a visibly proud and successful city.

The sea was vital for trade, and, as the quotation from Diodorus shows, was the source of wealth, along with the produce from the land. It was also, however, a source of fear, since Carthage, their main customer, was a constant threat. The career of the colony was punctuated by two Carthaginian attacks: the Battle of Himera in 480 BC was a glorious Greek victory – but the eventual return of the Carthaginians in 409 BC resulted in the destruction of Akragas and other Sicilian Greek cities. The victory at Himera was achieved by the combined forces of Theron (tyrant of Akragas), and his brother-in-law, Gelon (tyrant of Syracuse). Two temples were then built: at Himera by Theron, and at Syracuse by Gelon, both in a similar classic fifth-century style. The very different temple of Zeus at Akragas could have been a third victory monument, but more likely was begun earlier. Dinsmoor suggests a date of *c.* 510 BC (Dinsmoor 1975, p. 101, also Coulton 1977, p. 82). Many scholars suppose that Diodorus (Diod.11.25.3) implied a start for the temple of Zeus following the battle of 480, when he mentioned that large numbers of Carthaginian captives were used for stone-quarrying. It would perhaps be tempting to think of the Olympieion as a victory monument, built by a tyrant, but there is no proof of this. Diodorus also tells us that, after the resounding victory of Himera (480 BC), the defeated Carthaginians were made to pay outright for two 'victory temples' (Diod.11.26.2).

As it is known that the two very similar classical Doric temples were built at Himera and Syracuse, it seems extremely likely that these were the victory temples. Diodorus writes elsewhere with some excitement about the Olympieion at Akragas, so he surely would have mentioned it in this connection if it were connected. Instead, he says it was the Agrigentines's first major project, and it has been suggested that the trigger was the colossal temple started at neighbouring Selinus in the late sixth century. Dinsmoor's date thus seems the most likely. If the project had already been started as early as the late sixth century, it would in any case have been boosted by the victory at Himera, not least by the new funds and the huge captive work-force. As the vast work of construction would have continued for a very long time, whoever conceived this showy temple must have counted on a long-term source of income and a stable situation.

The surroundings of the temple of Zeus

At the bottom of the ridge known as 'the Valley of the Temples' is the older sanctuary area of the chthonic deities. This is a pleasant site with several attractive smaller temple buildings and a complex layout of different-shaped altars and bothroi. It gains significance from its purpose – the shrine of Demeter and Persephone was home to the city's women-only **Thesmophoria** with its complex three-day fertility rituals.

Beyond the area of the chthonic deities was a most remarkable feature, where the ground falls off suddenly into a deep natural gorge. According to Diodorus Siculus, the tyrant Theron had some of the city's famous underground water system diverted to this spot to create a large artificial lake: 'into this they brought water from rivers and springs and it became a well-stocked fishpond supplying basic food and delicacies; when flocks of swans also settled there, it turned out to be a most pleasant sight' (Diod.11.25.4). This feature was called the **Kolymbethra**. As well as a fish-lake, it also contained rare and useful plants, and was a shady and sheltered place, offering refreshment to the public. (This lovely amenity, open to the public, has recently been restored with ecological planting by the Italian FAI – or Italian National Trust.) Although the artificial lake eventually silted up and disappeared, the ancient underground water-courses are still running, and supplying irrigation for all the new orchards and other planting.

Above the temple of Zeus is the late-sixth-century temple of Hercules (cf. Cic. *Verr.* 2.4.94). This regular Doric temple, gains visually by the superior height of its position as one looks up the ridge from the Zeus sanctuary. Yet higher along the path are two fifth-century Doric temples of uncertain identity. The so-called temple of Concord is the better preserved. Most of its exterior is complete (now restored) and, more unusually, its cella walls still rise to full height, including the pronaos and opisthodomos walls. Interestingly, the stone towers for the staircases each side of the entrance to the cella are intact, as are the doorways and stairs themselves; and in the triangular attic wall behind the tympanum, at each end of the cella, is a shaped arch surrounded by a simple carved moulding, giving access between what were the roof-spaces. These archways can give a clue to the purposes (probably ritual) of the staircases to the roof-space, which were prevalent in Western temples (Miles 1998/9).

At the top of the ridge is the so-called temple of Juno or Hera Lacinia, another fifth-century Doric temple, raised on a stone platform to enhance its prominence. These temples succeed conspicuously by their position along the sky-line.

The temple of Olympian Zeus

The location of the colossal temple of Zeus is well-chosen. In contrast to the other temples along the ridge which rear up dramatically against the sky, this one is heavily grounded. Where the ridge descends to flatter land there is plenty of room for a very large installation with its surrounding amenities including the huge altar. The temple as seen now nestles in trees and bushes. On two sides the ground falls away, exposing the huge height and solidity of the **crepidoma**. On the other sides, the ground is level, supporting the building. The current state of the ruins gives only a very partial idea of the original experience. The height and strength of the platform can be seen, holding up vestigial parts of the outer colonnade (Fig. 110). Inside, small parts of the 'cella' walls remain. Sadly, the full height of the colonnade is entirely gone, and the architectural detail is largely lost. In 1401 AD, after years of gradual collapse, an earthquake caused the remaining walls to crash outward, falling in an immense cataract of stone, obscuring the original contours and ground levels. Thereafter, the site was inevitably treated as a vast stone quarry.

To the east of the temple, some 50 metres off, is the stepped altar of Zeus, facing east. As might be guessed, this altar is unusually large at 17.50 × 54.50 metres, matching the width of the temple. There is plenty of room here for very large numbers of sacrificial cattle to be managed, and equally for thousands of worshippers to attend, as would have been needed in a large city.

The exterior

The temple of Olympian Zeus is all about size and has many features designed to maximise the aesthetic effect of its magnitude – and many features designed to cope structurally and logistically with the extra mass of stone. For example, to facilitate transport of stone to the site, and then to help with the difficulty in lifting and placing, the components of the temple are divided into blocks: the capitals are not made from the usual single round piece, but are composed of sections and the columns are not made up of the usual drums but of segmented blocks.

The temple stood on an enormous platform (Fig. 109b), measuring 52.74 × 110 metres, and composed of five high steps instead of the normal three, arranged quite steeply, more like a stepped wall about 5 metres high. The top step was double height

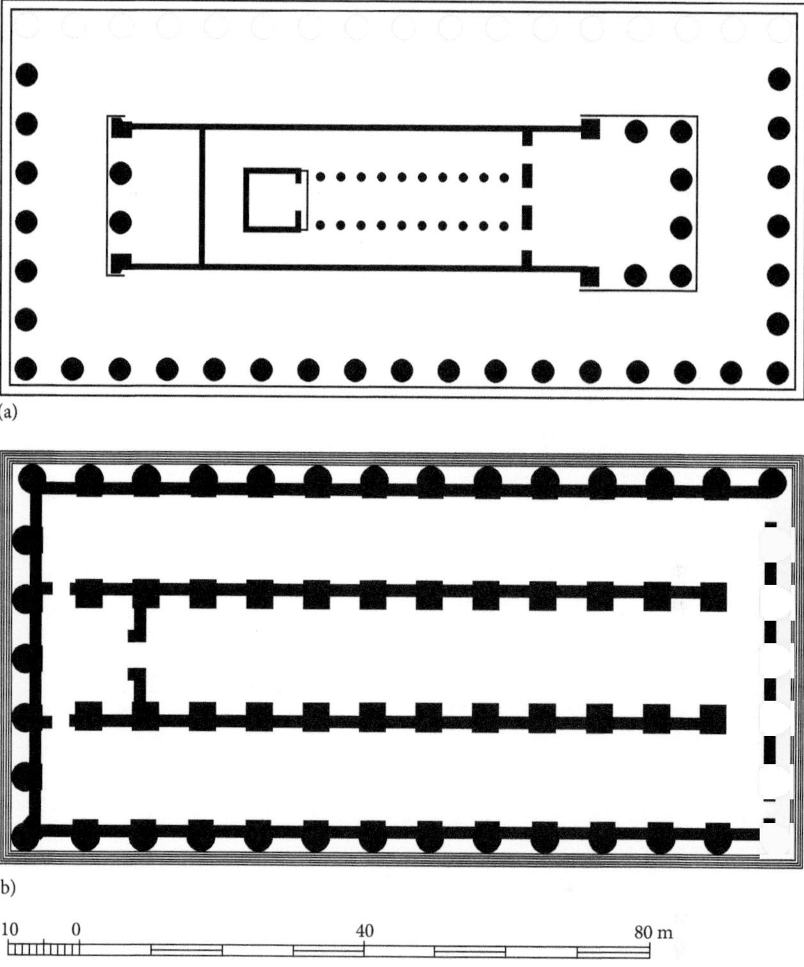

Fig. 109 Ground plans drawn to same scale: a) Temple G, Selinus (*c.* 520–409 bc); b) Temple of Zeus, Akragas (*c.* 510–409 bc). (Based on Coulton 1977).

with possibly a protruding lip (Fig. 110). With this arrangement, the visitor was not invited to approach the sides; the only approach would have been at the front, where provision for entry seems to have been at the corners. Planned in a double square of 7 × 14 columns, the front is wide in proportion to the length: most Western temples, like standard Doric temples, are more elongated. This width gave an unusually large frontage, an appropriate backdrop for the extensive sacrificial area.

The temple was to be so huge, it must have seemed to the planners that it would not hold up using the normal construction methods. Therefore, instead of the normal peristyle colonnade, it had a false colonnade of half-columns, linked by a massive connecting wall (Fig. 111). These columns were incredibly large and high – over 18 metres high – and (as said) were made up of sizeable shaped blocks rather than the

Fig. 110 Temple of Zeus, Akragas: 5-stepped platform.

Fig. 111 Temple of Zeus reconstruction model, east end, detail, Agrigento Archaeological Museum.

normal drums. The formation can still with difficulty be made out from the ruins, but the following comment from Diodorus is very helpful in establishing exactly what the arrangement was. It is interesting that Diodorus analyses the design as a fusion of two possible methods of temple building:

> And while other people build their temples either with peripheral walls or with a ring of columns to enclose the inner shrine, this temple combines both these methods; for the columns were built into the walls, the part outside the temple being round and the part inside, rectangular; and the circumference of the outside part of the column is 6 metres and a man's body can fit inside the fluting, while the inner part measures 3.6 metres. (Diodorus Siculus 13.82.3)

Diodorus measures the semi-circumference as 6 metres. In fact, the columns were just over the half-round, so they probably appeared to be actually imbedded in the wall rather than being half-columns. The designer seems to have emphasised their mightiness by using only 7 along the facades, and only 14 along the flanks. The space between them was scarcely greater than their width, a tremendously heavy proportion. Presumably this was quite deliberate as he could equally well have used a weightier wall, and slimmer and more frequent columns. Diodorus comments that a man could stand inside one flute, and this is true. The capitals were normal Doric in appearance. Above each round echinus in two parts was the square abacus in three parts, supporting the architrave and the triglyph-metope frieze.

Each column had a semicircular base made up of several Ionic-style mouldings piled at least 1.5 metres high, and these mouldings were continuous along the bottom of the wall between the semi-columns (Fig. 111). This gives some 'ballast' to the bottom of the colonnade, and binds it together, just where it might have seemed lightweight compared with the heavy entablature above.

(A similar effect, still complete, can be seen on two very small Roman temples. The first is the temple of Portunus (Fortuna Virilis) in the Ionic order, found in the Forum Boarium, Rome, and dated *c.* 120–80 BC. The other is the well-preserved Maison Carrée, in Nimes, Provence, France. This is a highly decorative Roman temple in Corinthian style, finished about 6 AD, dedicated to Gaius and Lucius Caesar, grandsons of Augustus and 'princes of youth'. Both these temples are raised on a high steep platform with steps only at the front, leading to a deep, columned prostyle porch. Round the sides and back of the buildings, the 'colonnade' is a solid wall, punctuated with semi-columns, and a high moulding running round the bases and along the walls.)

The Agrigentine Olympieion had an odd number of columns (7) to the front and back, therefore entrance to the building could not be central (as at Hera I at Paestum). The entrances seem to have been at the east front only, and were placed in the two final intercolumniations to the left and right (Fig. 109b). (There may have been an additional entrance halfway down the south flank wall between the seventh and eighth columns.) As the ground plan shows, these entrances would lead straight into the lateral roofed areas of the temple, which corresponded to the open colonnades in regular temples, while the place usually occupied by the cella was probably an unroofed courtyard that could not be directly approached.

The solid wall blocked the view into the temple from outside, (a scheme very different in feel from that of the standard Greek temple which was partially open to view all round, and which often consisted quite largely of that outer walkway, the accessible pteron). On the inner side of the solid wall, corresponding to the huge semicircular columns, were shallow rectangular **pilasters**, only visible from the interior. The wall was therefore buttressed on both sides, the larger supports being outside.

The roof

Although Diodorus assumed that the temple was unfinished, there is good evidence that it may have been finished as planned. Painted ridge tiles found in the ruins show that at least part of the roof was completed (Fig. 112). Since ridge tiles are the crowning element of a tile roof, it seems likely that each end was roofed right across behind the pediments, covering the pronaos and opisthodomos. Then the long stoas or side aisles would have had a pitched or a sloping roof. The central 'cella' area was most likely **hypaethral**, that is, an unroofed courtyard (Fig. 113).

The inner courtyard wall had deeper pilasters, backing and buttressing the slimmer ones in the 'stoas'. Again, this suggests a tiled roof over the stoas, since the support is aimed in their direction. Diodorus's use of the word 'stoas' in his description of the temple also suggests roofed corridors.

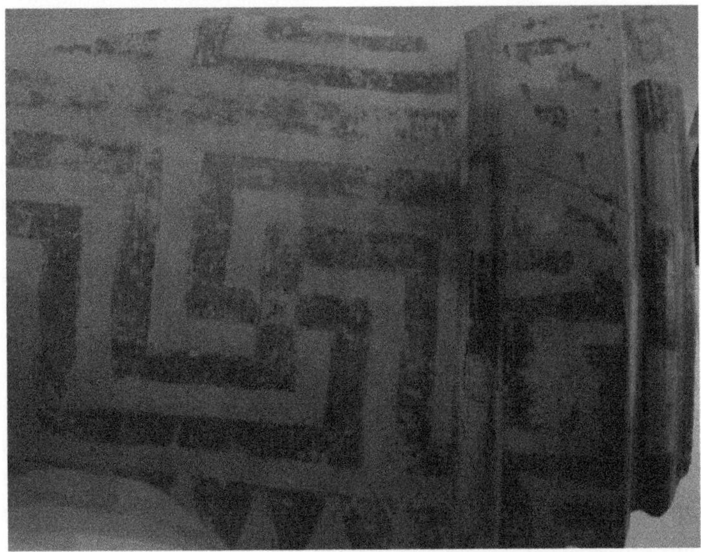

Fig. 112 Painted ridge tile from temple of Zeus, Akragas, Agrigento Archaeological Museum.

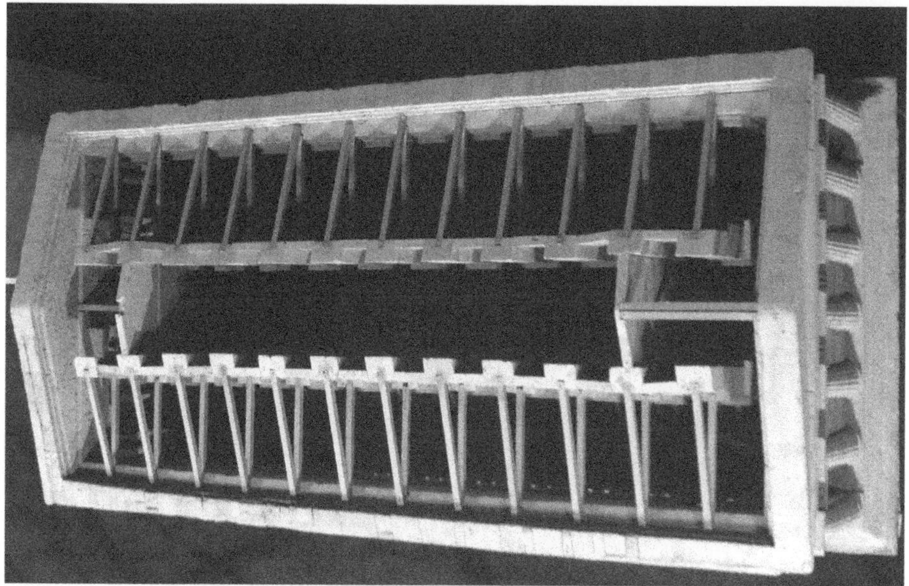

Fig. 113 Temple of Zeus Akragas: suggested reconstruction of roof. Agrigento Archaeological Museum. (Author photo)

The Telamons

Not yet mentioned is the most stunning and original feature of the temple – the **telamons**. The human figure, often carved in relief as temple decoration, for example in friezes, is also occasionally used in Greek architecture as part of the structure, for example the Siphnian Caryatids. Here at Akragas, a series of giants was employed to help support the temple. Unique male figures, 7.6 metres high, made up of blocks, were found in the ruins of the temple; being in fact columns, they were built in a similar way to the semi-columns. One telamon has been reconstructed and assembled in the Museum at Agrigento; even in the very large, two-storey hall in the Museum, the figure looks astonishingly tall (Fig. 114). However, the examples that are still lying among the ruins of the temple do not look large. They just hold their own in the huge site (Fig. 115).

The purpose of these giants on the building has been controversial, ever since they were rediscovered in the early nineteenth century. At first it was thought they were interior decoration. However, a place and purpose has been suggested for them that seems entirely logical, on the exterior. The massive columns and the connecting wall together bore the huge weight of the entablature. The architrave as usual protruded slightly; but, being made up of separate blocks rather than the usual single long block, it needed extra support halfway along each intercolumniation, at the joint. Iron bars were inserted under the architrave from abacus to abacus, indicating some anxiety on the part of the architect. But the problem was also met in a more spectacular way. Part-way up each connecting section of wall was a simple ledge. An egg-and-dart moulding may have underlined the

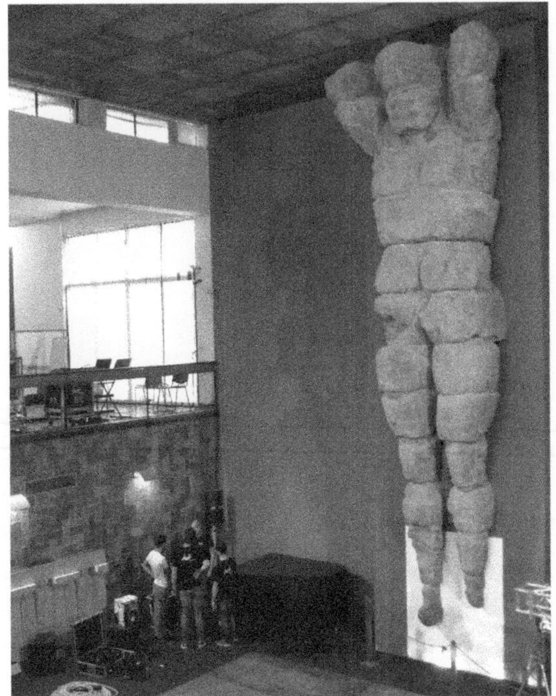

Fig. 114 A reassembled telamon displayed in the museum, indicating scale. Agrigento Archaeological Museum.

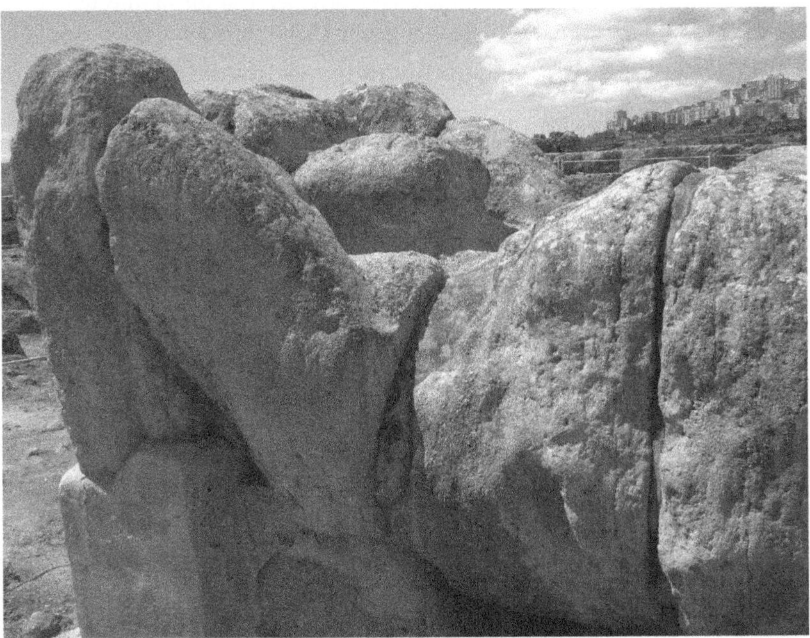

Fig. 115 Recumbent torso, on the site of the temple of Zeus, Agrigento.

ledges (Dinsmoor 1950). (Compare the egg-and-dart under the Erechtheum Caryatids's plinth (Fig. 72).) On top of each ledge stood a giant whose head and raised arms did real work, reinforcing the weak part of the architrave – at the joint. So, all round the temple was a rhythmic alternation of muscular telamon and fluted column: an elegant solution to the weight problem.

The figures – which are now badly eroded – would seem to hover between archaic and severe style. The bodies are robust. Their weight is firmly equal on both legs. Their arms are lifted and folded back to take their burden. This has the effect of raising the chest convincingly. Their heads are bowed to take the weight, and this has the effect that they may make eye-contact with the viewer, far below.

Some of the heads are fairly well-preserved (Fig. 116), and one can see that the hair is neat and wavy, the mouth gently smiles, the eyes look down. The carving slightly differs on each: some telamons are bearded, some clean-shaven – mature or youthful. It is thought these would have alternated. It is just possible, too, that the leg position may have varied, being closer together or further apart, but always with equal weight distribution; not like kouroi, who step forward, but in the static stance of korai, feet

Fig. 116 Head of telamon: badly worn. Agrigento Archaeological Museum.

together. A step forward would hardly be appropriate, while the feet-together stance speaks of stability and permanence. These are not robots. The somewhat crude effect is probably deceptive because much detail may be worn off; originally their facial details would have been painted naturalistically. The tawny tufa stone of the figures, and of all the buildings of Akragas, wears poorly. Originally a fine layer of stucco protected them from weather, but the unprotected surface breaks up (Fig. 117). For this reason, it takes a bit of imagination to 'restore' the appearance of the telamons.

As said above, of the many arrangements that have been suggested, the most satisfactory is that the figures stood on a simple recessed ledge, about two-thirds up the wall, and supported the architrave directly. What remains in doubt is whether the wall each side of them was continuous, or was pierced with apertures for light. If pierced, a slim pier may have reinforced the backs of the figures. The reconstruction model in the Museum is made in this way. Since the interior needed some kind of light, it is tempting to imagine the long series of slit-like windows, patterning the stoa inside with dramatic

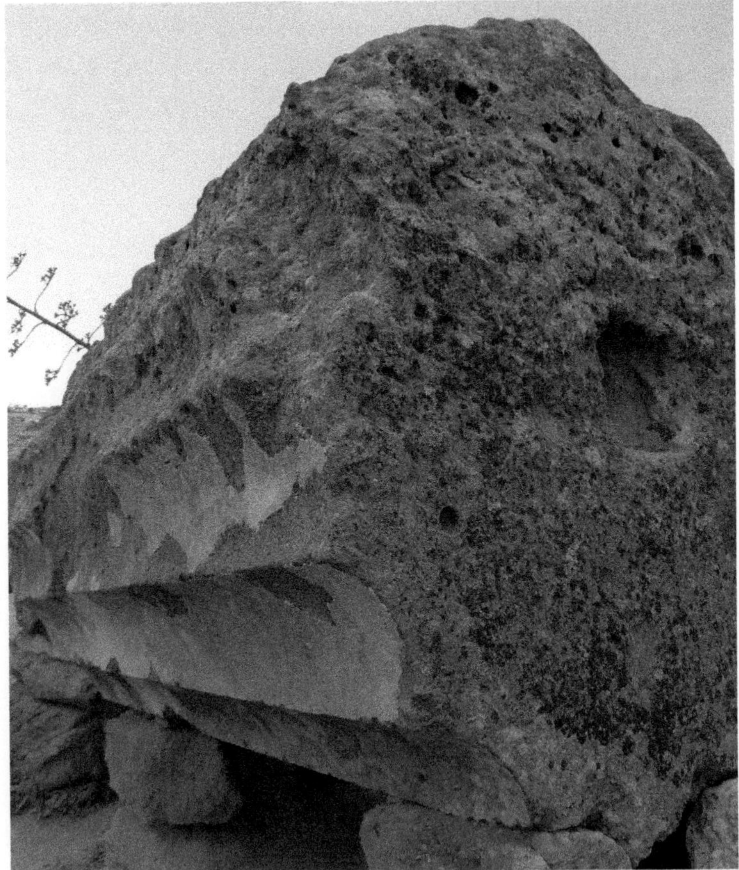

Fig. 117 Fallen column drum, showing weathering and remains of stucco protective layer, Agrigento.

strips of bright sunshine and alternating shadow. A possible alternative is that light came in from gaps in the screen walls of the 'cella' (or even from both directions).

A confirmation of the arrangement suggested for the positioning of the giants may be seen in an unexpected setting – the Forum Baths at Pompeii, built *c.* 60 BC (Fig. 118). These baths are extremely elegant and architectural; in the tepidarium, storage niches at shoulder height – probably for bathing equipment – are guarded by small-scale male figures constructed of stuccoed terracotta. They stand on a ledge on little plinths, as though supporting an entablature with an egg and dart immediately above them, leaning against the ends of spur walls that divide the niches. These mini-telamons are sturdy bearded figures, wearing little furry or leafy loin-cloths. The witty designer must have been aware of the giants of the Temple of Zeus at Agrigento. Here he has provided clothed figures to guard the lockers of naked bathers, and he has provided giants in miniature. More tongue-in-cheek, he has compared the sublime to the trivial – very effectively.

It is often asserted that the giant telamons represented Carthaginian captives from the Battle of Himera who were put to work on the building. Diodorus tells how these captives were used for stone-quarrying and also were used in constructing the underground water-system devised by engineer Phaiax for the tyrant Theron. Although slave labour might well be employed in building a temple, especially one this big, it would hardly have been considered tasteful to display images of captured slaves on a Greek sacred building – although for someone like Diodorus writing in the Roman era, first century BC, it would be a natural assumption (Oestenburg 2009). While the Romans certainly displayed

Fig. 118 Small-scale telamons, Forum baths, Pompeii, first century BC.

captives on, for example, the arch of Constantine, or the forum of Trajan, as in a Triumph, the Greeks did not do this. These figures, nude and without any accessories or attributes, represent **Atlantes**, non-human figures of immense strength and size, capable of holding up a weight like the heavens, in the service of Zeus. They honour the god, and proclaim his greatness. They are the Doric equivalent of the glamorous jewel-laden maidens at Delphi who hold up porches. Instead of charm and fashion, they exemplify naked power. (The meaning of the telamons will be discussed further below). Another difference between telamons and caryatids is the pose – telamons support their burden with raised arms and bowed head, while caryatids stand very straight and queenly, not noticing their burden.

The Pediments

The main evidence for the pediments is found in Diodorus Siculus (13.82.4) who tells us that the east pediment had a Gigantomachy with carvings of 'outstanding size and beauty', while the west had a Fall of Troy, 'showing each of the heroes crafted to appear as he really would have been'. These pediments are problematic in that only scanty traces of them exist as fragments of relief carving (de Waele 1982).

Diodorus gives no information about the construction of the Zeus pediments except that they were made with 'carvings'. The Greek term he uses (*glyphai*) sounds more like relief carving than like free-standing statues, and this accords with the fragments found. The stone of the tympana could possibly have been carved in a quite deep relief like the Gorgon pediment at Corcyra, but, even if shallow, would have been stuccoed and brightly coloured. Like this, the design would have shown up well, with large, clear figures in the large field of the tympanum. A lion was part of the composition – only its tail is preserved (Barbanera: Fig 47) – and its varied shape would have added to the interest (cf. the Siphnian gigantomachy). Generally, the width of the narrative pediments combined with the height of the columns and their alternating giant figures would have resulted in a rich and impressive temple. Diodorus in his description emphasises the words 'size', 'height', 'magnificence', 'magnitude', 'largest in Sicily', 'outstanding in size and beauty'.

A beautiful marble torso and helmeted head of a nude warrior, crouching or bending as though in the midst of battle, was found stuffed into a cistern in the temple of Zeus. (The marble would have been imported since it is not found on Sicily.) This warrior could have come from a pediment, and it is tempting to think that the Olympieion pediments could be reconstructed from the figure – but at under life-size its scale would be far too small for such a large space. It could, instead, be from the normally sized pediment of the adjacent temple of Heracles. To include this warrior in the Zeus temple, a combination of stone relief and free-standing marble figures has been proposed; this could be compared with the well-known fifth-century acrolithic metopes of temple E in Selinus where the women's faces and limbs are marble inserts while the rest of the metope is limestone relief (de Waele 1982). But the marble warrior is too small for the site, and the proposed system seems unlikely.

Regarding the subject matter as recorded by Diodorus, the Gigantomachy on the east front emphasises divine order, and Zeus as king. Highly appropriate to a temple of

Zeus, this message would hold true whether in a tyranny or a democracy. Temples were built to last for a very long time; iconography could not be designed as a rapid response to current events, as things could change and the investment of effort and finance was long-term. Here the topic may possibly have had political meaning and could certainly recall the Carthaginian invasion, but it is also perennial. Looking at the whole temple, in the context of the pedimental Gigantomachy it would have been reassuring to the average citizen viewer to see all the Atlantes – the 'good' giants – so calmly and orderly supporting the status quo.

The west pediment featured the Fall of Troy, namely the triumph of the Greeks in their human endeavours. This too was a useful 'trope' of wide application. These two topics were often paired in architectural sculpture, for example they were later used on the Parthenon metopes and the temple of Athene Nike pediments in their very different mainland Greek setting.

The interior

To imagine the experience of approaching and entering this temple is difficult – since it was like no other. There was no pteron open to view, no intermediate position: the visitor was either in or out. Once having climbed the eastern steps and entered at one of the 'corner' doors at right or left, he/she would find themselves in an immense, long space, roofed, probably darkened. Like a vast, architectural tithe-barn, cut off from the bustle of the sanctuary, the contrast with the outside world would have been striking. This space would have been at least 18 metres in height, 110 metres in length, and about 12 metres wide. (These long indoor areas were perhaps the 'stoas' which Diodorus Siculus admired for 'size and height', in other words, roofed corridors. His admiration of them suggests he had access.) On one side of the corridor would be the rectangular pilasters backing the exterior semi-columns. On the other side, corresponding pilasters lined the inner walls (or screen walls) that defined the inner cella space. There is no information about what would have been inside the stoas, whether cult statue or decoration, or light source, other than this strong, regular pattern of shallow rectangular pilasters.

There were two of these long stoas, one each side. What is most strange about the division of space in the temple is the passage from the stoas to the central area. A look at the plan (Fig. 109b) will show that the inner screen walls run nearly to the outer end walls (east and west). Of course, there is in reality plenty of room to pass from one area to the other, as the scale is so huge. But in terms of the whole layout, and remembering the huge heights involved, the narrowness of this connecting space is disconcerting.

Looking at the plan, it can be seen that the stoa, or what would be the colonnade in a conventional temple, would notionally have run around all four sides with uniformly wide measurement – except that, on the east and west ends, that width has been cut into by the final section of each interior screen wall. The last sections of the screen walls at each end (from pilaster to pilaster/anta) come close to the outer wall creating a porch-like space or 'pronaos' between them. As there is no outlet at the centre of the *outer* wall, the 'porch' is closed where it would be expected to be open. The way forward will be *inward* to the centre space, or 'cella'.

So, the visitor who has entered the stoa, and now wishes to move to the inner courtyard or unroofed 'cella', must retreat to the east (or west wall), slipping round the final pilaster (or anta), into the (presumably) roofed space of the 'pronaos' (or 'opisthodomos'). Once there, he will emerge, into the central, daylit walled space. It is not clear from the current state of the site, whether cross-walls defined the 'front porch' section from the 'cella' area. If the 'porches' were roofed, this would be a definition in itself. However, there may have been walling as well, making a front porch, and also possibly separating off an adyton on the west, for priestly purposes.

The courtyard walls were punctuated with heavy pilasters, backing the slimmer ones on the inner walls of the stoas, and reinforcing them, buttressing the weight of the roof. But, what else was there is unknown. Was there an impressive statue? Plantings, trees, or pot-plants? A pool? A display of many offerings and small votives, with the full range of showy goods that could be found in sanctuaries – or a small, roofed inner shrine? A **naiskos**, sheltering a cult statue, would have suitably ended the vista and blocked the west-end gap, shown on the plan. No clue has survived. Any or all of the above are likely, by parallel with Ionian temples. And because of the closed stoas, there would be a particularly strong experience of the changes from darkness to daylight, and from roofed to open, and to the spacious sacred enclosure. As Zeus is god of the sky, it could be considered that a courtyard open to the sky is manifesting the god himself. This experience has been heightened by the preparatory darkness (comparatively at least) of the stoas, and the cramped entry via the narrow gap between walls. A further effect might have been extra silence, or an insulated hushed background to any ritual speech or sound (cf. McMahon 2013).

A question to be asked about this completely closed-in temple concerns the access: Who was allowed in? It is usually assumed that the public did not freely enter temples, or even not at all. Some hints about public access exist, for example, the viewing gallery in the temple of Zeus at Olympia reported by Pausanias (Paus 5.10.10). The Agrigentine temple of Zeus seems to suggest that at least some limited access must have been available in order to make any use at all of the vast hidden interior. In the above discussion, the term 'visitor' must cover 'any person who would be permitted to enter', whether priest, choral singer, worshipper or member of the public. Diodorus seems to have entered in the first century BC, if indeed he did enter the stoas he so admired. Sacred personnel obviously had to enter the temple and do what needed doing there. It would be surprising if the access was this limited to a civic building of such immense grandeur and expense and which was so expressive of the wealth and well-being of the city.

Influences

The temple of Zeus at Akragas is unlike any other Greek temple. Where could the designer have got his ideas from?

The first characteristic is the size. Colossal temples typically were Ionic and mainly found in the Greek east, in Ionia. Major Ionic temples with their slender proportions and their forests of columns were impressive and huge, yet they were light and airy; their **ptera** were wing-like and floating. The space they held seemed greater than their mass, the marble or limestone material was bright and held a sharp edge. They were decorated and decorative. Above all, the colonnades were very open on all sides to the visitor, even though extra emphasis was laid on the front and the deep entrance way.

The Agrigentine architect might have heard about, or even seen, the Archaic temple of Apollo at Didyma (540 BC), linked with Miletus, which, in style was very different from the Zeus temple, being dipteral with elegant Ionic columns giving the airy 'forest of columns' effect. In size, the dimensions were close (51 × 110 metres) but giving a small win to Akragas. It also had deep rectangular pilasters around its inner unroofed courtyard or 'cella', reinforcing a very large wall. (This feature was later repeated in the even larger Hellenistic rebuild of this temple (Lawrence 1996, Fig. 237).) The temple of Didyma had its inner courtyard planted with trees, and sheltered a naiskos or small shrine, housing a cult statue. This oracular temple also enclosed a sacred spring, maybe the original source of the oracular cult.

We have briefly looked at the religiously important limestone temple of Hera at Samos (*c.* 525 BC) (Fig. 5), the birthplace of the goddess. As the cella contained two rows of 10 columns each, a roof was probably planned. Although possibly never finished, this temple was still immensely influential. It was slightly larger than Zeus at Akragas at 54.5 × 111.2 metres, and perhaps was the largest of all Greek temples.

A third colossal Ionic temple was the marble Artemision of Ephesus, *c.* 560 BC; at 46 × 115 metres it was not larger than Akragas, but was doubtless finer and more splendid, with rich sculptural decoration. The mid-sixth-century version of this famous shrine received financial backing from the rich king Croesus. Like Didyma, it was probably hypaethral, having an inner unroofed cella despite the surrounding forest of columns.

These three famous temples situated in a close geographic triangle (see Map 2) provided incentives for rivalry between themselves in terms of size, above all, but also of decoration. Each was rebuilt more than once, becoming greater each time. These sixth-century versions would certainly have been well-known in architectural circles throughout the Greek world of their day as bench-marks of great temples.

Another colossal temple nearer to home that could have provided inspiration was the temple of Olympian Zeus at Athens, begun by the sons of Peisistratus in about *c.* 520 BC. Although this temple was in fact to be abandoned at the fall of the Peisistratids in 510 (Dinsmoor's date for the Akragas Olympieion), it still could have set, in its huge scale, a mainland target to be achieved and surpassed by others, especially by tyrants. The Athenian temple was to be Doric in style, but Ionian-inspired in layout, again emulating Samos, Ephesus and Didyma: it was to be dipteral, with an additional row of columns on the ends. The columns were 8 across the ends and 20 on the sides. The measurements of the platform were 41 x 108 metres, so they were surpassed in Akragas by a definite margin (53 x 110 metres). It seems the columns were **poros** rather than marble, so perhaps were quite heavy in design (Wycherley, 1964, Lawrence/Tomlinson,

1996). Some of this temple was probably intended to be **hypaethral** (unroofed) due to the size, and the fact that this was common with Ionian temples. This temple also was situated in a low-lying position, near, but in contrast to, the lofty setting of the Acropolis. The visual aim must have been similar to that of the Olympieion of Akragas, that is to appear vast and grounded, making a virtue of its great weight.

(The unfinished Athens building later received attention from Antiochus Epiphanes (175–164 BC), and was finally completed in marble by the Philhellene emperor Hadrian on the old ground plan, but in colossal Corinthian style with a chryselephantine Zeus, satisfying at once both Hadrian's love of Greek culture and the Roman taste for gorgeousness.)

The designer of the temple of Zeus at Akragas came up against problems of competition with the great eastern temples. He had to work with a stone that was naturally a muddy colour and incapable of a lasting smooth finish. And it was not as strong as marble, so it needed to be bulky. Quantity of stone, however, was not a problem: he was able to foreground the merit of enormous mass. He was also working with the Doric style, which suited the type of stone much better than fine Ionic. He had to privilege the virtues of overwhelming size and strength, while rivalling the greatest sacred buildings so far built. By using the concept of giants, and matching them with gigantic architectural forms, he solved his problems, both practical and aesthetic, and created an atmospheric and striking building indeed.

The architect also had to do honour to his patron. Nobody praises a puny building or an insufficient offering to the gods. The building had to represent a 'money no object' attitude. It had to proclaim a wealthy and powerful city – a city that stood out among the rich and powerful cities of Sicily. Diodorus says that this temple exemplified 'magnificence' (Greek – *megaloprepeia*) – that is: the desirable Aristotelian quality of rich men who build appropriately to their station in life (e.g. Aristotle: *Nic Eth*, IV, 2).

According to Dinsmoor (1950) and Coulton (1977), the immediate competitor and inspiration was not in Ionia but in neighbouring Selinus, another successful Sicilian city with a plethora of temples (Fig. 109a). The colossal building known as temple G was begun near the end of the sixth century and was not yet finished when the Carthaginian attack in 409 put a stop to all building. Some of the huge column drums, half-quarried and still unfluted, can still be seen, today, in the quarry known as Cave di Cusa, 13 kilometres from Selinunte/Selinus. They lie, just where they were abandoned on the day of the Carthaginian attack (Fig. 119). The half-finished temple itself is a huge pile of tumbled masonry, thrown down by earthquake. At 50.07 × 110.12 metres, it was equally as long but not quite as wide as the Agrigentine Olympieion. Temple G was planned as Doric octostyle **peripteral**, with a deep inner porch of 4 columns across, with 2 behind, and deep antae, leading, by a 3-door entrance to a large inner 'cella' or court. According to Ross Holloway (2000) this court was probably to be unroofed, while the 'peristyle was thought of as a colonnade around a court (Ibid p. 71-2)' in which stood a free-standing **naiskos**. This inner open courtyard, though different in design, could be a direct precedent for the temple at Akragas. Yet a glance at the ground plans will show how different the effect would be. Akragas is heavy, bold and extremely simple with impressive spaces, each

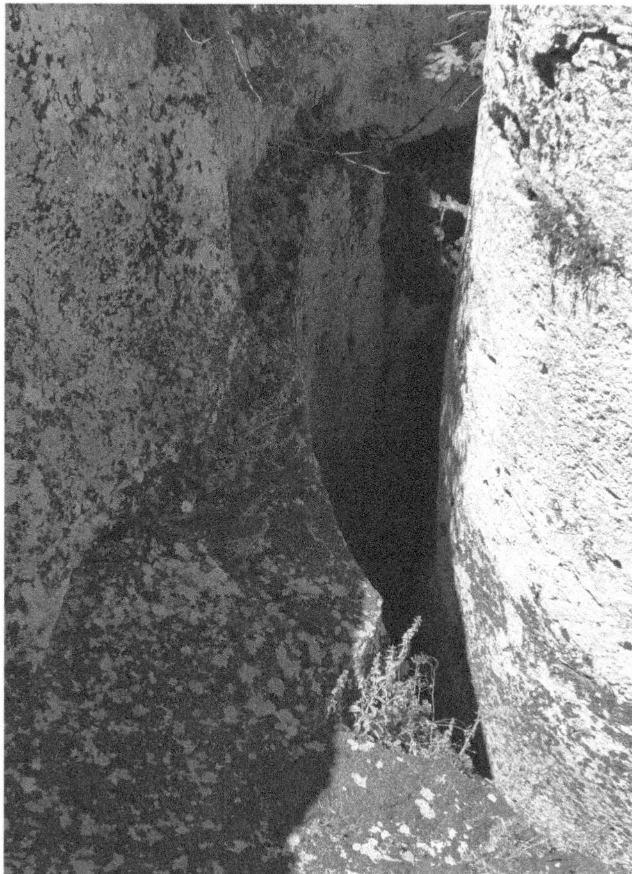

Fig. 119 Half-quarried tufa column drum, intended for Temple G, Selinus, Cave di Cusa, Sicily.

one closed-in and repetitive in treatment. Selinus, though Doric, has an Ionic complexity of layout, with its variety of column sizes and combination of colonnades and solid walls. According to the reconstructed elevations of the two temples given by Coulton (1977 Figs. 28 and 29), the entablature and pediment were slimmer and lower in Selinus, the weight far less. At Selinus, though massive by most standards, the columns were far less so than at Akragas, and they were combined with open spaces and sight-lines piercing through colonnades. Besides this, the platform of the temple of Zeus was higher and more massive with its 5 cliff-like steps and the use of the multiple moulding to thicken the bases of the columns and walls. By comparing the ground plans and elevations, it is easy to see that the architect at Akragas was determined on a temple that would match his conception of giants, and would give a very physical idea of the greatness of Zeus.

Another feature of the Olympieion can be found in Selinus at a smaller temple known as Temple F. This collapsed building has been reconstructed with stone screen walls linking the columns of the colonnade. These walls rose to a height of 4.6 metres or so, making it impossible to see into the corridor of the peristyle from outside, although the upper half was still open. The screens were fashioned with a 'false door' between each column, really a decorative panel, but giving the effect of a concealed entrance. Each panel would remind the outside viewer that entrance was closed to him/her, although presumably any ritual sounds would be perfectly audible. It has been suggested that this temple was designed for a mystery religion, only for initiates. Although this factor was presumably irrelevant to the worship of Zeus at Akragas, the idea of supporting-walls in the colonnade was obviously very useful structurally. The concealment of the interior also made this temple appear different from any other Greek temple.

What about precedents for the colossal human figures, the unique telamons? Several of the Ionian temples featured **columnae caelatae:** these were columns with one drum carved with large deep relief figures, like a frieze. (In some temples, this would be the lowest, but, in others, the topmost drum.) Such was the scale of the temples that the figures on the column could be life-size. One example from the later-fourth-century Artemision at Ephesus is in the British Museum (interpreted as Alcestis being abducted by Death). The earlier archaic Ephesus temple patronised by Croesus already featured sculpted columns (Dinsmoor, 1975, Fig. 48). Ian Jenkins suggests the earlier version included scenes from a ritual procession honouring the goddess. He puts this forward as a precedent for the Parthenon frieze, as an image reflecting contemporary life and worship (Jenkins, 2007). These large-scale sculpted columns can also be seen as a precedent for the large-scale human figure as temple decoration. Another precedent would be the life-size Delphic Caryatid maidens (Fig. 11). From life-size to colossus is just another step. Another possible predecessor for the telamons is the ubiquitous colossal kouros. One example would be the kouros found at the Heraion of Samos, over 5.5 metres in height and a personal votive offering (Kyrieleis, 1993), or another even bigger example on Delos (Hurwit, 1985). The colossal kouros, even when offered by an individual person, and usually not part of a state-sponsored plan, would still become a conspicuous landmark in a sanctuary, part of the visual impression of the built environment. With these predecessors in mind, it does not seem such a big jump for the architect at Akragas to include colossal statues as an integral part of his temple design.

It is sometimes claimed that the design of the Zeus temple derives from the Egyptian or Carthaginian style. Of course, the origins of Greek architecture are not unrelated to Egypt with its ancient stone-working skills and monumental pillared courts. As for Carthaginian temples, none has specifically been cited, although a pilastered inner courtyard has been identified in Sardinia. It has been shown here that the peculiar features of the Agrigentine Olympieion can all be accounted for by reference to other Greek temples, so there is no need to look elsewhere for sources. Even so, this temple is a unique enterprise, and shows what could be achieved by new arrangements of familiar features.

Further thoughts on the Telamons

The telamons stood like kouroi, but with feet together in a fixed posture, arms above and behind their heads in a static posture of steady exertion. A familiar mainland sculpted figure stands just like this, and the resemblance can hardly be a coincidence. As has often been pointed out, Heracles in metope 10 of the temple of Zeus at Olympia resembles a telamon turned sideways. The designer would seem to have had knowledge of the Agrigentine figures, and have been prepared to adapt a well-known architectural motif for use in his very different narrative work. In the metope, Heracles is standing in for Atlas, so this seems like a clue as to how the Agrigentine figures should be understood. Atlas was an immortal: although his role of holding up the heavens was not necessarily pleasant for him, it was vital for the Kosmos, and for the continuation of the races of gods and men. He separated sky from earth, making sure that the horror of Chaos could not happen. Akragas faced south across the Mediterranean towards Africa and the Atlas Mountains where it was supposed the giant deity was located. He was almost a neighbour. So, it may be more accurate to think of the weight-bearing figures on the temple of Zeus at Akragas as Atlantes, a series of Atlases. It was commented about the temple of Athene at Paestum - which has stars in the coffers of its soffit - that the roof of a temple might be thought of as a stand-in sky (p. 204). So, the Atlantes would then be doing their proper job; by holding up the architectural sky, they would represent sustaining the world-order of which Zeus is the commander-in-chief. They would be demonstrating his rule and offering a visible metaphor for things being as they should be, and guaranteeing that they would remain so. This is rather different from the idea of resentful Carthaginian slaves creating a permanent artistic record of their slave labour. It is more appropriate, more uplifting and far more truly honouring of Zeus.

Looking at the physical resemblance between the Agrigentine telamons and Heracles at Olympia, it is very noticeable that the pose is the same, the braced stance, the raised arms, the lowered head and gaze. The beautiful musculature of Heracles may once have been more reflective of the Sicilian figures than it is today. We have seen that the Agrigentine stone weathers poorly when unprotected, so the surface of the figures may have been far more worked and nuanced than it is now. What can still be seen is a more human and muscular treatment of the torso from certain angles, for example in Fig. 115, where the lift of the chest as a response to the effort being made is very natural, and is the same as can be seen in Heracles. Another point of similarity is the beard. On the temple of Zeus at Akragas, the figures alternated with beard and non-beard, mature and youthful. Possibly the sculptor of the Olympic metopes got the idea from here, that his Heracles could start youthful, beardless, and exhausted - and be seen to mature and change as a character. Normally a repeated personage in a series would look the same each time, for easy identification. It is an original factor in this series that Heracles is allowed to look different at different times, and this factor demands that the viewer observe very carefully. Of course, by metope 10 the hero *has* matured, and his beard is rendered in the same flat scoop-shape as those on the telamons (Fig. 116).

It has often been observed that the Heracles metope of the Apples of the Hesperides at Olympia is very architectural and can be compared with a triglyph, with its 3 upright parallel figures (Fig. 36). Further, it appears that Heracles (with the aid of Athene) is holding up the actual entablature, which is of course the same task as the Atlantes/telamons do. The metope is narrative, which changes its format: the bearing figure is in profile, whereas as a caryatid figure in architecture it would be frontal. The other two figures are also in profile (apart from Athene's body) because they are interacting with the hero. There is a certain quality of wit in the design: Athene is a one-handed caryatid, with a light hand; Atlas, the real bearer of the heavens, is moonlighting; Heracles, in carrying out one Labour, has got landed with another unscheduled one. Nevertheless, the design is full of dignity, pathos and heroism. The face of Heracles is possibly the most profoundly human touch in this whole, very human, metope series. His resignation and patience after so much suffering, with the apples of immortality coming towards him, and still a hiatus of how he is going to be given possession of them – it all is very moving to any viewer who confronts the scene thoughtfully. It backs the message of Olympia that there is no gain without pain and self-control. It goes further than athletics: this message applies to every viewer and every life.

At the same time, this metope may speak in a special way to one regional group, those from Sicily, especially Akragas. Olympia was of course greatly frequented by Western Greeks (Shepherd, 2000) and it is often said that different metopes from the series represented various quarters of the Greek world, as well as the Peloponnese itself. In this metope, Sicilians could recognise their own temple figure brought to life in a very significant narrative, supported by a graceful Athene. Intriguingly, the Atlas figure has changed places with the greatest of hero figures, Heracles, who is seen here at his weakest - and yet at his strongest, because he is doing the job of an immortal. Heracles, the greatest Greek hero, represents all Greeks; but also, as we have seen, he can at times especially represent travellers and exploration, and therefore, colonists. Another metope, the fight with three-bodied Geryon, might also have reference to the colonisation of Sicily, the three-cornered island. The Atlas Mountains, the Hesperides, and Geryon with his cattle, all lay in the west. Western visitors would likely have been gratified to approach the great central temple of Zeus and find a personal, inclusive greeting incorporated into very fabric of the temple itself.

The above discussion is made on the assumption that temples and their decoration were not only very carefully designed, but that viewers were generally well aware of visual detail and were prepared to recognise the significance for themselves. Some readers may object that people would not be aware. Certainly not all would be, but considering the vast public expense and attention given by the Greeks to such things, it seems most likely that they were meaningful to most people on some level. It is also made on the assumption that whoever designed the Heracles metopes knew about the Agrigentine temple, either from seeing it, or from close description. The Agrigentine temple of Zeus, though perhaps still under construction when the Olympia temple was conceived, would have been new enough and big enough to be reckoned with by any other temple-builder of the period.

Conclusion

The temple of Olympian Zeus at Akragas was an ambitious and successful project, now sadly all but lost to us. Its scheme has not been repeated, probably because the scale of it would be too challenging, not because it was unimpressive. However, the closed nature of its relation to the worshipper/visitor may also have been a factor not to repeat. It goes counter to the spirit of almost all other Greek temples, which were open to view and to circumambulate.

The designer and the patron who conceived the project were clearly in competition to augment the prestige of Akragas, as well as of Zeus himself. They made their temple larger than temple G in neighbouring Selinus, larger than the Olympieion in Athens, larger than most temples in Ionia.

However, size was just the beginning of it. Stylistically, they were determined on creating something very different. The gigantic conception at Akragas is the Doric answer to the Ionian colossal temples of Samos, Didyma and Ephesos. It retains a Doric spirit and Doric styling, while achieving something new, not just an upsizing of the 'same old thing'. With it, they have achieved what Diodorus calls 'magnificence', the appropriately imaginative scale of expenditure of a very rich city. This urban temple, the first major building project in Akragas, was clearly built to impress. As a result, the citizen of Akragas could feel himself to be a 'citizen of no mean city' when consorting with others across the Greek world.

It is a pity that this unique temple has all but vanished from sight. Despite the numerous undeniable vestiges of it, the original impact can only be appreciated in imagination. As a temple of Zeus, it conveyed the power of the king of the gods through architectural means. It is possible that an echo of this powerful vision is also felt at Zeus's satisfyingly massive Doric temple in mainland Olympia. There the heavy colonnade and the preserved east pediment with its columnar figures (though narrative and characterised rather than generic) shared something of the solemnity and weight of the Agrigentine Olympieion.

CHAPTER 17
LOOKING AT ART IN SANCTUARIES

How did the ancient viewer look at art and architecture? We have already made some guesses from the evidence of the art itself. We have tried to re-imagine the ancient experience of visiting sanctuaries as spectacles, and how the individual buildings might impact the viewer aesthetically; what they might have meant to him or her, in actual life, and why money was spent on them. We have given some consideration to the needs of patrons and the challenges faced by designers in helping them achieve their objectives. We have also looked at how designers could use the art of the past to create new ideas, for example, the archaic temple of Apollo at Bassae and its late-fifth-century update, or the Siphnian frieze updated in the Parthenon frieze.

The artists were experts, schooled in their task and involved in developing their field. What of the ordinary person, the 'consumer' (as it were) of sanctuaries? And how did the unschooled viewer respond to sculpture and the decorative and narrative parts of architecture? A few scattered clues can be found in literature. For example, there is one unusual extended dramatic passage worth examining, as it represents the 'public' in the act of looking at art in a sanctuary.

A visit to Delphi is featured in Euripides's play, *Ion* (mentioned in Chapter 11). Queen Creusa, daughter of Erechtheus, has come from Athens with her husband King Xouthos to consult the oracle about their childlessness. Creusa also has a secret sorrow: as a young girl, she was raped by Apollo, and the resulting baby she bore in secret and hid in a cave under the Acropolis. That baby disappeared and, without her knowledge, has been brought to Delphi by the god Hermes: it is Ion, now the young temple servant.

Towards the beginning of the play is a scene-setting passage (Euripides, *Ion* 185–237) in which the Chorus of women from Athens look around at the various buildings and sculptures; they are slaves, the hand-maidens of Queen Creusa. Here, they are visitors, having a day out. These women are having a wonderful time.

The scene is set in the forecourt of the temple of Apollo, where Ion, the temple servant, is carrying out his duties. The women behave in the scene as tourists. They are clearly not very experienced or well-travelled, and everything is new and surprising to them. Their first response to the sanctuary is to compare it with what they already know:

> CHORUS: Not in blessed Athens only
> are there finely columned temples,
> and worship of Apollo of the Gate-Post.
> Also at the shrine of **Loxias** (Apollo),
> son of Leto, from twin faces
> shines the light of lovely eyes. (Euripides *Ion*, 184–9)

They note two architectural features at Delphi – colonnades and pediments – which they relate with pleasure to their experience at home in Athens. (Anachronistically, they are seeing what the contemporary audience would see. At the date of the play (*c.* 413 BC) the Parthenon temple would be their major point of comparison.) They see the temple fronts as faces, representing the presence of the divinity. The strange expression, 'light of lovely eyes', assures us that their response to the new building is positive, and they see the god as favourable.

Having identified the temple building and briefly noted its basic architectural points, their interest is caught by sculptured representation of myths. Their focus is on story:

> CHORUS: See this, take a look!
> It's the Lernaean Hydra:
> the child of Zeus is slaying it
> with golden scythe.
> Look, darling! (Eur: *Ion*, 190–3)

They examine what is probably a typical series of metopes, including 'Heracles killing the Hydra'. (Neer (2004) identifies one fragmentary metope from the real Apollo temple as the cattle of Geryon, so the Heracles series described by the Chorus was quite possibly correct.) Their method is to keep looking till they can identify all the details. They name individual scenes, and are ready to follow the story into the next panel if appropriate.

> CHORUS: I see. And near him, another
> holds up a flaming torch;
> surely he is armoured Iolaos,
> who comes in the story
> told us at our looms. (Eur: *Ion,* 194–9)

Just as we would do, they begin with the many-headed monster whose opponent is necessarily Heracles, and from him logically they can name the hero's faithful companion, Iolaos, 'whose story is told to us at our looms'. Their pleasure is in finding and naming, in an unfamiliar place, familiar stories already associated with their intimate daily routine. As suggested earlier, the life of women has its own delight and value: here they recall their domestic work of weaving together, while a story-teller or singer entertains them.

They enjoy the process of identification. The more clue-giving details there are, the better. Iolaos has no real attributes of his own except his torch: he could not stand alone as a character, but he is a sort of attribute of Heracles; so, they can read along the line of metopes, linking the connected panels within the story. They also respond to the story-telling skill of the sculptor since they use heightened vocabulary to describe the scenes, such as 'blazing … fire-breathing … terrible double-flaming … burning up with fire.' They find these sculpted narratives not only lifelike but exciting. In truth, they have enhanced the sculptures from their own imaginations in a surprising way: the adjectives they have chosen are not so much about colour, but rather refer to the brilliance and action of fire. The naïve viewer may even have felt that the story was actually unfolding before their very eyes, moving, like a movie. Knowing the stories, they can add context and sequence, as they know what has happened and what will happen next; they can mentally add movement, lurid colour and light, sensation, even speech (cf. *Iliad* 18.490 ff.). The job of the sculptor has been to trigger this imaginative process by which the viewer will even add elements that cannot be sculpted, including fear, admiration and awe, for gods, heroes and monsters.

The dramatic text lays an enormous stress on the act of seeing. Partly, this encouraged Euripides's theatre audience to 'see' what the Chorus is supposed to be seeing, as presumably the young 'women' flit about the stage, miming the act of seeing. They say: 'Look, take a look, see … I see, oh, do gaze at, I follow my eye, see, we are looking, do you see? I see, I see' (lines 190–215). This is a lot of emphasis on the one idea of *seeing*, in a small passage. If it is at all realistic (as it seems intended to be), it suggests that visitors to sanctuaries were keen on detail, keen to look around, and did not by any means take the sculptures and narratives for granted, as is sometimes suspected by scholars. We can imagine the visitors at, for example, Foce del Sele going all round the temples, taking in each individual scene and giving it some thought – or maybe linking the topics, once identified, with their own place of origin, or with moral issues, or possibly just with a pleasurable complacency at the presence, in some form, of the powerful goddess they worship.

The idea of art as imitation, and recognition as the goal of art may seem childish or primitive. But Aristotle, writing in the latter half of the next century, still equates art with imitation, and the pleasure taken in art with identification:

> Thus the reason why men enjoy seeing a likeness is that in contemplating it they find themselves learning or inferring, and saying perhaps, 'Ah, that is he'. (Aristotle *Poetics* 4)

This is exactly what the Chorus so enthusiastically does as they call out: 'That is Heracles, etc.' Their pleasure lies in the mental act of processing and naming what is seen. 'However,' as Aristotle continues, 'if you happen not to have seen the original, the pleasure will be due not to the imitation as such, but to the execution, the colouring, or some such other cause' (ibid.). Normally (says Aristotle), the pleasure of art is in recognition of the imitation, and in identification. However, the thing imitated may not ever have been seen by the viewer. In that case it will be recognised by inference – maybe descriptions, or hearsay. But if the thing imitated actually has never existed, for example the Lernaean Hydra, it is the image itself which comes nearest to this non-existent entity. At this point, the viewer will enjoy the qualities which appear to lend it reality – 'the execution, the colouring, or …' (ibid) whatever aesthetic qualities make the image convincing. It is the skill of the artist which comes into play at this point, to make the viewer believe in the incredible. In the case of the Hydra, the viewer will probably have seen a real snake, and has heard of the Hydra; this pictured snake has seven heads, so there will be a leap of understanding from the known to the imagined. The snakelike qualities of the representation will be helpful, and so will the viewer's remembrance of the story. In the passage, the women identify the story from the obvious Hydra: Heracles, killing it, then need not wear his trademark lion-skin, and Iolaos with his torch is recognised as the companion of Heracles.

These women themselves regularly spend time weaving – a household necessity, but sometimes also an art-form. Helen of Troy in the *Iliad* wove the story of the battles in which men were dying for her. Andromache wove flowers. In real-life Athens, the Arrhephoroi wove the peplos for Athene which was figured with the Battle of Gods and Giants. Athenian women may well have been fascinated with this public artwork which employed their own special skills in its creation, and which was probably redesigned for each Panathenaic cycle. We can try to imagine from the evidence on pots what these designs might have been like: they must at least have been fairly narrative and clearly 'readable'. (We might also wonder what design was on the peplos given to Hera.) Here the Chorus' fascination is with the already known story; with its recognisability in the new setting and the translation to a different medium from the one they use. Euripides links weaving with this scene because the stories are told to groups of women at their daily weaving work. They may in fact be illiterate, but the stories are known to them by oral means.

The group turns next to the pediments, and must now be imagined as moving to the back of the temple. Most welcome to them there is the sight of 'my Athene'. Athene, like them, is a weaver – the best (*Odyssey* 13.300 ff.) and the recipient of woven gifts (her peplos). But here she appears in her guise of powerful warrior, since she figured on the back of the Delphi temple in the Battle of Gods and Giants, a subject of particular interest to Athenians. They enjoy (again) the recognition of the characters, naming the individual gods and giants: 'See the battle of the Giants/ … the mighty blazing thunderbolt in the … hands of Zeus. / I see … the furious Mimas/ and … Bacchus with his ivy staff … (Eur: *Ion*, 205–219.)'

As residents of Athens, they take a special delight in the greatness of their patron goddess and her success in the battle. They are all the more delighted with it because the same scene was familiar to them on the Acropolis, in the high-classical east metopes of the Parthenon, although here it appears in a less realistic late Archaic pediment. It was also painted inside the shield of the Parthenos, for those who had access to see it, and in fact would have been reflected in vase-painting too, as a popular subject. (The rather similar late Archaic pediment which had been part of the destroyed Athene Polias temple on the Acropolis was perhaps still known about and spoken of, even if not any longer visible.) However, artistic period and style is of no concern to these viewers, only clarity and recognition. It is noticeable that, although they know this is Apollo's temple, the group is most interested in Athene, their own goddess, and her exploits. In the Athenian telling of this story, it was Athene who did the most remarkable deeds.

> CHORUS: Do you see her shake her shield,
> her Gorgon-faced shield over giant Enceladus?
> – I see Athene, my own goddess! (Eur. *Ion* 230)

Athene is their goddess: she is here in Delphi too, and they delight to meet her. Although they are slaves and not citizens, they have identified themselves as Athenians in their loyalties. Similarly, a local visitor to the temple of Zeus at Olympia, might – if a woman – exclaim: 'My Hippodameia!' or – if a man – look up at: 'My hero, Pelops!' Equally, a visitor from elsewhere could salute the strong pivotal figure of Zeus. These enjoyable sculpted stories can involve the range of personal, civic and Greek identity. Here, the women are away from their home and city, but they are still in the presence of their god and – to that extent – feel themselves at home. The original audience of the play would certainly have been in tune with this Athenocentric approach. (Ironically, the sixth-century temple of Apollo at Delphi, extant in 413 BC, was the Alkmaionid temple and in that sense, Athenian. However, the women seem unaware of this connection and their pleasure would presumably apply to any sanctuary experiences.)

Next, the women ask the guide, Ion, a typical tourist question:

> CHORUS: Does Phoebus' temple truly stand on the navel-centre of the earth?
> ION: Yes, dressed in garlands, Gorgons all around.
> CHORUS: Just what we've always heard! (Eur. *Ion,* 223–5)

As typical tourists, they are happy to be given the kind of information they expected, and happy to look at 'what is allowed.' Since they may not go into the temple itself without paying for the sacrifice of a sheep, they will enjoy looking round outside: 'what is outside, delights our eye'. The display of the ornamental buildings and monuments that we know about, as well as plenty that we don't, was enough to keep the ancient visitor happy for many hours.

When Creusa, their royal mistress, joins them, Ion notices that her behaviour is very *un*typical:

> ION: The sight of Apollo's sanctuary has made you weep! ... Everyone else is happy when they gaze at the god's house, but you – your eyes run with tears. (Eur: *Ion,* 244–246)

Poor Creusa is suffering heartbreak and needs serious answers from the god. Together with her husband, she has a typical errand to Delphi, such as – 'Should I marry?' and here: 'Will I have a child?' Such questions were frequently put to the oracle. However, for herself secretly, Creusa of course has special issues with Apollo – her rape and the loss of her baby – she needs to know whether Apollo can be just to her. (By the end of the play, she will have her own child and her husband Xouthus will be happy with his 'son', and Athens will have its true-born ancestor, Ion. A rather peculiar theodicy will be explained publicly, not by Apollo, but by Athene, the deity who cares most for Athens.)

Euripides has employed an unusual method of scene-setting for his drama, by using the 'spontaneous comments' of the Chorus on art. Lacking onstage scenery, he has the Chorus comment in some detail, making the audience feel they are in a 'dramatic' Delphi. Many of the audience would have been to the real Delphi, and would have an idea of the setting. For the purposes of his play, Euripides has surely made the scene as plausible as possible, contrasting the care-free Chorus with the tragic heroine, Creusa, by reflecting the kind of comments really made by the general public: their main interest is clearly in story-identification and in relating what they see to their previous experience. There is also throughout the scene an emphasis on simple enjoyment and pleasure in the experience of visiting a shrine: this response would be applicable to all the sanctuaries we have looked at.

The Chorus of women does not distinguish between what is religious, aesthetic, cultural or social. For them, all these experiences are wrapped up together. They enjoy the leisure of the visit, the display of art, the expression of Greekness in the temples and the arrangements for worship – and the unseen presence of Apollo. This is a day out, a holiday, and there is something for everyone. By definition, a visit to a sanctuary for most visitors – except for athletes, priests, employees, etc. – would be a leisure experience, 'time-out' from normal duties. The beauty and charm of special buildings and monuments would be enthralling, seductive and refreshing to most people from whatever standpoint.

BIBLIOGRAPHY

Adornato, G.: 'Delphic Enigmas? The Gelas anasson, Polyzalos and the Charioteer Statue', *AJA* 112: 29–55 (January 2008)

Arafat, Karim: 'Pausanias and the Temple of Hera at Olympia', *The Annual of the British School at Athens*, 90: 461–73 (1995).

Ashmole, B: *Architect and Sculptor in Classical Greece*, Phaidon, London (1972).

Barbanera, Marcello: *Il Guerriero di Agrigento*, 'L'Erma' di Bretschneider, Rome (1995).

Barletta, Barbara: *The Origins of the Greek Architectural Orders*, Cambridge University Press, Cambridge (2001).

Barletta, Barbara: 'In Defense of the Ionic Frieze of the Parthenon', *American Journal of Archaeology*. 113 (4): 547–68 (October 2009).

Barletta, Barbara: 'Reconstructing the "Treasury," or Temple of Hera I at Foce del Sele', in *Stephanos: Studies in Honour of Brunilde Sismondo Ridgway*, edited by Hartswick, Kim J. and Sturgeon, Mary C., The University Museum, University of Pennsylvania, for Bryn Mawr College, Philadelphia (1998).

Barletta, Barbara: 'The Architecture and Architects of the Classical Parthenon', in *The Parthenon from Antiquity to the Present*, edited by Neils, Jenifer, Cambridge University Press, Cambridge (2005).

Barringer Judith M: 'The Temple of Zeus at Olympia, Heroes, and Athletes', *Hesperia* 211–41 (2005).

Barringer, Judith M.: *Art, Myth and Ritual in Classical Greece*, Cambridge University Press, Cambridge (2008).

Barringer, Judith M.: 'Making Heroes in the Athenian Agora: A New Interpretation of the Hephaisteion', in *Structure, Image, Ornament: Architectural Sculpture of the Greek World*, edited by Schultz, P. and von den Hoff, R., 105–20. Oxbow Books, Oxford (2009).

Baumbach, Jens David: *The Significance of Votive Offerings in Selected Hera Sanctuaries in the Peloponnese, Ionia* and *Western Greece. BAR International Series 1249*. Archaeopress, Oxford (2004).

Bell, Malcolm: 'Stylobate and Roof in the Olympieion at Akragas', *American Journal of Archaeology*, 84(3): 359–72 (July 1980).

Berve, Helmut and Gruben, Gottfried: *Greek Temples, Theatres and Shrines*, Thames and Hudson, London (1963).

Blundell, Sue and Williamson, Margaret, eds: *The Sacred and the Feminine in Ancient Greece*, Routledge, New York and London (1998).

Blundell, Sue: 'Marriage and the Maiden', in *The Sacred and the Feminine in Ancient Greece*, edited by Blundell, Sue and Williamson, Margaret, Routledge, New York and London (1998).

Boardman, John: *The Greeks Overseas, their Early Colonies and Trade*, new edn. Thames and Hudson, London (1980).

Boardman, John: 'Heracles, Theseus and Amazons', in *The Eye of Greece, Studies in the Art of Athens*, edited by Kurtz, Donna and Sparkes, Brian, Cambridge University Press, Cambridge (1982).

Brommer, F: *Die Metopen des Parthenon, Katalog und Untersuchung*, Deutsches Archäologisches Institut, Verlag Philipp von Zabern, Mainz (1967).

Buitron-Oliver, D., ed. *The Interpretation of Architectural Sculpture in Greece and Rome*. Studies in the History of Art, 49. Center for Advanced Study in the Visual Arts, Symposium Papers XXIX, Hanover and London (1997).

Camp, J. M.: *The Athenian Agora*, Thames and Hudson, London (1986).

Castriota, David: *Myth, Ethos and Actuality: Official Art in Fifth-Century B.C. Athens*, The University of Wisconsin Press, Madison, WI (1992'.

Connelly, Joan Breton: *The Parthenon Enigma: a Journey into Legend*, Knopf, New York (2014).

Coulton, J. J.: *Ancient Greek Architects at Work*, Cornell University Press, Ithaca, New York (1977).

Davidson, John: 'Olympia and the Chariot Race of Pelops', *Sport and Festival in the Ancient Greek World*, The Classical Press of Wales, Swansea (2003).

Dillon, Matthew: 'Did Parthenoi Attend the Olympic Games? Girls and Women Competing, Spectating, and Carrying out Cult Roles at Greek Religious Festivals', *Hermes* 128. Bd., H. 4, pp. 457–80 (2000).

Dillon, Matthew: *Girls and Women in Classical Greek Religion*, Routledge, London (2002).

Dinsmoor, William Bell: 'The Athenian Treasury as Dated by Its Ornament', *American Journal of Archaeology*, vol. 50, no. 1, pp. 86–121 (January to March 1946).

Dinsmoor, William Bell: 'The Internal Colonnade of the Hephaisteion', *Hesperia: The Journal of the American School of Classical Studies at Athens*, vol. 37, no. 2, pp. 159–77 (April to June 1968).

Dinsmoor, William Bell: *The Architecture of Ancient Greece*, Reprint of 3rd edn (1950) New York (1975).

Dontas, George S: 'The True Aglaurion', *Hesperia: The Journal of the American School of Classical Studies at Athens*, vol. 52, no. 1, pp. 48–63 (January to March 1983).

Dunbabin, T. J.: *The Western Greeks*, Clarendon Press, Oxford (1948).

Ekonomakis, R., ed.: *Acropolis Restoration: The CCAM Interventions*, Academy Editions, London (1994).

Ekroth, Gunnel: 'Blood On The Altars? On The Treatment Of Blood At Greek Sacrifices And The Iconographical Evidence', *Antike Kunst* 48. Jahrg, pp. 9–29 (2005).

Ekroth, Gunnel: 'Pelops joins the Party: Transformations of a Hero Cult within the Festival at Olympia', in J. Rasmus Brandt and Jon W. Iddeng: *Greek and Roman Festivals: Content, Meaning and Practice*, Oxford Scholarship Online (2012).

Edlund, Ingrid E. M.: 'The Sacred Geography of Southern Italy in Lycophron's *Alexandria*', *Opuscula Romana* XVL2 (1987).

Ferrari, Gloria: 'The Ancient Temple on the Acropolis at Athens', *American Journal of Archaeology*, vol. 106, no 1, pp. 11–35 (January 2002).

Ferris, I. M.: 'The Pity of War: Representations of Gauls and Germans in Roman Art', in *Cultural Identity in the Ancient Mediterranean*, edited by Gruen, Eric S., Getty Publications (2011).

Franzen, Christina: 'Sympathising with the Monster: making Sense of Colonisation in Stesichorus' *Geryoneis*', *Quaderni Urbinati*, vol. 2, p. 55 (2009).

Gaifman, Milette: *Aniconism in Greek Antiquity*, Oxford Studies in Ancient Culture & Representation, Oxford University Press, Oxford (2012).

De la Genière, Juliette, Greco-Maiuri, Giovanna and Donnarumna, Roberta: 'L'Héraion de Foce del Sele, découvertes récentes', *Comptes rendus des séances de l'Académie des Inscriptions et Belles-Lettres*, vol. 141, pp. 333–50 (1997).

Gerding, Henrick: 'The Erechtheion and the Panathenaic Procession', *American Journal of Archaeology*, vol. 110, no. 3, pp. 389–401 (July 2006).

Gill, David W. J.: 'The Decision to Build the Temple of Athena Nike' ('IG' I3 35) *Historia: Zeitschrift für Alte Geschichte*, Bd. 50, H. 3, pp. 257–78 (3rd Qtr., 2001).

Goldberg, Marilyn Y.: 'The Amazon Myth and Gender Studies', in *Stephanos: Studies in Honor of Brunilde Sismondo Ridgway*, edited by Hartswick, Kim J. and Sturgeon, Mary C., The University Museum, University of Pennsylvania, for Bryn Mawr College, Philadelphia (1998).

Glowacki, Kevin T.: 'The Acropolis of Athens before 566 BC', *Stephanos: Studies in Honour of Brunilde Sismondo Ridgway*, edited by Hartswick, Kim J. and Sturgeon, Mary C., The University Museum, University of Pennsylvania, for Bryn Mawr College, Philadelphia (1998).

Greco, Emanuele: 'On The Origin Of The Western Greek *Poleis*', *AWE*, vol. 10, pp. 233–42 (2011).

Harrison, Evelyn B.: 'Athena at Pallene and in the Agora of Athens', in *Periclean Athens and its Legacy: Problems and Perspectives*, edited by Barringer, Judith M. and Hurwit, Jeffrey M., University of Texas Press, Austin (2005).

Hedrick Charles, W. J.: 'The Temple and Cult of Apollo Patroos in Athens', *American Journal of Archaeology*, vol. 92, no. 2, pp 185–210 (1988).

Hoff, Ralf von den: 'Heracles, Theseus and the Athenian Treasury at Delphi', in *Structure, Image, Ornament: Architectural Sculpture of the Greek World*, edited by Schulz, Peter and von den Hoff, Ralf, 96–104, Oxbow Books, Oxford (2009).

Hollinshead, Mary B.: 'The North Court of the Erechtheion and the Ritual of the Plynteria', *American Journal of Archaeology*, vol. 119, no. 2, pp. 177–90 (April 2015).

Hurwit, J. M.: *The Art and Culture of Early Greece, 1100-480 BC*, Cornell (1985).

Hurwit, J. M.: 'Beautiful Evil: Pandora and the Athena Parthenos', *American Journal of Archaeology*, vol. 99, no. 2, pp. 171–86 (April 1995).

Hurwit, J. M.: *The Athenian Acropolis: History, Mythology and Archaeology from the Neolithic Era to the Present*, Cambridge University Press, Cambridge (1999).

Hurwit, J. M.: *The Acropolis in the Age of Pericles*, Cambridge University Press, Cambridge (2004).

Hurwit, J. M.: 'The Parthenon and the Temple of Zeus at Olympia', in *Periclean Athens and its Legacy: Problems and Perspectives*, edited by Barringer, J. M. and Hurwit, J. M., University of Texas Press, Austin (2005).

Jenkins, Ian: 'The Parthenon Frieze and Perikles' Cavalry of a Thousand', in *Periclean Athens and its Legacy: Problems and Perspectives*, edited by Barringer, J. M. and Hurwit, J. M., University of Texas Press, Austin (2005).

Jenkins, Ian: *Greek Architecture and its Sculpture in the British Museum*, London (2006).

Jenkins, Ian: *The Parthenon Sculptures*, Harvard University Press, Cambridge, MA (2007).

Kelly, Nancy: 'The Archaic Temple of Apollo at Bassai: Correspondences to the Classical Temple', *Hesperia: The Journal of the American School of Classical Studies at Athens*, vol. 64, no. 2, pp. 227–77 (April to June 1995).

Korres, M: *From Pentelicon to the Parthenon*, Melissa (1995).

Kowalzig, Barbara: *Singing for the Gods: Performances of Myth and Ritual in Archaic and Classical Greece*, Oxford University Press, Oxford (2007).

Kyrieleis, Helmut: 'The Heraion at Samos', in *Greek Sanctuaries: New Approaches*, edited by Marinatos, Nanno and Hägg, Robin, Routledge, London (1993).

Kyrieleis, Helmut: 'Zeus and Pelops in the East Pediment of the Temple of Zeus at Olympia', in *The Interpretation of Architectural Sculpture in Greece and Rome*, Studies in the History of Art 49, edited by Buitron-Oliver, D., 13–27, National Gallery of Art, Washington DC (1997).

Kyrieleis, Helmut: 'The German Excavations at Olympia: An Introduction', in *Sport and Festival in the Ancient Greek World*, The Classical Press of Wales, Swansea (2003).

Lapatin, K: *Chryselephantine Statuary in the Ancient Mediterranean World*, Oxford University Press, Oxford (2001).

Lapatin, K: 'The Statue of Athena and Other Treasures in the Parthenon', in *The Parthenon from Antiquity to the Present*, edited by Neils, J., Cambridge University Press, Cambridge (2005).

Larson, J: *Ancient Greek Cults: A Guide*, Routledge, London (2007).

Lawrence, A. W.: *Greek Architecture*, fifth edn, revised. R. A. Tomlinson, Yale University Press Pelican History of Art (1996).

Lefkowitz, Mary: 'Women in the Panathenaic and other Festivals', in *Worshipping Athena*, edited by Neils, Jenifer, The University of Wisconsin Press, Madison, WI (1996).

Lomas, Kathryn: *Rome and the Western Greeks, 350 BC-AD 200:Conquest and Acculturation in Southern Italy*, Routledge, London and New York (1993).

McInerney, Jeremy: 'Parnassus, Delphi, and the Thyiades', *Greek, Roman and Byzantine Studies*, p. 263 (Fall 1997).

McMahon, Augusta: 'Space, Sound and Light: Towards a Sensory Experience of Ancient Monumental Architecture', *American Journal of Archaeology*, vol. 117, no. 2, pp. 163–79 (April 2013).

Marconi, Clemente: *Temple Decoration and Cultural Identity in the Archaic Greek World: The Metopes of Selinus*, Cambridge University Press, Cambridge (2007).

Marinatos, Nanno and Hägg, Robin, eds: *Greek Sanctuaries: New Approaches*, Routledge, London (1993).

Mark, Ira S., Mellink, Machteld, J. and McCredie, James R: 'The Sanctuary of Athena Nike in Athens: Architectural Stages and Chronology', *Hesperia Supplements*, vol. 26, pp. i ff. (1993).

Mertens, Dieter: 'Some Principal Features of West Greek Colonial Architecture', in *Greek Colonists and Native Populations*, edited by Descoeudres, Jean-Paul, Clarendon Press, Oxford (1990).

Mertens, Dieter: *Der Alte Heratempel in Paestum und die Archaische Baukunst in Unteritalien*, Zabern, Mainz (1993).

Miles, Margaret M: 'Interior Staircases in Western Greek Temples', *Memoirs of the American Academy in Rome*, vol. 43/44, pp. 1–26 (1998/1999).

Miles, Margaret M: 'The Propylon to the Sanctuary of Demeter Malophoros at Selinous', *American Journal of Archaeology*, vol. 102, no. 1, pp. 35–57 (January 1998).

Miles, Margaret M., ed.: *A Companion to Greek Architecture*, Wiley Blackwell, Hoboken (2016).

Morgan, Catherine: 'The Origins of Pan-Hellenism', in *Greek Sanctuaries: New Approaches*, edited by Marinatos, Nanno and Hägg, Robin, Routledge, London (1993).

Mylonopoulos, Ioannis: 'Divine Images "behind Bars": The Semantics of Barriers in Greek Temples', from Current Approaches to religion in ancient Greece: Papers presented at a symposium at the Swedish Institute at Athens, edited by Matthew Haysom and Jenny Wallenstein (17–19 April 2008'.

Neer, Richard: 'Framing the Gift: the Politics of the Siphnian Treasury at Delphi', *American Journal of Archaeology*, vol. 105, no. 2, p. 296 (April 2001).

Neer, Richard: 'The Athenian Treasury at Delphi and the Material of Politics', *ClAnt*, vol. 23, pp. 63–93 (2004).

Neils, Jenifer: 'Reconfiguring the Gods on the Parthenon Frieze', *The Art Bulletin*, vol. 81, no. 1 (1999).

Neils, Jenifer: *The Parthenon Frieze*, Cambridge University Press, Cambridge (2001).

Neils, Jenifer: '"With Noblest Images on All Sides": The Ionic Frieze of the Parthenon', in *The Parthenon: From Antiquity to the Present*, edited by Neils, J., Cambridge University Press, Cambridge (2005).

Neils, Jenifer, ed.: *The Parthenon: From Antiquity to the Present*, Cambridge University Press, Cambridge (2005).

Neils, Jenifer and Schultz, Peter: 'Erechtheus and the Apobates Race on the Parthenon Frieze (North XI–XII), '*American Journal of Archaeology*, vol. 116, no. 2, pp. 195–207 (April 2012).

Palagia, Olga: 'First Among Equals: Athena in the East Pediment of the Parthenon', in *The Interpretation of Architectural Sculpture in Greece and Rome*, edited by Buitron-Oliver, D., National Gallery of Art, Washington 29–49 (1997).

Palagia, Olga: *The Pediments of the Parthenon*, Brill, Leiden, Boston, Koln (1998).

Palagia, Olga: 'Meaning and Narrative, Techniques in Statue Bases of the Pheidian Circle', in *Word and Image in Ancient Greece*, edited by Keith Rutter, N. and Sparkes, Brian A., Edinburgh University Press, Edinburgh (2000).

Palagia, Olga: 'Fire from Heaven: Pediments and Acroteria of the Parthenon', in *The Parthenon from Antiquity to the Present*, edited by Neils, J., Cambridge University Press, Cambridge (2005).

Parke, H. W.: *Festivals of the Athenians*, Thames and Hudson, London (1977).

Pausanias: *Guide to Greece*, vols 1 & 2, trans. Peter Levi, Penguin, London (1979).

Pavlou, Maria: 'Pindar *Olympian* 3: Mapping Akragas On The Periphery Of The Earth', *The Classical Quarterly*, vol. 60, no. 02, pp. 313–26 (December 2010).

Pedley, J. G.: *Paestum: Greeks and Romans in Southern Italy*, Thames and Hudson, London (1990).

Pedley, J. G.: *Sanctuaries and the Sacred in the Ancient Greek World*, Cambridge University Press, Cambridge (2005).

Philips, David J.; Pritchard, David, eds: *Sport and Festival in the Ancient Greek World*, The Classical Press of Wales, Swansea (2003).

Polignac, François de: *Cults, Territory and the Origins of the Greek City-State*, translated by Janet Lloyd, University of Chicago Press, Chicago and London (1984).

Pollitt, J. J.: Art and Experience in Classical Greece, Cambridge University Press, Cambridge (1972).

Pope, Spencer and Schultz, Peter: 'The Chryselephantine Doors of the Parthenon', *American Journal of Archaeology*, vol. 118, no. 1, pp. 19–31, Archaeological Institute of America (January 2014).

Rhodes, R. F.: *Architecture and Meaning on the Athenian Acropolis*, Cambridge University Press, Cambridge (1995).

Ridgway, Brunilde Sismondo: 'Notes on the Development of the Greek Frieze', *Hesperia: The Journal of the American School of Classical Studies at Athens*, vol. 35, no. 2, pp. 188–204 (April to June 1966).

Ridgway, Brunilde Sismondo: 'Archaic Architectural Sculpture and Travel Myths', *Dialogues d'histoire ancienne*, vol. 17, no. 2, pp. 95–112 (Année 1991).

Ridgway, Brunilde Sismondo: *Prayers in Stone: Greek Architectural Sculpture ca. 600-100* BC, Sather Classical Lectures, Berkeley (1999).

Ridgway, Brunilde Sismondo: '"Periclean" Cult-images and their Media', in *Periclean Athens and its Legacy*, edited by Barringer, Judith M. and Hurwit, Jeffrey M., University of Texas Press, Austin (2005).

Ross Holloway R.: 'Panhellenism in the Pediments of the Zeus Temple at Olympia', *Greek, Roman and Byzantine Studies*, vol. 8, no. 2, p. 93 (Summer 1967).

Ross Holloway R. 'Early Greek Architectural Decoration as Functional Art', *American Journal of Archaeology*, vol. 92, no. 2, pp. 177–83 (April 1988).

Ross Holloway R.: *The Archaeology of Ancient Sicily*, Routledge, London (1991).

Rozokoki, Alexandra: 'Some New Thoughts on Stesichorus' Geryoneis', *Zeitschrift für Papyrologie und Epigraphik* (2009).

Schultz, Peter: 'The Acroteria of the Temple of Athene Nike', *Hesperia*, vol. 70, pp. 1–47 (2001).

Schultz, Peter: 'The Date of the Nike Temple Parapet', *AJA*, vol. 106, pp. 294–95 (abstract) (2002).

Schultz, Peter: 'The Iconography of the Athenian Apobates Race: Origins, Meaning, Transformation', in *The Panathenaic Games*, edited by Palagia, Olga and Choremi-Spetsieri, Alkestis, Oxbow Books (2007).

Schultz, Peter: 'Divine images and Royal Ideology in the Philippeion at Olympia', in *Aspects of Ancient Greek Cult, Context, Ritual and Iconography*, edited by Jensen Tae, Jesper, Hinge, George, Schulz, Peter and Wicckiser, Bronwen (Aarhus Studies in Mediterranean Antiquity) Aarhus University Press, Denmark (2009).

Schwab, K.: 'Celebrations of Victory: The Metopes of the Parthenon', in *The Parthenon from Antiquity to the Present*, edited by Neils, J., Cambridge University Press, Cambridge (2005).

Scott, Michael: *Delphi and Olympia: The Spatial Politics of Panhellenism in the Archaic and Classical Periods*, Cambridge University Press, Cambridge (2010).

Scully, Vincent: *The Earth, the Temple and the Gods*, revised ed. Yale University Press, New Haven and London (1979).

Shear, I. M.: 'Kallikrates', *Hesperia*, vol. 32, pp. 375–424 (1963).

Shepherd, G.: 'Greeks bearing Gifts: Religious Relationships between Sicily and Greece in the Archaic Period', in *Sicily from Aeneas to Rome*, edited by Smith C. J. and Serrati, J., Edinburgh University Press, Edinburgh (2000).

Shoe, Lucy T.: 'Dark Stone in Greek Architecture', *Hesperia Supplements*, vol. 8, Commemorative Studies in Honor of Theodore Leslie Shear (1949).

Spawforth, A.: *The Complete Greek Temples*, Thames and Hudson, London (2006).

Stewart, Andrew F.: 'Pindaric "Dike" and the Temple of Zeus at Olympia', *Classical Antiquity*, vol. 2, no. 1, pp. 133–44, University of California Press, Berkeley (April 1983).

Stewart, A.: *Art, Desire and the Body in Ancient Greece*, Cambridge University Press, Cambridge, (1997).

Symeonoglou, Sarantis: 'The Doric Temples of Paestum', *The Journal of Aesthetic Education*, vol. 19, no. 1, Special Issue: Paestum and Classical Culture: Past and Present, pp. 49–66 (Spring 1985).

Van Keuren, Frances: *The Frieze from the Hera I Temple at Foce del Sele*, Giorgio Bretschneider, Rome (1989).

Walsh, John: 'The Date of the Athenian Stoa at Delphi', *American Journal of Archaeology*, vol. 90, no. 3, pp. 319–36 (July 1986).

Williams, Charles K. and Bookidis, Nancy: *Corinth, the Centenary, 1896-1996*, The American School of Classical Studies at Athens (2003).

Wilson-Jones, Mark: *Origins of Classical Architecture: Temples, Orders and Gifts to the Gods in Ancient Greece*, Yale University Press, New Haven (2014).

Winter, F. E.: 'Tradition and Innovation in Doric Design I: Western Greek Temples', *American Journal of Archaeology*, vol. 80, no. 2, pp. 139–45 (Spring, 1976).

Winter, Nancy A.: *Greek Architectural Terracottas from the Prehistoric to the end of the Archaic Period*, Clarendon Press, Oxford (1993).

Wonder, John W: 'What Happened to the Greeks in Lucanian-Occupied Paestum? Multiculturalism in Southern Italy', *Phoenix*, vol. 56, no. 1/2, pp. 40–55 (Spring to Summer, 2002), Classical Association of Canada.

Wycherley, R. E.: 'The Olympieion at Athens', *Greek, Roman and Byzantine Studies*, vol. 5, no. 3, p. 161 (Fall 1964).

Yeroulanou, Marina: 'Metopes and Architecture: The Hephaisteion and the Parthenon', *The Annual of the British School at Athens*, vol. 93, pp. 401–25 (1998).

Zancani Montuoro and Zanotti-Bianco, *Heraion alla Foce del Sele*, Roma (1951).

Zeitlin, Froma: 'The artful eye: vision, ecphrasis and spectacle in Euripidean theatre', in *Art and text in ancient Greek culture*, edited by Goldhill, Simon and Osborne, Robin, Cambridge University Press, Cambridge (1994).

GLOSSARY

abacus – square member of a Doric capital, just above the echinus and below the architrave; also used in Ionic and Corinthian but with concave sides.
acanthus – frequently used design motif based on the acanthus thistle leaf.
acrolithic – type of statue where only head, arms and feet are of stone, with a wooden body.
acroterion (plural **acroteria**) – sculptural flourish, floral or figurative, topping each of the three corners of a pediment.
adyton – innermost chamber of a temple.
aegis – a garment worn only by Athene, resembling a poncho worn centrally or sometimes asymmetrically over the shoulders. It is edged with snakes and may have a Gorgoneion (Gorgon's head) in the centre. Its function is to protect friends and terrify enemies.
agora – civic centre, similar to the Roman Forum.
amphiprostyle – prostyle façade on both back and front of a building.
amphora – two-handled pot, of clay or metal.
anathyrosis – smooth worked band on masonry intended to fit perfectly with adjacent masonry. The rest is cut slightly deeper so as to require less exact work.
aniconic – non-representational.
anta (plural **antae**) – projection of sidewall beyond a corner; or decorative pilaster marking termination of a sidewall.
antefix – repeated terracotta or marble ornament covering the lowest tile ends of a roof.
anthemion – floral border design, same as lotus-and-palmette.
anulet – thin ring around the top of a Doric column shaft – 'necking ring'.
apobates – competitive chariot race in which an armed contestant (apobates) jumps on and off the chariot, while the charioteer continues to drive.
apoikia – colony (see p. 187).
apse – rounded end to a building.
architrave – 'main beam' lying on top of colonnade supporting entablature and roof.
arris – the sharp edge of the flutes on a Doric column.
ashlar masonry – regular courses of blocks cut to neat rectangles.
atlantes – male version of a caryatid.
base of a column – absent in Doric style; in Ionic can be quite elaborate.
bead-and-reel – moulding design (see Fig. 12).
bouleuterion – council chamber.
bothros (plural **bothroi**) – a stone-lined pit near an altar in a sanctuary, to receive rubbish after a sacrifice.
capital – the decorative top member of a column; indicates its 'order'.
caryatids – architectural term for columns in the form of women.
cella – main chamber of a temple; also called naos.
chiaroscuro – artistic effect of dark and light.
chiton – Ionic dress of elaborately folded and pinned cloth.
chora – territory belonging to a city.
chryselephantine – sculpture made with gold and ivory plates on a wooden core.
chthonic – pertaining to the underworld
chthonic deities – mainly Persephone, with her mother, Demeter

coffering – method of making a decorative ceiling, using diminishing square steps like boxes; either marble or wood.
columnae caelatae – columns with sculpted drums
Corinthian – decorative order of architecture: capitals have small volutes and bands of acanthus foliage running underneath, otherwise similar to Ionic; first noted at Bassae.
cornice – a protruding section like a frame above a wall or surrounding a pediment; both decorative and protective.
crepidoma – platform on which a temple stands, composed of two, three or more high steps.
cult statue – statue focusing devotion in a particular cult: fixed focal statue in a temple.
Cyclopean – Mycenaean-age wall construction named after giants, consisting of massive boulders fitted quite roughly together with small stones filling gaps.
demos – the people; 'democracy' = rule of the people.
dentils – design of small square blocks alternating with spaces, an Ionic feature.
diapeton (plural – diapeta) – stone 'statue' believed to have fallen from the sky, possibly a meteorite.
dipteral – a temple with a double colonnade all round.
distyle in antis – arrangement of porch columns where two columns stand between the antae or short spur walls, the normal Doric arrangement; see Fig. 3.
Doric – plain order of architecture, mainly used on mainland Greece; see Fig. 2.
Doric frieze – horizontal element above the architrave; divided into triglyphs and metopes.
dressed stone – masonry neatly cut to shape on the front face.
drum – cylindrical section of a column, or any cylindrical form.
echinus – literally 'cushion': simple rounded member, characteristic part of a Doric capital; or small equivalent at top of an Ionic capital.
egg-and-dart – moulding design (see Fig. 12).
Eleusinian marble/limestone – dark stone from Eleusis, used for colour contrast.
entablature – entire superstructure supported by columns: or architrave + frieze + cornice.
entasis – subtle curve of columns.
euthynteria – levelling course, foundation layer under the stereobate, making a level base.
fillet – narrow flat strip; used of flat member between Ionic flutes.
finishing layer – extra stone protective surface removed only at the last stage.
flute, fluting – vertical decorative channels on columns.
frieze – horizontal member above the architrave; may or may not be sculpted.
geison – same as sima.
guilloche – a plaited moulding design (see Fig. 71).
guttae – small decorative stone knobs found under Doric mutules; they resemble wooden pegs.
heroon – hero shrine.
hexastyle – façade or inner porch with six columns.
hipped roof – roof sloping on four sides, without gables or pediments.
horos – boundary stone, especially marking out a sanctuary.
hubris – arrogance, pride that offends the gods.
hydria – water pot.
hypaethral – unroofed, partially unroofed.
in antis – describes arrangement of porch columns between the antae.
intercolumniation – distance between columns in a colonnade.
Ionic – decorative order of architecture originating in eastern Greece; see Fig. 4.
Ionic frieze – continuous 'ribbon' frieze found above the architrave; may or may not be sculpted.
island marble – marble imported from islands, usually Naxos or Paros.
kore (plural **korai**) – archaic statue type of a standing maiden, often holding an offering.
kouros (plural **kouroi**) – archaic statue type of a nude youth stepping forward with clenched hands held close to his sides.

lifting bosses – protruding lumps on stone blocks that were used to facilitate lifting. Usually removed at the last stage.
limestone – cheap stone, usually local; related to marble but much coarser.
lintel – horizontal beam spanning a door frame or supported on columns.
lotus-and-palmette – floral moulding design (see Fig. 12). Same as anthemion.
Loxias – name of Apollo, linked with idea of speaking (oracularly or even riddlingly).
metope – rectangular or square flat section between triglyphs; can be painted, plain or sculpted.
monolithic – made of a single piece of stone.
moulding – decorative carved border.
mutules – flat blocks decorated on the underside with guttae found under the Doric cornice.
naiskos – small free-standing shrine. Could shelter a statue.
naos – the main inner chamber of a temple = cella. (In Greek can mean the whole temple.)
Naxian marble – marble from Naxos; tends to be greyer and more loosely crystalline than Parian.
Nike (plural **Nikai**) – Victory or winged figure of victory.
numinous – emanating a natural impression of a spiritual presence.
octostyle – describes a façade or inner porch with eight columns.
oikist (Greek: oikistes) – leader of a colony.
opisthodomos – rear porch of a temple; sometimes a back-chamber.
orthostates – upright slabs forming the lowest course of a wall; usually double the height of the subsequent courses.
palaistra – peristyle building used for athletic and other educational activities.
Parian marble – marble from the island of Paros; pure, translucent white marble.
Pentelic marble – marble quarried in Attica from M Pentelicon; the marble of choice for Athenians from the second quarter of the fifth century onwards; very fine texture and warm colouring.
peplos – long dress made of folded and pinned rectangle of cloth. A plain mainland style.
peribolos – wall surrounding a temenos.
peripteral – temple with colonnade running all round exterior.
peristyle – outer colonnade of a temple; sometimes inner colonnade of a courtyard building.
phiale (plural **phialai**) – flat libation dish, either plain or lobed.
pier – squared column or pillar.
pilaster – flat squared or half-round column, stuck to wall.
polis – city-state.
polygonal – irregular but closely fitting masonry style; particularly used in earthquake zones.
polos (plural **poloi)** – a pill-box hat, worn usually by goddesses.
poros – a type of stone; a word sometimes used generally for limestone, a soft, course stone.
pronaos – front porch of a temple.
propylaia – a more elaborate propylon.
propylon – monumental gateway.
prostyle – arrangement of façade columns where colonnade stretches right across platform.
prytaneion – civic building with committee and dining facilities.
pteroma – corridor between colonnade and cella walls of a temple.
pteron (plural – ptera) – flank colonnade of a temple (i.e. not the front or back porch).
raking cornice – slanting/angled cornice, usually edging upper sides of pediment.
reeded – carved with horizontal grooves or convex flutes.
refinements – system of deliberate deviations from straight lines for optical effects.
regulae – same as mutules.
ridge – horizontal sharp edge on top of a roof, where sloping sides meet.
riser – vertical part of a step.
rosette – flat circular flower-shaped decoration.

scotia – concave section between two toruses on an Ionic column base (see Fig. 71).
shelly limestone – a local limestone found near Olympia with a loose texture owing to its fossilised shell content.
sima – a gutter, often highly decorative, edging a roof where the slope meets the walls.
sofa capital – capital including a small pendant cylindrical element like a bolster cushion. A mini-volute.
soffit – horizontal element masking the underside of the roof overhang. Sometimes decorated.
stereobate – the three-stepped platform of a temple.
stoa – roofed building with open colonnaded front.
stucco – a lime-plaster, to protect mud-brick walls, or mixed with marble dust, to mask the impurities of limestone and make it look like marble.
stylobate – platform on which columns sit; top step of a stereobate.
symposium – dinner party.
tainia – 'garland': a thin projecting band along the top of a Doric architrave.
telamon – male version of a caryatid.
temenos – designated sacred area.
tetrastyle – façade or inner porch with four columns.
theoria - sacred voyage, embassy to a sanctuary.
theoxenia – practice of welcoming the gods at sacrifices and festivities with laid out tables and chairs.
Thesmophoria – all-women festival in honour of Demeter and Persephone, aimed at promoting fertility of the city. This festival was held in many Greek cities.
tholos – circular building.
torus – cushion-like member of an Ionic column-base or convex moulding (see Fig. 71).
travertine – name for shelly limestone, very common building material in Italy.
tread – flat part of a step.
treasury – small building found usually in a Panhellenic sanctuary, like a mini-temple but made to hold valuable offerings given by a city or by its individual citizens. Usually of lavish architecture but without a colonnade.
triglyph – slab with three vertical raised strips, part of Doric frieze, alternates with metopes.
tripteral – temple, or one side of a temple, enclosed by three colonnades.
tympanum – the vertical triangular wall of a pediment which may be carved or against which sculpture may stand.
volute – scroll ornament found on Ionic columns and door frames.
votive offering – offering made at a sanctuary; very often a miniature terracotta version of the cult statue.
xenia – the host/guest relationship, hospitality.
xoanon (plural - xoana) – early archaic wooden statue.
xystos – running track covered by colonnaded roof.

INDEX